Cross-Country
Ski Routes

Oregon

Second Edition

Klindt Vielbig

THE
MOUNTAINEERS

This book is dedicated to a future generation of skiers—to Arianna, Hannah, and Emma, my granddaughters, and also to Tory, Dillon, Shea, Ian, Karen, Brooke, Molly, and the many other skiers of that young generation.

Published by
The Mountaineers
1011 SW Klickitat Way
Seattle, Washington 98134

8 7 6 5 4
5 4 3 2 1

Published simultaneously in Canada by Douglas & McIntyre, Ltd., 1615 Venables Street, Vancouver, B.C. V5L 2H1

Published simultaneously in Great Britain by Cordee, 3a DeMontfort Street, Leicester, England, LE1 7HD

Manufactured in Canada

Edited by Heath Lynn Silberfeld
Maps and photographs by the author unless otherwise noted
Book design and typesetting by The Mountaineers Books
Book layout by Nick Gregoric

Cover photograph: Mount Hood from Ghost Ridge

Library of Congress Cataloging-in-Publication Data
Vielbig, Klindt.
Cross-country ski routes, Oregon / Klindt Vielbig. -- 2nd ed.
        p.   cm.
Rev. ed. of: Cross-country ski routes of Oregon's Cascades. c1984.
Includes bibliographical references and index.
ISBN 0-89886-404-6
1. Cross-country skiing--Cascade Range--Guidebooks. 2. Cascade Range--Guidebooks. I. Vielbig, Klindt. Cross-country ski routes of Oregon's Cascades. II. Title.
GV854.5.C27V53   1994
796.93'2'09795--dc20
                                        94-22204
                                        CIP

CONTENTS

Map Symbols 4
Route Information 5
Acknowledgments 19
Introduction 21

PART I: THE SOUTHERN WASHINGTON CASCADES 39
           Chapter 1: Mount St. Helens 40
           Chapter 2: Upper Wind River 66
           Chapter 3: The Crazy Hills 79
           Chapter 4: Trout Lake 83
           Chapter 5: Mount Adams Backcountry 94
           Chapter 6: Glenwood Valley 99
           Chapter 7: Other Southern Washington Tours 103

PART II: MOUNT HOOD AND VICINITY 109
           Chapter 8: Hood Lowlands 112
           Chapter 9: Government Camp and Timberline 118
           Chapter 10: Trillium Basin 138
           Chapter 11: Salmon River Basin 153
           Chapter 12: Frog Lake and Blue Box Pass 159
           Chapter 13: Clear Lake and Mount Wilson 163
           Chapter 14: Barlow Pass 172
           Chapter 15: White River 181
           Chapter 16: Bennett Pass 186
           Chapter 17: East Fork Hood River Region 192
           Chapter 18: Cooper Spur 207
           Chapter 19: Clinger Spring and Brooks Meadow 212

PART III: THE CLACKAMAS HIGH COUNTRY 219
           Chapter 20: The Clackamas High Country 220

PART IV: THE SANTIAM REGION 229
           Chapter 21: Santiam West 230
           Chapter 22: Santiam Pass 248

PART V: THE CENTRAL CASCADES 261
           Chapter 23: The Bend Area 262
           Chapter 24: Newberry Crater 280

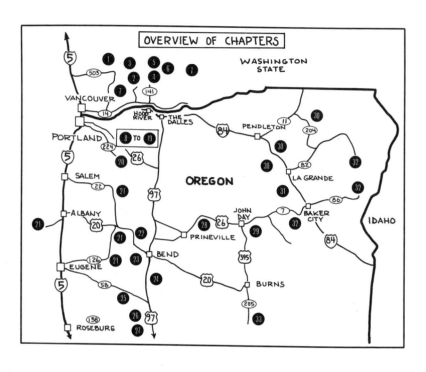

OVERVIEW OF CHAPTERS

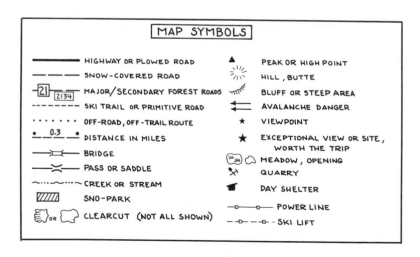

MAP SYMBOLS

HIGHWAY OR PLOWED ROAD	▲ PEAK OR HIGH POINT
SNOW-COVERED ROAD	HILL, BUTTE
MAJOR/SECONDARY FOREST ROADS	BLUFF OR STEEP AREA
SKI TRAIL OR PRIMITIVE ROAD	AVALANCHE DANGER
OFF-ROAD, OFF-TRAIL ROUTE	★ VIEWPOINT
0.3 DISTANCE IN MILES	★ EXCEPTIONAL VIEW OR SITE, WORTH THE TRIP
BRIDGE	MEADOW, OPENING
PASS OR SADDLE	QUARRY
CREEK OR STREAM	DAY SHELTER
SNO-PARK	POWER LINE
CLEARCUT (NOT ALL SHOWN)	SKI LIFT

4

Chapter 25: Willamette Pass 287
Chapter 26: Diamond Lake 300
Chapter 27: Crater Lake National Park 308
Chapter 28: The Ochoco Mountains 314

PART VI: EASTERN OREGON 325
Chapter 29: The John Day Region 326
Chapter 30: The Blue Mountains and Vicinity 343
Chapter 31: The Elkhorn Mountains 347
Chapter 32: The Wallowa Mountains 354
Chapter 33: Steens Mountain 371
Resources 373
Index 377

ROUTE INFORMATION

DEFINITIONS FOR MATRIX STANDARDS

Difficulty Rating: Categories are N, I, A, BC—Novice, Intermediate, Advanced, Backcountry. See the Trail Difficulty and Skill Level section of the Introduction for definitions. Where a tour is near the upper edge of a rating, a dual rating is often given as a warning that difficulty may exceed the lower rating. In general, children will do well on Novice tours, and if athletic may be capable of skiing some Intermediate tours.

Length of Tour: Length represents maximum distance for the tour and is for round trip from the sno-park. If the trail, loop, or connector starts away from the sno-park, distance is given from the sno-park. Where parking is at the snow line, a range of distances is given to reflect snow-line fluctuations. A range is also given when more than one access route exists.

Elevation: A: 0–500 feet gain; B: 500–1,000; C: 1,000–2,000; D: 2,000+

Campsite: A combination of factors was used to select suggested locations—accessibility, safety, isolation, and scenic attributes were considered. Be aware that cars parked overnight anywhere are vulnerable to break-ins.

PAGE		DIFFICULTY	DISTANCE	ELEVATION	CAMPSITE	MAP
	I. THE SOUTHERN WASHINGTON CASCADES					
	1. MOUNT ST. HELENS					
44	Wapiti Trails	N–I	1–12	A		3
44	Swift Creek Overlook	I	4	B	•	3
46	Swift Creek Trail	I	6	B	•	3
46	June Lake	I	6	A		3
47	Marble Mountain	I	14	C		3
48	Beaver Ponds Loop and Marble Mountain Summit	N–I	7	A	•	3
48	Sasquatch Trails	I	8–12	B	•	3
49	Worm Flows Buttress	A	12	C		3/4
51	Muddy River Lahar	I–A	10–14	B		3/4
52	Monitor Ridge	I	8	B	•	2
53	Redrock Pass and Lava Plateau	N	5	A	•	2/5
55	Butte Camp Loop	BC	15	D	•	2
56	Summit Ski Ascent	BC	10	D		3
58	Goat Marsh	I	4–8	A	•	5
59	McBride Lake	N–I	9	C		2/5
60	Kalama River Trail	N	3–6	A		5
61	Blue Lake	I	4–6	C		2/5
61	Blue Lake Mudflow	I	6–12	C		2/5
62	Cathedral Grove	I	8–10	C		2/5
62	Escape Ridge	I–A	14–20	D	•	2
64	Spirit Lake Memorial Highway	N–I	2–4	A		1
64	Windy Ridge to Bear Meadow Viewpoint	I–A	9	C	•	6
65	Mosquito Meadows	I	10	C		6
	2. UPPER WIND RIVER					
68	Scenic Loop: Trail 148	N–I	6	A		7
70	Old Man Loop	N	2	A		8
70	McClellan Meadows to Indian Heaven Trail	I	4–9	A		7
70	Valley Ski Trail to McClellan Meadows Trail	I	4	A		8

PAGE		DIFFICULTY	DISTANCE	ELEVATION	CAMPSITE	MAP
73	Hardtime Loop	I	11	B		7/8
73	Hardtime Creek Trail and Loop	I	12	B		7
74	Lewis River Overlook	I–A	10	B		7
74	Hardtime Cutoff Trail	I–A	8	B	•	7
74	Termination Point	I	12	B	•	7
75	Point 3670	A	14	B		7
75	Termination Ridge Cutoff	A	10	B		7
75	Outlaw Creek Clearcuts	I–A	8–10	B	•	8
76	Rush Creek Clearcuts	N	3	A		8
76	Lone Butte Quarry Viewpoint	I	6	C	•	8/9
78	Sawtooth Mountain Clearcut	I	8	C	•	9
	3. THE CRAZY HILLS					
79	Rush Creek Tour	N	3	A	•	9
80	Lone Butte Meadows	I	6	A		9
80	Skookum Meadow	I	8	A	•	9
81	Loco Pass Loop	I	10	B	•	9
82	Burnt Peak	I	8–10	B		9
82	Skookum Peak	I–A	6–11	C		9
	4. TROUT LAKE					
84	Mann Butte	I	10	B	•	11
85	Natural Bridges	I	8	A		11
86	Peterson Ridge and Lost Meadow	I	13	B	•	11
86	Peterson Prairie and Prairie Ridge	N–I	5–9	B		11
87	Sink Holes	N	1–2	A	•	12
87	Cave Creek	N	1–2	A		12
90	Eagle Loop	N	3	A		14
90	Big Tree Loop	N–I	5	A		14
90	Lava Loop	N–I	4	A		14/15
90	Pipeline Loop	I	6	C		14/15
92	King Mountain	I	8	B		14
93	Twin Buttes	N–I	2	A	•	14

PAGE		DIFFICULTY	DISTANCE	ELEVATION	CAMPSITE	MAP
	5. MOUNT ADAMS BACKCOUNTRY					
94	Aiken Lava Flow	A	12	C	•	14
94	Sleeping Beauty	A	12	C	•	17
96	Stagman Ridge	BC	14	D	•	17
97	Mount Adams Timberline from Morrison Creek and Cold Springs	I–A	6–12	C	•	18
	6. GLENWOOD VALLEY					
99	Outlet Falls	N	4	A	•	19
100	McCumber Place Loops	N–I	2–8	A		19
100	Conboy Lake National Wildlife Refuge	N	2	A		19
102	Diamond Gap	A	8	D		19
	7. OTHER SOUTHERN WASHINGTON TOURS					
103	Larch Mountain (Washington)	I	4–6	B	•	20
105	North Ridge	A	8–12	C	•	21
107	Simcoe Mountains	A	8–12	C	•	22
	II. MOUNT HOOD AND VICINITY					
	8. HOOD LOWLANDS					
112	Larch Mountain (Oregon)	N–I	8	C		23
113	Old Maid Flat	N	2–4	A		24
113	Ramona Falls	I	11	B		24
115	Lost Lake	I–A	6–12	B		25
	9. GOVERNMENT CAMP AND TIMBERLINE					
118	Mirror Lake	I	3	B		26
119	Enid Lake Loop	N–I	2	A	•	26
119	Glacier View Loop	N–I	2	A		26
122	Camptown-Crosstown Trail	I	6	A		26
122	Summit Trail and Multorpor Meadows	N	4	A		26
124	Multorpor Meadows	N	1–2	A		26
124	West Leg Trail	N–I	11	C		27

PAGE		DIFFICULTY	DISTANCE	ELEVATION	CAMPSITE	MAP
130	White River Canyon	N–I	4	B		39
130	Timberline Lodge to White River	A	7	C		27/39
131	Wy'east Trail	I–A	20	C		28
132	Snow Bunny Trail to Tie Trail	N–I	C	A		29
132	East Leg Area	N	4	A		29
133	White Away Trail	N	3	A		29
133	West Yellowjacket Trail	I	5	A		26/29
134	Yellowjacket Trail	A	12	B		29
	10. TRILLIUM BASIN					
140	Snow Bunny Hill	N–I	1	A		32
140	Red Top Meadow	N–I	1	A		32
140	Hemlock Trail	N–I	2	A		32
142	Barlow Trail	I	4	A		32
142	Trillium Lake Loop	N–I	5	A	•	32
143	Sherar Burn and Trillium Lake Dam Loop	A	9	B		32
143	Mud Creek Ridge and Porcupine Trail	I	8	A		32/33
146	Mud Creek Ridge Overlook	I	8	A		32/33
146	Salmon River Overlook	I	9	A	•	32/33
146	Quarry Loop	I	9	A		33
147	Mount Jefferson Loop	I	9	A		33
147	Lostman Trail and Loop	I	10	A	•	33
150	Wapinitia and Salmon River Overlooks	A	12	A	•	33
150	Sisu Loop	A	11	B		33
151	Veda Butte	A	10	B		33
151	Sherar Burn to Kinzel Lake	A	24	D	•	34
	11. SALMON RIVER BASIN					
153	Beaver Marsh and Pioneer Woman's Grave Loop	N	3	A		29
155	Buzzard Point Trail and Barlow Road Loop	N–I	4	A		29
155	Barlow Road Trail	I	3	A		29
155	Buzzard Point Trail	N	4	A		29

PAGE		DIFFICULTY	DISTANCE	ELEVATION	CAMPSITE	MAP
157	Upper Salmon Basin	I	4	A		29
157	Salmon River Meadows	N	2–4	A	•	35
	12. FROG LAKE AND BLUE BOX PASS					
159	Frog Lake	N	2	A	•	36
160	Frog Lake Loop	N	2	A		36
160	Frog Lake Buttes	I–A	6	C		36
	13. CLEAR LAKE AND MOUNT WILSON					
164	North Shore Tours	N	2–5	A	•	36/37
165	Corridor Tour	N–I	4	A		36/37
165	Lakeshore Tour	N–I	3–7	A		36
165	Westside Tour	N–I	6–10	A		36
166	Clear Lake Butte	A	11	B		36
166	Little Crater Meadows and Lake	A	13	A	•	36
167	Big Meadows	I–A	14	A	•	38
168	Big Meadows Loop	I–A	18	A		38
168	Clackamas Lake Historic Ranger Station	A	16	A		38
170	Mount Wilson Summit—Eastside Approach	A	15	D		38
171	Mount Wilson Summit—North Approach and Westside Overlook	I	16	B		38
171	Mount Wilson—High Loop	A	24	C		38
	14. BARLOW PASS					
172	Twin Lakes Trail and Loop	I	8–10	C		37
173	Lower Twin Lake	I	5	B	•	35
174	Ghost Ridge	I	4	B		35
175	Palmateer Overlook	I	6	B		35
175	Devils Half Acre Loop	I	3	A		35
177	Mineral Jane Trail	I	6	A		39
179	Panorama Dome and Boy Scout Ridge	I	6	A	•	39
180	Barlow Ridge	I	6	B		39
	15. WHITE RIVER					
181	Gravel Pit Tour	N	1	A		39

PAGE		DIFFICULTY	DISTANCE	ELEVATION	CAMPSITE	MAP
182	Powerline Tour	N–I	3	A		39
183	White River Glacier Moraines	I	4	B		39
183	Yellowjacket and White River Trails Loop	I	2	A		39
184	White River to Mineral Jane to Barlow Saddle to Boy Scout Ridge Loop	I	5	A		39
184	Mineral Jane Trail to Barlow Pass	I	6	A		39
184	Mineral Jane Trail East to Bennett Pass	I	4	A		39
185	White River Trail and Barlow Creek Pioneer Road Loop	A	19	B		39
	16. BENNETT PASS					
186	Bennett Ridge Trail	I	8	B		40
189	Bonney Butte and Meadows	I–A	12	B		40/41
190	Camp Windy	I	10	B		40/41
	17. EAST FORK HOOD RIVER REGION					
192	Nordic Center Groomed Tracks	N–I	2–10	A		42
194	Hood River Meadows and Sahalie Falls	N	2–3	A	•	42
194	Heather Canyon Trail	I	5	B		42
195	Elk Meadows Trail	N–I	6	A		42
196	Clark Creek Trail	N–I	4	A		42
197	Rocky Trail	N–I	3	A		42
197	Spruce Loop	N	2	A		42
197	Lamberson Butte	A–BC	13	D		42
198	Gates of the Mountain	I–A	8	C	•	42
199	Newton Creek Trail and Loop	I	7	A		42
201	Robinhood Creek Loop	N	4	A		42
201	Horsethief Meadows	N	4	A	•	42
202	Teacup Lake Groomed Tracks	N–I	2–12	A		40
202	Meadows Creek Trail	I	7	A		40
203	Teacup Lake Trail	I	3	A		40
203	Pocket Creek Trails	N	6	A		40
205	East Fork Trail (Pocket Creek)	I	6	A		40
205	Fat Lady Trail and Fat Lady Saddle	I	8	B	•	40/41

PAGE		DIFFICULTY	DISTANCE	ELEVATION	CAMPSITE	MAP
206	Windy Peak Traverse (Camp Windy Connector)	A	10	C		40
	18. COOPER SPUR					
208	Weygandt Basin	N–I	5	A	•	43
209	Cloud Cap Inn	I	3–9	D		43
211	Old Wagon Road	I–A	2	B		43
	19. CLINGER SPRING AND BROOKS MEADOW					
213	Clinger Ridge	I	6–10	B		44
213	Volcano View	I	6–10	B	•	44
213	Surveyor Trail	I	6–10	B		44
215	Brooks Meadow	I	6–10	B		44
215	Aqueduct Loop	I	8–14	B		44
216	Dog River Butte	I	8–14	B		44
217	Perry Point	I–A	12–20	B		44
217	Fivemile Butte	I–A	12–20	B		44
218	Lookout Mountain	BC	12–19	D		44
	III. THE CLACKAMAS HIGH COUNTRY					
	20. THE CLACKAMAS HIGH COUNTRY					
221	Cache Meadow and Cripple Creek Lake	I–A	8–12	C		45
223	High Rock	I–A	10–14	D		45
224	Low Rock	I–A	10–14	D	•	45
225	Black Wolf Meadows and Anvil Lake	I–A	12–14	C		45
226	Hidaway Lake and Shellrock Lake	I–A	12–16	C		45
227	Indian Ridge	A–BC	12–20	D		45
	IV. THE SANTIAM REGION					
	21. SANTIAM WEST					
230	Jefferson Park	BC	12–14	D	•	—
231	South Breitenbush Gorge Trail 3366	I	4	A		—
231	Elk Lake and Gold Butte Lookout	I	4–8	B		47
232	Pamelia Lake	I	7–12	B		48

PAGE		DIFFICULTY	DISTANCE	ELEVATION	CAMPSITE	MAP
233	Coffin Mountain	I	6–12	C	•	49
233	Fay Lake	N–I	6	A		50
235	Big Springs Trails	N–I	2–6	A		50
236	Lava Lake East Access Trail	I	6	A		50
236	Mountain View Trail West	I	5	A	•	50
237	Mountain View Loop	A	10	B		50
237	Middle Loops	N–I	2–7	A		50
238	Maxwell Loop	A	5	B		50
238	Lava Lake Trails	N–I	1–3	A	•	50
239	Little Nash Trail	N	2	A		50
241	Jack Pine Road Trail	A	4	B	•	51
241	Lost Lake	N	3	A	•	51
241	Civil (Iron Mountain) Tour	I	4	B		52
242	Lost Prairie and Heart Lake	I	7	B		52
242	Tombstone Prairie Trail	N	4	A		52
242	Prairie View Loop	N–I	6	A	•	53
244	Isaac Nickerson Loop	N–I	4	A	•	53
244	Old Santiam Wagon Road	I	8	B		53
245	Indian Ridge	A	12–18	C		54
246	Frissell Point	A	8–15	C		55
246	Marys Peak	N–I	6–12	C		56
	22. SANTIAM PASS					
248	Nordic Center Trails	N	3	A		51
248	North Loop	I	5	A		51
249	South Loop	N–I	7	A		51
249	Eastside Trails	N–I	2–12	A		51
249	Circle Lake Trail	I	8	A	•	51
249	Hayrick Butte Loop and Hoodoo Butte Plateau	I	4	A		51
252	Round Lake Trails	N–I	12	B		51
252	Round Lake Trail Loop	N–I	5	B		51
254	Camp Sherman Ski Trails	N–I	2–12	A		57

PAGE		DIFFICULTY	DISTANCE	ELEVATION	CAMPSITE	MAP
254	Metolius River Headwaters	N	4	A		57
255	Black Butte	A–BC	8–14	D		57
256	Three Creek Trail	I	8	B	•	58
256	Snow Creek Trail	I	8	B		58
257	Three Creek Lake and Tam McArthur Rim	I	10	C	•	58
258	McKenzie Pass Lava Fields	I	16	C		59
259	Cache Mountain	BC	14	C		51
259	Hoodoo to McKenzie Pass Traverse	BC	20	C		51/59
	V. THE CENTRAL CASCADES					
	23. THE BEND AREA					
264	Mount Bachelor Nordic Sports Center	N–A	30	A		60
264	Dutchman Flat Connector	N	2	A		60
264	Todd Lake Trail	N–I	7	A	•	60
266	Big Meadow Trail	I	5	A		60
266	Todd Ridge Trail	I	9	A		60
267	Swampy Lakes and Flagline Trails	I	8	B		60
267	Lost Valley Off-Trail Route	I	8	A	•	60
267	Broken Top Crater	I–A	10	B	•	60
268	Tam McArthur Rim	A	16	C		60
269	Green Lakes	BC	20	C		60
269	Sparks Lake	A	10	B		60
269	Moraine Lake	BC	18	D		60
272	Swampy Lakes Shelter Loop	N–I	5	A		62
272	Emil Nordeen Shelter Loop	I	5	A		62
272	Swede Ridge Shelter Loop	I	9	A		62
273	Vista Butte	I	7	B		62
275	Tangent Loop Trail	N	4	A		62
275	Knotweed Trail	N	3	A		62
275	Wednesdays Trail	N	4	A		62
276	Tumalo Falls	N	5	A		62
278	Novice Trails	N	1–5	A		63

PAGE		DIFFICULTY	DISTANCE	ELEVATION	CAMPSITE	MAP
278	Edison Butte Other Trails	I–A	2–12	B		63
279	Wanoga Butte	I	8	A		63
279	Kuamaksi Butte	I	6	A		63
	24. NEWBERRY CRATER					
282	Nordic Trail No. 9	N–I	6	A		64
282	Nordic Trail A	N–I	6	A		64
282	Paulina Peak	I	8–14	C		64
282	Lake Trail	I	3–9	A		64
282	South Lakeshore Trail	N	3–8	A		64
283	Big Obsidian Lava Flow	A	5–15	C		64
285	Hot Springs Lava Flow	I	8–10	A		64
286	The Dome	A	8–12	B		64
	25. WILLAMETTE PASS					
287	Westview Loops and Pengra Pass	N–I	2–3	A		65/66
287	Westview Loops	N–I	4	A		65/66
289	Bechtel Creek Trail	I	6	A		65/66
289	Midnight Lake, Diamond Peak Wilderness, and Yoran Lake	I	6–8	B		65/66
290	Gold Lake and Marilyn Lakes	N	5	A		65/66
290	Rosary Lakes	I	6	B		65
291	Maiden Peak	BC	14	D		65
292	Fuji Creek Trail	I	8	C		67
293	Waldo Lake	A	18–20	B		68
294	Odell Lake Resort and Crescent Lake Trail	N	8	A		69
295	Crescent Lake Flats Trail	N	7	A		69
296	Fawn Lake	I–A	11	B		69
296	Odell Butte and Little Odell Butte	I–A	11	C		70
297	Diamond Peak	BC	16	D		71
298	Northside Route	BC	18	D		71
299	Walker Mountain	A	6–12	C		72

PAGE		DIFFICULTY	DISTANCE	ELEVATION	CAMPSITE	MAP
	26. DIAMOND LAKE					
301	Nordic Center Trails	N	4	A		—
301	Round-the-Lake Loop	I	12	A		—
301	Vista Trail	N	4	A		—
303	Howlock Mountain Trail	I	7	B		73
303	Spruce Ridge Trail	I	6–8	B		73
303	Mount Thielsen Trail	A	3–8	C		73
303	Cinnamon Butte and Wits End	I	8–10	B–C		73
305	Pacific Crest National Scenic Trail (PCT)	BC	8–12	C		73
305	Crater Lake—North Rim	I–A	18	C		73
306	South Shore Trails	N	2–6	A		74
307	Horse 'N Teal Trail	N	3–6	A		74
307	Silent Creek Trail	N	4	A		74
	27. CRATER LAKE NATIONAL PARK					
309	Wizard Island Overlook Trail	N–I	2–6	A	•	75
309	Hemlock Trail	N–I	2	A		75
310	Raven Trail	I–A	2	A		75
311	Sun Notch Trail	N–I	9	B		75
312	Motor Nature Trail	I	14	C		75
312	Crater Peak	A	10	C		75
312	Garfield Peak	BC	8	C		75
313	Crater Lake Rim Trail	BC	30	C		75
	28. THE OCHOCO MOUNTAINS					
316	Ponderosa Loop	N	2	A		76
316	McGinnis Creek Loop	I	4	A		76
316	Ochoco Way	I–A	4	A		76
317	View Point Butte	I–A	10–12	C	•	76
318	Crystal Creek Valley and Grant Meadows	N	3–5	A	•	76
318	Walton Lake and the Sheep Corrals	I–A	10–14	B		76
318	Crystal Creek Route to Sheep Corrals	I–A	10	B		76

PAGE		DIFFICULTY	DISTANCE	ELEVATION	CAMPSITE	MAP
319	Lookout Mountain	I–A	6–13	C		77
321	Round Mountain	A–BC	14	C		77
323	Sherwood Saddle	N–I	2–8	A		79
324	Tower Point	A	8–10	C	•	79
324	Teaters Road and Sheep Rock Creek	I	4–10	B	•	79
	VI. EASTERN OREGON					
	29. THE JOHN DAY REGION					
328	East of Highway 395	N–I	2–12	A	•	81
329	Dry Soda Lookout	I–A	18	B		81
329	West of Highway 395	N–I	2–8	B		81
329	Cattle Drive Trail	I	2	A		81
330	Dixie Butte	I	10	D		82
330	Lower Road Loops	N–I	2–4	A		82
331	Bates Creek	N	4	A		83
331	Vincent Creek	N	4	B	•	84
332	Greenhorn and Vinegar Hill	I–A	8–14	C	•	85
333	Strawberry Mountain	I–A	8	C		86
334	Strawberry Lake	N	2	A		87
335	Logan Valley and Summit Prairie	N	2	A		87
335	Logan Valley	N	2–6	A		87
335	Summit Prairie	N	2	A	•	87
336	Deardorff Mountain	A	4–12	B		88
339	Snowshoe Creek Loop	N–I	6	B		91
340	Fields Peak	A	10–12	C	•	92
341	Aldrich Mountain	BC	20	D		93
	30. THE BLUE MOUNTAINS AND VICINITY					
343	Deadman Pass State Park	N–I	2–6	A		94
344	Emigrant Springs State Park	N–I	1–3	A		94
344	Meacham and Squaw Creek Overlook	N–I	1–3	A		94
345	Grande Ronde River Valley and Starkey	N	1–4	A		94

PAGE		DIFFICULTY	DISTANCE	ELEVATION	CAMPSITE	MAP
345	High Ridge Lookout and Horseshoe Prairie	I–A	3–10	B		94
346	Spout Springs	N–I	2–8	A		94
	31. THE ELKHORN MOUNTAINS					
347	Anthony Lakes Groomed Tracks	N–I	2–8	A		95
349	Grande Ronde Lake Basin	N	2–4	A		95
350	Hoffer Lakes	I	3	A		95
350	Black Lake and Elkhorn Crest Trail	I	3	A		95
350	Angell Basin and Ridgecrest	A	6	C		95
	32. THE WALLOWA MOUNTAINS					
356	Devils View Loop	N	2	A		97
356	Summit Groomed Loop	N	2	A		97
356	Divide Groomed Loop	I	2	A		97
356	Mountain View Loop	I	4	A		97
357	Wagon Road and Tenderfoot Trails	I	10	A		97
359	Aneroid Lake Basin	BC	16	D		98
360	McCully Basin	BC	12	D		98
362	Pine Valley Groomed Tracks	N	4	A		100
363	Cornucopia	I	12	C		100
363	Holbrook and Tunnel Creeks Tour	I	4–6	B		100
364	Summit Point	A	10–18	D		100
365	Cornucopia Peak	BC	12–18	D		100
367	Eagle Creek, Horton Pass, and East Lostine River Traverse	BC	30	D		98
368	Aneroid Basin, Tenderfoot Pass, Imnaha River, and Cornucopia Traverse	BC	30	D		98
369	Cornucopia, Hawkins Pass, and West Fork Wallowa River Traverse	BC	30	D		98
370	Beaver Mountain	N	3–4	A		101
370	Bald Mountain	A	10	B		101
	33. STEENS MOUNTAIN					
371	Westside Steens Mountain	BC	48	D		102

ACKNOWLEDGMENTS

Many individuals contributed to this guidebook. First, I want to express appreciation to Nancy Chapman, a strong skier and my patient wife. She not only accompanied me on many explorations of new areas, but also shared her computer expertise and advice with me in the final preparation of the manuscript.

The wide range of territory covered by this guidebook required information from many individuals. Special recognition goes to the following, who offered significant information on trails and routes, often in remote areas: Ted Fremd, Skylar Rickabaugh, Jennifer Stein Barker, Bob Ratcliff, Doug Ironside, Pete Krystad, Verle Duckering, Pat Wick, Jim Blanchard, Darryl Lloyd, Jeff Jendro, Dave Clemens, and Doug Newman, my predecessor and author of the first Oregon ski trails guidebook, now long out of print.

Others who contributed include Jill Dougherty, Bill Kerr, Darvel Lloyd, Harold Cole, Jana Ratcliff, Dr. Roger Sanders, Mark Hauter, Jacqui Bostrom, Steve Staloff, Bill Sullivan, George Wallenstein, Chuck Hinkle, Warren Aney, Jim Knoll, Dave Minor, Owen Bentley, and Brett Vielbig.

I want to express my gratitude to the editorial staff of The Mountaineers Books, who shared my vision of a definitive guidebook. My thanks to Donna DeShazo, a stern but appreciated taskmaster, and to Heath Lynn Silberfeld, the editor who helped mold the vast amount of copy into a coherent product and who worked most closely with me. Her abilities at rearranging tours into logical order and her judgment on word usage were invariably intelligent and appreciated. In addition, thanks to Marge Mueller for advice and assistance regarding map design.

A special word of appreciation is given in memory of John S. Day of Central Point and Medford, Oregon, who introduced Oregon to Nordic skiing in 1965. Since then, John Day's vision of "citizen skiing" for the general public as a life sport has become a reality. He directed his unfailing enthusiasm, resources, and considerable efforts to the promotion of Nordic skiing in its early years, and maintained close touch with the sport's growth. His own life, dedicated to a wide range of sports, set an example for all of us who had the privilege of knowing him. He was a charter member of the Oregon Nordic Club.

It also seems fitting to extend recognition to the following people, who have made significant contributions to the growth of modern Nordic skiing in Oregon: Bill Pruitt, Jay Bowerman, Virginia Meissner, Ron Radabaugh, Ed Park, John Craig, Homer Blackburn, Vilho Bjorn, George Korn, Emil Nordeen, Tom Gibbons, Gary Grimm, Doug Newman, Jim Blanchard, Frank Moore, and Bob Venner.

Many staff members of the U.S. Forest Service were helpful over the many years required to assemble information on new trails and sno-parks, skiers' day-use huts, trailhead relocations, and many other details. Without their many contributions, the completeness of this revision would not have been possible. The following Forest Service personnel provided invaluable information:

Mount Hood: Kevin Slagle, Mary Ellen Fitzgerald, Paul Norman, Paul Koehler, Laurel Skelton, Bruce Haynes, Wendy Evans

Mount St. Helens: Randy Peterson, Jim Nieland, Stefan Nofeld, Francisco Valenzuela, Leo Zacker

Wind River: Joe Koshko, Russell Plaeger

Trout Lake and Mount Adams: Greg Page, Mary Bean

Santiam Pass: Kirk Metsger, Bill Jones, Mike Kelly, Paul Engstrom, Steve Otoupalik, Jay Moore

Bend and Newberry Crater: Chris Savo, Mike Underwood, Tom Carlson, Marvin Lang, Art Hearing

Willamette Pass: Chris Jensen, Ray Christ

Diamond Lake: Debi Church, Terry Klingenberg

Ochocos and Maurys: Larry Friesen, Chuck Hedges, Barbara Smith, Bob Harrison

John Day: Tim Jones, Dan Ermovick, Debbie Ried, Jacque McConnell

Elkhorns: Dale Hough, Rich Tobin, Lynn Roehm

Wallowas: David Clemens, Roger Averbeck

INTRODUCTION

In the years since the first edition of this guidebook appeared there have been dramatic additions to the ski trails of both Washington and Oregon national forests. This is partly due to the decline in timber harvesting, and to an increased emphasis on forest recreation. The result has been hundreds of miles of new marked ski trails, many of which are not on existing roads but have been cut out of the forests, resulting in well-designed ski routes that provide a quality winter experience.

Mount St. Helens National Volcanic Monument alone contains over 30 miles of specially constructed and marked trails. In addition, it seems that every ranger district that has snow now has ski trails. The Santiam Pass region has some 70 miles of trails scattered among six separate trail systems, not counting the original trail complex near Hoodoo Ski Area. Willamette Pass offers ski trails in all directions, with a number of attractive day-use log shelters, as do the Santiam Pass and Bend ski areas. Added to this are the machine-groomed tracks at Upper Wind River in Washington and Mount Hood in Oregon, with Mount St. Helens planning not only additional trails but also groomed trails in the future.

This second edition has been greatly expanded over the first one that appeared in 1984, and now includes all the major skiing areas from Mount St. Helens to Crater Lake, then east from Central Oregon clear to the Wallowa Mountains on the Idaho border. This is a vast area that offers a wide range of skiing experiences. The present book describes about 500 ski trails and areas totaling about 2,000 miles of skiing.

A significant effort has been made to describe ski areas in such a way as to disperse the growing number of skiers, to offer loops and alternative routes so that there is less human impact on everyone's personal experience. Hopefully, many skiers will be encouraged to leave the usual, crowded trails and explore in isolation less-used areas. In addition, the trails are rated for difficulty (Novice, Intermediate, Advanced, Backcountry), thereby minimizing the chance of getting onto trails that are difficult or of little interest.

Most skiers seldom venture farther than 4 miles from the trailhead. The many hundreds of miles of trails described here, some not marked and requiring route-finding skills, provide opportunities to expand skiing skills and experience a more self-reliant attitude and appreciation of the sport. Those who are more comfortable with skiing out and back on the same trail will find the concept of loop skiing a challenging and refreshing experience. Loops and connector trails are included wherever possible to encourage different and more efficient use patterns, particularly in some of the more popular areas. This revised and enlarged edition will hopefully make many emerging Backcountry skiers happy, too.

There are a good number of one-day tours, in many parts of the two states, including Mount St. Helens and Mount Adams, that will take skiers to remote, unique, and scenic areas that usually include climbs to high areas and often to fire-lookout sites.

Although the thorough coverage of this guidebook may lead you to conclude that it covers every road, trail, and viewpoint, leaving nothing to the imagination, be assured that there are still many interesting places to discover. In every aspect of life or sport, there should always remain a little of the unknown.

The growth of Nordic skiing in the Pacific Northwest has nearly outpaced the development of skiing areas, trails, and sno-parks. It is in the interest of all skiers to be concerned about and involved with future planning by the Forest Service and outdoor clubs for Nordic skiing. Without suitable additions and improvements to existing areas, the problem of crowding will worsen and result in a reduction of skiing quality.

People who have skied in several states will attest that each region has its own special mood and physical qualities. Those who have skied the mountains of Washington and Oregon almost always speak of the unique natural beauty and variety of the areas covered in this guidebook. No other skiing region offers more variety or a greater concentration of skiing routes. Our Northwest volcanoes, extensive and beautiful forests, and accessible backcountry are remarkable assets to be valued.

For first-time skiers in this region the descriptions and trail ratings should serve to make initiation pleasant. No more wasting time on dull, snow-covered roads that lead nowhere, or skiing to within a few yards of a fine viewpoint but missing it because you didn't know it was there and didn't ski quite far enough. For help in choosing tours appropriate for you, see the matrix of tours at the end of this book.

The bonanza of new ski trails mentioned earlier carries with it some responsibilities, however, for every skier. We have been given these trails by the Forest Service, some built with the aid of volunteers, but the maintenance will be more and more our own responsibility due to lack of Forest Service funds. We must volunteer, both individually and through our clubs and environmental organizations, to help with this eternal maintenance on a year-by-year basis. Every year many trees fall onto trails due to wind or age, and countless blue-diamond trail markers pop off as tree growth forces the diamonds over the nail heads. These must all be replaced, and, of course, brush and small trees must be periodically trimmed and cleared from trails. Volunteer work is good exercise and a rewarding and pride-producing community effort. One of the great pleasures of work parties is meeting others who share your interests and becoming familiar with new skiing areas. Call one or more ranger districts and volunteer at least one or two days of each summer—guaranteed, you will not regret it and you will feel a great sense of involvement and accomplishment.

TRAIL DIFFICULTY AND SKILL LEVEL

Each trail in this guide has been rated according to the level of skill required to ski it comfortably:

Novice. Can be skied with reasonable ease and safety by a first-time skier of average athletic ability. The trail is easy to follow, often marked, and seldom longer than 3 or 4 miles. It is restricted to gentle terrain. A Novice skier often has little stamina, partly from lack of efficient skiing technique, and has little or no knowledge of winter survival. The Novice has little ability to ski downhill, turn, or control speed.

Intermediate. Can be skied by skiers who have mastered basic gliding, turning, slowing, and stopping techniques. The trail may involve some minor route finding, downhill skiing on moderate to moderately steep slopes, and distances up to 10 miles round trip. An Intermediate skier has some knowledge of map reading, route finding, and winter survival. He or she is confident on tours, has suitable equipment and clothing, and has developed a good sense of skiing and skiing conditions.

Starting across Terrible Traverse on Bennett Ridge Trail; Gunsight Ridge and Windy Peak behind

Advanced. Can be skied only by skiers with good stamina and highly developed skiing skills. The Advanced skier is able to ski in all snow conditions and to ski safely and with control on most slopes. He or she is skilled with map and compass and is able to travel safely in all weather conditions and over all types of terrain and understands avalanche safety and conditions.

Backcountry. Should be attempted only by properly equipped skiers who can assume sole responsibility for their own comfort and safety. In addition to being proficient in skiing on all slopes and conditions, they are also skilled in compass use and map reading, know proper route selection, are fully aware of the complex factors of avalanches, know the symptoms and prevention of hypothermia, and know first aid.

A word of caution in rating one's own skill level: the number of times or years one has skied is by itself not an indication of skill. Skill lies in technique and relates to the number of miles skied and types of terrain on which one has skied. Most skiers tend to consider themselves Intermediates after only a few times on skis, whereas they really lack the skills to qualify for that category. Many self-appointed Intermediates are truly Advanced Novices. A flat-terrain expert is rarely more than a Novice on varied terrain. Many times around Trillium Lake does not an Intermediate make.

TERRAIN STEEPNESS

Although skiing uphill can be taxing, most people find skiing down the same hill more difficult to master. Therefore, the following categories describe slope steepness in terms of downhill difficulties.

Gentle. Only average athletic ability required to handle this terrain with ease, but under fast conditions may exceed a Novice's ability.

Moderate. Too fast for most Novice skiers, and under fast conditions may challenge the ability of Intermediates. The Intermediate skier can easily handle moderate steepness in average snow.

Moderately Steep. Usually too fast for most skiers skiing straight downhill. Skills demanded to control speed are the use of turns, stems or snowplow maneuvers, and effective use of edging. On open slopes, descending traverses and kick turns are often used.

Steep. Cannot be skied straight downhill under control by any skier. Dangerous for Novices and very difficult for Intermediate skiers. Advanced skiers may have difficulty. Descent is usually with traverses and kick turns, sidestepping or walking down. Turns are very difficult unless conditions are perfect.

These terms are used on all tour descriptions and are uniformly applied so that you can compare the terrain of various trails. You will find that skis and body easily and quickly come to learn these terms.

At best, however, such terms are difficult to apply because of the many factors that affect slope conditions and skiing speed. The same slope may change greatly from one day to the next, or even from early morning to late afternoon. Insofar as possible the trail descriptions include commentary on such changes when they seriously affect slope conditions along a particular trail.

NOMENCLATURE

The lack of names for natural features in some areas has made it necessary to apply names for convenience in descriptions. Some may think that assuming such a prerogative is pretentious. To them I can only say that doing so was unavoidable. In selecting names, I have attempted to remain within the bounds of accepted practice and good taste, using logical associations or, as in the case of the Trillium Basin, using names from Norse mythology. Examples of such place names following geographical or historical guidelines are Barlow Saddle, Weygandt Basin, Trillium Pass, Knebal Pass, Wy'east Trail, and Boy Scout Ridge. Only the test of time will tell whether these will be accepted. I hope that skiers will find such names appropriate and relevant. I am confident that no local or common names for an area or feature have been overlooked, and that names I have selected for descriptions do not conflict with established customs.

MAPS

The sketch maps in this book are as current as possible, and often display roads and features not on National Forest and USGS maps. The sketch maps will often be all you need for Novice-rated tours. However, should you get off the described route, intentionally or otherwise, become disoriented, or decide to explore off the trail, a map showing a larger area will be invaluable. In fact, such maps will add enjoyment to any trip by identifying more features of the area. This author recommends always carrying a Forest Service, USGS, or Green Trails map, or any other map available from the Forest Service. The preceding is also true for Intermediate, Advanced, and Backcountry tours, only more so.

All marked Forest Service trails are identified by trailhead signs and usually are found at sno-parks. Trail maps are often posted at trailheads, and sometimes a supply of free printed maps can be found in a box nearby.

The book's sketch maps are occasionally simplified and distorted slightly to make interpretation easier. Some features may be omitted. These maps are not intended for compass work, but you will find them necessary for your tour. If you do not carry them, you may become confused at junctions and side roads if the trail is unmarked.

Mileages on the sketch maps are accurate and are derived from several sources. Many are obtained from the Forest Service or are derived from driving and biking the roads or trails and recording distances. Off-road and off-trail routes are derived from hiking or by measuring from large-scale maps.

For Backcountry skiing you should always carry both a National Forest and a USGS map. The USGS topographic maps usually do not include the latest logging roads, so the National Forest maps are an important adjunct. In fact, for Backcountry skiing where there are roads, an even more important map is a Forest Service "transportation map," often called a "fireman map." These maps of ranger districts are large scale and display all roads in detail. They are usually up-to-date and often contain elevation contour lines. Transportation maps are essential for Backcountry tours, useful for any long tour, and particularly so if your objective is changed en route on skis, or when you find the road you want is not drivable. They will often make finding an alternative route easier. In the future, National Forest maps will reflect a new wildlife ethic—the elimination of many roads from maps as they are closed to vehicles for wildlife protection.

Green Trails topographical maps, available for many areas of the Cascades, are the most useful maps for skiers. They are based on USGS maps and have all the same contours and topographical features. In addition they have summer and winter ski trails shown clearly, and they are more complete than USGS maps with regard to logging roads. They are available in many sporting-goods stores.

Leaving maps at home or in the car has ruined more than one potentially good tour. The best advice to all skiers is to always carry a map or two of the area in which you plan to ski.

In the Pacific Northwest, most ski trails gain elevation to their final destinations and descend on their return trips. If there are significant ups and downs along the way to a higher, final destination, these elevation changes are added to the basic start-to-finish gain to give a realistic value to the expenditure of energy. This consolidated total is expressed in the text as a cumulative elevation gain. Although most trails have some ups and downs, these usually do not result in significant additional use of energy and are therefore not added to the basic elevation gain for most trails.

SNO-PARKS

Oregon and Washington each operate sno-park programs between November 15 and April 30. During this period, each vehicle must display a sno-park permit. Both daily and annual permits are sold at many sporting-goods shops and at many facilities near winter recreation areas. Parking in designated sno-parks without a permit will result in a fine. Oregon, Washington, and Idaho have reciprocal agreements wherein each state honors the others' permits. Parking outside sno-parks is sometimes possible if the vehicle is outside the roadside fog line or off the pavement or travel area, not on a curve, and does not obstruct normal snowplowing. Although a sno-park may be full, parking outside on the road may be illegal, such as at Mount St. Helens. Always check with authorities before taking a chance. Unfortunately, the county sheriff or state patrol may not always be around to advise.

DRIVING

Winter weather changes quickly, so be prepared for snow and ice, and watch for black ice in shady areas. Drive cautiously and defensively. Even though you have studded tires, front-wheel or four-wheel drive, carry tire chains and a shovel. If you are driving on unplowed roads do not be tempted to drive too far to gain distance and elevation before parking. The snow will get deeper and it may become difficult to proceed or turn around. If you are planning to Backcountry ski from such roads, call the appropriate ranger district beforehand for road information. If a road has been plowed for winter logging, be cautious driving on weekdays. Always have alternative plans (and maps) as you may not reach your prime objective.

Note: The Forest Service refers to the violation of your car at trailheads or sno-parks as "car clouting." It is an unfortunate result of a loss of the ethic that respects the property of others. Break-ins are happening at an alarming rate. If possible, do not leave anything showing in your car. Hiding things under a sweater or cover is not effective. Put belongings in your trunk, and never leave money, credit cards, or keys in your car or trunk—carry them with you. Always report break-ins immediately to county sheriff or state patrol. If you are parking overnight in ski areas, be especially careful—many cars are "clouted" at night.

SNOWMOBILES

In spite of the high cost of this sport, it is not dying, and in some areas there are many snowmobilers and you will have to share roads or trails. As these vehicles are now much quieter than they used to be, you must be alert to unexpected encounters with them, particularly on winding roads where there is only a short line-of-sight. Always ski near the edge of the road or trail. Be a good neighbor and do not show hostility. In general, snowmobilers are friendly, family-oriented people who do not want to disturb you. However, do not hesitate to report "maverick" riders who threaten your safety or enter closed areas.

BACKCOUNTRY AND WILDERNESS ETHICS

This guidebook is aimed primarily at Novice to Intermediate skiers, although many tours described are for Advanced skiers. Oregon has remarkable opportunities for Backcountry skiers with access to spectacular high country from the major highways. As the skiing population grows more experienced and confident, the number of skiers venturing farther into the backcountry will increase. Many will find a quality wilderness experience, but to maintain this we must all practice no-trace skiing by leaving the areas we visit as we found them. Our attitudes are often affected in winter by the covering of snow that reduces our awareness of human impact.

Never cut branches except in survival situations when you need insulation. If you need wood, use only what is dead and down. Keep any fires small; build only in existing fire rings, and only where safe and legally permitted. Consider using a stove even where food fires are permitted. Carry all litter out. Don't burn it. Do not mark, spray paint, blaze, or hang plastic markers. If you must use plastic, take it with you when you leave. Crepe paper is biodegradable and is therefore better for marking a difficult route.

These rules of conduct require discipline, are good wilderness habits, and benefit both winter and summer visitors. Any sign of your passing will reduce the quality of the wilderness experience for those who follow.

Some tours rated as Advanced may appear to you as Backcountry—there is often a fine line in judging a tour, and the skier must be able to judge his or her own skills and limitations. There are comments and suggestions throughout the book on Backcountry skiing, so only a couple of additional points will be made here beyond the obvious, common sense that is required:

- Always use runaway straps to prevent ski loss.
- Carry ski climbers.
- Be prepared for any eventuality.
- Carry shovel and tire chains even though your tires may be studded.
- Above all, be totally self-reliant.

If your tour will take you onto unplowed roads, get information on conditions before you leave so that you can plan alternative goals if you cannot achieve your primary objective. Be wary of any advice, especially from non-skiers, and remember that all information is not current. What was plowed yesterday may not be plowed today after more snowfall. Being properly equipped will ensure greater confidence and a greater chance of success.

SANITATION

A conspicuous abuse of the winter scene is uncovered human waste. This creates a health hazard, and mars otherwise beautiful areas. Use backcountry toilets when available. Always dig a hole with your boot or ski pole and relieve yourself in it. Carry out toilet paper in a plastic bag or bury waste at least 200 feet from any water source. Remember, toilet paper will remain long after the spring thaw. When selecting a toilet site, avoid lakes and streams, frozen or otherwise, and always get well away from trails, roads, and other facilities.

TRAIL COURTESY

The quality and enjoyment of the skiing experience can be maintained if we all show sensitivity to other skiers and minimize the effects of our passage through the silent winter landscape.

- If you stop to rest, eat, or wax, step off to the side without damaging the continuity of the track. When skiing in a group, do not block the track.
- If you fall, fill in the depression (sitzmark) your body makes and re-establish the track. The sitzmark may cause others to fall. Just scrape snow into it and tamp the snow down.
- Step aside to permit faster skiers to pass.

- Avoid walking across or in an established track. Snowshoers and snow players should not walk on ski tracks. Snowmobilers should not ride on ski tracks.
- When skiing uphill, always give the right-of-way to the skier coming downhill by stepping out of the track.
- Carry out your own litter and that of others. Litter should not be dropped on the snow or buried. It diminishes the outdoor experience for all. If you pack it in, pack it out. Use a plastic bag. Practice no-trace skiing.
- Enjoy the quiet outdoor world without yelling, shouting, or whistle blowing, except to solicit aid.
- Avoid downhill runs in ski areas. If you must cross one, do so rapidly, or try to stay near its margins.
- If there is more than one set of tracks, ski in the right-hand track. If trails are marked for skiing direction, proceed in that direction only. Keep poles close to the body when near another skier.
- If an accident occurs, render assistance. If you saw the accident, establish your identity as a witness.
- Avoid use of fire. If you require a warm meal on day tours, use a thermos bottle or carry a stove. If a fire is absolutely necessary, keep it small and use only lower, dead limbs. Do not cut trees or boughs. Do not cut dead snags, which are a picturesque part of the winter scene.
- Respect private property, and do not block driveways.
- If you must ski with your dog, ski where there are no other skiers. Dogs ruin good tracks. Better yet: leave your dog at home.

Note: The Forest Service discourages pets in cross-country areas. Dogs get in the way on narrow trails and usually walk on, and ruin, ski tracks. They also pose a hazard to skiers, particularly Novices, who cannot easily maneuver out of the way. Dogs chase wildlife and mess up skiing areas with their urine and feces. Skiers who insist on bringing their dogs should ski in areas that are not heavily used and should restrain them when other skiers approach. Dogs should not be permitted to urinate or defecate on or near ski tracks, and dog owners should clean up after them. If possible, leave your dog at home.

SETTING A TRACK

Always set a good track for yourself and for those who follow. If you are following a track, maintain it or improve it. The tracks ahead of you often do not permit pleasurable skiing because they have been carelessly set by inexperienced skiers. If you are breaking trail, look back at your tracks. If they wander or waiver, then you are skiing inefficiently, and not leaving an enjoyable track for those who follow, or indeed for your own return trip. Learn to set a good track, as straight as possible, with skis about six inches apart. A group of skiers should ski in the same track, each improving the track ahead. Bad tracks are difficult to ski, and destroy the rhythm of forward movement.

Emil Nordeen Shelter in Swampy Lakes area; Newberry Crater in distance

CASCADE WEATHER

To the uninitiated, particularly skiers from the Rockies, the mild winter weather of the Cascades may be both a surprise and disappointment. Typical Cascade winters are overcast, with air temperatures often hovering near freezing. The result is wet snowfalls, particularly at 3,500-foot to 4,500-foot elevations, where most Nordic skiing is done. These warm conditions on occasion cause problems with staying dry and also with waxing skis. On the other hand, every winter delivers many fine skiing days, so it balances out well if you are prepared with the proper clothing and attitude.

Although there are many days of cold snow and weather, there are others when air temperatures allow occasional rain. Depending on weather conditions on the west side of the Cascades—for example, at Government Camp on Mount Hood—it is sometimes worth altering skiing plans to seek out better weather. By driving to Timberline Lodge, for example, you may get above the damp weather into snowfall, or even above the clouds. With threatening forecasts and weather, driving to the east side of Hood—to the White River or Pocket Creek areas, or perhaps even to Clear Lake—often results in improved weather. Sometimes the difference in weather is startling: from cloudy with rain to broken skies with no rain. Of course, this is not always the case, but it is often enough to justify driving east to look for better conditions.

Skiing in the Cascades does develop in some skiers the ability to make at-home weather forecasts. These can often result in an exceptional day of skiing even when visible conditions would indicate otherwise. Do not always judge the area where you plan to ski, which probably has its own micro-climate, by local forecasts for nearby lowlands or other mountain areas. It is often worth taking a chance in spite of bad forecasts. Careful attention to snow level, freezing level, weather reports, ski-area reports, common sense, and knowledge of basic weather patterns and cloud formations over a period of time will lead one to quite accurate analysis of mountain weather. Oddly, some of the best skiing days have been when weather in Portland was at its worst.

Recent years have seen unusual weather patterns for much of each winter in the Cascades. The normally low maritime cloud masses, predictable and solid, seem to have given way to atypical patterns, with thunderstorms, rapidly changing weather fronts, and cloud forms of surprising variety. The winter of 1982–1983 saw heavier-than-average snowfall above 5,000 feet, but less-than-average below, in the Nordic skiing zone. The previous winter, with above-average snowfall at all elevations (8 feet at Summit Meadows in mid-April), contrasted with the five preceding snow-drought years, when the maximum depth at Government Camp was 5 feet and the average was less than 2 feet, with many periods of bare ground. The winter of 1992–1993 saw a heavy snow pack, after eight drought years when snow was seldom deep for any length of time.

The snowline on Mount Hood and in the Bend area is typically near the 3,500-foot elevation, fluctuating up or down on a short-term basis. Above 3,500 feet, the depth of snow increases rapidly. As there are no sno-parks in the Clackamas, and therefore no snowplowing above the snowline, fluctuations in the 2,000- to 3,000-foot zone will affect your skiing plans more than other areas. The Mount St. Helens and Upper Wind River areas, also subject to snowline fluctuations in recent years due to unstable weather patterns, typically have a lower snowline than Mount Hood. Southern Washington has an average 3,000-foot snowline. All areas in this guidebook generally have good skiing into April and, in the Bend backcountry, into May. Spring skiing on St. Helens is usually shorter, however, as most of the ski routes on south-facing slopes have less protective tree cover. Fluctuations and snow depth are often unpredictable, however, and therefore there is no sure way of knowing exact conditions until you go to the area you want to ski.

The west slopes of the Cascades receive heavier snowfall and experience more cloudy weather than the east slopes. As moist air from the Pacific Ocean reaches the Cascades, it rises and cools, producing heavy precipitation. The east side of the Cascades receives less precipitation and enjoys fairer weather. The Bend area benefits from this advantage and is considered by many skiers to be a haven from the damper weather and snows of the west side—an occasional delusion, however, as even in Bend the weather is not always ideal.

The preceding comments certainly hold true also for the Santiam Pass and Willamette Pass areas, where driving eastward from the passes during bad weather may lead to better conditions. Across the Santiam area lie Suttle Lake, Camp Sherman, and the Sisters region with numerous trails at a range of elevations. At Willamette Pass, going east for better weather might take you to Crescent Lake, Odell Butte, Big Marsh, or even as far as Walker Mountain.

EASTERN OREGON WEATHER

Although weather in Eastern Oregon is usually more stable and colder than in the Cascades, you can also encounter unseasonable periods of warm weather similar to the Cascades, and also periods of extreme cold. Some of the tours in Eastern Oregon will take you to high, windy areas and, if you are there in conjunction with a cold wave, you will want to be prepared with proper clothing—that is, clothing to pull over your regular "Cascade outfit," such as wind pants, windproof jacket, and good mittens. To keep your feet warm, try pulling old socks (not cotton) over your boots with cutouts for the pin holes. A ski mask or balaclava for bitter-weather protection is also important. Be prepared for a range of conditions, or your trip may be ruined.

ICING UP

Because the vast majority of Northwest cross-country skiers use waxless skis, it may seem strange to devote space to the subject of waxing. Temperatures near freezing cause the greatest problems, and skis with bases dampened by wet snow or from picking up moisture during the drive to the mountains are likely to "ice up."

Icing up refers to the formation of frostlike patches on ski bases, and just one such patch affects gliding significantly. Such a problem usually gets

On Tam McArthur Rim with north side of Broken Top and South Sister beyond

worse unless the patches are scraped off with a flexible putty knife or other scraper. The application of paraffin or other wax, even over the gripping area, will help, and is best finished by smoothing all areas of the base with a waxing cork. The smoothing process distributes the wax more than it polishes the surface. If the gripping area is not covered as well as possible, it may ice up. A commercial wipe-on liquid product for skis is usually helpful. The process in most cases has to be repeated. The slightest icing is frustrating and energy consuming, so have the right tools and wax in your pack on every tour.

AVALANCHES

Avalanches are rare in most areas covered by this book, unlike the precipitous North Cascades, where avalanches are commonplace. The Cascades of Oregon and Southern Washington feature quite gentle terrain at skiing elevations—generally from 3,500 feet to 6,000 feet. Most of the ski routes described here are through forest and on trails and roads below timberline. Of course many of these ski routes do ultimately lead to open slopes and high country, where cornices and slab avalanches pose a threat. Where danger exists, it has been duly noted in the trail descriptions. Where avalanches are not mentioned, the potential can be considered low to nil.

Infrequent evidence of avalanches on some of the ski routes described, however, does not mean that they never occur. Skiers should always be alert to possible avalanche danger. Any slope steeper than 25 degrees is vulnerable to avalanches, but most slides occur on slopes of 30 degrees to 45 degrees. Any slope, however, may avalanche under the right conditions, and it is imperative that all skiers have some knowledge of those conditions and of what to do should an avalanche bury oneself or a fellow skier. Such knowledge may save your life or that of a friend.

The time of greatest avalanche activity is during or immediately following a storm. Eighty percent of all slides occur then. At such times skiers should avoid steep slopes, especially those on the leeward side of a ridge, where windblown snow can form large, unstable drifts and cornices. Ridgetops are generally safer than the slopes on either side, but skiers must avoid venturing, perhaps unwittingly, onto cornices. Stay well away from the edge of cliffs and steep leeward slopes, where the extent, location, and stability of cornices may not be apparent.

When skiing in valleys, stay on the flat, well away from the slopes. Learn to recognize avalanche signs, such as fracture lines and steep, open chutes through the forest. If hardpacked snow sounds hollow, keep off!

If you must travel on a dangerous slope, do so one person at a time. Before proceeding, loosen your equipment. Avoid traversing the slope; if possible, ski or walk directly up or down. Under no circumstances should you cross a convex slope. If you must traverse, stay as near the top as possible and use dense woods or scattered trees as islands of safety. As each person ventures onto the slope, others in the party should watch and wait, staying alert to the sights and sounds that may signal an imminent slide.

If you are caught, get rid of whatever equipment you can. Skis, poles, and pack can trap you. Make a vigorous effort to swim, staying near the top and side of the flow. When you come to rest, keep snow from packing against your face. Try to form an air pocket as the movement decreases. If buried, try to stay calm to conserve air and strength.

If you have seen someone swept away, mark the spot where the person was last seen. Search directly downhill from there. If there are several survivors, one should go for aid while the others organize a systematic search. Use the handle of your ski poles to probe carefully into the snow. Remember, after one hour, the victim has only a 50 percent chance of survival.

If planning a tour in avalanche-prone terrain, be sure to call the Northwest Avalanche Center hotlines for current snow avalanche information (Oregon and Southern Washington: 503-326-2400, Washington: 206-526-6677).

CLOTHING

The clothing you wear is the most basic item of all your cross-country equipment. Your comfort and enjoyment to a large extent depend on what you wear. In severe weather proper clothing can ensure your survival. Yet clothing selection is also a personal matter, and a wide range of styles will be seen on the trails. Whatever style you prefer, your clothing should keep you warm and dry while permitting maximum freedom of movement.

As a general rule avoid cotton, which absorbs moisture, conducts the cold to your body, and dries slowly. Instead dress in wool or suitable synthetic fabrics. Keep your clothing light and flexible, dressing in layers for warmth rather than relying on heavy, cumbersome garments. In the Northwest it is also important to carry good rain gear, either breathable or fully-coated waterproof fabrics. If your jacket is light, it can double as a windbreaker. Modern, thin, tight, light clothing has little insulation value and requires backup covering for bad weather. Gaiters, a basic item of clothing, are designed to keep your feet dry by keeping snow from entering boot tops. Although in wet snow it is impossible to keep any boots and socks dry, gaiters are necessary. Low gaiters are entirely adequate for most skiing. High gaiters are absolutely necessary for Backcountry skiing, and for skiers who wear slacks, jeans (cotton, and really unacceptable), or long pants.

WHAT TO TAKE

Winter is fickle, a season of rapid and often unpredictable weather changes. Every skier should hope for the best weather and prepare for the worst. Winter, while beautiful, is quick to punish the unprepared—at best, you will be miserable if ill-equipped, and at worst you will find yourself unprepared in a survival situation. Each pack should include at least the "ten essentials":

1. Extra clothing
2. Extra food
3. Sunglasses
4. Knife
5. First-aid kit
6. Fire starter
7. Matches in a waterproof container
8. Flashlight/headlamp, with spare bulbs and batteries
9. Map
10. Compass

An eleventh essential for ski tours is a repair kit (see below for what to take and how to use the items).

In addition, day skiers should also have the following in their packs: closed-cell foam seating pad, lunch and full water bottle, snow scraper, paraffin or wax, toilet paper, litter bag, rain suit, extra mittens, extra gloves and socks, and a sweater.

For day tours rated Advanced, take the following items in addition to the above: survival food, whistle, two plastic garbage bags for emergency cover, container for melting snow, small nylon-tarp shelter, heat tabs or stove, heavy sweater or pile or down jacket.

REPAIR KIT AND HOW TO USE IT

There should be at least one complete repair kit with every party. Carry it in a compact stuff sack or other container. You may not have to repair your own equipment, but someone else, perhaps a stranger on the trail, will be eternally grateful for your repair kit. It does not add significant weight to your pack and will inevitably be needed at some time or another. The repair kit should include the following items:

Spare ski pole basket. If necessary, use tape or wire to attach securely.

Plastic ski tip. The tip that broke off may not be found in a bad fall.

Binding bail. For rugged skiing, some skiers tie the binding bail to the binding to eliminate accidental loss; they may also run a "runaway strap" from the binding to the boot or ankle to secure the ski in event the binding opens on a steep slope.

Swiss Army knife. It must include an awl for drilling screw holes; a binding torn from a ski may have to be placed elsewhere on the ski to ensure a snug fit; use an awl for making new screw holes; for a tighter fit stuff the holes with steel wool or match sticks; in extreme situations, drive bolts through the ski to hold the binding—this will certainly make skiing difficult, but it will ensure your retreat to the trailhead.

Needle-nose pliers. Choose a small size, with wire cutter; an essential tool for cutting and manipulating wire.

Screwdriver. Stubby type; make sure the head fits the screws on your skis.

Screws. Carry a small assortment; you will need at least three to fit the usual binding.

Thin bolts and nuts. For where screws fail.

Steel wool. For reinforcing screw holes.

Wire. Use to attach binding, support broken pole or basket, attach new basket, or splint a cracked ski or delaminated tip.

Fiber tape. For same use as wire; in addition, it is essential for mending torn clothes or boots.

Nylon cord. Useful for tying a shelter together, repairing clothing, holding a boot in a binding, dangling a container over a snowbank for water, etc.; where friction would wear out a cord or where elasticity is undesirable, use wire.

Short nylon strap. For replacing broken pole strap.

2 long (30-inch) nylon straps. Useful for attaching boot to ski if a bail breaks or is lost.

Large safety pins.

Skiing with this additional gear may seem troublesome, but a piece of tape or spare pole basket can make the difference between an easy return to your car and a difficult, tiring, even dangerous experience. The extra ounces of repair equipment are an important investment in your enjoyment, peace of mind, and perhaps survival.

HYPOTHERMIA

Hypothermia is caused by exposure to cold, but not necessarily freezing temperatures, and is aggravated by wet, wind, and exhaustion. It is the number-one killer of outdoor recreationists. Shivering is the first sign that the body core temperature has dropped to the critical level. The following signs occur afterward and may not be recognized by the victim: slurred speech, memory lapse, stumbling, drowsiness, and loss of hand control. Hypothermia alters the brain functions and creeps up without warning. Without treatment it can lead to collapse and eventual death.

A few precautions to prevent hypothermia: avoid sweating, stay dry, do not wear cotton clothing of any sort, be aware of your partners' conditions, carry extra clothes (in the Northwest climate, waterproof clothes are essential), eat often.

The first step in treating hypothermia is to get the victim to shelter, and out of the wind. Set up a shelter tarp or windbreak of snow. Try to warm the victim. Build a fire, prepare warm liquids, give quick-energy food, and apply additional layers of dry clothes. If that does not help, make skin-to skin contact to transfer body heat. Putting the victim into a sleeping bag alone will not help; an external heat source is needed.

FROSTBITE

While not common in the Cascades, frostbite is a hazard to be aware of. In frostbite, body tissues actually freeze. If you have cold fingers, nose, chin, ears, or toes, warm them immediately. If there is no sensation, it may be frostbite, and immediate warming is essential. Never rub frozen skin. If toes are cold, do not add extra socks as this will reduce blood supply. Warm affected body parts and cold toes against a partner's bare, warm skin. The stomach area works well.

A NOTE ABOUT SAFETY

Safety is an important concern in all outdoor activities. No guidebook can alert you to every hazard or anticipate the limitations of every reader. Therefore, the descriptions of roads, trails, routes, and natural features in this book are not representations that a particular place or excursion will be safe for your party. When you follow any of the routes described in this book, you assume responsibility for your own safety. Under normal conditions, such excursions require the usual attention to traffic, road and trail conditions, weather, terrain, the capabilities of your party, and other factors. Keeping informed on current conditions and exercising common sense are the keys to a safe, enjoyable outing.

The Mountaineers

Part I
THE SOUTHERN WASHINGTON CASCADES

The Cascades of Southern Washington—from near the town of Goldendale in the east to Larch Mountain in the west—offer skiers many destinations that add variety to the usual type of Northwest skiing. They include Larch and Silver Star Mountains, the incomparable Mount St. Helens, the Upper Wind River–Crazy Hills region, the Trout Lake–Mount Adams–Glenwood area, all in the Gifford Pinchot National Forest, and to the east of these the Simcoe Mountains. For Portland–Vancouver skiers, skiing Mount St. Helens requires driving no farther than to the trails on the east side of Mount Hood, and the Trout Lake–Mount Adams area is not much farther.

Opposite: *Mount St. Helens and ash cloud from Muddy River Lahar*

Chapter 1

MOUNT ST. HELENS

On May 18, 1980, a devastating volcanic explosion destroyed the beautiful symmetry of Mount St. Helens, removing some 1,300 feet of the summit, reshaping the mountain in a few moments to a somewhat squat, domelike peak. The incredible blast destroyed miles of roads and leveled 150 square miles of forest. Nordic skiing on the mountain's north side was eliminated due to the subsequent closure of large areas for public safety.

Skiing interest was then diverted to the south side of the mountain, which is readily accessible from the Vancouver (Washington) and Portland (Oregon) metropolitan area. Excellent roads lead to the skiing areas, only 65 miles from the Columbia River bridges at Portland. The most direct route from Portland is to cross the I-205 bridge, then take the Orchards exit onto Highway 503, which leads northward via Highway 503 past Battleground, through Amboy, past the headquarters of the Mount St. Helens National Volcanic Monument near Chelatchie Prairie, then north to leave Highway 503 at "Jack's Corner." Here the route turns east to the village of Cougar. Continue east on Road 90 6.7 miles, then turn left onto Road 83, which provides access to the southside ski tours. An alternative route to St. Helens from the Portland/Vancouver area is via Interstate 5 north to Woodland/Highway 503 (Exit 21), then east on 503 to Cougar. This route is 10 miles longer than the route through Battleground. The driving routes to St. Helens's south-, west-, and northside ski routes are described later in this chapter.

BACKCOUNTRY SKIING ON ST. HELENS

The magnificent open slopes of the mountain are a great attraction, and as interest in adventure skiing increases more skiers will be trying their skills out by exploring the backcountry, most of which is easily accessible on one-day ski tours. Marked ski trails in several places lead to such areas, and by leaving the trails the upper slopes and outer reaches of the mountain are gained within two or three hours. Of greatest advantage for skiers wishing to access timberline areas are the numerous steep-walled but skiable ravines and canyons which appear to be obvious routes through forest to the higher areas. Springtime ski tours are particularly rewarding as the snowline rises, days are longer and warmer, and the snow consolidates.

Be fully knowledgeable about snow types in all temperatures and avalanche factors, or stay on the marked trails. Read the section about avalanches in this guidebook, then study a book devoted to the subject.

Skiing above 4,800 feet, the approximate timberline, requires a permit from the Forest Service, and after May 15 climbing permits for mountaineering or ski ascents are required for any trip above 4,800 feet. These are restricted to 100 per day of which thirty are available on a first-come basis at Jack's Restaurant west of and near Cougar. For up-to-date information on roads, snow, snowline elevation, and permits, contact Mount St. Helens National Volcanic Monument Headquarters, 42218 N.E. Yale Bridge Road, Amboy, WA 98601–9715, 206-247-5473, or the after-hours recorded message at 206-247-5800.

MAPS OF ST. HELENS

(Map 1) Most skiers and climbers will be well served by the Green Trails topographical map titled Mount St. Helens NW, which shows most of the roads and ski trails and the mountain itself. The prime USGS map for the area is Mount St. Helens. Maps for Goat Mountain and Smith Creek Butte cover areas west and east, and the Mount Mitchell map covers areas to the south. For the Randle side of the mountain, refer to the Spirit Lake East and French Butte quadrangles.

SOUTHSIDE MOUNT ST. HELENS

The south side of Mount St. Helens offers a variety of unique tours and scenery grouped in two general skiing areas, both accessible from Road 83: the Ape Cave–Monitor Ridge–Red Rock Pass area, and the Marble Mountain–Sasquatch Loops–Muddy River Lahar area.

For geographical convenience in describing the many ski tours on St. Helens, Redrock Pass has been chosen as the dividing line between westside and southside ski tours. As this is an arbitrary choice, be advised that several ski tours are reached by crossing the line regardless of which side you park on. Crossing over may depend on the extra miles you are willing to ski and, of course, the location of the snowline on the west side will also be a factor.

Sno-parks are maintained in three places: (1) near Ape Cave at the junction of Roads 8303/83, (2) at Cougar Sno-Park—also known as Irongate,

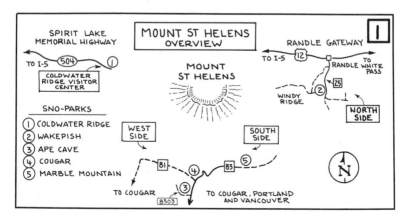

and (3) Marble Mountain Sno-Park, the highest at 2,650 feet at the end of plowed Road 83. Marble Mountain Sno-Park has a warming shelter and toilets. At this time there is no sno-park on the west side. Washington or Oregon sno-park permits are required.

Southside ski tours offer amazing variety and in general are very scenic with sweeping views due to the many years of clearcut logging that created vast, open areas. Although the marked skier-only trails are designed for Novice–Intermediate skiers, there are many miles of off-road ski routes for the more experienced skier. In many cases these do not require Backcountry ski experience. St. Helens offers greater variety in terrain and scenery than any other skiing area of similar size in the Northwest, with the possible exception of the Bend area in Central Oregon, where many miles of trails have been added in recent years.

APE CAVE TO NORTH CINNAMON PEAK

(Map 2) The unmarked road above Ape Cave is rated Novice to Interme-diate with an optional round trip of up to 13 miles to a high point of 4,000 feet and elevation gain of 2,000 feet. The route provides many sweeping vistas of the southern part of the state and of St. Helens, Adams, and Hood. Depending on your goals, the tour can turn around at any point.

Drive up Road 83, turning left on Road 8303, the side road to the cave area and site of turnout parking and a future sno-park. Ape Cave is 1.1 miles from Road 83. From there the road travels through thick second growth for about 3 miles, where clearcuts open up to impressive views that improve as you ski higher. The road continues to the somewhat steep final slopes at the summit of the peak, where Goat Mountain and St. Helens dominate the scene, while in the distance Hood and Adams ap-pear over countless ridges and blue hills. On the way to North Cinna-mon Peak, 4.5 miles from the trailhead, you will reach a bend and an obvious, wide saddle at 3,280 feet. Here at Cougar Saddle, for an excep-tional view, leave the road and climb an obvious, open, low ridge to the east. Actually, there are three open, parallel ridges here that invite ex-ploration, and are a worthy goal for the day. To the northeast, through second growth, lies an unpleasant route with shallow ups and downs to the end of a scenic ridge and fine views. From the saddle itself, a short 80 yards north leads to a view of St. Helens.

LAVA CAST FOREST

(Map 2) This small area of several acres is a summer point of interest where log casts are seen in the lava flow that once covered this forest. In winter it is an interesting, short side trip for poking around. From Road 83

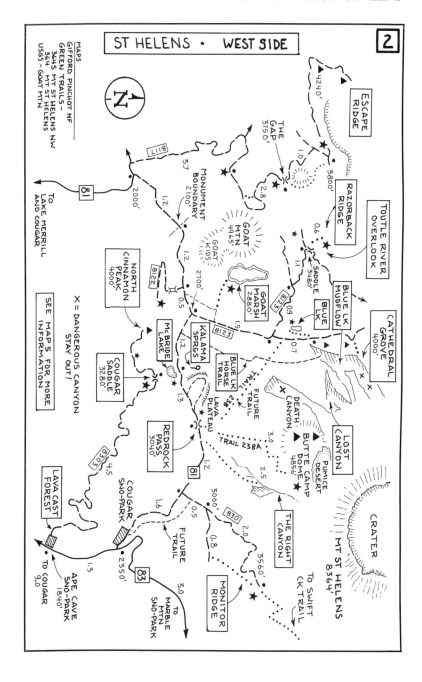

ST HELENS · WEST SIDE

2

MAPS
GIFFORD PINCHOT NF
GREEN TRAILS -
364S MT ST HELENS
364S MT ST HELENS NW
364 MT ST HELENS
USGS - GOAT MTN

X = DANGEROUS CANYON
STAY OUT!

SEE MAP 5 FOR MORE
INFORMATION

ESCAPE RIDGE

4240'

THE GAP 3750'

8117

3.7

MONUMENT BOUNDARY 2100'

2.8

1.0

3800'

RAZORBACK RIDGE

TOUTLE RIVER OVERLOOK

81

TO LAKE MERRILL AND COUGAR

2000'

1.2

1.2

1.2

GOAT MTN 4965'

GOAT KIDS

0.6

SADDLE 3480'

BLUE LK MUDFLOW

1.1

NORTH CINNAMON PEAK 4000'

8122

2700'

GOAT MARSH 2880'

3282'

0.9

BLUE LK

CATHEDRAL GROVE 4000'

0.5

8123

1.5

0.7

McBRIDE LAKE

KALAMA SPRGS

BLUE LK HORSE TRAIL

LAVA PLATEAU

862

FUTURE TRAIL

X

DEATH CANYON

X

X

COUGAR SADDLE 3280'

1.2

1.3

3.0

BUTTE CAMP DOME 4856'

PUMICE DESERT

LOST CANYON

REDROCK PASS 3040'

TRAIL 238A

2.5

8303

4.5

81

1.2

MT ST HELENS 8364'

CRATER

LAVA CAST FOREST

COUGAR SNO-PARK

1.6

0.5

3000'

830

2.0

THE RIGHT CANYON

TO SWIFT CK TRAIL

FUTURE TRAIL

0.8

3560'

1.3

2350'

83

3.0

MONITOR RIDGE

TO COUGAR 9.0

APE CAVE SNO-PARK 1840'

TO MARBLE MTN SNO-PARK

it is 0.2 mile west to the first bend on Road 8303 to Ape Cave. At the bend, enter the forest and explore. A future sno-park in this area may alter access to the Lava Cast Forest. Suitable for Novices. Mostly level, round trip less than 1 mile.

MARBLE MOUNTAIN SNO-PARK TRAILS

(Map 3) From the sno-park going east lies the beautiful Pine Marten Trail, which parallels Road 83, a snowmobile route. Paralleling the Pine Marten ski trail and above it are two short trails that form interesting loops. These are connector trails to the Swift Creek Trail, the 244 (Lower Swift Creek) and the 244B (Fir). The 244B Fir Trail is particularly worthwhile as it passes through towering old-growth timber.

Across Road 83 at the sno-park entrance is Road 8312, where a view of Mount Adams can be seen by skiing a short distance. And on the same side of Road 83 a fine view of the Swift Creek valley can be enjoyed by skiing an unmarked road almost opposite the sno-park entrance. Ski this road only 200 yards to the edge of the valley and explore either left or right.

Wapiti Trails. (Map 3) The Wapiti Trails are the first ones many skiers will visit on St. Helens as they start at Marble Mountain Sno-Park. The trails are rated Novice-Intermediate, are essentially level, and offer numerous loops, the longest being 4 miles. At the north foot of Marble Mountain lies a series of meadows with splendid views and through which flow two streams; one is Swift Creek, and the other is Wapiti Creek.

The Wapiti Trails, in a series of loops, pass through this marvelous area, going from meadow into forest then back into meadows. The gentle, rolling nature of the terrain is perfectly suited for cross-country skiing. There have been rumors that this area may have trails groomed in the future, as in the Upper Wind River area to the east.

With the Pine Marten Trail and the four loops of the Wapiti system there are over 7 miles of trails. Within 3 miles or so of the sno-park are an additional 12 miles of marked ski trails, and many more miles of excellent touring on roads and through clearcuts. The south side of St. Helens has few equals in the entire Northwest for skiing variety and scenery.

To find the Wapiti Trails follow signs out of Marble Mountain Sno-Park (south side) and cross the nearby snow-covered Road 83 to the trails. Refer to the map for more details on the four loops. Note that there are three "tie" connectors from the Pine Marten Trail, which starts at the northeast corner of the sno-park. Pine Marten forms even more loops when skied in conjunction with the Wapiti system. Guaranteed, you will not get bored with all these loops and the scenery.

Wapiti is the Chinook word for "elk," and the meadows are a calving area for elk in spring.

Swift Creek Overlook. (Map 3) This short, Intermediate, unmarked tour

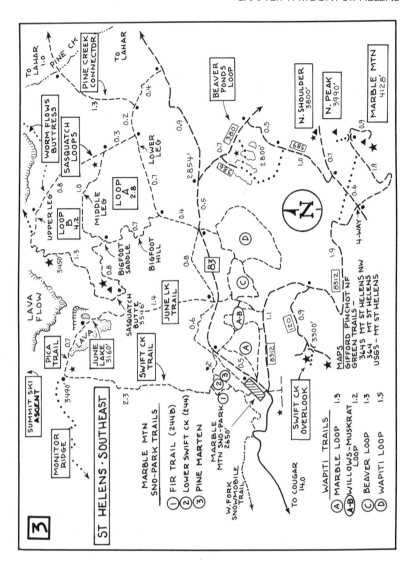

takes you 2.3 miles one way to the most dramatic viewpoint near Marble Mountain Sno-Park. The final views are breathtaking. Do not confuse this ski tour with the Swift Creek Trail across the valley. Elevation gain is 650 feet.

Ski the Wapiti Trails and exit onto Road 8312 eastward to Road 120. Turn right onto this road and ski up moderate grades past several views to a pass below a clearcut, where there are two short, steep roads, one going downhill 400 yards, and the other more scenic route going uphill 150 yards. Both lead to superb views of Cinnamon Peak, Redrock Pass, Goat Mountain, and, of course, St. Helens. If you have time, cross the pass and descend southward through forest only 400 yards to a remarkable view to the west and south. Be sure to have your camera on this tour.

Swift Creek Trail. (Map 3) The trail is a direct, strenuous uphill route to a scenic, open ridge with grand views of St. Helens and Hood. Rated Intermediate-Advanced, it is 2.7 miles one way, gaining 840 feet to a high point of 3,490 feet.

With adequate snow depth it is possible to ski down to June Lake on the Pika Trail, crossing a lava flow. Due to steepness of the uphill trail, return by way of June Lake. The loop length is 5.4 miles.

The Swift Creek Trail is the official winter-climbing route to the summit of St. Helens, which is why you may see all sorts of odd people with big packs, often stomping holes in your trail. From the high point they keep going up, while you turn east to June Lake.

From Marble Mountain Sno-Park take Trail 244 (Lower Swift Creek), then Trail 244B (Fir) through old growth to the main trail, which at first is a road that climbs steeply and relentlessly. Simple polypropylene homemade rope climbers will help you farther up where otherwise you might have to herringbone or sidestep. In several places you will be on the ridgecrest for views both east and west. Close on the west are the steep, clearcut slopes of Monitor Ridge.

A low, steep, lava-flow face, a good place for lunch, is the high point from which the trail continues east to June Lake. Backcountry explorers may want to continue upward for another mile or so over spectacular terrain and open lava flows at timberline.

The Pika Trail over to June Lake is at first demanding, drops steeply to a lava flow, climbs onto the lava flow surface, then descends moderately to the lake.

June Lake. (Map 3) This Novice–Intermediate marked trail is relatively easy, gains 510 feet to a high of 3,160 feet, and takes you on a 5-mile round trip. The trail goes up a scenic valley and ends at a lovely pond, which is probably why it is the most popular tour on St. Helens—and definitely the most used and abused trail of all. The abuse is from skiers, their dogs, and people who take skis off and walk because they find the trail too difficult near the lake. Unfortunately for serious skiers, the intruders walk all over the trail and destroy the surface, dogs are not kept away from skiers, and kids wander along the middle of the trail. This is an excellent trail on which to study other skiers' personal ethics, or the lack of them.

Obviously, skiers not sure of their skills should ski first on the nearly level Wapiti Trails before attempting the June Lake Trail.

From Marble Mountain Sno-Park ski east on the Pine Marten Trail 1.1 miles to the June Lake Trail. The Pine Marten "connector" trail was constructed to make it safer for skiers and to eliminate conflicts with snowmobilers who use Road 83.

South side of Mount St. Helens with steam puff, viewed from top of Marble Mountain

From the June Lake trailhead at the end of Pine Marten ski upward through meadows then up easy to moderate grades as the trail parallels the creek coming from the lake. On the way you'll see both St. Helens and Marble Mountain. The lake is in a rugged, peaceful setting with cliffs on one side and a lava flow on the other where the Pika Trail crosses to Swift Creek Trail and ridge for a loop return to the sno-park, a loop recommended only to Advanced skiers.

On your return down the trail, short, steeper sections may intimidate you. If you must walk, walk along the edges, not in the trail, and don't use your dogs or kids as bowling pins for skiers descending the trail. Many skiers who visit the lake are inexperienced and aren't aware that the down-hill skier has the right-of-way. Even the experienced need to be prepared for problems and ski in control.

Marble Mountain. (Map 3) The easily reached 4,128-foot summit of this dormant volcanic peak, rising massively above the Wapiti Trails and Marble Mountain Meadows, offers sweeping views. The tour, on unmarked roads after leaving the Wapiti Trails, gains 1,500 feet to the summit, a round trip of 11.6 miles. Extensive timber harvesting, typical of St. Helens, has opened up most of the upper slopes, which provides opportunities for off-road routes and shortcuts to the summit. The road, the most skied route, circles to the very summit from which four major volcanoes can be seen. Share this mountain with snowmobilers and keep to the right when they pass.

There are two routes to the summit. The most direct is up Road 8312 across from the entrance to Marble Mountain Sno-Park and takes a scenic

5.8-mile route up. The other route is the Beaver Ponds Loop, which is more challenging and offers a one-way distance of 8.5 miles and the option to return by the first route. Skiing an off-road route from the four-way junction at 3,400 feet directly to the summit will shorten both routes by a mile or more. Read the Beaver Ponds Loop description for additional information on Marble Mountain and its northside viewpoints. Study the guidebook map carefully to orient yourself on this route.

Beaver Ponds Loop and Marble Mountain Summit. (Map 3) An interesting alternative route to Marble Mountain, these multi-level ponds and meadows are a worthy goal in themselves. After skiing to the end of the Pine Marten Trail, you can follow unmarked roads to the pond area, then climb to the summit, gaining 1,500 feet on a round trip of 14.3 miles. Rated Novice to the ponds, Intermediate to the summit.

From Marble Mountain Sno-Park ski the Pine Marten Trail 1.9 miles, then 0.5 mile east on Road 83. Turn onto Road 380 at an obvious wide junction and ski southeast 0.7 mile to the ponds. If there is good snow cover, ski across the ponds to a meadow behind. Climb into a clearcut beyond and climb to a road above. (If there is not sufficient snow, continue a short distance beyond the ponds, turn right onto Road 389, a primitive road where you start climbing seriously. This is the road you would ski to if crossing the ponds and meadow.) Two miles above the ponds join an east-west road, turn right, and ski 0.6 mile to a four-way junction. Turn left onto Road 8312 and ski south and up as it hairpins then circles on a scenic route to the east side of the peak through forest, around to the south side, and up to the top.

Before you cross the saddle (on the mountain's north side) to the east side, from the saddle climb a short, steep pitch to the north to a grand view and onto a short spur eastward for better views. This is the North Peak, and it is a splendid consolation prize if you do not go on to the summit.

Another shortcut near the beaver ponds is Road 386 (see map) to the clearcut previously mentioned. Or, from this clearcut, drop down into the beaver ponds for a short loop.

Sasquatch Trails. (Map 3) These Novice to Intermediate marked trails lead to good views and as much skiing as you can handle in one day. The trails total 6.5 miles and form two loops. Heavily logged in the past, the area is open with many views. The loops are reached by skiing the Pine Marten Trail 1.9 miles from Marble Mountain Sno-Park. At 3,546 feet, Sasquatch Butte is the highest point of the trail system. Its open summit is reached by climbing steeply 100 yards from the trail.

The Sasquatch Trails form two loops, one above the other. The Upper Loop (B) is 3.8 miles long, and the Lower Loop (A) is 2.6 miles long and is connected to Road 83, a snowmobile route, by two legs. The trails follow old logging roads and are uncrowded. Grades seldom exceed gentle to moderate, although Novice skiers should first ski the Wapiti Trails to gain experience before skiing here. The Upper Loop provides easy access to timberline areas of the mountain. Ski through the forest fringe on the uppermost leg to encounter a series of lava-flow faces. The steep faces can be climbed to the rolling top surfaces for unlimited Backcountry opportunities.

To reach the Sasquatch Trails, ski the Pine Marten Trail east from the sno-park for 1.9 miles, paralleling Road 83, then turn left onto a lower-trail leg that leads to the Lower Loop. At the first junction go left for the most direct route to the Upper Loop and Sasquatch Butte. The route winds upward to Bigfoot Saddle on moderately steep grades. This leg is best skied uphill due to steepness, with descent made along the east leg. The best view of St. Helens, rising 5,000 feet above, is 100 yards west of the east leg on the middle leg heading for Sasquatch Saddle. The middle leg is a pleasant, gentle, uphill pull to the saddle. At the saddle you meet the middle leg, shared by both loops.

From Bigfoot Saddle, turn left and climb a winding road to a turn below nearby Sasquatch Butte for excellent views. Continue around the west side of the butte onto the upper leg, which is a winding route through wide, open, almost level areas with sweeping views. The leg bends around the tops of several minor canyons. From the east leg of the Upper Loop it is all downhill, sometimes quite fast and exciting.

The summit of Sasquatch Butte at 3,546 feet is an inspiring viewpoint. On a clear day you can see Mount Adams, 20 miles east, and to its north the Dark Divide, the Indian Heaven high country, Mount Hood, nearby Marble Mountain, hills, ridges, and a reservoir farther west, then Cinnamon Peak and Monitor Ridge and St. Helens itself. Directly below and out of sight is June Lake and its lava flow, which leads up to the top of Swift Creek Ridge, another ski route. The best route for reaching the summit of Sasquatch Butte is from the northeast side with sidestepping up the steeper sections. From the top you will have a feeling of great height, a reward in itself. In good weather, this is an enjoyable spot for a leisurely snack or lunch.

Worm Flows Buttress. (Maps 3 & 4) For a superb, easy Backcountry experience ski to the flat-topped summit of this prominent feature north of the Sasquatch Trails. Partly on marked trails, this 10-mile round trip gains 1,850 feet to a high of 4,300 feet. It will probably exceed your greatest expectations.

From halfway across the upper leg of Loop B of the Sasquatch Trails ski north through the narrow fringe of forest to the steep foot of one of the many southside lava-flow lobes of St. Helens. Ski east to quickly find an obvious steep ravine and climb this into a small basin. Here you may have to take your skis off and climb the steep west face of the buttress. Ski to the top of the wide, flat buttress for a view of Mount Rainier, the upper reaches of the Muddy River Lahar, and the Plains of Abraham. To complete the 3-mile loop from the marked trails, ski down steep, wide slopes on the northeast side of the buttress and follow the base of the buttress around to where you obviously head back to the upper leg 1.7 miles from the top of your high point.

For another, even more adventuresome, backcountry tour from the upper leg, follow directions for the Worm Flows, ski to the foot of the lava flow, and follow its lower edge westward along the route of the Loowit

Trail, which is clearly shown on the Green Trails map of St. Helens. There will be several surprises along the way and some decision making, but do not drop down to June Lake because of the many cliffs. Go beyond the lake at least 0.5 mile before dropping down.

This route can also be followed farther west to descend onto Swift Creek Ridge and pick up the marked trails there, then down the ridge or eastward on the loop trail to June Lake.

Still another adventuresome backcountry tour from the top of the Worm Flows Buttress is to ski off the north side into the shallow basin, which is the head of the south fork of Pine Creek, and then to descend to Road 83 to complete a loop. An alternative to this loop is to ski a longer loop by not descending Pine Creek but continuing north, roughly skiing the 4,200-foot contour in and out of shallow ravines, in some places traversing short, moderately steep slopes. You will cross several minor rounded ridges along the spectacular route to the north fork of Pine Creek (which can be descended easily) or on to the edge of Shoestring Canyon on the Muddy River Lahar. This trip should not be attempted if the snow is hardpacked or deep since some slopes will be dangerous. If you ski higher than 4,200 feet you will encounter steep, difficult canyons.

On any backcountry tour always carry a map and compass and ski only in good weather. Be sure you understand snow types and the mechanics of snow related to depth, steepness, and temperature. Even a short, steep slope can avalanche with dangerous results.

Pine Creek Connectors. (Maps 3 & 4) The Muddy River Lahar on St. Helens is the southeast side's most awesome natural feature. The Pine Creek Connectors offer a shortcut to the lahar. Rated Intermediate, the route is on both marked and unmarked terrain, climbs 500 feet, and is 10 miles round trip.

See the Sasquatch Trails description, then ski the Pine Marten Trail, ski east on the lower leg of Loop A, leave the loop, and briefly descend toward Road 83. Turn left and climb a steep, low bank 0.4 mile from Road 83 and ski northeast through second growth on an obscure primitive road, and go left at a junction. Head for the forest stand and ski around its lower end to a creekbed crossing, then ski 100 yards to another creekbed, which is Pine Creek. Ski up the east bank of the wide creek, then bear gently east 0.8 mile to the lahar at 3,360 feet, about 1.5 miles above the lahar's lower end. The scale of the scene as the lahar sweeps directly to St. Helens's base is one of the great sights of the Northwest.

A second shortcut route to the upper lahar is to ski east on Road 83 to the Pine Creek bridge 4.1 miles from the sno-park. Ski up the twisting creekbed to join the first connector's route. If the creekbed is not skiable, enter the forest to the east and follow the summer trail, if possible, as it parallels the creek 0.4 mile to a rustic, elusive, three-sided log shelter located 100 yards from the creek. Skiing close to the creek will only lead you into thickets. Continue uphill on gentle grades to the lahar, first through second growth, then through old growth.

Muddy River Lahar. (Map 4) On a clear day, with the towering mass of St. Helens rising dramatically above the mile-wide lahar, you can witness one of the Northwest's most dramatic scenes. With the distant views, the magnificent open areas, and an occasional puff of steam from the mountain's crater, this is the crowning ski tour of St. Helens. Rated Intermediate, 10 miles round trip, elevation gain 350 feet to a high point of 3,000 feet.

The lahar, extending 3 miles from the Road 83 summer viewing site at 3,000 feet to the very base of the mountain at 4,400 feet, offers a number of destinations. The south side of the lahar is bounded by Pine Creek and the north by the impressive, steep-sided and forested Ape Canyon ridge. The surface of the lahar is smooth, rises gently for its entire length, and is cut lengthwise by two prominent canyons in its upper reaches. Starting high on the mountain, 40 feet deep with near-vertical sides, the two descend and gradually become shallower until they disappear a mile from the lower end of the lahar.

The lahar (an Indonesian word meaning volcanic mudflow) was formed in prehistoric times, and the 1980 eruption caused a giant flood of Shoestring Glacier ice, melted snow, rocks, and debris over 40 feet deep traveling at 70 miles per hour. The destructive mixture uprooted and carried away thousands of trees. The massive, speeding flow sloshed up and scoured the walls of the northside ridge and Flattop Butte, which turned the flow southward. In places the depth of the flow can be seen on the sides of surviving trees.

The canyon on the lahar's south side is Shoestring Canyon, which takes its name from the glacier that occupied the prominent notch on the crater rim. The parallel canyon to the north is the Muddy River Canyon. If your plans are to cross from one side of the lahar to the other, do so near the lower ends of the canyons before they deepen. Farther up they become steep-walled and dangerous. The canyons are both channels for huge avalanches that have been known to flow 2 miles down the lahar. Use care and judgment when crossing them.

On your first visit to the lahar you will probably want to ski up the flats and explore the canyons' edges. Flattop Butte at the foot of the lahar is an exceptional viewpoint. It is a total of 5 miles from the Marble Mountain Sno-Park to the lahar. At first, ski the Pine Marten Trail or the Wapiti Trail, then ski Road 83.

The south side of the lahar leads up eventually to a contouring route to the Worm Flows Buttress. The north side of the lahar leads to rounded, bare buttes at 4,400 feet, speckled by ghost snags killed by the 1980 blast. These buttes are great viewpoints down onto the lahar, and northward to the Plains of Abraham, which extend north almost 2 miles. There are views of Spirit Lake and Windy Ridge if you climb Windy Pass Peak. To reach these buttes cross the Muddy River Canyon low.

On the side of Ape Canyon Ridge north of this canyon are two prominent alcoves or bays. Getting around the foot of the upper alcove, a rocky, bulging buttress, is intimidating but possible. The steep bulge is at the edge

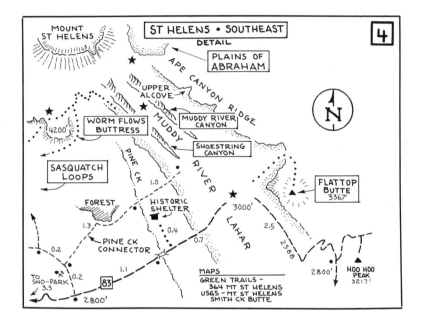

of the canyon, and may have to be crossed on foot. However, the safest way to bypass this buttress is to enter the canyon, bypass the bulge, and climb out above it.

Flattop Butte. (Map 4) If you want a remarkable view of the lahar, Rainier, Adams, and Hood, this low, forested butte at 3,367 feet is for you. From the lahar it is less than a 400-foot climb, mostly on logging roads.

After crossing Pine Creek on Road 83, exit the forest and head directly across the lahar 1.2 miles to its far edge and ski to an alcove beyond Flattop Butte. Climb 200 yards to the low pass then turn south 100 yards to a gully that you ascend about 50 yards. Then turn south again into open areas and a ridgetop road that climbs to a saddle. Ski onto a spur ridge for a fine view, then ski 0.3 mile to the highest point of the butte.

MONITOR RIDGE

(Map 2) This massive, essentially treeless ridge is, in summer, the access route for summit climbers. In winter it offers maximum views for the least miles, tying with Marble Mountain for scenic honors. The tour is rated Intermediate, is on unmarked roads, climbs 1,380 feet to a high of 3,600 feet, and is 8 miles round trip.

From Cougar drive 10.2 miles to Cougar Sno-Park (2,650 feet), historically known as Irongate Sno-Park by many because this was the end of road for plowing and an iron gate blocked four-wheel traffic beyond. Ski up Road 81 1.6 miles and turn right onto Road 830. Although you will have already had a few views, from here on you will climb through square miles of logging-ravaged mountainside with views at every turn. In 0.5 mile a side road to the right leads into a giant, rolling clearcut with many skiing opportunities, including a shorter but steeper route to your destination at the top of the ridge near the summer climbers' camp.

Following Road 830, however, is less steep and scenically rewarding. The views from the top are panoramic—St. Helens, Adams, Hood, Marble Mountain, and blue, endless ridges to the horizon.

For more views ski northeast, climbing gently into another vast open area where you look down into Swift Creek and over June Lake to Sasquatch Butte. For adventurers, ski north to the edge of forest, descend an ever-steepening open slope down to Swift Creek. If you continue across the upper Swift Creek-June Lake loop system, you'll need a car shuttle from Marble Mountain Sno-Park. In reverse, it is possible to ski to Monitor Ridge from June Lake and Swift Creek Ridge where ski trails exist.

Future trail development plans include a forest trail for skiers from Cougar Sno-Park paralleling Road 81 to join with Road 830 up Monitor Ridge. The purpose is to separate machines from skiers and provide a safer, more pleasant skiing experience.

REDROCK PASS AND LAVA PLATEAU

(Maps 2 & 5) Presently this road tour is unmarked and gains 420 feet to the pass at 3,040 feet over a one-way distance of 2.8 miles. The future will see a skiers-only trail parallel to Road 81 from the sno-park. The pass, which divides this guidebook's sections on St. Helens into southside and westside sections, is a worthwhile goal for the views along the way, particularly from the nearby, easily reached lava plateau. Ski to the pass from Cougar Sno-Park, then climb the short, steep face of the lava flow to the north to gain the undulating plateau where you will enjoy a superb view. To the west you'll see distant ridges and Goat Mountain, then up to Butte Camp Dome and, of course, St. Helens. The plateau offers access to summer trails 238 and 238A, not marked at this time for skiing and hard to follow. Trail 238 leads to Road 8123 and is scheduled to be marked for skiing in the future with the Blue Lake Mudflow at its upper terminus.

To explore the plateau ski north across the lava into meadows with scattered alpine firs, then turn west to the far edge for views. Ski a loop to enjoy different perspectives.

Trail 238A to Butte Camp Dome. (Maps 2 & 5) This unmarked summer trail starts at Redrock Pass, climbs 1,600 feet over 2 miles to a timberline pumice desert at 4,600 feet, and is strictly for Backcountry skiers. The level desert lies behind the Butte Camp Dome, a pair of prominent, forested buttes.

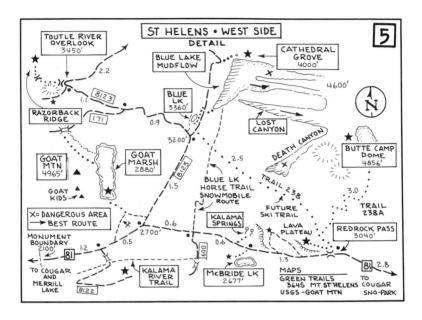

The trail is usually hard to follow, but an experienced Backcountry skier will have few problems forging a route upward, and the reward will be the unique area of the Dome and pumice desert.

To locate the trail ski across the plateau and meadows and find the trail as it enters second growth. As the forest opens up, the trail will become hard to follow. Keep working uphill—ski climbers will help. Keep well east of the Dome, which will not be seen for quite some time at first. When you reach the pumice desert you will have several choices for a return route—via the Blue Lake Mudflow, or east above timberline to The Right Canyon, or on to Monitor Ridge, or by your upward route, all requiring Backcountry skills.

Trail 238 to Blue Lake Mudflow. (Maps 2 & 5) Presently this is an abandoned summer trail that will in the future be marked for skiers to provide access to areas not easily reached since there is no sno-park on the west side (Road 81). The trail goes through mature forest, then into jack pine, crosses a small lahar (which leads up into Death Canyon, a dangerous gully), then at 2.5 miles crosses the Blue Lake Horse Trail, which leads to the Blue Lake Mudflow but is only for snowmobiler use. Continue westward to the standard route to the mudflow (see Blue Lake Mudflow), a distance of 3 miles from Redrock Pass.

The lahar coming out of Death Canyon climbs into an ever-narrowing, steep-sided, dangerous ravine prone to rock fall and avalanches. Partway up is a 20-foot vertical step. Stay out of this canyon!

To find Trail 238, cross the lava plateau and meadow, turn left at the meadow's northwest corner, and follow an old road 250 yards into a large clearcut. Here, keep right along the north edge 50 yards to find the trail as it enters the forest.

BUTTE CAMP LOOP

(Maps 2 & 5) There are many loops for the Backcountry skier on St. Helens, and the number is limited only by a skier's creativity. The southwest and west sides of St. Helens are particularly interesting when you use the pumice desert east of Butte Camp Dome as the halfway point. A recommended loop for a starter experience is to ski up The Right Canyon to timberline, across timberline to the pumice desert, then down Lost Canyon to the Blue Lake Mudflow. Descend the mudflow to Road 8123, then find Trail 238 to Redrock Pass, or ski down Road 8123 to Road 81 then east on 81 to the pass to complete the loop. When Trail 238 is marked for skiers, the climb up Redrock Pass's west side will be eliminated and the loop shortened. Skiing this loop as described offers the easiest route finding. Total loop distance is 12 miles.

Snow above timberline may be crusty or windpacked, whereas the canyons may have perfect conditions. Ski climbers are recommended, but metaledged skis are not required—regular skis are usually adequate.

THE RIGHT CANYON

(Map 2) This snow-filled gully is the most direct and easiest route to timberline from the Redrock Pass area, and gives access to the Butte Camp Dome area. The route requires confidence and Backcountry experience, although it is not difficult. The first part of the route is up a clearcut, then you have to find the route through forest to find the "right" gully.

Ski toward Redrock Pass from Cougar Sno-Park. Two hundred yards before the pass turn right into a large clearcut, follow its west side upward for 0.5 mile, enter the forest, and bear slightly west as you climb until you find a shallow, 30-foot-wide canyon. Downed trees across the canyon can be bypassed. The canyon climbs gently to timberline at 4,500 feet. Turn west and ski 0.7 mile to the pumice desert plateau east of Butte Camp Dome.

In descending The Right Canyon be sure to follow your uphill route and don't be deceived by a wide, gentle lahar that will take you to the wrong canyon, a tree-choked gully. Bear left at the inviting lahar and follow the canyon to the left.

Another ascent route for The Right Canyon is to ski to Redrock Pass, climb the lava edge to the plateau, follow the right (east) edge, then enter a ghost forest. Ski upward through this to find The Right Canyon.

SUMMIT SKI ASCENT

(Map 3) The summit of Mount St. Helens at 8,365 feet, with its wrinkled southside snow slopes sweeping upward to the crater rim, appears to be a close and easily ascended destination but is actually just the opposite. Many adventuresome skiers are lured each year by the goal of standing on the crest of this major Cascade volcano.

Although the mountain is climbed by several thousand people every year, and several hundred use their skis during spring and early summer, do not let "piece-of-cake" advice from friends convince you that this is an easy mountain. The ski ascent to the summit is for Backcountry skiers only who have strong downhill skills. Mountaineering experience is recommended. This is not a ski trip—it is a mountaineering climb on skis. Elevation gain is an impressive 5,700 feet with 10 miles traveled for the round trip. As on any major mountain, skill and good judgment are required. So is the strength to endure the long, monotonous ascent of almost 6,000 feet that may take six hours or more.

With ideal snow conditions and weather, it is safe for a skier/climber who is properly equipped. If the weather is not good and the snow is crusted or windpacked, beware, and stay off the mountain. Even in clear weather, skiers have wound up miles from their cars on distant roads due to careless route finding in the descent.

The safest and best time in most years to climb the mountain on skis is April and May, although bare ridges and blowing dust may already be evident. Days are longer and warmer, and the snow consolidated, with cornsnow surfaces after morning softening. Of course, many days will be overcast, perhaps cold, and snow conditions not good even in late spring.

Although the mountain's west side is skiable (see Blue Lake Mudflow description) and other southside routes are occasionally used (see Redrock Pass, The Right Canyon, Monitor Ridge), the most accessible and direct route is from Marble Mountain Sno-Park.

See the Swift Creek Trail description and ski or carry skis directly up that trail. At the top of the trail, where it turns eastward to descend to June Lake, continue upward. The ascent route is obvious, up an open, wide gully, past a lava flow on the right. This leads into a shallow, wide basin on the south slopes of the mountain. The surface is corrugated by many minor ridges, really just minor wrinkles. From the basin, select the easiest route up, traversing as slopes steepen. The true summit is westward on the crater rim several hundred yards from where most climbers reach the rim. Enormous cornices overhang the steep-walled crater, and from your position these overhangs appear as safe snow highways. Stay far from the rim to avoid the possibility of cornice collapse.

Certain equipment is recommended for this ski ascent: proper clothing for all weather types, at least one ice ax per group, crampons for all, a rope,

Making turns on volcanic ash-covered snow

and ski climbers, be they mohair or inexpensive polypropylene rope. Metal edges are advised, but not necessary if the surface is not hardpacked or icy. Use runaway straps on your skis. The ten essentials, including map and compass, should be carried. It is important that you register for the ascent as well as sign out upon your return, wherever you registered for the ascent.

Summit climbs are controlled by the Forest Service. Until May 15, unlimited permits are available at Jack's Restaurant on Highway 503 east of Cougar. After May 15, only 100 permits are issued per day, 70 on a preissued, reserved basis, and 30 on a first-come, first-served basis after 11:00 A.M.

WESTSIDE MOUNT ST. HELENS

(Map 5) Although there is no sno-park west of Redrock Pass, there are many adventuresome ski tours on St. Helens's west side, and there are several easy, scenic tours suitable for Novice skiers. The usual practice here is to drive to the snowline, then start skiing. Due to the fluctuation of the snowline the length of the ski tours can vary considerably, sometimes adding miles to the tour if the snowline is low. In general, a snowline between 2,500 and 3,000 feet provides good access to the more distant points, such as the Toutle River Overlook and the Blue Lake Mudflow. Some westside tours may be reached by skiing over Redrock Pass from Cougar Sno-Park, and the future marking of Trail 238 will shorten distances considerably.

Most westside tours, however, are best reached by driving up Road 81, a paved road, past Merrill Lake to the snowline. One mile before reaching Cougar, turn left onto Road 81. If there is snow on the road the first few miles, turn around—you will be too far from the tours. After two or three trips up Road 81 you will get a feel for the snowline and distances, and you will gain confidence. The junction of Roads 81 and 8123 at 2,697 feet is 11.4 miles from Road 90, the Cougar Highway, where Road 81 begins.

GOAT MARSH

(Maps 2 & 5) This scenic, Novice, 4-mile round trip follows unmarked roads and forest trail with a gain of up to 580 feet. The large marsh at the steep foot of Goat Mountain is exceptionally scenic.

Drive to the snowline and ski up Road 81 to an open area and side road 0.4 mile below the 81/8123 junction. Ski the side road (1.2 miles above the Monument sign) to a quarry, then continue uphill into old growth. Ski 0.5 mile through rolling forest to the edge of the southern lake at 2,880 feet. A wonderful view of St. Helens and the marsh greet you. If frozen (rare), cross the marsh 0.5 mile and on the northwest shore enjoy the immense noble firs. In years of deep snow, cross the marsh, stay on the west side of the outlet stream that flows north, ski to the bridge in 0.5 mile, turn right, and follow Road 171 up to Road 8123 for a long loop return adding 3.5 miles to your tour.

ROAD 8122

(Maps 2 & 5) Incorrectly shown on some Forest Service maps as Road 8022, this road climbs steadily to wonderful viewpoints. Following an unmarked road, the 5-mile round trip gains 800 feet to a high point of 3,290 feet.

Follow Goat Marsh directions, ski 1.1 miles above the Monument sign, turn right onto Road 8122 at 2,542 feet, and ski 0.3 mile to the bridge. From here, the first view is another 0.7 mile, but continue still another 0.7 mile to the high point, where you will find the best view of St. Helens and a spectacular vista of Goat Mountain and the precipitous descending ridge called the Goat Kids. The Blue Lake Mudflow is visible, as is twin-topped Butte Camp Dome at timberline on St. Helens. Continue 0.8 mile to the end of the road for more views.

McBRIDE LAKE

(Maps 2 & 5) The lake setting is scenic, and best appreciated by skiing to the lake's west end for the St. Helens view. A Novice-to-Intermediate road tour of up to 8.5 miles round trip, the cumulative gain from Cougar Sno-Park is 1,160 feet, and only 300 feet from the west side. The lake is at 2,677 feet.

Practice extreme caution if skiing on the lake, particularly near inlet or outlet areas. This low-elevation lake is not safe. The meadow at the west end is worth exploring, particularly for the good view of St. Helens.

Follow directions for Goat Marsh, ski to the 81/8123 junction (1.7 miles above the Monument boundary sign), turn right, and ski east 1.2 miles to the lake. Ski down the steep road bank at the lake's west end to reach the lake. The lake also may be reached by skiing over Redrock Pass, an 820-foot climb, then descending 340 feet for a total one-way distance of 4.2 miles.

Kalama Springs and Overlook. (Maps 2 & 5) The headwaters of the Kalama River, a number of springs quickly forming a wide, flowing river, are unique. Follow directions for McBride Lake. The springs are almost directly across Road 81 from the lake and just a little west. The springs are at the north end of an interesting ghost forest of silver snags, called "buckskins" in Eastern Oregon. From Road 81 ski 400 yards through the snags and forest.

East and directly above the outflowing river is an 80-foot wall of lava, the top of which provides a view of Cinnamon Peak, Goat Mountain, Escape Ridge, and St. Helens. Beyond this wall is a plateau beneath yet another lava-flow wall extending from Redrock Pass. The small plateau offers open skiing, and the perimeter road shows you several wild dips near the overlook edge. This overlook plateau is reached by skiing 0.5 mile west and below the pass.

KALAMA RIVER TRAIL

(Map 5) This summer trail starts almost 6 miles below McBride Lake and climbs to Redrock Pass. The section between the pass and the lake is steep, dangerous, and unskiable. West of the lake, however, it enters level, mature forest and passes through beautiful areas paralleling the Kalama River, which rises out of Kalama Springs. The marked trail is rated Novice, and Intermediate if the snowline is low. The distance can exceed 6 miles round trip. Elevation gain is nominal.

Road 600, a short side road off Road 81, is the best access to the trail. This road lies 1.9 miles west of Redrock Pass and 0.6 mile east of the junction of 81/8123. Ski 0.3 mile on Road 600 and turn left or right onto the trail near the river. To the west (right) it follows the north side of the river, and to the east (left) it follows the south side and is steep and dangerous as it crosses a rock face. Westward, ski 1 mile to Road 8122. West of there the trail is steep and difficult.

TOUTLE RIVER OVERLOOK

(Maps 2 & 5) The exceptional view from Razorback Ridge over the South Fork Toutle River valley makes this long tour worthwhile. The crest of the narrow, steep-sided, heavily-scalped ridge is your destination. An Intermediate tour of up to 12 miles round trip on unmarked roads, the tour climbs 1,500 feet to a high point of 3,480 feet.

From the Monument boundary sign on Road 81 it is 6 miles to the viewpoint. Ski up Road 81, then up 8123 to where it turns west near the Blue Lake Trail and goes along a sidehill with a view of Goat Mountain and Goat Marsh. Enter old growth and ski to an obvious hairpin turn around the end of a ridge. At the saddle leave the road and take a side road directly across the steep face of the ridge as it descends to another saddle then turns and climbs along the top of Razorback Ridge to a viewpoint 0.5 mile from the hairpin turn. The view is marvelous—west to Escape Ridge, down and across the Toutle River and the northwest ridge of St. Helens. Although much of the region to the north was logged before 1980, you can see some of the blast zone.

Back at the hairpin, take the left fork onto the south side of the ridge going west a short distance for views of Goat Mountain, the marsh, and Mount Hood.

If you still want to explore, from the hairpin go north down Road 8123 toward the Toutle 2.2 miles for a view down the valley. The road then turns east, climbs steeply for a mile or more for more views, and leads to summer trail No. 240, which goes into the blast zone but is too steep to ski.

BLUE LAKE, BLUE LAKE MUDFLOW, AND LOST CANYON

(Maps 2 & 5) The Blue Lake Mudflow, just east of Blue Lake, blocked the shallow valley 600 years ago and formed the lake. The eruption of 1980 enlarged the mudflow, technically a lahar. The mudflow is the easiest route to timberline on the west side, requiring little route finding. The lake sits at 3,360 feet, and the mudflow goes up to 4,600 feet.

Ski up Road 81 to the junction of 81/8123 then up 8123 1.5 miles to the bend in the road, where the next five tours all begin.

Blue Lake. (Maps 2 & 5) The summer trail to Blue Lake is not recommended for skiing due to steep hillside traverses. To reach the small, attractive lake safely, start from the turn in Road 8123, leave it, and ski straight north along an old roadbed called "the wash," which soon becomes deeply rutted and washed out. At one point the wash splits into two deep, washed-out routes that reunite. Ski 0.7 mile to where the Blue Lake Mudflow almost reaches the wash, your route. A fairly obvious opening, which soon widens to the right (east), is the foot of the Blue Lake Mudflow. To find the elusive lake, however, continue about 100 yards to another washed-out channel cutting back to the left. Follow this 200 yards to the lake.

Blue Lake Mudflow. (Maps 2 & 5) See Blue Lake above for directions. At first narrow, the mudflow widens and climbs gently for over a mile to its widest point, where it turns toward the mountain and splits into a north and south flow, both climbing and eventually entering narrow gullies as they climb more steeply to timberline at 4,600 feet.

If your goal is adventure, timberline, and marvelous views, do not ski up the north mudflow unless you seek danger. This branch of the mudflow narrows into a steep-sided, steeply climbing gully that is hard to climb out of.

To reach timberline safely, ski up the south branch, the first you see to the right. As it climbs gently, then moderately, it eventually narrows into a deep, steep-walled canyon, but it is easy to ascend. Climbers are helpful. At timberline turn right and ski on an ascending route for views to the south as you cross minor ridges and wide, gentle basins.

The view of the Butte Camp Dome peaks with Mount Hood behind is spectacular. It is 1 mile to the pumice desert between the buttes and the sweeping rise of the mountain. An adventurous loop descends by way of Lost Canyon.

If you are uncertain of snow conditions in the south gully, climb the ridge immediately beside and south of it. Ski up the mudflow until you find a slope to climb onto the moderately steep ridge.

On any Backcountry venture, be constantly thinking of snow conditions and air temperature. Recent, heavy snowfall or warm days, particularly on south-facing slopes, may create dangerous conditions. Snow can slide or avalanche on slopes as gentle as 30 degrees.

Lost Canyon. (Maps 2 & 5) This mudflow and canyon is the most direct route to timberline on the west side of St. Helens, a distance of only 1 mile from the Blue Lake Mudflow to timberline. Lost Canyon descends from near the north side of the Butte Camp Dome. However, do not confuse Death Canyon with Lost Canyon if you are descending from the pumice desert. Death Canyon is immediately beside and below the steep north face of the buttes. It will lure you down but becomes steeper and steeper, then goes over a 20-foot vertical step. Below this step, the canyon is subject to avalanches and rock falls. Lost Canyon is about 400 yards north of Death Canyon and is not obvious at its upper end due to the wide snow slopes and shallow basins that join out of sight farther down to form the canyon. It is not a narrow gully but an obvious, easy route down.

To find the hidden lower end of the mile-long Lost Canyon when you are skiing up the Blue Lake Mudflow, ski to the obvious, solitary, tall, "land-mark" fir tree in the center of the mudflow. Enter the forest to the right. In 200 yards you will reach the lower end of Lost Canyon. There are no other mudflows in the forest to confuse you.

Cathedral Grove. (Maps 2 & 5) A unique grove of giant Noble fir trees is just off the bend of the Blue Lake Mudflow at 4,000 feet, a mile above the mudflow's lower end. The grove is majestic and inspiring.

There are two routes to it. In bad weather you might consider the protected route that goes up through forest beyond the lower end of the mudflow. Stay on "the wash," the deeply washed-out roadbed, and continue up beyond the turnoff to the mudflow. The going soon becomes easier as the road above is not washed out and climbs through beautiful forest for 1.3 miles above the Blue Lake Mudflow turnoff. At a sharp bend in a ravine, leave the road, enter the ravine, climb the steep bank, and enter the beautiful giant tree grove in 200 yards. If you do not turn off at the ravine, but continue upward on the road into a clearcut, you will find beautiful old growth on the north side in the wide saddle.

For the alternative route, ski up the Blue Lake Mudflow to its bend and enter the forest cathedral there. This will give you the maximum effect as you enter the grove from the widest part of the mudflow at the bend. You will feel the special effect of the stillness and isolation.

ESCAPE RIDGE

(Map 2) You will enjoy extensive views from the denuded crest of this relatively unvisited, flat-topped ridge west of Mount St. Helens and Goat Mountain. This is an easy, but long, unmarked Intermediate road tour, with a climb of 2,000 feet or more to 4,000 feet. Skiing distance may exceed 12 miles round trip. The higher you climb the more views open up for you.

Drive up Road 81 past Merrill Lake to Road 8117 8.3 miles from the Cougar Highway. Ski 3.7 miles up 8117 through clearcuts and second growth to the first views just beyond a quarry. Another 2 miles and you see Mount Hood, the ridges around Merrill Lake, and the first views of the ridgetop you are skiing to. At 6.5 miles you reach The Gap, a saddle, and your first view of Mount St. Helens, a breathtaking sight.

At The Gap you can either continue up the road or ski around the east side of the low ridge north of The Gap on open slopes to the plateaulike ridgetop. On the plateau you'll have a panoramic view of the region. If you have energy left, continue higher, 1.8 miles more to the highest point of Escape Ridge.

If you leave your camera home, you are guilty of sheer negligence. You'll see Rainier, Hood, Marble Mountain, and other views beyond your expectations. The first miles of the tour are monotonous, but dogged perseverance will pay dividends.

NORTHSIDE MOUNT ST. HELENS

(Maps 1 & 6) Most of the mountain's north side is inaccessible to skiers due to unplowed winter roads. Of interest to skiers, however, are several areas on the north side where plowed roads offer access to wonderful views of the devastation zone and the mountain itself.

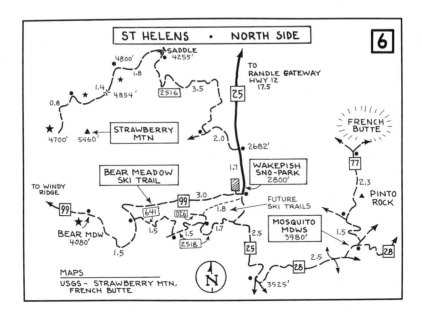

SPIRIT LAKE MEMORIAL HIGHWAY

(Map 1) The Memorial Highway (Highway 504) opened in 1993 and is primarily for summer visitors who wish to view the devastation zone and St. Helens from the north, looking directly into the steaming crater. The views across the lahars and into the crater are unforgettable. The highway is open year-round.

At this time there are no plans for the Monument to build or mark ski trails on this side of the mountain. However, "dispersed" use for both hikers and skiers will be permitted. As there is no vegetation here, there is no groundcover to hold the snow, and it is believed that winds will blow the snow off many areas. The quality of skiing here is untested at this time.

The highway follows a ridge-hugging, spectacular route from Toutle to the large visitor center at Coldwater Ridge only 8 miles from the crater, and 43 miles from I-5. Plans include extending the highway to Johnston Ridge near Spirit Lake.

To reach the Memorial Highway from the north, take Interstate 5 (Exit 60) onto Highway 505 then to 504. From the south, drive 60 miles from Portland to Exit 49, then drive east to Toutle. You will reach the Mount St. Helens National Volcanic Monument Visitor Center 5.5 miles from I-5. The exhibits here are well worth the visit.

RANDLE GATEWAY

(Maps 1 & 6) There are several ski tours in the Monument south of Randle that offer spectacular views and experiences. These are the Windy Ridge-Bear Meadows area (Road 99), Strawberry Mountain (Road 2516), and Mosquito Meadows. From Portland it is a 143-mile drive to Wakepish Sno-Park, which services this side of the mountain. For skiers from Seattle, it is a drive of 163 miles. Drive Interstate 5 to Highway 12 south of Chehalis, then drive east 48 miles to Randle, then 19.2 miles south into the Monument to Wakepish Sno-Park at 2,800 feet.

Windy Ridge to Bear Meadow Viewpoint. (Map 6) The route follows a marked road 4.5 miles to the viewpoint, best for Intermediate skiers as there is an elevation gain of 1,280 feet. This route follows Road 99 through old-growth forest to the viewpoint. If you ski farther, you will enter the 1980 blast zone with ghost trees leaning near the road. There are extensive views over shamelessly logged valleys, and across to Windy Ridge, barren and spectacular, another result of the 1980 eruption.

From Randle, drive 19.2 miles on Road 25 to Wakepish Sno-Park (pronounced wake-eh-pish) at 2,800 feet. Ski Road 99 westward and up to Bear Meadow Viewpoint (4,080 feet) for the first view of St. Helens, and a good campsite for overnighters.

Another 1.9 miles brings you to the edge of the living forest and your first closeup view of the "death zone." The superheated air from the eruption blast laid flat some 150 square miles of forest in just moments, killing 64 people and all life in the area except small animals under the snow cover. From the edge of the ghost forest it is 2.6 miles to Meta Lake, 9 miles from the sno-park. It is another 8 miles to the end of Road 99 on Windy Ridge. Share the road with snowmobilers.

A skiers' trail to Bear Meadow Viewpoint may be constructed in the future to allow a route without snowmobiles. The route will mostly follow logging roads south of Road 99. The precise route is not available at this time, but the general route is shown on the sketch map. The first 1.2 miles from the sno-park will be on a forest trail paralleling Hemlock Creek. Sno-Park to Bear Meadow will be approximately 6.5 miles.

Mosquito Meadows. (Map 6) From Wakepish Sno-Park the distance is 10 miles round trip on easy roads with a gain of 1,200 feet. Ski south up Road 25 2.5 miles toward Elk Pass, then turn east onto Road 28 at 3,525 feet and ski 2.5 miles to Mosquito Meadows. Along the way there are views to Mount Rainier and of Pinto Rock and its bare ridge to the north. If you have time, ski beyond the meadows north to the Pinto Rock-French Butte ridge, a fire-devastated area that was not capable of regenerating. This additional leg of the tour northward demands, however, a minimum commitment from Mosquito Meadows of 2.5 miles and at least an additional 800-foot elevation gain.

Strawberry Mountain. (Map 6) There are magnificent views from the end of this Advanced tour at 4,700 feet, 9.5 miles from Road 25 and a gain of 2,000 feet. This mountain is a high point on a long ridge northeast of St. Helens. The sweeping views overlook the blast zone and miles of devastated valleys and mountains. Here at the edge of the devastation, you'll see a clean line of living forest edging the ghost forest. Views from this tour, following Road 2516 to its end below the top of Strawberry Mountain, also include other major Cascade volcanoes. This is the most spectacular ski tour on the north side of St. Helens.

Drive 17.5 miles from Randle on Road 25 to a turnout plowed at Road 2516 (2,682 feet). Drive up 2516 as far as possible. You will at first pass through old growth, then into clearcuts and through unattractive second growth to the saddle 5.5 miles from Road 25. There are good views here at 4,255 feet, but keep going, crossing east-facing slopes with increasingly good views of Mount Adams. About 2.5 miles above the saddle, the road passes through another saddle at 4,854 feet, then goes onto steep north-facing slopes.

Continue climbing to the end of the road at 4,700 feet, 9.5 miles from Road 25. The views are magnificent. In heavy snow years, be alert to snow stability on the last 3 miles.

Chapter 2

UPPER WIND RIVER

The Upper Wind River area, 76 miles from Portland and 26 miles north of the Columbia River at Carson, offers many trails and views in generally rolling, heavily clearcut, and forested areas. This continues to be a little-known Nordic skiing area with many scenic surprises and superb views of Mount Adams, Mount St. Helens, and Mount Rainier.

Crossing Outlaw Creek with Mount St. Helens beyond

Because of the area's relatively low elevation (3,000 to 4,000 feet) you should verify snow depth in winters of light snowfall by calling the Wind River Ranger Station before making the trip. Still, the area generally has more snow than might be expected for its modest elevation.

Special recognition should be accorded Harold P. Lange, District Ranger, Wind River Ranger District, and his recreation specialists Russell Plaeger and Joe Koshko, for the exceptional variety of marked ski trails in the Upper Wind River area. Mr. Lange had the unusual foresight in 1975 to recognize the growing need for Nordic ski trails. In annual increments he developed an outstanding area with assistance from local skiers, and with considerable sensitivity separated snowmobilers from skiers in most areas.

From downtown Portland to Carson, Washington, it is 50 miles, and from Carson to the Upper Wind River Winter Sports Area it is 26 miles. Drive east on I-84, cross the Columbia River on the Bridge of the Gods at Cascade Locks, and drive east on Highway 14 for 6.7 miles to the Carson exit. After exiting, enter Carson and drive northwest on the Wind River road (the street on which you enter town) past a fish hatchery 13 miles north of town. Just past the hatchery, at a junction, turn right onto Road 30 and drive 13 miles to Old Man Pass. The road is paved, but the last 5 miles to the pass are fairly steep, gaining 1,500 feet of elevation.

Road and snow information is available from the Wind River Ranger Station during business hours, Monday through Friday, 509-427-5645, or from the Skamania County Sheriff non-emergency telephone: 509-427-9490. The ranger station is 9.3 miles north of Carson and off the Wind River road to the west. An outside information board is posted with current trail, snow, and road information. Leave home with a full tank of gas.

Road 30 is generally plowed Monday through Friday only, rarely on weekends. Be prepared to drive through snow. Tire chains may be required, and a shovel always proves handy. During heavy snowfall at lower elevations, county plows may not be able to plow Road 30 because residential areas have priority, a good reason to call for current road conditions. As dire as all this sounds, experience has shown that there is seldom a problem getting to the ski area for the average, well-prepared skier.

There are seven sno-parks in the area, and they are labeled A through G by the Forest Service. The sno-parks are named as follows, from south to north (numbers in parentheses indicate vehicle capacity):

Sno-Park A: Road 31 (5)—share with snowmobilers

Sno-Park B: Old Man Pass (25)—skiers only, toilets, access to all marked trails

Sno-Park C: McClellan Meadows (10)—skiers only, access to Pete Gulch, Outlaw Creek Clearcuts

Sno-Park D: Road 3050 (6)— skiers only, access to Scenic and Hardtime Loops

Sno-Park E: Curly Creek (6)—share with snowmobilers, access to Indian Heaven, Outlaw Creek Clearcuts

Sno-Park F: Road 6507 (25)—access to Rush Creek routes
Sno-Park G: Lone Butte (25)—toilets, share with snowmobilers, access to Crazy Hills
Note: Sno-Parks E and F may not always be plowed.

Parking is permitted only in sno-parks, which are located along a 6-mile section of road. A Washington or Oregon sno-park permit is required. Please do not block snowmobile unloading ramps. Parking may be crowded, so please use space efficiently. Carpooling is encouraged.

Road 30, between Old Man Pass and the end of plowing at Lone Butte Sno-Park, a distance of 4.7 miles, cuts through the center of the Upper Wind River skiing area. The westside routes (west of Road 30) are more numerous. However, in addition to marked eastside routes, there are a number of exceptional, scenic, unmarked routes here.

The most useful map of the area is the Forest Service trail map, and next most useful are the two Green Trails maps. The latter are easier to use than the USGS map and are more complete.

The Upper Wind River area, with 40 miles of marked ski trails, offers tours for all tastes and skill levels. In addition, there are miles of unmarked, rewarding ski routes, many of which are described in this chapter.

In some open areas, routes are marked by tall poles. Many miles of the trails are groomed weekly and tracks set by machine by the Forest Service. There is no charge for skiing the groomed tracks. Novices can glide along short, easy trails on gentle terrain. Advanced skiers can enjoy extended tours requiring downhill and route-finding skills. Numerous loops are possible. Use your creativity to join various trails. All Forest Service and many unmarked ski routes are shown on the sketch maps.

SCENIC LOOP: TRAIL 148

(Map 7) This scenic and varied Intermediate 5.7-mile loop offers forest trails, meadows, and a vast, flat clearcut with views of Mount Adams. There is also some gentle downhill skiing. The loop should be skied counterclockwise to keep steep grades to a minimum. The loop is usually groomed, and there is an elevation gain of 400 feet.

The usual trailhead is Old Man Pass (3,000 feet), or you may start at Sno-Park C by crossing the road and skiing down to the nearby loop. The trail goes north from Old Man Pass, parallels Road 30, and follows old skid roads. When the trail reaches the north end of the loop it turns west into a huge clearcut that invites exploration to its far side for the best views and a sense of isolation. The trail turns south in the clearcut, reenters forest, passes through a meadow with cottonwood trees, then follows a long, moderate, uphill zigzag course to a high, rolling area (3,200 feet) where a future clearcut will provide views. Here, the loop

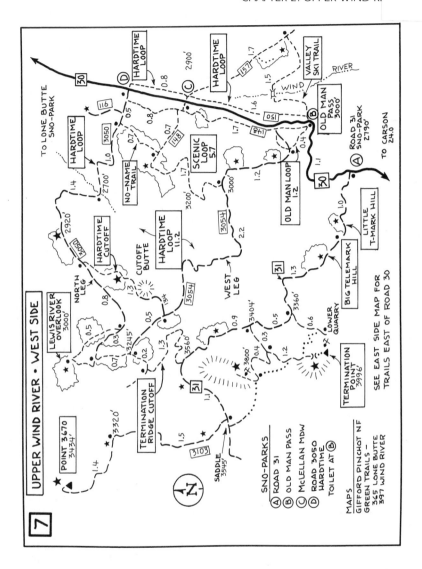

joins the west leg of the Hardtime Loop for 1.2 miles then reaches a junction with the Old Man Loop. Turn uphill to the right, ski over a low divide and then a gentle downhill to Old Man Pass.

The loop can be extended by skiing straight ahead and not turning west at the north end, then skiing to Road 3050, then west on the Hardtime Loop 0.5 mile to the No Name Trail, which you ski south into a huge clearcut to rejoin the Scenic Loop.

OLD MAN LOOP

(Map 7) Starting at Old Man Pass (Sno-Park B) this Novice 1.2-mile loop through forest is best skied counterclockwise. Most of the loop is machine groomed, making the loop safer and easier. Ski Trail 148 paralleling Road 30 northward 0.4 mile where you turn west and ski across a 400-yard flat, climb a modest hill (easier counterclockwise), cross a road, and follow forest back to the sno-park. Partway around the loop, where you cross the road, ski out the road a short distance for a view from a clearcut.

McCLELLAN MEADOWS TO
INDIAN HEAVEN TRAIL

(Map 8) This Novice marked trail (Trail 157) is the most popular route to McClellan Meadows, a 3.6-mile round trip. From there it is rated Intermediate as it climbs 3.8 miles as Trail 159 through forest, with a gain of 1,000 feet, to Road 65, where grand views are enjoyed from the upper end of the Outlaw Creek Clearcuts. Indian Heaven is a roadless, Backcountry area above and east of Road 65. Not recommended for the average skier, it is a confusing area to ski because there are few landmarks. If you enter this area, start with a compass bearing and map. See the Thomas Lake Trail description.

From Old Man Pass drive 1.6 miles north to Sno-Park C. Follow a road (Trail 157) southeast up a long, gentle hill to flat terrain as you pass a long clearcut to the right, about 1.2 miles from the sno-park. For a fine view ski into the clearcut to its northwest corner. You are now at the edge of a long cliff forming the western edge of the clearcut and offering the best views of the area. The forested, deep valley of the Wind River goes south and is impressive. Ski with care along the edge of the clearcut, then turn to the meadows where you will see Mount Adams to the northeast above a forested ridge.

Back on Trail 157, at the end of McClellan Meadows, the road continues south into a clearcut. Turn left there, climb left along the far edge onto Trail 159 where St. Helens comes into view. Entering forest, the trail winds and twists across rough terrain and through dense growth of alder and cedar. After 0.5 mile or so, however, the trail enters semi-open second growth and from there to Road 65 becomes most attractive. A side road 1.5 miles below Road 65 leads north into the immense, scenic Outlaw Creek Clearcuts. From McClellan Meadows to Road 65 and the upper Outlaw Creek Clearcuts is 4 miles, and a climb of 1,000 feet.

VALLEY SKI TRAIL TO McCLELLAN
MEADOWS TRAIL

(Maps 7 & 8) Of the two marked trails into McClellan Meadows, this Intermediate, 4-mile round trip is the most challenging. It first descends

On Road 65 at upper edge of Outlaw Creek Clearcuts

150 feet to the Wind River, which it crosses on a footbridge, then climbs out the other side. The trailhead is across the road from Old Man Pass Sno-Park. Take the right-hand trail, which immediately heads east on a gentle descent through forest. Do not take the left-hand trail—Hardtime Loop Trail 150, which from here goes north while paralleling Road 30.

After several hundred yards the Valley Ski Trail makes an abrupt left turn to the north, traversing the slope and clearcuts and descending to the river, which here is just a creek. Cross the river on a footbridge and turn southeast into a long clearcut, following its bottom edge to near its far end. There, the trail turns uphill and climbs steeply. Near the top the trail dodges into trees then emerges onto a road—Trail 157 at the south end of McClellan Meadows. For an interesting 4.8-mile loop, follow Trails 157 and 150 back to Old Man Pass. Or cross Road 30 at Sno-Park C and pick up Trail 148.

PETE GULCH TRAIL

(Map 8) From McClellan Meadows the Pete Gulch Trail, a round trip of 6.6 miles and a 600-foot gain, climbs along narrow, winding summer trail 157 to Road 65 where it ends. Several places are moderately steep, and this trail is only for experienced skiers with route-finding skills.

The trail starts at the bottom of the clearcut just south of McClellan Meadows, where the Trail 157 road ends. From there the trail enters forest and winds gently to moderately upward through second growth, along the way crossing three bridged streams. At 1.7 miles the trail crosses the top of a clearcut. Turn right 100 yards for a view of St. Helens. After more forest

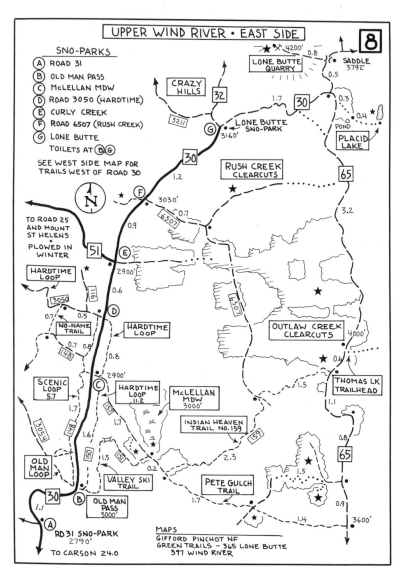

travel where the trail is easy to miss, it eventually reaches Road 65. Turn left onto 65 and ski 0.9 mile north to a side road leading 200 yards into several clearcuts with fine views—a side trip worth taking.

A shorter, more interesting route to this clearcut area with views begins back at the clearcut 1.7 miles up the Pete Gulch Trail. From there turn left and follow the clearcut road uphill into the forest to a large clearcut with a view of St. Helens. An opening at the top of the clearcut in a fringe of forest leads to yet a higher one, with direct access to Road 65, 400 feet above and 1.5 miles from where you left the Pete Gulch Trail. A clearcut to the south from the upper clearcut—and through a screen of trees—has a fine view of Mount Hood, Mount Jefferson, and nearby Red Mountain in Indian Heaven.

For a loop tour ski north on Road 65 to the upper end of the Outlaw Creek Clearcuts, returning to Sno-Park C on Trail 159, then Trail 157.

HARDTIME LOOP

(Map 7 & 8) Starting at Old Man Pass this 11.2-mile Intermediate loop goes through rolling forest and clearcuts. The total accumulated elevation gain is about 700 feet. It is unfortunate that its 4.3-mile-long west leg is generally uninteresting as it travels along a wide road, but the north leg, also on a wide road, has several exceptional views and interesting side trips (see Hardtime Creek Trail). The entire loop is usually machine groomed with a double track. Since there are few demanding hills it is a popular ski tour. For skiers with limited time and energy, the more interesting east leg and north leg are recommended. Or ski the east leg of the Scenic Loop to Sno-Park D.

To ski the loop as marked by the Forest Service, cross the road at Old Man Pass and ski north on Trail 150 on the east side of Road 30. Ski this primitive road 2.4 miles to Sno-Park D, cross Road 30, and ski west on the Hardtime Creek road, the north leg of the loop. At the west end of the north leg 4 miles from Sno-Park D the trail leaves the road, turns abruptly south, and climbs a clearcut to the loop's highest point at 3,245 feet. Pass through a band of forest to find Road 3054, then west along the final leg. There are several "screamer" hills along the west leg going south, particularly if the snow is fast or icy.

Hardtime Loop Connector (Trail 150). (Maps 7 & 8) This Novice trail, descending gently northward as it parallels Road 30 on its east side, goes 1.6 miles through beautiful forest along a primitive road to Sno-Park C. It continues 0.8 mile on to Sno-Park D, and serves as a connector and/or a leg for several loops, including the Scenic Loop, by crossing Road 30 at Sno-Park C.

Hardtime Creek Trail and Loop. (Maps 7 & 8) There are striking vistas of three volcanoes, as well as other fine views, along this 4-mile road that is also the north leg of the Hardtime Loop. For Novices, the gentle grades and wide road offer a scenic 5-mile round-trip tour to the principal viewpoint with a cumulative elevation gain of 400 feet. The combination of large clearcuts, forest, valley, and mountains make this one of the most scenic tours of the area.

To reach the trailhead ski or drive to Sno-Park D (Road 3050) 0.8 mile north of Sno-Park C. From Sno-Park D ski west on the road that soon descends to Hardtime Creek (1.5 miles), then climbs and in 1 mile reaches a steep clearcut with stunning views of Rainier across deep valleys, St. Helens, and nearby Crazy Hills and Adams behind. This road ends in a clearcut another 1.5 miles west. From the road end the loop continues upward through a clearcut, then onto Road 3054, the west leg of the Hardtime Loop.

There are four side trips off the Hardtime road worth knowing about, including Road 116, No-Name Trail, Lewis River Overlook, and the Hardtime Cutoff Trail.

Road 116. (Map 7) Only 0.3 mile west of Sno-Park D, a side trip northward on this road goes 1 mile, at first level, then descends to a clearcut with a view of Hardtime Creek and St. Helens.

No-Name Trail. (Map 7) This side trip goes south into clearcuts. Ski 0.5 mile west from Sno-Park D, turn south onto the No-Name Trail, and ski 0.7 mile across rolling, open clearcuts to the north leg of the Scenic Loop.

Lewis River Overlook. (Map 7) From the north leg of the Hardtime Loop a short, unmarked side trip leads to another fine viewpoint. From Sno-Park D ski west on the Hardtime road 3.7 miles, then ski into a clearcut below the road (see map), just 0.3 mile from the end of the Hardtime Loop north leg. Follow along the almost-level top of the clearcut, enter beautiful old growth and climb to another clearcut. The best views are from the upper edge of the clearcut. To the west is the end of a forested ridge, the end of Point 3670. Also seen are St. Helens, the Lewis River valley, Rainier, Adams, and the Indian Heaven high country.

An alternative route to this viewpoint is from the end of the Hardtime road where the loop turns abruptly south. Here, go west on an old road and follow as it turns and descends northward to the viewpoint clearcut.

Hardtime Cutoff Trail. (Map 7) This 1.3-mile, unmarked, Intermediate off-road route shortens the Hardtime Loop by 0.7 mile, is easy to follow, and most importantly is scenic. From the steep clearcut with views 2.4 miles from Sno-Park D, ski to the west end of the clearcut, and go another 200 yards. Then turn uphill on a side road through forest, then into a large clearcut, a vigorous but scenic climb. The upper clearcut is meadowlike and gently sloping and an excellent, scenic spot for an overnight camp. From here, ski through an 80-yard band of trees, find a road, and ski around the north side of Cutoff Butte. Follow the road down, then up to the west leg of Hardtime Loop. If you are looking for downhill runs, ski this cutoff from the west leg to the north leg.

TERMINATION POINT

(Map 7) At 3,996 feet, this easy Backcountry tour ensures isolation as few skiers or snowmobilers visit the open ridge and its fine views. The modest 4 miles one way and 1,200-foot elevation gain to the scenic final saddle just below the peak provide rewards other than just scenery.

From Road 31 (Sno-Park A) ski uphill and west from Road 30 2.8 miles to a side road that leads uphill 0.3 mile to a junction (not obvious under snow). The left fork goes 1.2 miles directly to Termination Point, and the right fork zigzags steeply up to a quarry with views of Rainier and Adams.

From the quarry floor it is possible to ski directly to Termination Point through a large clearcut in a broad saddle, an excellent camp spot. Enter the forest and ski up a moderately steep road to the saddle at the very foot of Termination Point, whose summit is only 200 yards above, and from where St. Helens can be seen. If you climb the very steep ridge to the summit, you will see Hood, Adams, Rainier, and all of the Upper Wind River area.

If the snow is good, it is possible to ski 600 feet down from the saddle through an old clearcut to the lower quarry, then out to Road 31.

Point 3670. (Map 7) This Advanced, 16-mile round-trip tour on unmarked roads leads to a ridge end with panoramic views across to St. Helens, Rainier, and Adams. You'll also be looking down at Swift Reservoir almost 3,000 feet below.

Follow directions toward Termination Point but continue on Road 31 until you are 4.8 miles from the sno-park, where you reach a junction in a flat, open saddle. Ski this road (3103) north, switching sides of the ridge to the final views at the road's end.

Termination Ridge Cutoff. (Map 7) This 1.5-mile route on a steep, primitive road climbs 300 feet from the Hardtime Loop to Road 31 3.7 miles from Sno-Park A.

Telemark Hill. (Map 7) Skiers looking for Telemark skiing will find an exceptional clearcut hillside 1.5 miles up Road 31 from Sno-Park A. The huge south-facing clearcut, 300 feet high, has angles and variety to suit any T-marker.

OUTLAW CREEK CLEARCUTS

(Map 8) This Intermediate tour on unmarked routes climbs 1,000 feet to a high point of 4,000 feet at the west edge of Indian Heaven after 4 miles of moderate uphill skiing. It offers a unique opportunity to ski through vast open areas with an almost ethereal quality. There are views of distant ridges and a superb view of St. Helens.

From Old Man Pass drive north 3.9 miles to Sno-Park F (Rush Creek). Ski the snow-covered road eastward as it climbs through forest to a Y-junction 0.7 mile from the sno-park. The left fork goes to the Rush Creek Clearcuts, and the right fork is your route. The second clearcut you enter is the bottom (west end) of a system of huge, connecting clearcuts that leads upward to excellent views of St. Helens and the high, forested ridges of the Wind River area.

Road 65, a major forest road, crosses the upper end of these clearcuts at the 4,000-foot level, 1,000 feet above the sno-park. On this tour you will find hills to ski, streams to cross, and an ever-changing spectacle of distant forest borders silhouetted against ridges and sky.

THOMAS LAKE TRAIL TO INDIAN HEAVEN WILDERNESS

(Map 8) This 1-mile summer trail is the most direct route into the heart of the Indian Heaven Wilderness. The only problem is that you have to ski 4 miles and climb 1,000 feet to get to this trail—but the effort expended is rewarded. This tour of at least 10 miles round trip is rated Advanced.

The summer trail avoids the dense forest found along most areas of the west boundary of the wilderness, and leads to extensive, level meadows near Rock Lakes at the west foot of East Crater. Other approaches are remote, steep, and difficult. There are few viewpoints in the wilderness, so your trip here is more an exercise in Backcountry travel than in seeking vistas, except for the stunning views from the upper Outlaw Creek Clearcuts.

Drive to Sno-Park F (Rush Creek) and see directions for Rush Creek and to the huge clearcuts. The summer trailhead for the Thomas Lake Trail is not easy to find unless you have previously scouted it out in summer to facilitate winter route finding. If you ski into the Indian Heaven Wilderness, be aware there are no marked trails and few landmarks to help you navigate. Use a map and compass to orient yourself in the forest and complex meadow systems, and be sure to identify your return route carefully.

RUSH CREEK CLEARCUTS

(Map 8) If you have a minimum amount of time to ski or want a second ski tour of less than 3 miles round trip for the day with maximum views for a modest effort, then this is the route for you. The views are great, and the gentle downhill will glide you back almost to the sno-park. This area is rated Novice.

See the Outlaw Creek Clearcuts directions, then ski to the Y-junction 0.7 mile east of the sno-park, go left, and climb out of the forest into the clearcuts. In just under 0.5 mile from the Y-junction you will get your first views, which get better as you climb. A 9-mile loop, best left to Advanced skiers, is possible by skiing 3 miles to Road 65, then south 2 miles to the upper Outlaw Creek Clearcuts, then down through the cuts to the sno-park.

Views from the Rush Creek Clearcuts include the Crazy Hills, Lone Butte (the "China Hat" cone to the north), St. Helens, and Mount Adams. A large clearcut across Road 30 from the sno-park offers good views, particularly if you climb to its upper levels. This is an easy tour for Novice skiers.

LONE BUTTE QUARRY VIEWPOINT

(Maps 8 & 9) The most conspicuous landmark of the entire Upper Wind River, the forested, symmetrical cone of the Lone Butte area (4,780 feet) rises

1,700 feet above its base and towers over the nearby Crazy Hills. The quarry, high on the south side, providing sweeping views, is a 1,000-foot climb and a 3-mile tour for strong Intermediate skiers.

Lone Butte Sno-Park at the end of plowed Road 30 is the access point for the Crazy Hills, the enormous clearcuts behind Lone Butte and Placid Lake. The sno-park is also the center of snowmobile activity for the entire region.

To ski to the quarry ski up Road 30 east of the sno-park 1.7 miles to the junction with the north end of Road 65, then to the left 0.5 mile to Lone Butte Saddle (3,792 feet). Turn left onto a narrow road and climb moderate grades 400 feet through forest 0.8 mile to the quarry. For the best views, go around the west side and climb a bit on the edge of the pit. You will see St. Helens, all of the Wind River ski areas to the south, including the massive clearcuts of Rush Creek and Outlaw Creek. Mount Hood is barely seen behind Red Mountain.

The summit of Lone Butte, a very steep 580-foot climb above the quarry, is best left to Backcountry skiers who will probably do most of it off skis.

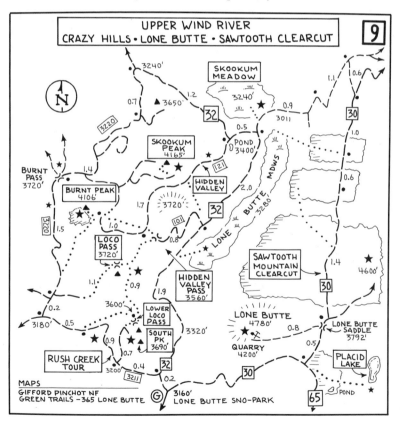

UPPER WIND RIVER
CRAZY HILLS • LONE BUTTE • SAWTOOTH CLEARCUT

9

SAWTOOTH MOUNTAIN CLEARCUT

(Map 9) From Lone Butte Saddle (see Lone Butte Quarry) a huge clearcut sweeps upward over 2 miles to 4,600 feet and extends a mile northward and downward behind Lone Butte to Lone Butte Meadows—a gigantic, denuded area attesting to pre-environmental logging practices. The views from the upper clearcut are stunning. The round-trip ski tour of up to 8 miles is for Intermediate skiers willing to climb up to 1,500 feet.

Ski to Lone Butte Saddle and at a fork just beyond in the forest go right, uphill, and enter the Sawtooth Clearcut with Sawtooth Mountain rising above. As you climb, the scene expands and you will see St. Helens and Rainier.

LONE BUTTE MEADOWS AND LOOP

(Map 9) The vast clearcuts behind Lone Butte and the meadows below the butte, extending 2 miles to Skookum Meadow north of the Crazy Hills, provide an area that is wide open to creative loop skiing.

From Lone Butte Saddle (see Lone Butte Quarry) ski to the nearby junction and turn left and ski north on Road 30 into the center of the Sawtooth Clearcut. The road follows a snakelike, wandering route across several huge clearcuts separated by forest fringes. Two miles from the saddle turn downhill, descend the clearcut, and make your way to Skookum Meadow.

On your return, the meandering stream through Lone Butte Meadows is interesting to follow if the snow is deep enough and the marshes covered. There are no obvious ways to cross the small stream that flows ultimately into Rush Creek unless it is bridged by snow. The meadows connect with Skookum Meadow, forming a wide, gentle valley over 2 miles long. The easiest return to the sno-park is to ski from the meadows to Road 32, which goes along the east foot of the Crazy Hills just above the valley bottom.

PLACID LAKE

(Maps 8 & 9) This small, lovely lake is surrounded by deep forest and is easily reached by Intermediate-level skiers from Lone Butte Sno-Park in just over 2 miles with an elevation gain of 500 feet. The tour is good practice for inexperienced skiers who wish to learn some Backcountry skills and gain confidence in off-road skiing. From Lone Butte Sno-Park ski east on Road 30 1.7 miles, turn right, ski south on Road 65 briefly, then climb the clearcut above the road to a shallow drainage at its top. Follow the drainage for 0.4 mile into the Indian Heaven Wilderness to the lake.

Chapter 3

THE CRAZY HILLS

The Crazy Hills comprise an unusually compact area north of the main Upper Wind River trail system. This little-known but remarkable area offers a number of surprises. Although all routes are unmarked for skiers, there are excellent viewpoints, passes to cross, a beautiful hidden valley, off-road skiing, and many loops. The entire area is encircled by a gentle, easy-to-follow road that forms the longest loop. The fascinating area invites off-road exploration.

There is generally no problem in route finding unless you try off-road skiing on the ridges. The area is so compact, however, that skiing downhill in any direction will always take a disoriented skier to the perimeter road, which is obvious and ultimately leads back to the sno-park.

Avalanche danger is almost nonexistent in the Crazy Hills, except possibly for the south slopes of Skookum Peak. Ongoing logging and the growing of second growth in clearcuts affect route descriptions. If confused while skiing, keep going, use judgment, and reinterpret descriptions.

The Crazy Hills are open to snowmobilers and see a lot of snowmobile use. Fast-moving machines are always a danger to skiers. Step aside, watch their approach, and be sure their drivers are aware of your presence.

Until you are familiar with the Crazy Hills, carry a map of the area. There is only one sno-park for all the Crazy Hills tours: Lone Butte Sno-Park (Sno-Park G), with toilet facilities, is the northernmost in the Upper Wind River skiing area. From Old Man Pass drive Road 30 north 4.7 miles to its end at the sno-park.

RUSH CREEK TOUR

(Map 9) If you are looking for a Novice ski tour of 3 miles round trip with only a 60-foot elevation gain that offers the maximum open space and views for the least effort, try this tour. Exceptional sweeping views are a unique aspect. From Sno-Park G ski north on Road 32 0.2 mile and turn left onto Road 3211. You will soon be looking down and across several draws and the Rush Creek valley to a scene unfolding to the south. As you progress along the level, sidehill road, the views become more striking and soon the entire Upper Wind River basin comes into view, gently sweeping upward to the east and ending in the massive ridge of the Indian Heaven backcountry. To the north, above the road, are slopes leading to a ridgecrest. For a description of this area see Lower Loco Pass/South Peak.

LONE BUTTE MEADOWS

(Map 9) At the east foot of the Crazy Hills lies a series of meadows and marshes that offers off-road, exploratory skiing for those interested in a short, undemanding tour. The 6-mile round-trip route is rated Novice and gains only 160 feet.

From Sno-Park G ski north on Road 32 about 1.5 miles to where the road levels out. Then descend through a screen of trees into the meadows. The road continues north paralleling the meadows, so enter them wherever it is convenient. Brushy areas, marshes, and small streams are the only obstacles. The tour is best when there are 3 feet or more of snow.

The meadows may be followed north to Skookum Meadow. There are no good stream crossings unless bridged by snow. This is a tranquil area, perhaps the most relaxing tour of the area.

SKOOKUM MEADOW

(Map 9) Skirting the east foot of the Crazy Hills this Intermediate 8-mile round trip offers views, streams, and meadows with a cumulative elevation gain of only 440 feet. From Sno-Park G ski north on Road 32. Once over the initial low hill—called "Misery Hill" as it must be wearily recrossed on the way home after a long tour—an essentially level route leads to the meadows. At 2 miles, views open out onto the wide valley of streams and marshes that comprise Lone Butte Meadows. Continuing north you eventually arrive at Skookum Meadow, a wide, open area with a view of St. Helens. Skookum means "large" in Chinook, a fitting name for this area. From the meadow's west end, Adams can be seen, and there are better views if you ski south and uphill into the clearcuts of the Crazy Hills.

LOWER LOCO PASS TO SOUTH PEAK

(Map 9) This short Intermediate 3-mile round-trip tour provides unexcelled views with an elevation gain of only 530 feet. The route follows a moderately climbing road to views of Hood, Adams, Goat Rocks, and St. Helens.

From Sno-Park G ski north on Road 32 0.2 mile, then turn west onto Road 3211 following the Rush Creek Tour route. At 0.6 mile from the sno-park you will reach a 200-foot-wide level spot on the road and a nearby large stand of old-growth trees. Opposite this spot is an obscure side road heading north into well-established second-growth conifers. Follow this road upward for a 490-foot vertical climb to the two open knobs of South Peak. The southern knob is higher and has the best unobstructed views. To the north, across Lower Loco Pass, connecting clearcuts lead to Loco and Hidden Valley Passes. Beyond lies the scalped top of Skookum Peak. The high area of clearcuts to the north lends itself to easy exploration.

Crazy Hills from east; Skookum Peak on right and Mount St. Helens beyond

CRAZY HILLS LOOP

(Map 9) Surrounding the Crazy Hills is a 10.8-mile loop road, much of it nearly level, with several long, gentle hills on the west side where it crosses Burnt Pass (3,720 feet). This is an Advanced tour with a cumulative gain of 640 feet. Roads 32, 3220, and 3211 comprise the loop. The best views are from the north end and from high on the west side, near the pass.

From Sno-Park G ski north to Skookum Meadow, then west past the road to Hidden Valley to beautiful forest where the loop turns south to climb to the pass. At the pass, a side road goes to a good viewpoint. After a 500-foot drop the road levels near the side road to Loco Pass.

If you are short on time, just ski the south and west legs to Burnt Pass, only 3.7 miles from the sno-park, for the views. The loop can be shortened by taking side roads across the Crazy Hills.

LOCO PASS LOOP

(Map 9) The Intermediate Loco Pass Loop of 9.7 miles round trip is the most scenic tour of the Crazy Hills, offering a great variety of terrain and vistas, crossing two passes, and providing some off-road route finding. Elevation gain is 520 feet, and the high point is 3,680 feet.

Follow directions for Skookum Meadow. At the north end of the loop, turn south onto Road 121, skiing through wide, open areas and past a small pond, then gently upward through old growth and past steep hillside clearcuts. This is Hidden Valley, offering a delightful, scenic tour as the road winds gently upward into an ever-narrowing defile.

At the upper (south) end of Hidden Valley, 6.3 miles from the sno-park, the road turns right (southwest) and climbs through clearcuts and forest to Burnt Peak. At the turn, leave the road and climb up and to the left to wide, flat Hidden Valley Pass. From the pass climb upward and southwest then south into a large clearcut, then up open slopes to the broad saddle of Loco Pass (3,680 feet). West of the pass the route (the road is lost under snow) generally follows the edge of the forest, then leads downward to Road 3220, which leads to Road 3211 and back to the sno-park.

BURNT PEAK

(Map 9) On the west edge of the Crazy Hills, the 4,106-foot summit of Burnt Peak, the second-highest point of the Crazy Hills and site of a former fire lookout, no longer offers good views as the forest has reclaimed the summit. However, the clearcut on its south side is worth climbing for views. This is a round trip of 9 to 14 miles, rated Intermediate.

The most direct route is over Hidden Valley Pass (4.5 miles each way). Ski north on Road 32 toward Skookum Meadow for 2.1 miles to Road 101 to the left. Follow this road upward, circling southward then around to Hidden Valley Pass, which is crossed onto Road 121, which is followed upward or through paralleling clearcuts 1 mile from the pass to a large clearcut at the south foot of Burnt Peak. Climb this for views to the south, and west to St. Helens.

SKOOKUM PEAK

(Map 9) The ridgelike summit of this 4,165-foot peak is the highest point in the Crazy Hills, and there are good views in several directions. Although screens of trees block other views it is a worthwhile goal. Round trip is 6 to 11 miles for this Advanced tour that gains 1,000 feet.

The most direct approach is to follow directions for Burnt Peak to the clearcut on its south side just under the summit. Ski to the clearcut's northeast corner, enter the forest, and ski 200 yards to an old road that leads up to another road that takes you to the summit ridge and saddle of Skookum Peak. There are good views from the saddle, but ski east and climb the steep ridge 200 yards to its end for the best views.

Another route to the summit from the sno-park follows the Loco Pass Loop into Hidden Valley. The high point, west of the narrow valley with the prominent rock formations, is Skookum Peak. Climb the steep clearcut on its south slope to the saddle, or follow the south edge up a steep, open draw into forest onto the old road that leads to the saddle near the summit.

Yet another direct route is to ski to the junction of Roads 32 and 101, follow 101 up to where it turns south, leave the road, and ski west over the ridge and down into Hidden Valley, then up the southside clearcut route.

Chapter 4

TROUT LAKE

(Map 10) The area west of the village of Trout Lake in the White Salmon River valley offers several scenic marked trails and many miles of other tours. Although many snowmobilers use the area, their routes are separated from the marked trails. Atkisson Sno-Park, 5 miles southwest of Trout Lake, serves both users. Most trails follow roads, some to exceptional viewpoints.

The village of Trout Lake at 2,000 feet is reached from the Washington side of the Gorge by driving 21 miles north of the Columbia River on Highway 141 out of White Salmon. An alternative route from Hood River, Oregon turns right from the Hood River Bridge and leads east to nearby Bingen, then uphill through the town of White Salmon to connect with Highway 141.

Arriving at Trout Lake, you have the choice of driving straight ahead at the gas station, which will take you to the Smith Butte ski area (see Trout Lake East), or angling left into the village. The Mount Adams Ranger District headquarters is 0.8 mile to the left through the village, on the way to the west side and Atkisson Sno-Park. This sno-park is at 2,700 feet and 5 miles from the ranger station.

TROUT LAKE WEST

(Map 11)

TROUT LAKE MEADOW

(No sketch map) Suitable for Novice skiers, the 1-mile meadow at the northeast edge of Trout Lake offers a unique skiing experience when there

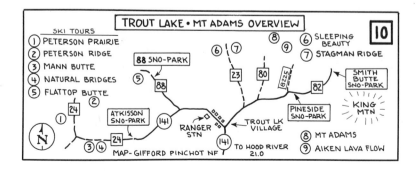

is adequate snow. Skiing in the meadow is not always possible because of the low elevation. The meadow, as it is called, is largely private land, but skiing is permitted. It is accessed by crossing a bridge to the village picnic park. From here, the flat meadow stretches out, surrounded by views of the distant ridges and Mount Adams rising to over 10,000 feet above and only 14 miles away.

The village picnic park is found by turning right onto a short dead-end side street before reaching the ranger station. Parking may be a problem as space is required by the tavern-inn-store located next to the bridge. Use good judgment.

The famed waterfowl viewing area of Trout Lake is located at the northwest edge of the meadow, but it is reached only by an unsigned side road just beyond the ranger station.

MANN BUTTE

(Map 11) The tour to Mann Butte, partly on marked roads and partly unmarked, requires little route finding, is suitable for Novice-Intermediates skiers, is 10 miles round trip, and climbs 700 feet to the top of the quarry at 3,440 feet. Although there are other good viewpoints on the west side, the Mann Butte quarry probably provides the best. Adams, the Simcoes to the east, the Trout Lake valley, and the Indian Heaven high country are all seen from the plateau at the upper quarry. From a distance, the red-colored cliffs below the upper quarry are a landmark.

From the west end of Atkisson Sno-Park ski west on the shared-use, marked trail 500 yards, then turn right onto a ski trail crossing Road 24 onto Road 020. Follow this about 0.2 mile, then turn left off the road into clearcuts and forest paralleling Road 24 to Road 2420 (the Peterson Ridge route). The trail briefly follows 2420 north, then turns left to cross Road 24 to Road 041, which goes south toward Mann Butte.

This seemingly complex route was laid out to avoid snowmobile routes. It is more interesting than following the snowmobile route west from the sno-park to Road 041 and is worth the extra effort. This winding route may be further altered as time goes by.

Ski 041 over a high point (the Natural Bridges Trails are to the west) and descend to a four-way junction 1.3 miles from Road 24. From here you can ski straight ahead 0.3 mile to the lower quarry for views. For the upper quarry, turn right onto 8620, ski 0.7 mile, turn left, and ski the road uphill through open areas. Turn left onto the final road for 1 mile to the plateau for views. A road continues uphill through old growth to yet another viewpoint on the butte's west side.

A shortcut from the four-way junction below the quarry goes up through open hillsides to the upper quarry road. When the snow is good, these slopes are a good descent route.

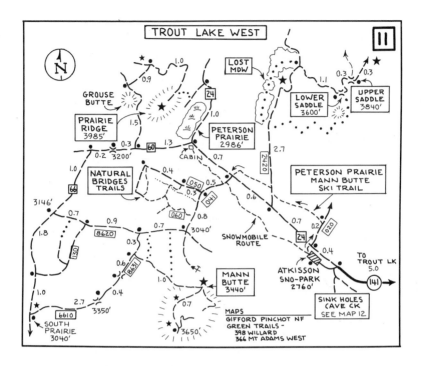

NATURAL BRIDGES

(Map 11) The Natural Bridges area is for Intermediate skiers, an 8-mile round trip on marked trails from the sno-park that gains 300 feet to a high of 3,000 feet. The three natural basalt bridges that span a collapsed lava tube are interesting, but the most rewarding part of this tour is the ski loop formed by nearby forest trails on the plateau south of the lava bridges. Shown on the sketch map are alternative loops and areas to explore on the plateau in addition to the marked trails.

See Mann Butte description for access to the Natural Bridges area. From Road 24 ski uphill on Road 041 0.5 mile, then turn right and ski west 0.3 mile, leave the road, and climb a steep bank to reach the east-west collapsed tube. The trail parallels the sunken tube past the bridges. The trail turns left onto a primitive road and follows a winding route through forest and loops around.

Most of the area is level, but the maze of primitive roads may be confusing if you lose the trail markers or if you try off-trail skiing. If "lost," ski east to Road 041.

PETERSON RIDGE AND LOST MEADOW

(Map 11) This Intermediate 13-mile round trip on marked roads climbs 1,200 feet to fine views. At the 3,840-foot high point you will see Mount Hood, the Trout Lake valley, and Indian Heaven. Along the way, a short side trip takes you into Lost Meadow.

Follow directions for Mann Butte and ski to Road 2420 where you turn northward, passing old growth and clearcuts and then entering an open, scenic valley. At first level, the road then climbs, then levels, with a large clearcut to the west. Enter the clearcut and ski to its north end. Pass through an opening in the forest that leads to Lost Meadow.

A narrow band of trees at the far end leads to a hillside clearcut, the top of which puts you back on the road and a junction with the road you want to follow upward onto Peterson Ridge. Ski to the lower saddle, then 0.3 mile to the upper saddle. Both saddles have good views. From the upper saddle descend eastward on a road 0.3 mile to excellent views of the Trout Lake valley.

If you ski above the upper saddle, the road goes from side to side of the narrow ridge. At 0.7 mile there is a good view westward and down onto your uphill route. The road then descends to a view of Mount Adams.

An alternative off-trail return route from the lower saddle takes an obvious road southward around a bare knoll, then curves westward to tall timber. Enter, contour west, go through a plantation to a saddle, and climb 50 yards to an open knoll. This is the top of the large clearcut you saw from the lower road on your way up. If icy or hardpacked, do not descend this slope.

PETERSON PRAIRIE AND PRAIRIE RIDGE

(Map 11) The marked trail to Peterson Prairie is a Novice tour, but the climb of the ridge beyond is Intermediate, a 9-mile round trip onto unmarked terrain. Peterson Prairie is a small meadow 2.7 miles west of Atkisson Sno-Park and the site of a ranger's cabin available for rent from the Forest Service. The meadow is not particularly interesting, but Prairie Ridge overlooking it to the west makes for a scenic tour. The long, bare, almost-level ridgetop has views of Mounts Rainier and Adams, the Trout Lake valley, Mann Butte, and other points of interest. The gentle backside of the ridge to the west offers extended touring on roads through logged areas. The top of the ridge is barely 5 miles from the sno-park and only a 1,300-foot climb.

Follow directions for Mann Butte and ski onto Road 041 after crossing Road 24, then go 100 yards and turn right onto an abandoned snowmobile trail that leads toward Peterson Prairie and the cabin at its south end.

Road 24 is often plowed beyond the sno-park for winter logging. If not plowed it can be skied, but it is used by snowmobilers and is less interesting than the marked ski trails. If plowed, there is usually a plowed turnout at Peterson Prairie for parking.

To ski to the top of Prairie Ridge, ski north on the road paralleling the edge of Peterson Prairie, and in 1 mile turn left into the forest on a road. Follow this 0.5 mile south or more then climb the steep east side of the ridge through open areas. Snow depth permitting, turn off the side road sooner and climb through old growth 400 yards into a clearcut at the north foot of the ridge. Ski south to the ridgetop.

SINK HOLES AND CAVE CREEK

(Maps 11 & 12) East of Atkisson Sno-Park are several unmarked roads worth exploring with forest, open spaces, and areas of geological interest. The route is nearly level and suitable for Novices. Round-trip distances are less than 2 miles.

Sink Holes. (Map 12) Ski only 0.8 mile to a series of fascinating "sink holes" caused by the collapse of lava tunnels. Walk or ski along the sno-park access road to within 20 yards of Highway 141, which continues westward as Forest Road 24. Turn east here at a small opening and ski east on a primitive road. In 20 yards another road branches off to the right—the Cave Creek road.

Ignore this side road and ski east 0.5 mile to a large, open area where 20 yards to your left you will find the first of several sink holes. Explore the area carefully as the holes are 20 feet deep with vertical dropoffs. Highway 141 is only 300 yards to the north. Other primitive roads to the south can be explored.

Cave Creek. (Map 12) See Sink Holes description for the start of this easy tour. Ski south through dense, attractive forest along the winding, primitive road. In 200 yards enter a large clearcut, skirt the west side, reenter forest, and ski to a Y-junction. Go left for the most interesting route, and ski 0.3 mile to Cave Creek where there are several open areas to explore.

Loop Tour. (Map 12) Ski east on the Sink Holes route, then turn right onto an obscure road and ski southwest 50 yards into the large clearcut that leads to the Cave Creek road.

FLATTOP MOUNTAIN

(Map 13) This Advanced unmarked 6.6-mile round trip climbs 1,600 feet to a high of 4,200 feet for exceptional views. Your goal is the north shoulder

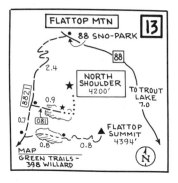

for views that are better than from the forested summit. The 4,394-foot forested butte northwest of Trout Lake is easily identified by its flat top and two snow streaks.

The actual summit of Flattop is gained not without considerable effort, and it is disappointing to find no views, although it is the site of a fire-lookout tower. The last 0.8 mile to the top is very steep. The north shoulder is your best goal on this mountain.

From the Trout Lake Ranger Station, drive 0.8 mile to an abandoned mill. Turn right onto Road 88, then drive 6 miles to its junction with Road 8821 where a sno-park at 2,600 feet is maintained primarily on an experimental basis for snowmobilers. Ski up Road 8821 past a view of Mount Adams 2.4 miles to Road 081 where you turn left and ski upward, climbing steeply eastward into a large clearcut. At a saddle in its upper end, enter forest to the left and ski to the large, level north shoulder. Views abound with St. Helens, Rainier, and Adams across a sweep of forest. The almost flat shield-volcano profile of the Simcoe Mountains near Goldendale appears above the Trout Lake valley. Ski eastward in the clearcut for the best views.

On your return descent, ski to the saddle then out into the upper clearcut for more views of Trout Lake. At the junction of 8821/081, leave the road and ski west 100 yards into one of the Deadhorse Meadows.

TROUT LAKE EAST

(Map 14)

SMITH BUTTE LOOPS

(Map 14) This fascinating area offers everything—wide, safe roads, twisting primitive routes, open forests, some groomed tracks and marked ski trails, and a few good, scattered views. If you are primarily interested in views, ski the King Mountain routes or the Trout Lake West area.

At this time there are four marked loops, all accessed from Pineside Sno-Park, in addition to many miles of roads. In fact, due to logging in the area, a labyrinth of small roads, most of which are interesting to ski, form many unmarked loops and provide considerable isolation.

There are two sno-parks here. Pineside Sno-Park at 2,800 feet is at a marginal elevation near the snowline, and 3.3 miles farther up the road is Smith Butte Sno-Park at 3,850 feet. The road is not always plowed beyond Pineside Sno-Park because of lack of equipment and regular funding.

The area is roughly triangular, about 6 miles across at the top, including the King Mountain area, tapering southward 4 miles to Pineside Sno-Park. Three major roads go roughly south to north, one penetrating up through the center, the other two forming the sides of the area. Within this triangle is a maze of smaller roads, most of which are very attractive to ski. Together with a complex system of low ridges and drainages, it is an easy area in which to get disoriented. Most of the roads do not appear on Forest Service maps, unless you have a "transportation" map that gives great detail. If lost, finding one of the major roads and skiing down it will always lead you to safety. The lack of landmarks and thick forest make orientation difficult. It is a wonderful area for off-road exploration if you are experienced, but be sure to carry a compass and head south, not west, if confused. After you have skied here several times you will gain confidence in exploring this complex area whose greatest attractions are the primitive roads, numerous small clearings, and loop-skiing opportunities.

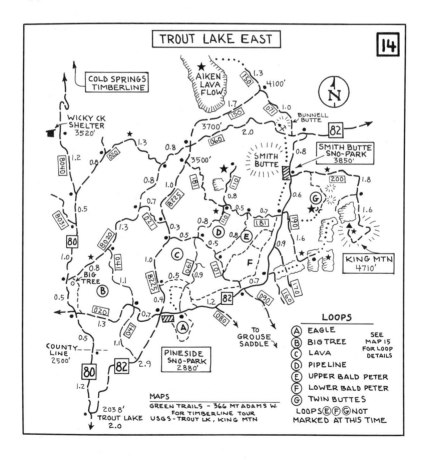

There are three public shelters—Wicky Creek, Morrison Creek, and Cold Springs—but they are all far from the popular ski routes:

Due to the complexity of roads in the area, the sketch map of this area lists all of this area's roads in three categories:

- major road—widest, straightest, and generally uninteresting
- forest road—narrower and winding
- primitive road—narrow, twisting, occasionally hard to follow

Eagle Loop. (Map 14) This marked Novice loop of 3 miles starts at 2,850 feet, gains very little, and travels through forest.

The trailhead is on the south side of Pineside Sno-Park. The loop has been changed several times, and the low elevation may cause elimination of the loop, which follows skid roads through forest. Roadside skiing may be necessary when Road 82 is plowed to Smith Butte. The loop will probably become irrelevant as other loops above 82 are added.

Upper Eagle Loops. (Map 14) There are several unmarked short loops above Road 82 across from the sno-park in generally level forest. Access is from Road 061, which is 0.4 mile up Road 82 from the sno-park. This attractive area invites exploration.

Big Tree Loop. (Map 14) This Novice loop following marked roads and a trail offers a variety of scenes, open forest, scattered openings, gentle terrain, and generally interesting roads. Elevation gain is 200 feet and round trip is 5.4 miles.

Ski west from Pineside Sno-Park 0.7 mile on Road 041 to a junction where the loop begins. At this four-way junction ski west on Road 020 1.3 miles, then turn right and ski uphill along an interesting primitive road to the Big Tree, a 7-foot-diameter, 200-foot-tall ponderosa pine. Ski up 8020, a beautiful route, past a brief view of Mount Adams, then south on 041 along a picturesque, shallow ravine to the four-way junction and the end of the loop itself.

Road 8020, the north leg of the Big Tree Loop, is a lovely road to ski. When skiing the loop, and before turning south on Road 041 (east leg), consider continuing northeast on 8020 to enjoy its beauty. If you ski up 2.1 miles beyond 041 you will reach 020 on the left. Ski out this road for a good view of Adams. Continuing on to Road 8225, then down it and onto Road 181, provides some great adventure skiing for a return to the sno-park.

Lava Loop. (Maps 14 & 15) This Novice–Intermediate marked loop will take you on a 3.7-mile round trip over a variety of roads, through beautiful forest, and on some gentle downhills if the loop is skied clockwise. Elevation gain is 150 feet and high point is 2,950 feet.

To ski the loop, ski from the Pineside Sno-Park up 8225 1.4 miles, then east on 101 to 061, a primitive road, down to the south leg and best part of the loop through open forest. Between the south leg and the sno-park are the unmarked Upper Eagle Loops, a compact, lovely area to explore.

Pipeline Loop. (Maps 14 & 15) The Intermediate loop itself is 2.6 miles, total 5.2 miles from South Butte Sno-Park and total 6 miles from Pineside Sno-Park, round trip, on marked routes. It is best reached going west on 181 from Smith Butte Sno-Park, which at this time requires unmarked skiing to Road 181, not a difficult feat. The loop and connector routes are rated Intermediate with a gain of up to 1,500 feet from Pineside. The west leg is through lovely forest and openings. A side trip up Road 110 north of the loop goes to large clearcuts at the west foot of Smith Butte for views of Adams. The east leg of the loop, Road 744, is a shallow valley with many meadows.

Bald Peter Loops. (Maps 14 & 15) Rated Advanced, the two round-trip loops are from 4.5 to 8.1 miles, depending on your choice of sno-park, and a gain of up to 1,500 feet. These two interesting loops circle near Bald Peter, a small, naked

Skier with gray jay

butte 1 mile south of Smith Butte. Following primitive roads in most places, the loops are exceptionally scenic, perhaps the best of the entire area.

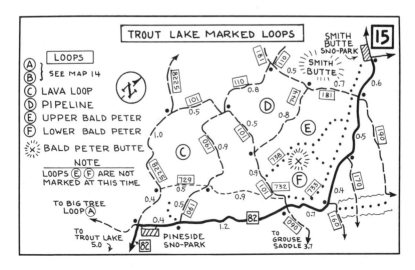

As these loops are not marked at this time except for the west leg of the Upper Loop, which is shared with the Pipeline Loop, they require off-trail route-finding skills. For the Backcountry skier, these loops will be a lot of fun—and a real challenge to others.

Upper Bald Peter Loop. (Maps 14 & 15) From Pineside Sno-Park, ski up Road 101 (see Grouse Saddle tour for directions) to Road 738, turn right, and ski through open forest and flat parkland, and climb a steep hill to the saddle in a clearcut at the north foot of Bald Peter Butte. Turn left (north), enter forest, and climb uphill on a winding road through small openings to where a road leads you up to Road 181. Turn left (west) and ski to 744, then down 744, within a shallow, narrow valley with many meadows, then left on 101 to finish the Upper Bald Peter Loop.

Lower Bald Peter Loop. (Maps 14 & 15) Follow the same route to Road 101. At 200 yards from Road 82 turn right onto 732 and ski a winding course uphill through several meadows for 500 yards into a more open valley and then to an obscure road going west (below Road 181). Turn left (west) and then down to Bald Peter Butte. Circle west around the north side, then west down a steep hill into flat parkland to Road 101.

To ski either loop from Smith Butte Sno-Park, enter a clearcut (regrowing rapidly) west of the sno-park and ski south parallel to Road 82, a route that will probably be marked in the future, to Road 181, then west to where the upper loop begins at Road 744.

KING MOUNTAIN

(Map 14) Unmarked roads and routes, for Advanced skiers, on the west side of King Mountain, and to its summit, offer a 7.5-mile loop with a gain of 860 feet. King Mountain at 4,710 feet is a forested shield volcano east of Road 82. There are three roads (160, 170, 190) that follow its western slope and lead to clearcuts and views. Although Road 200 goes directly from Smith Butte Sno-Park to the summit of King Mountain, the best views are from the western slope.

To ski the loop, ski east on Road 200 past a superb view of Adams, then turn southward, continuing on the road that climbs and circles the very summit of the mountain for views of Adams and the Simcoes. To continue the loop, either ski down the very steep northside slopes to a saddle below, or ski back down the road to where it flattens out. Then turn west into a clearcut and climb to the saddle.

From the saddle ski west down into an L-shaped clearcut to its southern end, enter forest, then ski south into another clearcut. Ski to its distant south end for views. For the loop, however, ski down to the clearcut's west edge, then enter old growth, find a road, ski down to Road 190 (or ski down a long clearcut to Road 170 or 160). Ski north on 190 through beautiful alpine

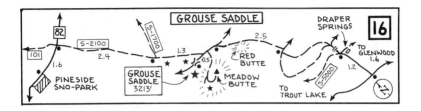

areas and meadows, cross Road 82, and ski unmarked routes up to Smith Butte Sno-Park.

Road 190 is a scenic, interesting ski tour in its own right for skiers not wanting to do the loop. Ski 1 mile from Road 82 to its end in a large clearcut.

Twin Buttes. (Map 14) Large clearcuts only 1 mile southeast of Smith Butte provide the finest views of the entire area. The unmarked route, climbing only 350 feet, at first follows old roads then open slopes to the exceptional viewpoint.

From the sno-park ski east 0.3 mile on Road 200 (King Mountain route) to a side road, then ski south into a level, second-growth lodgepole pine area. The road winds along, then angles southeast, climbs gently, and passes a side road to the south (right). The route continues climbing eastward, then curves southeast. Still in pines, ski past a high rock outcrop and climb moderately up a hillside clearcut to a lone, triple-topped ponderosa pine, the final viewpoint. To the west is Flattop Butte and, beyond, the full sweep of the Indian Heaven peaks. To the north is a splendid view of Mount Adams.

GROUSE SADDLE

(Map 16) This Intermediate, mostly unmarked route gains only 200 feet on an 11-mile round trip from Pineside Sno-Park to a wide, open saddle at 3,213 feet with views. The route to the saddle follows an old logging railroad grade (Roads 090 and S-2100) that makes the tour nearly level. Good views along the route and at the saddle are rewarding.

From Pineside Sno-Park ski Road 8225 to the south leg of the Lava Loop, ski east, then off the loop following obscure, unmarked skid roads and open forest eastward to Road 101, 1.8 miles from the sno-park. Ski to and cross Road 82 onto Road 090, and ski the railroad grade with scattered views 3.7 miles to Grouse Saddle. At 2.4 miles you will pass S-1700 climbing up King Mountain, and 0.5 mile from the saddle you'll have the best view of the tour, looking west and south at Indian Heaven, the Trout Lake valley, and Hood.

Chapter 5

MOUNT ADAMS BACKCOUNTRY

Mount Adams offers several exceptional, off-road, Backcountry, one-day ski tours. They are best attempted in spring when snow is consolidated and it is possible to drive closer to the mountain. They all require strong Backcountry experience, and previous knowledge of the routes gained in summer is helpful. None is technically difficult, although slopes of all degrees will be crossed, and knowledge of snow and avalanche conditions is necessary to be safe. Check with the Mount Adams Ranger District office in Trout Lake for road information and wilderness permits. Telephone 509-395-2501 during office hours.

AIKEN LAVA FLOW

(Map 14) This is a superb 16-mile round trip for Backcountry skiers, climbing 2,000 feet to a high of 6,400 feet for stunning scenery.

The 4-mile-long lava flow, descending from the upper end of Bird Creek Meadows at 6,400 feet to 3,800 feet in the Smith Butte area northeast of Trout Lake, is one of the Northwest's classic ski tours. Skiing the rugged, undulating crest of the lava flow offers views to the horizon across miles of forest. The tour takes you to the foot of the Gotchen Glacier moraines and South Butte. From here continue upward across the upper end of Bird Creek Meadows for stunning views of Mount Adams and Hellroaring Valley.

The most direct route is from Smith Butte Sno-Park (3,850 feet) on Road 82. Enter a clearcut to the west that is rapidly regrowing, ski along the east edge on a skid road, then onto Road 060 around Bunnell Butte, then onto 071, then up Road 150 to its end at 4,800 feet. Proceed through open areas and follow the vague route as it turns left and crosses a gully following an old road. This ends in several hundred yards. Enter tight forest and ski to the edge of the lava flow. This is the best route when the snowline is high.

In deep snow years, ski to the lava flow's snout where it touches Road 150, or ski the Snipes Mountain Trail, which parallels the flow's east edge, although this trail is steep in places. The trail climbs to timberline, never far from the lava flow. Of course, the top of the lava flow is more interesting and very scenic.

SLEEPING BEAUTY

(Map 17) When the snowline permits driving to the base of the ridge, this Intermediate tour climbs up to 1,800 feet and travels 12 miles round

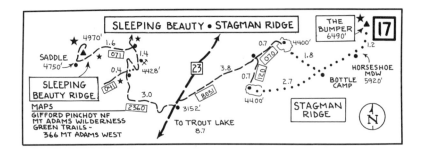

trip on unmarked roads to sweeping views. High point is 4,970 feet.

Sleeping Beauty, a small peak 8 miles northwest of Trout Lake, is a land-mark of the valley with its profile of a sleeping woman, the flowing hair and face formed by a rocky summit, the site of a former fire lookout. The reclining woman is, however, only the southern end of a long, heavily logged ridge. The high, ridgetop goal of this tour is far to the north of the reclining woman.

Drive north 1.3 miles from Trout Lake toward the Mount Adams Recreation Area-Smith Butte ski area, then turn left onto Road 23 2.4 miles north to a snow gate. Check with the Forest Service concerning the snow gate, which may be locked until spring.

Descending upper Aiken Lava Flow with Mount Adams behind

From the snow gate drive 5 miles to Road 2360 (3,152 feet), which climbs west onto Sleeping Beauty Ridge. At 3 miles from Road 23, Road 041 is reached. Although your route continues on Road 2360, you can climb a clearcut to the north to shortcut a long zigzag. Back on 2360 you will soon pass a quarry at 4,428 feet with grand views of Adams. Continue 4.4 miles from Road 23 to Road 071 and follow it south across huge, steep clearcuts, with views, to a saddle on the narrow ridge. North of the wide saddle is a bare knob, your objective. Ski around the west side of the ridge and follow a road 0.3 mile to the ridgetop.

You will see Rainier, Adams, St. Helens, and Hood. The sleeping-warrior profile of Adams is unmistakable from this direction. The Simcoes, Indian Heaven, Dark Divide, and Steamboat Mountain to the west are all visible. This is truly a remarkable viewpoint.

STAGMAN RIDGE

(Map 17) This rugged, Backcountry tour climbs 2,100 feet to a high of 6,500 feet on unmarked routes with a round trip of 12 miles. The above-timberline west side of Adams has vast, skiable, open slopes reached by skiing up Stagman Ridge on the mountain's southwest side. Due to the remoteness of the area, it is best skied in spring after the lower roads have melted out and the snowline has climbed to 4,000 feet or so. It is impressive to be on the open snowfields of a major volcano and ski for miles far above the surrounding country.

See directions for Sleeping Beauty and drive 50 yards beyond Road 2360, then turn right onto 8031, cross the White Salmon River, go straight at the next junction onto 070, and follow it to its end in a clearcut. Climb the clearcut, enter the forest at 4,400 feet, now the Mount Adams Wilderness, and join the Stagman Ridge Trail near Bottle Camp north of Grassy Hill. If snow is shallow, this route is brushy for a mile or so. This is the shortest route.

You will probably not find the summer trail, so use your map and follow the drainage uphill to a large meadow (5,360 feet) 0.5 mile beyond Bottle Camp. Continue upward through increasingly open forest. Angle up onto the ridge to the north and arrive at Horseshoe Meadow at 5,920 feet. Continue uphill through forest, up draws, and across side hills to the open slopes at timberline.

Turning northward, you will gain the seemingly endless, rolling plateau of snowfields that lead past the Bumper and the Hump. All the vast timberline areas of the west side are rewarding, and if you choose another direction you will be equally compensated with views and isolation.

When returning on your upward route, exercise caution. If you cannot find your tracks (probably melted out), a miscalculation may lead you far from your goal. Refer to your map and compass often. The Mount Adams Wilderness map is your best source, although the National Forest Map is necessary for following roads.

The alternative route is to ski the Stagman Ridge Trail. From Road 23 drive 3.8 miles on 8031 and turn right onto 120, then 0.7 mile to the Stagman Ridge trailhead at 4,400 feet in a clearcut. Follow the trail as well as possible over Grassy Hill and drop down to Bottle Camp.

MOUNT ADAMS TIMBERLINE FROM MORRISON CREEK AND COLD SPRINGS

(Map 18) This ski tour will be rewarding only if you reach timberline at the Round-the-Mountain (RTM) Trail, for the only views will be in the last mile. If the snowline requires skiing more than 6 miles uphill to timberline, perhaps an alternative ski tour such as the Aiken Lava Flow should be considered. The views from timberline are superb and skiing above the RTM trail is challenging, and particularly scenic if you ski 2.6 miles westward to Crofton Ridge, where a magnificent view of Adams's west side is seen.

The access route, Roads 80/8040, is not plowed in winter above Road 82. Most skiers to timberline wait for springtime for the snowline to rise, snow to consolidate, days to get longer, and weather to stabilize. Transportation over snow has been available in the past for skiers to Cold Springs by arrangement in Trout Lake and BZ Corner.

From Trout Lake, follow directions for the Smith Butte area and drive up Road 80 then Road 8040, which starts at Mile 0 at the 8031 junction. The large, three-sided Wicky Creek Shelter (3,520 feet) is 1.7 miles above the 8031/Mile 0 junction. Two miles above the Wicky Creek Shelter the wide, monotonous road becomes a one-lane primitive road that continues to Cold Springs. Grades seldom exceed moderate. From the shelter it is 3.6 miles to the Morrison Creek Campground at 4,680 feet. From there to Cold Springs is 3 miles and another 1.4 miles to timberline.

At Cold Springs (5,600 feet) the forest thins and numerous meadows appear, making the skiing less confined and more interesting. At the last sharp turn of the road at Cold Springs (large signboard, two toilets) follow the Climbers Trail to timberline. From the signboard the route proceeds at 320 degrees from magnetic north then curves eastward 700 yards to a hairpin turn to the left, now climbing more steeply. At 0.7 mile from Cold Springs numerous openings in the forest make following the trail more difficult.

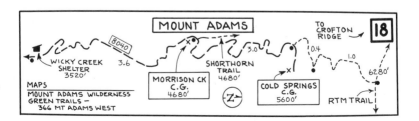

The trail is actually the old road constructed by a sulfur mining company that operated on the summit of Adams in the early 1900s. The trail is not marked, and in the last half mile or so views to the south and west open up to Hood and St. Helens. It is necessary to ski almost to the Timberline Trail (the RTM Trail) to get a view of Adams. The RTM Trail is at the first level opening (6,250 feet), triangular in shape, with whitebark pines to the west and firs to the east.

For the best views ski east, cross two low ridges, and reach a small, shallow basin with the best views of Adams. Climb for better views.

Crofton Ridge. (Map 18) The ridge is a spur on Adams's southwest side and is reached by skiing the Shorthorn Trail 3 miles from the Morrison Creek Campground. The elevation gain from the campground to the ridge's top near the RTM Trail is 1,500 feet. The ridge provides dramatic views. The trail is narrow, moderately steep, and requires strong Backcountry skills. A second route to the ridge is from the Climbers Trail above Cold Springs.

Follow the RTM Trail around to the west side of the mountain to Crofton Ridge. The trail, which is neither marked nor blazed, maintains a contour near 6,200 feet, with a number of long, gentle ups and downs passing through both old growth and meadows. Do not climb above 6,200 feet or you will encounter steep slopes. If you do reach Crofton Ridge, 2.8 miles from the Climbers Trail, climb the ridge only 300 yards westward to its high point for a marvelous view. An excellent, scenic camp spot is just west of the ridge's high point.

Chapter 6

GLENWOOD VALLEY

The Glenwood Valley, over a ridge and 16 miles east of Trout Lake, offers scenic, uncrowded ski tours. The valley is flat, wide, and the site of a federal wildlife refuge along a waterfowl migration route. Farm fields and old barns provide a colorful foreground for Mount Adams, only 12 miles away, rising majestically to the northwest. The village of Glenwood, one restaurant and no gas station, sits at the north edge of the valley.

From Highway 141 to Trout Lake, two roads lead to Glenwood. The most direct is from BZ Corner 10 miles north of the Columbia River. The other is from Trout Lake.

The long, forested ridge paralleling the south edge of the valley has the most scenic tours although none is marked. These tours all follow roads, with clearcuts providing the viewpoints. The Dead Canyon and Medley Canyon tours both climb quickly to clearcuts with exceptional views. The Diamond Gap tour climbs steeply to the highest point of a long ridge with the finest views, site of a former fire lookout.

Tours on flat terrain in the valley are Outlet Falls, the McCumber Place Loops, and the Conboy National Wildlife Refuge. The only marked trails in the Glenwood Valley are the McCumber Place trail system just north of Glenwood. Snowmobiles are not common, although all areas except the refuge are open to machines. The valley, at 1,900 feet, does not always have skiable snow, but the south ridge holds it well. There is a bed-and-breakfast in Glenwood as well as several in Trout Lake.

Be advised that there are no sno-parks in the valley and parking is roadside. The Klickitat County sheriff (Goldendale) has jurisdiction here and will ticket or even impound cars that block private property or in any way create a safety problem or traffic hazard. Do not block snow-plowing equipment, and do park off the roads and use common sense. Carry chains and a shovel as it may be necessary to improve your parking. Sounds like a lot of trouble, but all the tours are worth the extra effort.

OUTLET FALLS

(Map 19) The 80-foot falls are in a spectacular, vertical-walled canyon easily reached by Novice skiers traveling on almost totally level terrain. From Glenwood drive eastward on the Goldendale road 3.5 miles and turn left onto the Hatchery road. Drive 1.2 miles and park where an abandoned railway bed crosses. Ski southeast on the old railbed 0.7 mile to Outlet Creek, then enter open pine forest and ski east following the edge of the creek. In 0.5

mile you will reach the overlook east of the falls. Be wary of the clifftop viewing area as it slopes into the deep canyon. Continue eastward along the canyon edge 0.5 mile to the end of the ridge for a view into the Klickitat River Canyon. If snow is absent or shallow, this tour becomes a rewarding hike.

McCUMBER PLACE LOOPS

(Map 19) A 6.5-mile loop for Intermediate skiers follows roads north from the parking area 2.4 miles from Glenwood, then swings westward and descends southward along the primitive McCumber Springs road to the site of the McCumber Homestead meadow 1.4 miles from the end of the loop. If you are short on time or a beginner, an alternative 1.9-mile tour follows the main loop clockwise, west from the parking area through forest and open areas, then north up a gentle hill to the Homestead area, and loops back to your car.

Both loops are on state land and marked by widely spaced blue tags. The trails are groomed, conditions permitting. Recommended direction is counterclockwise. At 0.7 mile, a 1.6-mile side trail goes east, the Klickitat Canyon Trail, with a steep final descent to a clifftop view of the canyon.

Back on the main loop, follow logging roads north and at 2 miles from your car you will have a view of Adams. Here the loop starts swinging westward to the McCumber Springs road, then southward and downhill to the Homestead site in a large meadow where no buildings remain. Here the 1.9-mile Homestead Loop offers an easy loop for beginner skiers and a scenic digression from the main loop.

A free, more-detailed map of these loops is available from the Flying L Country Inn, which you will pass on the way to the parking area at the end of the county road 2.4 miles from Glenwood.

Note: The loops on the map in this guidebook are not to scale and are distorted due to space limitation.

CONBOY LAKE NATIONAL WILDLIFE REFUGE

(Map 19) The 10 square miles of the refuge cover a large part of the flat Glenwood Valley, and many thousands of waterfowl visit the area yearly on their migration routes. The access road to the refuge headquarters, and the start of skiing, is 5 miles southwest of Glenwood along the Trout Lake road, and 10 miles east of Trout Lake.

The 2-mile Willard Springs Nature Trail is open to skiers (and hikers when the snow is gone) and starts near the headquarters 1 mile from the Glenwood–Trout Lake road. The trail forms an easy loop through scenic, gently rolling pine forest bordering the refuge marshes. Although the refuge covers many miles, skiing is permitted only on the Nature Trail, which is not marked for skiing.

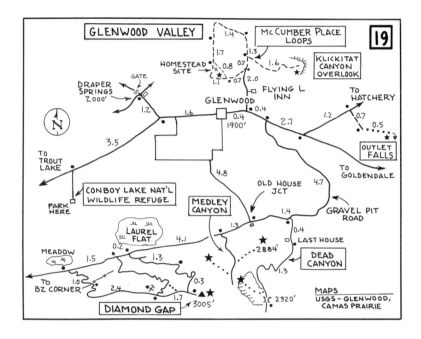

DEAD CANYON

(Map 19) Clearcuts near the top of the valley's south ridge offer sweeping views. The route is for Intermediate skiers, and is not marked. The elevation gain is up to 500 feet, with a round trip of 5 miles.

Drive to the Old House Junction (see map) on the BZ Corner road south of Glenwood on the south side of the valley, then drive east 1.4 miles on the Gravel Pit road. Park on the road, then hike or ski up the Snowden–Appleton road 0.4 mile to the last house (no parking) and continue upward on the moderately climbing road to 1.7 miles from the Gravel Pit road to the Dead Canyon pass at 2,320 feet. Near the pass ski westward, climbing a large clearcut to the open ridgetop for an exceptional view of the valley, Hood, Adams, Goat Rocks, and the Simcoes to the east.

An interesting, short side trip from the pass goes south and below the pass 0.3 mile to a primitive side road you can ski eastward. Turn around when it starts descending in earnest. There are no distant views, but it is a scenic area.

MEDLEY CANYON

(Map 19) This tour is for Intermediate skiers and similar to the Dead Canyon tour. Elevation gain is 500 feet, with a round trip of 5 miles.

From the Old House Junction (see Dead Canyon description, and map) drive west 1.3 miles to Bertchie Road. It is opposite a ranch house and large, old barn. Park carefully off the road and ski up the primitive road 2 miles, then leave it and climb westward to the open ridgetop for exceptional views similar to those from the Dead Canyon tour.

An even more scenic tour follows the first road to the left (east) as you ski up Bertchie Road. Ski uphill about 1 mile to an open hilltop at 2,884 feet for panoramic views.

DIAMOND GAP

(Map 19) Site of a former fire lookout and the highest point along the high ridge south of the Glenwood Valley, this is the area's most spectacular tour. There are sweeping views from Hood to Adams and of valleys below to the south and north. The tour is rated Advanced and climbs 1,000 feet to a high of 3,005 feet on a round trip of 10 miles on unmarked roads.

There are three routes to the ridgecrest. All follow roads that start from the BZ Corner–Glenwood road. The longest route is up the westside road, and the other two form the recommended loop, each starting only 400 yards from the other along the road. The roads are steep but easily followed. Conditions may require carrying skis at first. Do not block roads, and park off the main road.

The most direct route is the road starting at the four-way junction with the BZ Corner road and the one to Laurel Flat opposite a large meadow, 5.4 miles west of the Old House junction and 9.1 miles from BZ Corner.

Ski south up through forest, at first moderately then more steeply as the road turns eastward on south-facing slopes. Across the narrow side valley is the open, steep ridgecrest. At 1.3 miles take a breather from the unrelenting grade as you reach a broad, forested saddle with a view to the north.

Continue steeply upward around several bends on open slopes. Above the saddle 0.3 mile you reach the ridgecrest. Ski east to the nearby high point. The view is remarkable—Indian Heaven, Sleeping Beauty, Adams, the Glenwood Valley, the Simcoes to the east, the distant Columbia Hills southeast, all seen along with an isolated ranch directly below, and farther away the pyramid of Hood.

To add adventure to the tour, ski the loop route. Ski west on the ridgecrest, first on south slopes, then north slopes around a partially forested rise. The crest road then descends a moderately steep grade to an obvious quarry at the next saddle 1.7 miles from the summit. Here, a road leaves the ridgetop, dropping steeply northward into forest. At the BZ Corner road, turn east to find your car.

The west route to the summit is 5.1 miles long and follows the ridgecrest for about 2.5 miles. It offers nothing superior to the direct route, with the first 2 miles in dense, uninteresting forest.

Chapter 7

OTHER SOUTHERN WASHINGTON TOURS

Although the areas described here are little visited, they justify your interest. The scenic attributes and isolation offered by these tours are remarkable. If you have a spirit of adventure add these to your priority list. Even though there are no sno-parks here, the roads are good and are not difficult to drive. For success, select a time when the snowline is high in order to shorten the skiing distance.

LARCH MOUNTAIN (WASHINGTON)

(Map 20) This exceptional viewpoint is an easy tour for Intermediate skiers who are seeking a unique experience. You may ski 6 miles or less round trip and climb about 1,500 feet on roads that go to the very summit. Larch Mountain is only 30 miles in a direct line from downtown Portland and forms an impressive high-ridge mass with Silver Star Mountain, 4 miles to the northeast, easily seen from many miles away. Larch Mountain's 3,496-foot summit, however, collects adequate snow for skiing only several times each winter. It is worth waiting for it to look white, then testing its skiability, for the views will certainly reward you.

Although there is also an access route from the south to the Larch Mountain saddle on the mountain's west side, only the western approach is described here. The route from the town of Camas on the south is complex and difficult to describe, and available maps are not accurate.

The westside approach to the 2,000-foot saddle is an 18.6-mile drive from the north end of the I-205 bridge across the Columbia River, and it is only 4 miles longer than the southside route. Furthermore, the westside roads are plowed much farther.

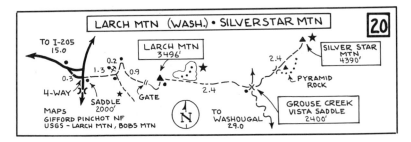

103

From Portland, cross the bridge and drive 3.3 miles to Orchards Exit 30, then 1.5 miles on Highway 500 to 4th Plain Road. Turn east onto 4th Plain, drive 1.7 miles to Ward Road, and follow this north 2.5 miles to a right onto Davis (which changes to 109th). Go 1.5 miles east to 212th Avenue. Go north 1 mile to Powell, angle up and eastward 1 mile to Rawson, and follow this 2.3 miles, in forest, climbing steadily, with beautiful farmlands behind, to a clearcut with views to the south. The Rawson road (the ridgetop road) is plowed to the Larch Corrections Camp for Youths just 2 miles below and north of the Larch Mountain saddle and four-way junction.

Proceed another 2.4 miles on the ridgecrest to another big clearcut, with a fine view of St. Helens and Rainier, now only 0.6 mile from the four-way junction at the saddle. At 0.3 mile before the saddle a fork appears. The left branch is plowed and goes to the corrections camp. Your route, however, is to the right at the fork. You may have to park here. Be sure to carry chains and a shovel for this tour.

Ski or walk up this 0.3-mile side road to the four-way junction—a good place to park if you can drive this far, for above here the road narrows and steepens. From the four-way in the broad saddle it is 2.6 miles to the summit, with several turnarounds for the adventuresome driver on this good gravel road. The road starts out moderately, then becomes steeper, climbing through dense, immature forest with views only along the last mile. For winter campers who want to witness the nighttime spectacle of the Portland/Vancouver area, there is a good, tree-protected camp spot on the large, level summit, and a spot on the lower road.

The summit is cluttered with relay-station antennae, and trees block much of the view. A large, beautiful meadow 350 yards northeast of the summit, however, is worth skiing to for more views. This requires an initial, steep drop down a narrow, turning road with a good outrun near the edge of the meadow. Climb left into the meadow and proceed 200 yards to its northeast edge for views of Rainier, St. Helens, neighboring Silver Star, Hood rising above the Columbia River Gorge, Jefferson, Three-Fingered Jack, and two of the Sisters! Part of this splendid view may also be enjoyed 0.2 mile below the summit on the way up, where there is an obscure road to the right. Downtown Portland is visible from this road, and good camp spots also are found here. Another side road, just above a quarry, 1.2 miles above the saddle, also offers views to the south. Ski 0.7 mile south on this road for views. The upper side road, however, is the better one for a scenic camp spot.

Immense, denuded areas on Silver Star attest to the Yacolt Burn of 1902, which caused streetlights in Olympia, Washington, to be used at midday. One hundred square miles of forest burned, and over thirty lives were lost.

Note on Maps: Both county and Forest Service maps of this area are maddeningly inconsistent, inaccurate, and confusing. Nevertheless, carry the Gifford Pinchot National Forest map for orientation and viewing the scenery.

SILVER STAR MOUNTAIN

(Maps 20 & 21) This beautiful mountain in Southern Washington is a neighbor to Larch Mountain. Its 4,390-foot summit boasts the best view of all the Southern Washington summits in this guide, with all the major volcanoes and the Columbia River visible in fair weather. Two routes are described here, with the north approach and north side being the preferred ski tour. The southside road to Grouse Creek Vista Saddle is about the same driving mileage as the north side. The northern approach offers alternative tours if you do not make it to the summit. All routes are rated Advanced.

The southside route could extend from 6 miles to 10 miles round trip, and the north side up to 12 miles, depending on driving conditions. Both routes will be close to 2,000 feet in elevation gain.

North Ridge. (Map 21) Once you reach the open north ridge you will experience a decidedly alpine area with rugged ridges and deep valleys to the east. The north ridge is moderately angled, wide, and open. This is the more scenic of the two routes to the summit. Surprisingly, a road now closed to all traffic in all seasons climbs to the very summit from both north and south, a result of lack of environmental concern from the Forest Service for many years. From the I-205 bridge across the Columbia River it is about 48 miles to Road 4109, the final ski route. In periods of low snowline you may not be able to drive this far, but an alternative tour up nearby Summit Springs Ridge (Road 4104) offers wonderful views.

This tour verges on Backcountry style, and familiarizing yourself with the area in summer is a good idea. This is a ski tour with adventure and isolation, requiring a self-reliant attitude both for the final drive and the skiing.

From the I-205 bridge drive north to Battleground (see Mount St. Helens description). Stay on Highway 503, drive north 5.6 miles, turn east onto N.E. Rocky Creek Road, and drive 8.4 miles to County Road 12. Climb south uphill on this road 2 miles and turn left (east) for 5.2 miles to Sunset Picnic Area. Drive south on Road 41, now on gravel, up a long series of curves 2.7 miles to Road 4104 on the left (east). Pass this side road, drive 0.9 mile, turn right onto Road 4109, descend to a creek bridge crossing, and climb 1.3 miles, often steep, to an obvious, wide parking area at 1,300 feet. A side road to the left branches upward. This is your summit route but is impassable to cars. Ski or walk up this road to snow. From here to the summit is 4.1 miles, most of which follow moderate grades along an old road. If you cannot go the full distance, ski partway for the fine views. The rugged scenery is a unique experience for most Oregon skiers.

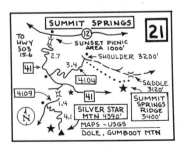

Near the top of the massive open ridge you ski under rock outcrops as you climb the ridge's west side, then descend into a forested saddle, then climb earnestly 0.3 mile to the open summit for sweeping views similar to those from Larch Mountain.

If you cannot get to the summit due to low snowline and shortened driving, two very scenic consolation tours are described below.

Summit Springs Ridge. (Map 21) Follow Silver Star directions and drive to Road 4104. Drive or ski up this one-lane, moderately steep road. There are a number of turnarounds for the adventuresome driver. From the turn-off on Road 41 it is a 1,950-foot climb over 4.7 miles to the final, open ridgetop with marvelous views. Ski to an obvious shoulder 3.4 miles from Road 41 and go 200 yards on a side road for views. You will also find good views 100 yards farther along the main road. Just below the shoulder on your upward tour is a side road to the right that goes 400 yards to a clearcut with views.

From the shoulder continue on the road as it descends gently 1.3 miles to a saddle. Climb the open slopes to the south for views, particularly 0.3 mile farther west in a clearcut for even better views. From this clearcut an off-road tour through old growth leads back to the shoulder, if you are an explorer. If you do not ski west to the clearcut from the saddle, ski the ridge eastward for more views.

Road 41 Views. (Map 21) Continue 0.9 mile beyond Road 4104 (see above) and do not turn onto Road 4109 to Silver Star, but continue on Road 41 as it climbs moderately on a steep, open hillside with wonderful views of Silver Star, its rugged east ridge, and down into Copper and Star Creek Canyons.

South Side. (Map 20) The southside driving route goes to Grouse Creek Vista Saddle on gravel roads, 29 miles from the I-205 bridge. If the snow is below the saddle, the ski tour up the road is scenic and suitable for Novice skiers. However, above the saddle the tour is very steep and for Advanced skiers only.

Drive Highway 14 east from the I-205 bridge 9.9 miles to Washougal and enter the town at the Highway 140 sign. Continue onto 15th Street, which changes to 17th and becomes S.E. Washougal River Road. Leave this road and turn left onto N.E. Hughes Road 6.6 miles from Highway 14. Hughes Road leads to N.E. 392nd Avenue, which climbs a long hill to a T-junction, where you turn right. In a short distance turn left off Skye Road onto 412th Avenue (Yacolt Recreation Area sign), then drive north to a nearby Y-junction 10 miles from Highway 14. Take a right fork at the Y at 1,000-foot elevation and drive 2.7 miles to a second Y-fork. Go left 5.7 miles to Grouse Creek Vista Saddle at 2,400 feet.

At the saddle a very steep 2.4-mile road goes west to the summit of Larch Mountain, a climb of 1,100 feet. Opposite this road, at the saddle, is another very steep road going almost 3 miles to the summit of Silver Star. At 3,100 feet the steep road to Silver Star eases off, as forest is left behind for open hillsides and ridgetop meadows with wide views. At the 3,400-foot saddle below Pyramid Rock, a prominent minor peak beside the upward road, the easiest and safest route to the summit follows along the east side of the ridge you are on. The summit is not the rocky buttress on the left horizon, which appears to be the highest, but the rounded ridgecrest straight ahead and east of the buttress.

Under some circumstances the upper open slopes may be subject to avalanche danger, and in the mornings the west slopes may be crusty or icy. If so traverse around the east side of Pyramid Rock. Beware of frosty or icy surfaces on the blacktop road, especially in shady areas, while driving to the snow zone.

SIMCOE MOUNTAINS

(Map 22) This little-known area north of Goldendale, Washington, offers a unique skiing experience. As the route is not marked, it is rated Advanced, but a determined Intermediate would enjoy the area. Depending on snowline, it could be up to 10 miles round trip with an elevation gain of 2,000 feet or more. The high point is 5,822 feet.

The Simcoes are a massive, gently rounded shield volcano, now covered with huge meadows and impenetrable forests. The views from up high include the rugged east face of Adams, as well as Rainier, Hood, and many volcanic cones that dot the flat farming valleys below. A boundary of the Yakima Indian Reservation runs along the top of the Simcoes.

If you are driving from Oregon, cross The Dalles Bridge and drive 35 miles to Goldendale. An alternative, more scenic route crosses the Columbia at Hood River, and proceeds to Lyle then up Klickitat Canyon to the rolling plateau above with many views. To fully enjoy either route, particularly the Lyle route, you should have a county map that details the county road systems not shown on the usual highway maps.

From Goldendale, take Columbus Avenue and drive west about 11.1 miles. Along the way you will be on Bloodgood Road and Cedar Valley Road. At the last houses, the Monument road leaves Cedar Valley Road at the first monument to Bolon, the Indian Agency official who was killed in 1885 by Indian renegades. From this first, small monument, drive up the dirt Monument road, at first through trashy clearcuts. Although the road is quite good, there are a few short, steep sections. Even if wet, the road is drivable with many turnouts. Three miles beyond the first monument the route goes right at a fork and gets steeper and narrower. You are now 1.3 miles from the cattleman's shack and barn, the start of the off-road tour. The fork may be a good place to start skiing or carrying your skis to the snowline. There is only one brief view of the Simcoes just 0.4 mile above the fork.

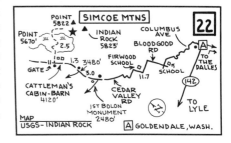

107

At the cattleman's cabin is the second Bolon monument, a small stone beneath a pine tree, marking the site of the murder. Here you have two choices for your upward route. Straight ahead leads to a locked gate and private property, the former route, and the easiest way up. The second route leads 100 feet north of the cabin and enters the dense forest on a jeep road that climbs steeply through forest, then a clearcut, then reenters forest on an unrelenting, erratic ascent into open forest, until it reaches the vast open meadows of the upper Simcoes, a climb of perhaps 600 feet.

USGS maps are absolutely necessary for this tour when you are in the high meadows—a rolling plateau of open spaces and large patches of dense forest without landmarks. The tour is a commitment in time and distance, and the map is a small investment to ensure success. The tops of Potato Butte and Point 5670 offer open skiing. The undulating, open area extends for miles and invites exploration.

From Point 5670, it is about 2 miles southeast to Indian Rock (5,823 feet), the highest point of the Simcoes, which is capped by a 50-foot pluglike rock formation rearing above the snowfield. On the way to Indian Rock, pass Point 5822 on its west side to avoid dog-hair growth—impenetrable small trees. The best time to ski this area is early spring, when roads are drier and snow is more consolidated.

The approach to the Simcoes from Satus Pass to the east is not recommended because the distance is long and almost entirely through viewless forest; you will need a compass and map for navigation even though you will be on a road of sorts.

Part II
MOUNT HOOD AND VICINITY

The inspiring symmetry of Mount Hood as seen from Portland is that of a classic volcano, possibly the most beautiful of all the Northwest peaks. At 11,239 feet, the mountain is a splendid landmark for Nordic skiers. In winter, Hood's eleven glaciers are shrouded in deep snow that smooths out the mountain's upper contours to form a distinctive profile—an eternal guardian of all that lies below.

To reach Mount Hood from Portland, drive east to Gresham, a suburban town, then follow Highway 26 to the mountain. Many skiers find it convenient to drive east on I-84 to the Wood Village–Gresham exit, about 13 miles from downtown Portland. From here drive 3 miles south to East Burnside Street, a major intersection, where a left puts you on Highway 26 to Mount Hood. Government Camp is 55 miles from Portland.

From Salem and the Willamette Valley, skiers drive north on I-5 then follow I-205 toward the east side of Portland. Some 5 miles north of Oregon City, pick up Highway 212 and drive east through Damascus and Boring, ultimately joining Highway 26 5 miles west of the town of Sandy. Total distance from Salem to Government Camp is about 92 miles, only a few miles more than the drive to ski areas at Santiam Pass.

From the north, the town of Hood River on the Columbia River is the only access point to the Mount Hood region. It is 43 miles by Highway 35 from Hood River to Government Camp, although several fine skiing areas, such as Cooper Spur, Pocket Creek, Bennett Pass, and Barlow Pass, are passed on the way.

The forested terrain at the mountain's base is gentle, sloping into major valleys on all sides. Fortunately for skiers, the most suitable terrain for skiing is also the most accessible—the west, south, and east sides. Surprisingly, in most areas evidence of logging is not troubling, and much of the skiing zone between the 3,500-foot and 6,000-foot elevations is covered with attractive forests. On the other hand, in areas such as the Trillium Basin and Clear Lake, clearcuts contribute to a sense of openness and freedom.

Between the few major creek and river canyons there are miles of forest for skiing, penetrated by logging roads and summer forest trails. Due to the dense forests there is not much off-road skiing except for clearcuts and where special trails have been built for skiing, but the variety, the viewpoints, and the meadows more than compensate for this circumstance.

East face of Mount Hood with Newton Clark Glacier and upper end of Newton Creek valley; Gates of the Mountain rock buttresses below

Although the three sides of Hood that skiers frequent are essentially gentle, ridges and valleys break up the terrain into a number of distinct, separate skiing areas. These are described in chapters to follow.

Fortunately, most of these areas are connected to one another by ski routes that are not always marked but are easily skied. The connectors also provide exceptional opportunities to ski longer, more challenging loops, a concept presented in this guidebook as an efficient way to enjoy many areas. Connectors also can be linked together for long-distance trails, the finest example being the Wy'east Trail, extending from west of Government Camp to lower Pocket Creek, a distance of some 20 miles.

The first section covers lowland ski tours, including the Larch Mountain and Old Maid Flat–Ramona Falls areas, which several times in a normal winter have sufficient snow for skiing.

On the south side, the Government Camp and Timberline areas, which are presented together, offer several excellent trails for Novices, together with a variety of challenging routes for experienced skiers. These are the first of the major skiing areas reached by road from Portland, so many casual skiers stop at one of the several sno-parks to enjoy the easy trails.

The next areas east of Government Camp (often affectionately referred to as "Govie") on Highway 26 are Snow Bunny and the Trillium Basin, both popular with Novice skiers and close to Govie. Both areas have many Novice trails, and in the basin there are two scenic ridge routes and numerous loops, short and long, including the scenic Trillium Lake tour. The Salmon River Basin to the east features unmarked tours at this time on the old pioneer road. South of this area the Frog Lake and Clear Lake areas offer views, lakeshore tours, and miles of gentle, rolling terrain.

Barlow Pass, just east of the Salmon River area, has a wide range of tours, mostly for Intermediates. From the pass skiers can climb a ridge to the north or south or ski down a road to Devils Half Acre. Connector trails go north to Barlow Ridge, paralleling Highway 35 and continuing on to White River and Bennett Pass.

White River, an immensely popular area in good weather, provides scenic views in all directions, being a flat, wide, open river valley, the only such area on Mount Hood. Bennett Pass, to the north, offers a ridgetop trail, a descending trail to Pocket Creek, and access to the Sahalie Falls Trail and Hood River Meadows. The Bennett Ridge Trail goes eastward to Gunsight Ridge, where challenging scenic tours go both north and south for miles.

The East Fork Hood River valley has many trails on both sides of Highway 35. Pocket Creek, just below Bennett Ridge, has many open areas and views, as well as many connector trails. These provide loops to the upper basin adjoining Gunsight and Bennett Ridges. The Clark Creek and Teacup Lake trail systems are superb for forest skiing. These trails are the result of foresight and excellent planning by the Hood River Ranger District.

Cooper Spur, on the northeast side of the mountain, and the Brooks Meadow-Lookout Mountain areas, across the deep Hood River valley, offer miles of forest roads to ski and spectacular viewpoints to enjoy. From these areas the land drops rapidly in elevation to the north.

Chapter 8

HOOD LOWLANDS

This group of tours is for skiers who want to try areas that are closer to home. The days following low-elevation snowfall are generally best for these tours, which at other times often lack adequate snow cover. Even then, you may have to gamble on snow depth, not knowing for sure until you are actually there to study the skiing possibilities. In most cases, however, you can, if necessary, easily alter your plans and, with little time lost, head for higher regions.

LARCH MOUNTAIN (OREGON)

(Map 23) Starting at a snow gate at 2,560 feet, this Novice to Intermediate tour climbs 1,500 feet on a round trip of 8 miles to a high point of 4,056 feet, if you go to the very summit. The summit of Larch Mountain, overlooking the Columbia River Gorge only 30 miles east of Portland, offers outstanding views in many directions. Snowmobilers and low elevation detract from the area's rewards. But it is near Portland, and under the right conditions can be worthwhile. Most of the skiing is on roads.

The road, when snow is low, is normally plowed to the last houses, although access to the Bull Run Watershed also requires some plowing. The last houses are about 8 miles from the summit. The snowline, however, is often above this level. The summit is unprotected, so ski at lower elevations when the weather is bad.

From Portland drive east on I-84 to either the Lewis and Clark State Park exit or Exit 22 (Corbett). Drive uphill to the small town of Corbett, then east 2 miles to a Y-junction, elevation 893 feet. Turn right at the Y onto the Larch

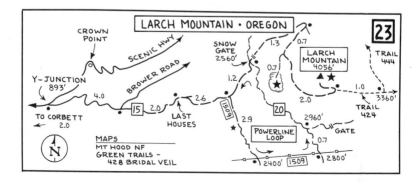

Mountain road. From there it is 13.8 miles to the end of the road near the summit. A snow gate is located 10 miles up the road and, depending on the snow level, skiing may start before or beyond this gate, elevation 2,560 feet.

Two miles past the gate, just beyond the 12-mile marker, a side road (3,200 feet) to the right descends gently then levels out into a large clearcut—with good views—only 0.7 mile from the main road. Lower Bull Run Reservoir is one of the sights visible far below. From the start of this side road it is only 2 miles uphill to the summit parking lot.

From the snowline the road to the top is a gentle climb, changing to moderate grades in the last mile or so and providing a good return glide. As you climb higher the snow usually improves, and the roadside trees can be quite beautiful. The road tour is completely enclosed in forest until the top. If possible, cross by trail 100 yards to the highest point northeast of the road end, often best done on foot. In fair weather the views of the Gorge and Hood are sweeping.

From the sharp bend just below the parking lot at the road end, adventurous Intermediate skiers can follow Trail 424 down moderate grades for about 1 mile, then turn left onto Trail 444, which is a most unusual and beautiful level route along an abandoned railroad bed. Although there is only one viewpoint along this trail, the trail itself is picturesque and worthwhile if the snow conditions are good. This is not a marked route.

Powerline Loop. (Map 23) An 8.4-mile loop is possible when the snowline is down to about 2,000 feet. This Intermediate tour on unmarked roads, with one leg climbing along a powerline swath, is scenic. Drive 8.6 miles from the Y-junction on the Larch Mountain road to Road 1509 (2,300 feet), going south. Ski this road as it climbs gently 1 mile, then rolls along to the first view at 1.7 miles. Continue another 1.2 miles to the obvious powerline lane, where you turn uphill and climb a primitive road up the "lane." It finally enters forest, then pops out just before suddenly starting steeply uphill into thick forest to join Road 20 in 0.7 mile at 2,960 feet. Turn left on Road 20 and ski down moderate grades to rejoin the Larch Mountain road 1.2 miles above your starting point. Road 20 may at times be plowed.

OLD MAID FLAT, LOST CREEK, AND RAMONA FALLS

(Map 24) For those few weeks each winter when low-elevation snow blankets this area at the west foot of Mount Hood there are unusual scenic opportunities for skiers. Composed of an ancient "lahar," or mudflow, the area is now covered by a struggling forest of stunted firs, and by some old growth farther up. It is a unique area.

Due to the length of the trail to Ramona Falls and minor route finding, the 12-mile round trip is rated Intermediate. The elevation gain is 1,480 feet. The Lost Creek Trail is shorter—2.8 miles one way—and suitable for Novice

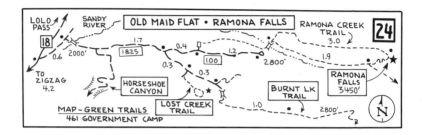

skiers since it is mostly on gentle road, but perhaps too long for first-time skiers. Elevation gain is 400 feet. The ancient mudflow, up to one-half-mile wide and curving downhill from Ramona Falls some 5 miles, offers uniformly gentle grades as it descends from 3,480 feet (at the falls) to 2,000 feet, where skiing usually starts.

To ski here, drive to Zigzag on Highway 26 about 44 miles from Portland, then turn north onto Road 18 (the Lolo Pass road) and follow it 4.2 miles to Road 1825 and the end of winter plowing. Turn right onto 1825 and drive or ski 0.6 mile to a bridge over the Sandy River where an iron gate stops four-wheelers and snow machines. Climb around or over the gate. Do not block private property and driveways. The turnaround near the last house is used by school buses and for skier parking. Do not block its use!

Old Maid Flat. (Map 24) From the iron gate at the bridge, Road 1825 invites you up gentle grades. The lovely, stunted forest here, home to pine martens, squirrels, and rabbits, provides unlimited areas of scattered trees and openings for exploration. If you are adventuresome, you may ski as far as the Lost Creek Trail or even try the Ramona Falls Trail.

Lost Creek. (Map 24) From the iron gate it is 1.7 miles to a junction with Road 100 (to the Ramona Falls Trail). Here the snow is significantly deeper than where you started. Turn right, remain on Road 1825 0.3 mile to another junction in an opening. Turn right and ski 80 yards to the Lost Creek Trail, a summer trail, which follows alongside the road and closely follows the edge of the creek, passing through tall forest. The trail is not obvious, but stay close to the streambank. In 100 yards cross a footbridge, then go another 200 yards to where alder and a side stream block your way. Turn left, and ski along the creek 50 yards to a marsh with a beautiful view of Mount Hood. Across the road from the start of this short trail is a picnic ground in a stand of ancient forest—explore also this streamside area.

Ramona Falls. (Map 24) This beautiful 100-foot-high waterfall, hidden in a forest grotto, is a prime scenic attraction. When snow depth is adequate, this is a lovely tour through stands of lodgepole pines.

From the iron gate it is 3.3 miles to the trail bridge across the Sandy River, the road end. At 2.1 miles from the iron gate a side road goes left (north) 0.2 mile to a large parking lot and the summer trailhead of the Ramona Falls Trail. Do not follow this road, or attempt the difficult trail from the parking lot. Instead, continue straight ahead on the main road for 1.2 miles to its end near the trail footbridge.

Cross the bridge to a trail junction and turn right. Both trails here lead to the falls, but the one on the right is shorter. If you prefer to ski a loop, ski the left one on your descent from the falls. For now, follow the trail to the right, which climbs moderately along and near the Sandy River. At 1.9 miles from the bridge you come to the junction with the Pacific Crest Trail (PCT). Turn left and in just over 0.5 mile enter the dense forest enshrouding the beautiful falls.

Return the same way or by way of Ramona Creek (the other trail down), keeping left at the nearby junction. Impressive rock cliffs soon appear, and in about 1.5 miles you leave the stream to enter lodgepole pine forest. At the next junction go left and ski 0.5 mile to the trail bridge. The Mount Hood Wilderness map will help you on these trails.

LOST LAKE

(Map 25) Lost Lake at 3,143 feet is the site of the classic postcard scene of Mount Hood. This Intermediate tour could be as long as 12 miles round trip, or more, or less, depending on the snowline. Elevation gain could be as much as 1,500 feet, but is usually less. If you are not up to a long tour into the lake, and the snow level is low or at the last house, you should consider going partway for there are some points of interest and one phenomenal scene, described later. There is also a 12.3-mile loop on roads around Lost Lake Butte that passes along the lake's east shore.

From Hood River in the Columbia River Gorge, drive south on Highway 35 and exit to Odell, a small town to the west. There, follow signs for Dee as the road winds through orchard country. From Dee, about 7 miles from Odell, follow signs for Lolo Pass (not open in winter to Zigzag) and Lost Lake. Drive southwest to Road 13 and follow it as far as possible to the lake. The road from Dee is plowed 3 miles to the last house (1,270 feet) during low-elevation snowfalls. The snowline, however, may be higher, making the tour much shorter than the 11.6 miles to

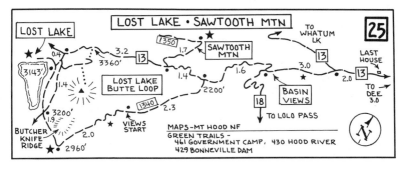

the lake from the last house. Lost Lake is 14.6 miles from Dee.

The road at first goes through logging-ravaged country that is pitiful to see, but soon enters attractive forest with few views. Once at the lake, however, you will be rewarded by the splendid scene of the lake nestled between high, forested hills and Mount Hood rising 8,000 feet above to the southeast. For the classic view follow a spur road that goes a short distance around the north end of the lake. The trail around the lake begins at the road end. If there is ice on the lake, stay off it, for ice is always unsafe at these low elevations. There are two shelters on the east side of the lake where the campgrounds are located.

Near the lake, where Road 13 goes right near a campground ticket booth, follow Road 1341 0.4 mile to the lake. Road 1340 also splits off here to go south above the lake's campground road along the shoreline.

If you cannot ski the full distance to the lake, there are many other attractions to the tour, so you can ski partway or select other objectives. Just 1.4 miles beyond the last house a side road to the left climbs into a series of clearcuts with good views. Only 2.1 miles beyond this side road, along Road 13, you will pass close to the top of a deep, cliff-sided river canyon—a spectacular site. From here the road climbs gently, then at 5 miles from the last house it drops into a wide, heavily clearcut basin with marvelous views of Hood and the high, scenic, surrounding ridges. If the lake is still too far for you, go just another mile or less toward the lake and gain some elevation for a better view of the scenic basin than is possible from the lower areas on the road. This basin contains the junction with Road 18, the Lolo Pass road, at 1,880 feet. From here the road climbs seriously and in 1.6 miles passes to the left a side road (Road 1340), the start of the Lost Lake Butte Loop. From Road 1340 it is 5 miles to the lake basin.

Sawtooth Mountain Road. (Map 25) Three miles beyond the Lolo Pass road junction in the basin and on the way to Lost Lake, a side road to the right at 2,720 feet leads to a fine consolation prize only 1.7 miles from Road 13. From the last house this is a long ski tour, so it is best done when the snowline permits driving several more miles. From Road 13 (11 miles from Dee) ski gently uphill on Road 1350 to the first good view at 0.5 mile. Another 0.9 mile along the south-facing slopes brings you to a big road bend. Take the first road to the right and ski east 0.3 mile along a ridgetop to the road's end, where the view makes the entire ski tour worthwhile. You will see Hood, Lost Lake Butte, the Columbia Hills across the Gorge from Hood River, and the Simcoe Mountains near Goldendale, Washington. The ridge you are on drops steeply on both sides to deep valleys. Elevation gain from Road 13 is only 240 feet!

Lost Lake Butte Loop. (Map 25) This 12.3-mile Advanced road-skiing loop completely circles Lost Lake Butte, a prominent, forested butte east of and immediately beside Lost Lake. The loop's elevation gain is 1,000 feet. The loop takes you past numerous viewpoints, some quite outstanding, and passes along the lake's east shore.

Starting 6.6 miles from the last house (see map) ski onto Road 1340 at 2200 feet—the start of the loop. In 2.3 miles there is a good view of Hood, and a better one 0.7 mile farther. At 3.9 miles from Road 13 there is a sweeping view of the West Fork Hood River valley all the way down to Dee, and of Hood. The road then turns around the south end of Butcher Knife Ridge, with views, and climbs to a saddle at 3,200 feet along a scenic hillside and narrowing valley. Ski the campground road along Lost Lake's east shoreline (Road 1340, which parallels the hillside). From the lake, climb to Road 13 past the ticket booth and in 0.9 mile cross a divide, then descend 1,000 feet to Road 1340, your starting point on the loop.

Chapter 9

GOVERNMENT CAMP AND TIMBERLINE

Government Camp is a small winter-sports-oriented village on the south side of Mount Hood that serves as the trailhead for many ski tours. The village gained its name in 1849 from an encampment of U.S. Cavalry soldiers en route between The Dalles and Oregon City. Government Camp is particularly popular with Novice skiers who are unfamiliar with other parts of Mount Hood and who find the area convenient in terms of rentals, parking, and a wide selection of trails.

The complex of touring trails at Government Camp (affectionately referred to as "Govie") has something for all skiers, from easy trails for the first-time Novice to fast trails for Advanced skiers. The trails offer scenic places to enjoy such as old-growth forest and nearby open areas to explore such as Multorpor Meadows, a peaceful place of frozen ponds, streams, and level areas. Challenging trails such as the twisting Barlow Road Trail and the Yellowjacket Trail will lure Advanced skiers. The Enid Lake Loop is one of the loveliest tours when there is adequate snow, and in combination with the Glacier View Loop offers considerable variety. Future plans by the Forest Service include circling Government Camp with a loop trail, the south half of which now exists from Multorpor to the Ski Bowl.

Government Camp serves as the primary access point for the Timberline Lodge area. Govie also provides access to the northern end of the Trillium Basin. Comprising some 8 square miles, the basin has 19 miles of snow-covered roads and offers a wide variety of terrain, including forests and clearcuts. Since most of this large area is suitable for Novice and Intermediate skiers it is the prime area on Mount Hood for future Nordic trail development. It is hoped that the future will see the basin set aside for quiet users, with the introduction of additional trails and huts to complete what could be a unique skiing experience for Portland skiers.

A Nordic ski center with groomed trails was in use on a trial basis in 1992–1993. The center is located near the top of the Summit Ski Area and is accessed by a chairlift or by skiing up the West Leg Trail. A fee is charged for skiing on its tracks.

MIRROR LAKE

(Map 26) Nestled in a scenic alpine basin this 3-mile round trip and 700-foot elevation gain for Advanced skiers offers a fine view of Mount Hood and serves as a starting point for high-country tours on Tom Dick

Timberline Lodge looking toward Ghost Ridge (right), *Frog Lake Buttes* (center), *and Mount Wilson in distance*

and Harry Mountain. The route to the lake is an unmarked summer trail.

The parking area and trailhead are 0.8 mile west of Ski Bowl and Glacier View Sno-Parks. Cross a footbridge to the trail, which climbs at a moderately steep grade to the lake. The trail crosses a rockslide with views twice and has five switchbacks. Since the trail is popular with winter campers and day hikers, usually traveling on foot or snowshoes, it is likely to be roughed up, rutted, and packed—not ideal for Nordic skiing. The trail is especially difficult to descend.

The lake lies in a shallow basin opening toward Mount Hood, a spectacular setting. For the Advanced skier the towering Tom Dick and Harry ridge rising over 900 feet above is a challenge. It is also possible to climb high and travel the contour east to the upper Ski Bowl area, a rugged trip for experienced off-trail skiers only! The steep, open areas of the upper basin are potential avalanche slopes.

ENID LAKE AND GLACIER VIEW LOOPS

(Map 26) Just west of Government Camp and across from the Ski Bowl access road is a relatively flat forest area with several ski trails. Loops range from 1.5 to 2.5 miles long and are rated Novice to Advanced. One trail gains 50 feet in elevation, then loses 200 feet. Access to all trails is from Glacier View Sno-Park.

There are three loops here that may be skied independently or together,

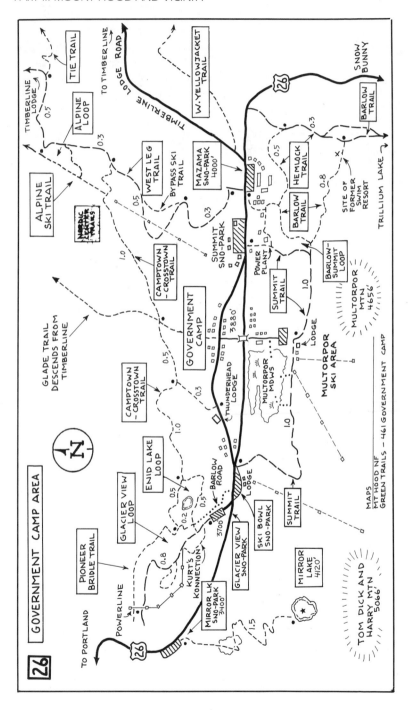

as they form figure eights. These loops offer something to every skier—uphill, downhill, open forest, a scenic lake with a view of Mount Hood, and a wonderfully preserved section of the old pioneer Barlow Road. There is both road and trail skiing to please any skill level. The Camptown-Crosstown Ski Trail that goes behind and north of Government Camp to the Summit Ski Area begins here, starting partway around the Enid Lake Loop. The area requires 2 feet of snow to be safely covered. Less snow and the skiing will be rough and brushy.

Historical Note: The Barlow Road of pioneer days crosses through this area, and it is recommended that you visit the area in summer to explore its route. In some places it has not been cleared or maintained.

Enid Lake Loop. (Map 26) This 1.2-mile Intermediate loop will seem much longer because of its great variety and numerous challenges. This is not a good loop for first-time skiers, and will tax all the resources of Novice skiers.

From Glacier View Sno-Park, ski along the snow-covered road about 200 yards (just beyond the third power pole), then turn right and enter the tall timber. Immediately to the right is a section of Barlow Road that goes uphill 0.3 mile to Highway 26. It is unmarked, but easy to follow.

Continue 200 yards on the loop to the lake and a view of Mount Hood. Wood-duck boxes have been placed on several lakeshore trees by the Forest Service. The trail goes along the south shore of the small lake then climbs gently eastward, turns and crosses a marsh, reenters forest, and soon meets the junction of the Camptown-Crosstown Trail to Govie. The trail continues on the loop descending through beautiful forest as it circles the lake to meet the Pioneer Bridle Trail from Rhododendron, which forms part of the Glacier View Loop. Turn left at this junction, climb a winding, moderate, uphill grade and return to the trailhead. Because of this last hill, the loop is best skied counterclockwise.

Glacier View Loop. (Map 26) This is a gentle downhill road tour, with an uphill return on the Pioneer Bridle Trail through lovely forest. The loop is just over 2 miles round trip, is rated Novice–Intermediate, and has an elevation loss and return of 200 feet.

The snow-covered road you first ski downhill on is a section of the former Highway 26 that eventually joins the present highway. About 250 yards from the end of the old highway section a powerline crosses the road. Just 50 yards prior to this is a tricky 80-yard trail section that takes you to the right and onto the Pioneer Bridle Trail. Follow the Bridle Trail uphill to the junction with the Enid Lake Loop, and then up the winding hill to the trailhead. For a more imaginative loop, consider skiing the north leg of the Enid Lake Loop back to the sno-park. The top of the winding hill is crossed by the pioneer Barlow Road that goes down to the top of nearby Laurel Hill (across the present highway) where wagons were lowered with ropes.

Kurt's Konnection. (Map 26) This trail forms a 1-mile loop with minimal elevation loss. It turns off the road not far beyond the sno-park, parallels the road through beautiful forest, then loops back on the road. The loop is suitable for first-time skiers but will be a challenge in several places.

This trail is an example of a "linear clearcut," purposefully designed to create a ski trail. Hopefully more of such planned logging will provide well-planned, safe ski trails in the future as alternatives to road skiing, and to serve as connectors to disperse the growing numbers of skiers.

CAMPTOWN-CROSSTOWN TRAIL

(Map 26) The total length of this Intermediate trail, sno-park to sno-park, is about 3 miles, but the trail's length from the Enid Lake Loop to the West Leg Trail is 2.5 miles. From its high point on West Leg Trail at 4,330 feet the trail at first follows the elevation contours then, from near the Glade Trail, descends moderately to the Enid Lake Loop for an elevation loss of 690 feet. In reality, with its many small ups and downs, the total loss is more. The trail is scheduled for completion the winter of 1994–1995, although the east half from Glade Trail may be delayed.

The west end of the trail starts 0.3 mile from Glacier View Sno-Park where it leaves the Enid Lake Loop. Then it climbs gently, then moderately, through thick forest, then into lodgepole pines. A connector trail starts 50 yards east of the Thunderhead Lodge, a motel that was the lower terminus of the ill-fated Timberline Tramway (see Glade Trail). It climbs 0.3 mile on a road going up the old tramway swath to the Camptown-Crosstown Trail. A half mile farther east from this connector, the trail crosses the Glade Trail at about 0.5 mile above and behind Govie.

From the Glade Trail the Crosstown Trail continues eastward through forest on a twisting, up-and-down course that is quite interesting, then joins the West Leg Trail, passing along the way the Nordic Center trail system. From the West Leg and the end of the Crosstown Trail it is about 0.8 mile down the West Leg Trail to Summit and Mazama Sno-Parks.

SUMMIT TRAIL AND MULTORPOR MEADOWS

(Map 26) This is the perfect introductory 4-miles-out-and-back tour for Novices. The marked trail is generally level, has views, gentle hills, forest, and an opportunity to visit beautiful Multorpor Meadows. If skied east to west there is a 300-foot elevation loss.

The west end of this trail begins at the east end of Ski Bowl Sno-Park, where a wide snow-covered road leads to the Multorpor Ski Area 1 mile away. The trail is a road tour all the way, and occasionally ski-area snow vehicles are encountered along the way. At the Multorpor Ski Area the trail follows a service road at the edge of Multorpor Meadows and just behind the various ski lifts and buildings.

For a pleasant side trip ski into and explore Multorpor Meadows. Although

Multorpor Meadows with otter tracks

the meadows are adjacent to a major ski area, the chairlift operations do not seem to intrude. Several streams meander through the meadows, a protected area owned by The Nature Conservancy, where there are several beaver dams and ponds. If you are observant, you may see beaver or otter tracks in the snow. About 3 feet of snow are necessary for stream crossings.

The meadow is effectively screened on most sides by fringes of forest, and even Highway 26 at the north edge goes unnoticed.

From the Multorpor Day Lodge, the trail continues as a road into tall trees and climbs slightly, then levels out and winds toward Highway 26, ending near Mazama Sno-Park just after passing the Government Camp auxiliary power plant, a square, metal structure. Circle the plant to the east and pass several Forest Service cabins to where the Barlow Trail starts into the Trillium Basin, only yards from Mazama Sno-Park. Both Summit and Mazama Sno-Parks give access to the east end of the Summit Trail.

MULTORPOR MEADOWS

(Map 26) Although mentioned in the previous trail description, another access point to this beautiful area merits description. From the main street of Govie drive across the Highway 26 overpass to Multorpor Ski Area and drive beyond the large condominium building on the right. Park just beyond this building or in the sno-park beyond. The access to the meadow is easily spotted west of the road and south of the condominiums. In low-snow times a narrow drainage ditch 80 yards from the parking area may offer a temporary access problem to the meadows.

WEST LEG TRAIL

(Map 27) The West Leg is a long 5.3-mile uphill tour starting at Government Camp and following a former highway to Timberline Lodge. Elevation gain is 1,950 feet if you go all the way. Good exercise, views at the upper end, and a long, thigh-burning descent are your rewards. This is a good tour for a car shuttle to get you uphill the easy way.

Starting from Mazama Sno-Park opposite the Timberline Lodge road, cross the highway to the north side and walk up a narrow plowed road 100 yards west of the Timberline junction. Go 50 yards up this side road, then climb the snowbank to the left onto the West Leg Trail. If Mazama Sno-Park is filled, park at Summit Sno-Park, just 200 yards west, and ski up through the ski area to join the West Leg.

As you ski upward the road winds and turns through the Summit Ski Area, and in one place a bypass trail off to the right side of the road allows you to avoid the hardpacked ski runs that follow and cross the road in several places. At 1.6 miles from and 600 feet above the sno-park the Tie Trail joins from the right at an obvious switchback. Just below here, and a short distance out on the Tie Trail, are several good viewpoints. Otherwise the West Leg is almost entirely enclosed by forest.

A short distance below Timberline Lodge the West Leg crosses chairlift runs so be alert to fast-moving skiers. Inattentive Nordic skiers in this area can easily become involved in serious collisions. To avoid the most congested areas leave the West Leg just above the last switchback, on a marked Nordic trail about 0.5 mile from Timberline Lodge, and ski the trail upward to join the upper Glade Trail, which leads to the lodge. With the Blossom chairlift operating near the area it is almost impossible, however, to avoid meeting downhill skiers streaking by. To further complicate your enjoyment, you may find that the alpine ski runs are often hardpacked and difficult to ski, particularly downhill.

If you wish to start your tour at Timberline Lodge, car shuttles will give you concentrated doses of downhill running and practicing of turning skills. See the Alpine and Glade Trails for other downhill ski routes.

If you are at Timberline Lodge, to find the West Leg Trail ski west of the lodge under the Magic Mile chairlift, then west 200 yards to a wide slope, the top of the Glade Trail and also a downhill ski run. Ski downhill following cross-country trail markers to the West Leg.

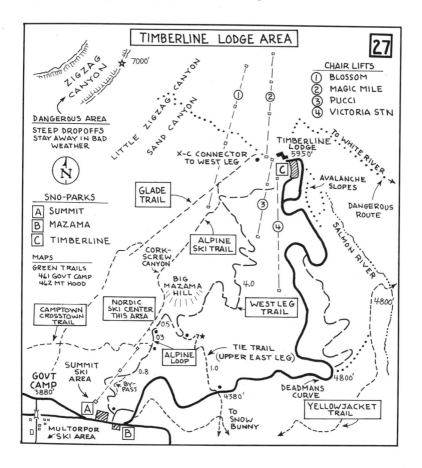

Skier and friend (Photo: Darryl Lloyd)

If the snow is hardpacked or crusty, descent of the West Leg can be frightening for a Novice and very unpleasant for even the best skier. Remember also when near downhill skiers that they are not always in full control and may not be able to avoid you. Be careful.

The Glade Trail, a wide swath through the forest to Government Camp, may be skied but requires strong turning and edging skills. Ski Glade only if the snow is perfect!

ALPINE SKI TRAIL

(Map 27) This 3-mile one-way descent from Timberline to the Summit Ski Area is very fast, direct, and unmarked. The elevation loss is 1,950 feet, and it is for Advanced skiers only! Formerly constructed for alpine skiers many years ago it is having a revival as snowboarders are discovering the winding, challenging route. Ski it only when the snow is perfect.

If you are planning to ski this trail uphill follow directions for the West Leg Trail and ski 1.3 miles up the West Leg, then turn left at a sign and go 50 yards to the Alpine Ski Trail through a narrow opening in the trees. Follow the trail up to the base of Big Mazama Hill (open slopes) and climb the hill to its top left corner. Follow the trail upward through Corkscrew Canyon, a tight, narrow gully, then up to its end at the bottom of the Blossom chairlift. The lower terminus of the chairlift is located just 100 yards west of a sharp switchback about 0.5 mile below Timberline Lodge.

If you are skiing down from Timberline, ski to this obvious switchback on the West Leg, then down and west through open areas into a wide, open clearing and the lower end of the chairlift. Below the chairlift there is an open area beside a gully. The open area may be marked with a large orange-painted sign marking the beginning of the Alpine Ski Trail.

ALPINE LOOP

(Map 27) This 2.6-mile round trip from the Summit area gains 400 feet and will challenge some Novice skiers. The short, pleasant loop has been greatly shortened by installation of the Summit chairlift. The loop is a nice change of pace from the uniformity of the West Leg Trail. The loop itself is only 0.5 mile long.

Ski up the West Leg Trail about 1.1 miles to where the Alpine Ski Trail, descending from the Timberline Lodge area, almost touches the West Leg. Leave the West Leg (signs) and cross 20 yards west to the Alpine Ski Trail. Once on the Alpine Ski Trail, ski downhill on the west leg of the loop to a side trail heading left just above the top of the chairlift. Follow this trail as it immediately turns uphill and winds gently for 300 yards to the West Leg. This portion of the loop is a narrow, twisting trail through the woods, passing a marshy, slide alder clearing. The loop is scenic and worthy of your attention.

GLADE TRAIL

(Map 27) The Glade Trail, best attempted only by Advanced skiers, or experienced Intermediates, descends 4 miles from Timberline Lodge to Govie in a most direct manner, losing 1,950 feet of elevation. There are continuing views on the way down, and you may have the sensation on the upper Glade of being suspended far above the country below—an interesting experience. It is rarely used in the uphill direction, but will see more cross-country downhill in the future. The trail demands good turning and edging ability, skills that many Nordic skiers do not have. For the descent to Govie from Timberline Lodge, however, the nearby West Leg Trail seems to be preferred by most skiers.

See the description of the West Leg tour for directions to the upper end of the Glade Trail. Once on the wide swath of the trail it is hard to stray off it. The irregular terrain drops relentlessly, demanding skills and strong legs.

For a way the trail follows the wide, former route of the ill-fated Timberline Tramway of 1950. An overhead cable suspended from many towers carried a city bus body with its own cable-climbing propulsion motor. The tram failed to operate properly and was soon a financial failure. The trail leaves the tramway swath to enter forest on the right, following a narrower trail to Govie, where it comes out onto the main street opposite the road to Multorpor Ski Area Sno-Park.

Snow is often a problem on this trail. The upper Glade is heavily used by downhill skiers to the bottom of the Blossom chairlift, resulting in a hardpacked surface. It is often rutted, and seldom smoothly packed. Due to elevation differential, the snow is not consistent from top to bottom. On those days when it is cold at Government Camp and there is a mantle of fresh snow, the Glade is a great run. If hardpacked or crusty, do not ski it. If the upper part is bad, the lower part may not get better, so head over to the West Leg Trail for a safer, more enjoyable descent.

TIMBERLINE LODGE

(Map 27) At 6,000 feet, Timberline is a popular area to ski because of the varied terrain, its beautiful frosted and snow-sculpted trees, and its remarkable panoramic view to the south of Trillium Lake, Mount Jefferson, and many minor Cascade peaks and ridges. Because there is almost no level terrain here, Timberline is not suitable for first or even second-time Novice skiers.

The Timberline area has a number of unique hazards. In poor weather it is easy to become disoriented as there are no landmarks in the forest below, and it is easy to ski out of the area without realizing it. The ravines and canyons have great potential for danger in poor visibility, when it would be easy to ski right off the edge into one. Finally, alpine skiers abound, and you will do well to stay off their runs if possible, and if you can't, you had better cross rapidly.

Historical Note: Timberline Lodge, located at the upper forest limit, was dedicated by President Franklin Roosevelt in 1937. The structure of the lodge is like no other in America. Every massive beam, every stick of furniture, every rug and painting and doorknob was fashioned by human hands. Like Mount Hood it is a priceless asset to all of us who enjoy the mountain sports of the area.

Lower Zigzag Canyon. (Map 27) The area west of the lodge attracts many skiers with its varied terrain and the beauty of its scattered islands of subalpine trees. Most of the skiing is for Intermediates, being up and down over challenging terrain.

From the lodge ski west crossing under the Magic Mile chairlift and past the top of the Glade Trail. Then ski up open slopes into scattered trees and across rolling terrain through the Blossom chairlift ski runs. Cross Sand Canyon, hardly noticeable, then Little Zigzag Canyon, about 50 feet deep. Continue to Zigzag Canyon, which is over 400 feet deep and about 1.5 miles from the lodge. Do not enter this canyon as it is often a dangerous avalanche area.

As you cross downhill ski runs, do so rapidly and with an eye to the streaking downhill skiers. This is their area, so they have the right-of-way.

Upper Zigzag Canyon. (Map 27) The 1.7-mile climb to the 7,000-foot point at the precipitous edge of Zigzag Canyon is truly a spectacular tour in good weather, and best done in spring when the weather is stable and the snow consolidated into corn form. Although not difficult, this tour is rated Intermediate due to the long descent to Timberline Lodge, which requires downhill skills.

From the lodge head west, under the Magic Mile chairlift, then climb steadily, above the top of the Blossom chairlift, then on the rolling, vast, open snow slopes upward to Little Zigzag Canyon, 30 feet deep with steep sides. It is best crossed near its upper end, which may require climbing along the canyon edge to reach it. Continue climbing to Zigzag Canyon, about even with the top of the Magic Mile chairlift, which can be used as a gauge for your elevation. The canyon is a 500-foot-deep gash on the southwest flank of the mountain. Steep, dangerous canyon sidewalls continue downmountain for over a mile. Directly across the canyon is Mississippi Head, a prominent cliff.

The view of the half-mile-wide canyon is awesome, and views to the

Climbing above Timberline Lodge to Zigzag Canyon

Central Cascades are most impressive. Mount Hood rises over 5,000 feet above. The 7,000-foot point is the best viewing site, and avoids crossing Little Zigzag down lower where it is often difficult.

White River Canyon. (Map 27) The area east of the lodge is not heavily used by Nordic skiers. Due to the difficulty of the terrain, it should be attempted only by Intermediate or better skiers.

Climb behind the lodge, then cross a very steep ravine to the east. This is the headwaters of the Salmon River, often dangerous due to avalanche potential. Beware of this steep, deep ravine during or immediately after heavy snowfall. Windblown snow piles up in deep unstable drifts at the edge of this and other ravines, making them dangerous for two days or more after storms.

Several hundred yards east of the Salmon River ravine is the White River Canyon, which has precipitous sidewalls and is almost always corniced with overhanging snow. This canyon is over 400 feet deep and is always dangerous regardless of snow or weather. *Do not go near the edge!*

Timberline Lodge to White River. (Map 27) This is an exciting, long descent to White River and Highway 35, requiring wilderness skills. It is all downhill except for the first 400 yards. This is a 3.5-mile, one-way, unmarked route with an elevation loss of 1,727 feet.

Do not attempt this tour except in good weather with good visibility. In fog or snowstorm it would be easy to become disoriented, even with map and compass. For the first mile or more the canyon is often corniced and abrupt. Do not ski near the edge at any time. The canyon wall is a dangerous avalanche slope much of the winter.

From the northeast corner of the upper parking lot at Timberline Lodge, cross the road and ski northward climbing gently for about 300 yards to a very steep gully. Cross this potentially dangerous gully and head southeast, along contours to another similar gully that also must be crossed. Continue to the near edge of White River Canyon, which is perhaps 700 yards from your starting point.

Follow the crest of a ridge downhill, keeping White River Canyon on your left. There are a few trees on this ridge, and you may find the upper parts quite rough going due to wind-formed snow convolutions on the ridge. There are fine views from here of the immense medial moraines of the White River glacier, and the mountain rising far above.

The ridge soon broadens as it continues its gradual descent, offering wide, shallow bowls for long traverses. Continue to about 5,200 feet (0.7 mile), where a descent may be made on steep, open slopes into the canyon. If snow appears unstable, continue down into the trees where the descent will be easier and safer.

Once on the flat floor of White River Canyon, follow it to the White River bridge by way of either the left or right side, where a bench with scattered trees descends to the Gravel Pit, then to the bridge.

WY'EAST TRAIL

(Map 28) This 20-mile trail, extending from Glacier View to lower Pocket Creek, is a composite ski route linking a number of shorter segments to form a unique challenge to the experienced skier. The trail crosses three mountain passes—Summit, Barlow, and Bennett—on its exciting course one-quarter of the way around the base of Mount Hood. The trail uses both marked and unmarked routes, reaches a high point of 4,674 feet, and has a cumulative gain of 1,750 feet and a cumulative loss of 1,400 feet. The name *Wy'east* was used in Indian myths and is said to be the legendary name for Mount Hood.

The Wy'east Trail starts at the Glacier View Sno-Park and ends at the Pocket Creek trailhead. Depending on how you ski this route—and there are several alternative trails—you will cross Highways 26 and 35 two to five times. There are now only two unmarked, off-trail segments that total about 1 mile. The future will, no doubt, see these sections cleared of brush, marked, and bridged.

Completion of such a long, unique trail will provide the Mount Hood region with a remarkable recreational opportunity. Long-distance skiing, like long-distance running, will attain increasing popularity, and this trail will grow correspondingly in importance. That it closely parallels major highways makes it even more available and safe to skiers.

The only undeveloped and unmarked segment at this time is from Snow Bunny Sno-Park to the Pioneer Woman's Grave. Although there are a number of route alternatives and variations, such as Boy Scout Ridge, the Yellowjacket Trail, and the Mineral Jane Trail, the classic as well as most practical route is to follow alternatives closest to the highways.

Over ten sno-parks along the Wy'east Trail permit you to select individual sections rather than the entire trail, thereby allowing you to become familiar with the route and to test yourself against the distance and terrain. The following is but a general description of the route. For details, read the appropriate trail descriptions that appear in other chapters and consult maps.

Before attempting to ski the full length of the Wy'east Trail, become familiar with the various segments. Then select good snow conditions for your trip. Since many of the segments are already popular tours, much of

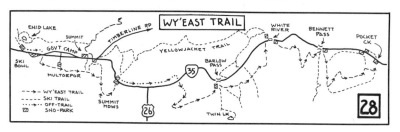

the total route will probably be tracked for you. The best direction in which to ski the Wy'east Trail is from west to east, starting at the higher end and saving the descent from Bennett Pass for last.

The trail is a serious undertaking and the length of the tour, particularly in less than ideal conditions, may cause stamina problems for skiers who are not in proper physical condition. There is no difficult terrain along the trail, but route-finding skills are required in several places. Carry maps and repair kit.

From west to east the classic route begins with the Glacier View Loop, then follows an unmarked powerline route on the north side of Highway 26 to the Ski Bowl. From there, ski the Summit Trail, Barlow Trail, Summit Meadows Trail, and Red Top Meadows Trail to Trillium Lake Sno-Park. Cross the highway and ski through unmarked forest to the Salmon River area, where a segment of the old pioneer Barlow Road (the Pioneer North Loop) continues to the Pioneer Woman's Grave. From there, ski the Buzzard Point Trail (or Barlow Road Trail) to Barlow Pass. Continue on the Mineral Jane Trail over Barlow Saddle to White River. Cross the highway bridge to White River East Sno-Park and ski Mineral Jane Trail East to Bennett Pass.

At the pass there are numerous choices for the final distance to Pocket Creek Sno-Park to complete the Wy'east Trail. Of all the options—Sahalie Falls, Clark Creek Trails, Teacup Lake Trail, Pocket Creek Trail—perhaps the East Fork and Meadows Creek Trails are the most scenic and interesting.

SNOW BUNNY TRAIL TO TIE TRAIL

(Map 29) Drive to Snow Bunny Sno-Park 2.2 miles east of Government Camp, across the highway from Trillium Lake Sno-Park. Walk to the trailhead past a snow-play area. Climb gently on this Novice route through forest for 1.6 miles to the Timberline road. This trail follows the former East Leg Road to timberline.

Cross the road, climb the snow bank, and proceed on the old road, now called the Tie Trail. Ski gently upward through lodgepole pines and second-growth firs 1 mile to a prominent switchback on the West Leg Trail, the second road built to Timberline Lodge. This switchback is 1.6 miles above Mazama Sno-Park. The scenic high point of this tour is near Still Creek, just 200 yards before reaching the switchback turn, where there are partially obstructed views of Hood and to the south of lesser peaks—Multorpor, Eureka, Veda, and Tom Dick and Harry.

EAST LEG AREA

(Map 29) Tours here range from Novice to Intermediate with a round trip up to 6.8 miles and an elevation gain up to 750 feet. Built in the 1930s, the East Leg road was the first to Timberline Lodge. Today it is the basis for a number of interesting loops ranging from 3.2 to 7.9 miles in length. In

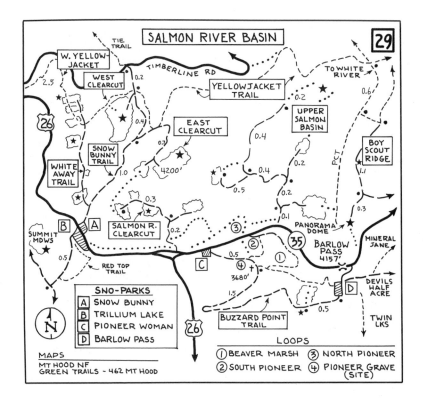

addition, there are two trails that can be skied out and back, and most of the trails of the area are marked. There is considerable variety for both Novice and experienced skiers. Several clearcuts offer views and off-trail skiing.

White Away Trail. (Map 29) This trail offers a 3.2-mile loop for Intermediates, or just an out-and-back tour along a road. Just 0.1 mile beyond the Snow Bunny trailhead you may notice a side road to the left, near the snow-play hill. This road is the White Away Trail, which ends 1.2 miles from the trailhead. A short way up the road, there is a clearcut with a view of Mount Jefferson, and near the trail's upper end several clearcuts have great views to the west. This road climbs through forest to a junction with the West Yellowjacket Trail, where by turning right to the Snow Bunny Trail and heading back to the trailhead, you can form a loop.

West Yellowjacket Trail. (Map 29) This rugged forest trail for strong Intermediate skiers starts near the Timberline road-Highway 26 junction, then travels through big timber 2.3 miles to where it joins the Snow Bunny Trail at a point 1.4 miles above Snow Bunny Sno-Park. Several loops can be formed by using this trail.

The trail, starting up the Timberline road about 80 yards from Highway 26, enters dense forest. It climbs steadily, with several bridged creek crossings, sidehills, and steep pitches before it reaches the White Away Trail, a road. It continues through the trees above the West Clearcut to the Snow Bunny Trail. The trail has many challenging ups, downs, and turns. From west to east it is generally uphill to the White Away Trail, and rolling from there to the Snow Bunny Trail. Several clearcuts on and just off the trail provide views. For details, see Yellowjacket Trail in Chapter 15.

Snow Bunny Clearcuts—East and West. (Map 29) The tours to these two scenic clearcuts will challenge most Novice skiers but are not difficult and are worth the effort. Each is a 4-mile round trip with an elevation gain of 500 feet, following a marked road. The two clearcuts offer views of Hood, Jefferson, and the Trillium Basin peaks.

From Snow Bunny Sno-Park walk to the trailhead then ski or walk up the Snow Bunny Trail past the snow-play hill. Put on your skis and ski 1 mile to a junction, where a side road goes to the right. From there it is 0.7 mile to the East Clearcut, which should be skied to its top for the best views.

Back at the junction, to reach the West Clearcut, either climb the steep bank to the west or continue uphill 0.4 mile to where signs mark the crossing of the Yellowjacket Trail. Immediately back, at a sharp reverse angle to the left, is a road that leads 0.4 mile to the West Clearcut and good views. This clearcut can be used as an alternative to the West Yellowjacket Trail by skiing along its top edge westward, then rejoining the Yellowjacket.

Snow Bunny Loops. (Map 30) There are numerous loop-skiing opportunities in this area, some of which will challenge even the hardiest Novice skier. In all there are five loop combinations, which may be skied from either Mazama or Snow Bunny Sno-Park. Loop 1 is the only one for Novice skiers; the rest are for Intermediate skiers. (See the map to view various loops.)

YELLOWJACKET TRAIL

(Map 29) Following a route cut through the forest from the Timberline road to the White River, the Yellowjacket Trail is a challenge against which to judge your skiing skills, for most of them will surely be required before the tour is ended. If you can ski this trail with aplomb, you may consider yourself an Advanced skier. It is a physically demanding trail and while marked along its entire length, some route-finding skills will be needed. This trail is a classic tour that every skier wants to ski for the notoriety it has acquired.

The trail is 6.3 miles one way, climbs 800 feet to a high point of 4,800 feet, and is a long, tiring tour for which a car shuttle is recommended. To make a 16-mile loop tour, however, you may return via Boy Scout Ridge or the Mineral Jane Trail to Barlow Pass, down the Buzzard Point Trail then across Highway 35 and through untrailed, unmarked forest to Snow

Bunny, then into the Trillium Basin and north to Mazama Sno-Park. From Snow Bunny the full loop is 14 miles and is less demanding.

The first leg of the Yellowjacket, here called the West Yellowjacket Trail, heads northeast through big timber 2.3 miles to the Snow Bunny Trail. The

Trailside cascade in upper Pocket Creek, Mount Hood area

SNOW BUNNY LOOPS

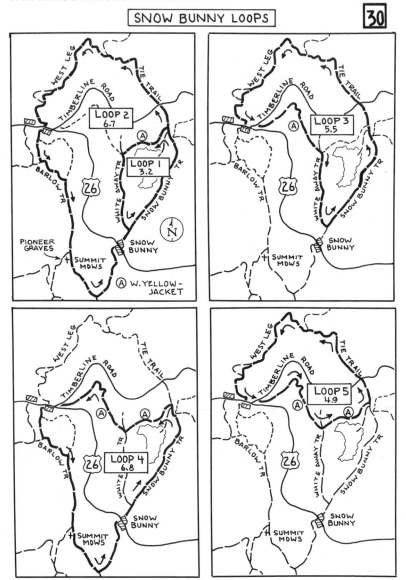

Loop 1: Snow Bunny, West Yellowjacket, White Away; Loop 2: Snow Bunny, Tie, West Leg, Barlow, Summit Meadows; Loop 3: Snow Bunny, Tie, West Leg, West Yellowjacket, White Away; Loop 4: Snow Bunny, West Yellowjacket, Barlow, Summit Meadows; Loop 5: West Yellowjacket, Snow Bunny, Tie, West Leg.

Yellowjacket then crosses the Snow Bunny Trail, turns south and goes down-hill, paralleling the Snow Bunny Trail, then popping out onto the east clearcut road to cross the West Fork of the Salmon River. It then continues uphill along the east side of the river before turning east.

If you are skiing the Yellowjacket from Snow Bunny, ski up the Snow Bunny Trail for 1 mile to the first side road on the right. Turn here and ski 200 yards to the first stream crossing. Look carefully for the trail markers, and follow them uphill along the east side of the Salmon River until the trail turns right and continues winding through the forest. The trail climbs and eventually reaches a ridge shoulder, then follows uphill along the west edge of the main and middle fork of the Salmon River, far above the stream itself. The Salmon River, little more than a creek here and farther up, usually offers little if any problem at the crossing.

Along the west edge of the canyon, the trail climbs steeply and seemingly without end, but finally descends to the river, at 4,800 feet, which is crossed on snow. Climb out of the canyon as the trail doubles back and descends through open forest. At the 4,500-foot level it turns left (north) and follows the contour toward the White River, reaching a meadow in about 600 yards.

The trail crosses the meadow and enters beautiful open forest. Continuing with more gentle ups and downs, it finally switchbacks sharply to the right and descends a moderately steep slope into and out of a deep gully. Crossing gentle terrain, the trail passes near the Gravel Pit, which is on the other side of a low ridge, and soon ends at the White River West Sno-Park. An eventful, tiring, but rewarding tour has ended, unless you are skiing a loop back to your starting point!

Skiing the Yellowjacket is easiest from west to east because in this direction the steepest hills are climbed, with mostly gentle slopes to descend to White River. The pleasure of this tour depends on selecting the right snow conditions. New, heavy snow would be very tiring. Late spring conditions may mean tree wells, dirty snow, and icy surfaces in the shade.

As with most advanced tours carry appropriate gear and an emergency repair kit. And be prepared to do some route finding. The trail, however, is well defined overall, and there should be few problems. Select a safe crossing for the Salmon River at the high point of the tour.

Historical Note: This trail was conceived by Homer Blackburn, who was instrumental in laying it out and in effecting its ultimate completion, after four years and 2,540 volunteer worker-hours. The Mazamas, Trails Club of Oregon, and the Skinny Ski Club, which was Blackburn's club, were the primary forces in the trail construction. The trail received its name from the many stings suffered by the trail workers. As originally constructed, it extended from the Timberline road. The first part of the trail has been called West Yellowjacket in this guidebook to minimize confusion in loop descriptions.

Chapter 10

TRILLIUM BASIN

(Map 31) The Trillium Basin is unique on Mount Hood: no other area on the slopes of Hood has Nordic skiing terrain of comparable extent, quality, and variety. Furthermore, the basin is convenient, being accessible directly from Government Camp, with its parking, ski rentals, public facilities, and other amenities.

Trillium Basin lies just southeast of Government Camp, extending 6 miles from north to south and covering 8 square miles. It is a heavily logged area of gentle, rolling hills and flats enclosed by two high ridges: the Eureka-Veda-Sherar Ridge on the west, and Mud Creek Ridge on the east. The two principal drainages are Upper Still Creek in the far northwest and Mud Creek, which flows south from the Trillium Lake dam. The Salmon River flows south along the east base of Mud Creek Ridge and then curves westward in the extreme south to encircle the basin on two sides.

Beautiful Trillium Lake also draws large numbers of skiers, and the lake loop is usually crowded. The lake area and the basin to the north are heavily used by Novice and Intermediate skiers seeking the safety of numbers, easy terrain, and comfortable skiing distances.

Aside from the lake and Summit Meadows, the basin is only lightly used by skiers. Yet away from the crowded and popular half-day tours lies an area of considerable beauty, fine views, and a variety of skiing experiences. There are 19 miles of snow-covered roads in the basin, providing tours of up to 14 miles. And by using clearcuts and connector routes it is possible to ski long distances without retracing your tracks. The ever-changing scenery, numerous views of Hood, Jefferson, the high peaks of the Clackamas, and the Salmon River valley are ample rewards for those who ski the longer tours.

If there is a problem with the basin, other than crowding on the popular tours, it is that all ski routes into the basin are downhill, and while short, they are somewhat steep for the Novice. The large number of Novices using the basin, however, suggests that the rewards are worth the exertion and adrenalin demanded by the initial hills.

Machine grooming of some trails in the Trillium Basin started in 1990 on an experimental basis, subject to available Forest Service funds and those from donations. Donations are made by Government Camp and Sandy businesspeople, and boxes are located at the trailheads for donations by skiers. Of course, all skiers are encouraged to donate. The grooming makes your skiing easier, more fun, and safer. If you skied Trillium Basin before the machine grooming you will remember how terrible the tracks were, often destroyed by inexperienced and unskilled skiers. The groomed tracks

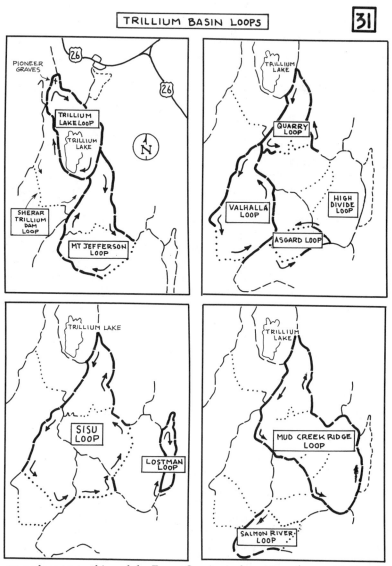

TRILLIUM BASIN LOOPS

31

are a pleasure to ski, and the Forest Service is deserving of support. Donate every time you ski the basin.

It may surprise most skiers to the basin that at one time it was a popular area for snowmobilers. Technically it remains open to snowmobile use but is rarely so used as there are many miles of snow trails groomed for such use in the Frog Lake and Clear Lake areas. Due to heavy skier use of the basin, the Forest Service will someday have to bite the bullet, face reality, and close the basin to snow machine use, except for trail grooming.

There are four routes leading into the basin—all downhill. These four—the Barlow, Hemlock, Snow Bunny Hill, and Red Top Meadow Trails—are all difficult for Novice skiers, who seldom have downhill skiing skills.

SNOW BUNNY HILL

(Map 32) This route follows a wide road down moderate grades. It is the shortest route to the Trillium Basin and the most popular for skiers of all skill levels. This route is recommended to Novice skiers as the most direct route to the trails of the basin.

Park at Trillium Lake Sno-Park (hereafter referred to as "the sno-park"), which is located on Highway 26 1.6 miles east of the Timberline road. At the trailhead you have a choice of two routes into the basin: the Snow Bunny Hill road (by far the most used) and the Red Top Meadow Trail (see below). The Snow Bunny Hill road descends several hundred yards, flattens out, crosses a creek, then reaches the airstrip junction in a few yards for a total distance of 0.5 mile. By turning right at the junction, you can go to Summit Meadows. By turning left (staying on the main road), you are headed for Trillium Lake. Snow Bunny Hill is generally packed hard, requiring you to snowplow to control speed. If you can't control your descent on skis, take them off and walk safely down the edge of the road out of the path of skiers and where your steps will not damage the skiing surface.

The airstrip junction is located at the south end of a former emergency airstrip for small planes. Near here was located a Civilian Conservation Corps (CCC) camp for the workers and artisans who built Timberline Lodge in the 1930s.

RED TOP MEADOW

(Map 32) Misnamed, this trail is never close to Red Top Meadow and is the least used of all the trails into the basin. To find the trail, ski down the Snow Bunny Hill route 50 yards then turn left (signs) and enter the trees. The first half of this 0.7-mile trail is on forest trail. Then it follows a primitive road, crosses a small meadow, and soon joins the Snow Bunny Hill route at the creek just before the airstrip junction. The route, although steep in places, is less direct but has scenic charm that the Snow Bunny Hill road lacks. It is an interesting alternative for your return trip.

HEMLOCK TRAIL

(Map 32) Originally named "Easy-Does-It Trail," this trail was in reality never "easy," but it does give fairly easy access to the north end of the Trillium Basin. Both it and the Barlow Trail use the same trail for several hundred yards until they diverge and go their own ways.

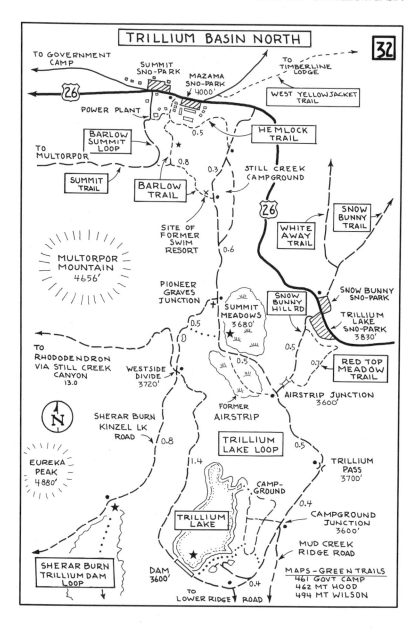

From Mazama Sno-Park at the Highway Department area, opposite the Timberline road, go to the west end of the sno-park and ski down and around several Forest Service cabins while watching for trail signs. At the south

141

edge of the cabin area a trail enters the forest, climbing a slight incline. This is the start of both trails. Ski down a moderate grade. The Hemlock Trail turns off to the left. It descends through forest to the summer campground road, then in 0.3 mile it joins the Barlow Trail to continue on the road to Summit Meadows 0.6 mile farther.

BARLOW TRAIL

(Map 32) Following the route of the historic Barlow Road, this beautiful forest trail travels through scenic old growth. Because of several short, steep sections it is recommended only to skiers with downhill experience. The trail goes 0.8 mile to the campground road then along this to Summit Meadows.

Follow directions for the Hemlock Trail but continue straight ahead at the junction with the Hemlock Trail. The trail twists and descends quickly at first, with an abrupt turn and several dips and tricky pitches and turns, then soon joins a trail coming down from the right. This side trail is a short connector to the Summit Trail just up the hill that permits a short loop back to your starting place.

The Barlow Trail now turns left and continues descending gently, then moderately through tall trees, twisting along the sunken, historic roadbed. So many skiers pass this way that the run is often packed smooth, resembling a wide toboggan run with rounded walls: for the good skier an exciting run!

There is one final steep pitch of about 50 yards before crossing a small meadow near the site of the former Swim Resort. In the early 1900s, the hotel and cabins were open year-round. Cross the small opening then cross Still Creek to the campground road. Turn right here and ski to Summit Meadows. A short side trail just above the last pitch to the small opening permits avoiding the steepest hill into the meadow. Many skiers fall on the steep turns before the meadow so ski carefully. If you fall, immediately get off the trail.

If Mazama Sno-Park is filled and you park at Summit Sno-Park, reach the Barlow and the Hemlock trailheads by crossing Highway 26 and taking a short spur road just a little east of the sno-park exit. This leads to an auxiliary power station (a square metal structure), where you turn left to the nearby Forest Service cabins and the trailhead.

TRILLIUM LAKE LOOP

(Map 32) The marked trails of this loop are suitable for Novice skiers. The round trip from Trillium Lake Sno-Park is 5 miles and from Mazama Sno-Park 7.2 miles. Elevation loss (and gain) is 450 and 620 feet respectively.

This is the most popular and crowded of all the trails of the basin. Proximity to sno-parks and constantly changing scenery and points of interest make this loop the first tour for many beginning skiers. The loop, however, is a bit long for some Novices, so exploring the Summit Meadows area is recommended to less aggressive skiers.

From the airstrip junction (see Snow Bunny Hill description) ski south down a wide, gentle road, before climbing up and over Trillium Pass at 3,700 feet. After descending a long, gentle hill, ski along a flat as it eventually curves right to a gentle descent to the dam at the foot of the lake (3,600 feet), a popular lunch and rest spot with a good view of Mount Hood. Farther along, reach the Westside Divide, the junction of the Sherar Burn and Still Creek roads. From the divide a moderate downhill run leads past a frozen pond and along the level, winding road across a flat leading to the Pioneer Graves junction, at the north end of Summit Meadows.

The white picket fence surrounding the graves is a scant 50 yards south of the junction. The small headstones date to 1882. Just 50 yards north of the junction is the site of the former Summit House, where the historic Barlow Road crossed the meadows.

If you are returning to Summit or Mazama Sno-Park, head north on the campground road. If your destination is Trillium Lake Sno-Park, follow the road or meadow south to the airstrip junction.

There are few hazards along this route. Under icy conditions the hills, though gentle, will be fast and dangerous for Novices. If the weather is bad or the Novice not in good shape, it is possible the tour will be too long. If so, turn around at the dam and retrace your route, foregoing the longer loop. The lake ice is not always safe, so it is best to stay off the lake.

SHERAR BURN AND TRILLIUM LAKE DAM LOOP

(Map 32) Marvelous views and steep clearcut skiing on this 8.8-mile Advanced round-trip tour will challenge the best skiers. The cumulative elevation gain of 1,000 feet provides the views and a good workout on this mostly road tour.

The loop itself is 4.6 miles and can be started at either of two places. Either way, ski to the Westside Divide (see Trillium Lake Loop) and ski up the Sherar Burn road 0.8 mile to the top of an almost mile-long clearcut. Descend on steep slopes into the clearcut over mixed, rolling terrain to its bottom at a crossing of Mud Creek. Ski 0.4 mile to the Lower Ridge road, and here, near the quarry, turn left and ski north to complete the loop after crossing the Trillium Lake dam. If your downhill skills are not strong, ski the loop clockwise and climb the clearcut to the Sherar Burn road.

MUD CREEK RIDGE AND PORCUPINE TRAIL

(Maps 32 & 33) This 8.2-mile Intermediate round trip leads you to views of the basin, Mount Jefferson, Mount Hood, the Salmon River ridges, and

Summit Meadows in Trillium Basin with Mount Hood behind

the Clackamas high country. The cumulative elevation gain is 1,200 feet. The last mile is along a lovely, primitive road where signs of elk are not uncommon.

From the campground junction east of Trillium Lake (see map) take the road angling uphill for a long, gentle climb to the Jefferson Viewpoint, 1.8 miles from the junction and 3.5 miles from the sno-park. On the way up there are several good views across the basin to Veda Butte and Eureka Peak. The road makes a sweeping turn at the viewpoint, where there is a good view of Mount Jefferson 40 miles to the south. Follow the road as it curves eastward. Where it starts to curve southward, leave the road and enter a

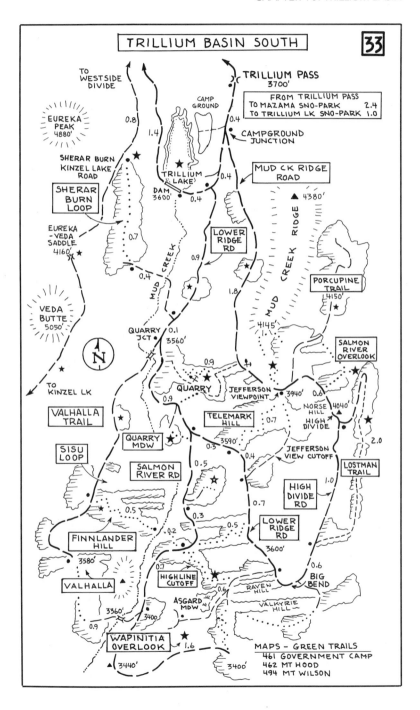

TRILLIUM BASIN SOUTH

33

TO WESTSIDE DIVIDE

TRILLIUM PASS
3700'

CAMP GROUND

FROM TRILLIUM PASS
TO MAZAMA SNO-PARK   2.4
TO TRILLIUM LK SNO-PARK 1.0

EUREKA PEAK 4880'

0.8

1.4

0.4

CAMPGROUND JUNCTION

SHERAR BURN KINZEL LAKE ROAD

TRILLIUM LAKE

0.4

MUD CK RIDGE ROAD

SHERAR BURN LOOP

DAM 3600

0.4

0.4

▲ 4380'

EUREKA-VEDA SADDLE 4160'

0.7

LOWER RIDGE RD

0.9

MUD CREEK

0.4

1.8

MUD CREEK RIDGE

PORCUPINE TRAIL 4150'

VEDA BUTTE 5050'

QUARRY JCT 3560'

0.1

4145'

SALMON RIVER OVERLOOK

N

0.9

QUARRY

0.9

JEFFERSON VIEWPOINT

3940'

0.6

NORSE HILL 4040'

TO KINZEL LK

0.9

TELEMARK HILL

0.7

HIGH DIVIDE

VALHALLA TRAIL

QUARRY MDW

3590'

JEFFERSON VIEW CUTOFF

2.0

SISU LOOP

0.3

0.4

LOSTMAN TRAIL

SALMON RIVER RD

0.5

HIGH DIVIDE RD

1.0

0.5

0.3

0.7

FINNLANDER HILL

0.5

0.2

0.5

LOWER RIDGE RD
3600'

3580'

0.6

VALHALLA

0.7

HIGHLINE CUTOFF

BIG BEND

3360'

3400

0.6

RAVEN HILL

VALKYRIE HILL

ASGARD MDW

0.9

WAPINITIA OVERLOOK

1.6

3400'

▲ 3440'

MAPS - GREEN TRAILS
461 GOVERNMENT CAMP
462 MT HOOD
494 MT WILSON

large clearcut to the north, following a primitive road that is visible if the snow is shallow.

The Porcupine Trail begins here, following a narrow road for 1 mile. Climb northeast in the clearcut and around the north side of a prominent tongue of forest on its east edge. After entering the forest, climb in a northerly direction along the side of Mud Creek Ridge, then descend into a final clearcut. The Forest Service has plans to eventually continue this trail on around the ridge to Trillium Pass to form a loop. There are many views along this route.

The Jefferson Viewpoint is a popular lunch spot. The large clearcut below, Telemark Hill, offers good skiing and is a connector route to the Lower Ridge road below and to the High Divide and Mount Jefferson Loops.

Mud Creek Ridge Overlook. (Map 33) Climb north from the Jefferson Viewpoint to the nearby top of the ridgecrest for sweeping views. Follow the contour around the west side to avoid dog-hair growth. The climb takes only 10 minutes or so and the view is rewarding.

SALMON RIVER OVERLOOK

(Map 33) Barely 300 yards off the main trail is an unexpected vantage point from which you can see the Salmon River valley and meadows. From the Jefferson Viewpoint follow the road east for about 200 yards to the bottom of a prominent clearcut. This rectangular patch extends east to the top of the ridge and the overlook. Ski to the northeast corner of the clearcut and follow openings 80 yards to the fine viewpoint. The beautiful Salmon River Meadows are spread out at your feet in their full length, with Ghost Ridge above and Frog Lake Buttes beyond. The highway leading to Wapinitia Pass is seen just above the meadows.

QUARRY LOOP

(Map 33) This Intermediate loop is one of the most interesting in the basin as it has fine views and goes through the terraced quarry with opportunities to try downhill skills. The 6.4-mile round-trip tour is mostly on roads and has a cumulative elevation gain of 700 feet. Most of the loop is machine groomed, but the best part of the quarry skiing is off the groomed tracks, making your way down from bench to bench. The loop itself is 4 miles.

From the campground junction east of Trillium Lake, ski up the Mud Creek Ridge road to a long, narrow clearcut below the road about 250 yards before reaching the Jefferson Viewpoint. Descend the moderate slopes of the narrow clearcut to the top of the quarry. Here a sharp left turn goes down a "screamer" hill (usually groomed) on a narrow road that circles the quarry. The more adventuresome route, however, does not take the sharp left but goes straight to the top of the quarry from where you can work your way down. At this time there are no vertical dropoffs, but a quarry always requires care. Do not ski it unless the visibility is good. Ski to the bottom of the quarry, gain the Lower Ridge road and return to the Trillium Lake Loop.

Quarry Meadow. (Map 33) While in the quarry area, consider skiing out of the quarry into a clearcut on its southwest side (before going to the Lower Ridge road), then descending this to Quarry Meadow across the road. This is a large, old clearcut. A primitive, obscure road leaves the Lower Ridge road 0.6 mile south of the Valhalla Road–Quarry Junction and descends gently 400 yards into the meadow for isolation and open, wide views. Leave the meadow by climbing the east edge to the road, or by the access road.

MOUNT JEFFERSON AND THE HIGH DIVIDE LOOPS

(Map 33) Many loops are described in this guidebook to encourage skiers to get off the beaten path, experience greater adventure, sharpen offroad and off-trail skiing skills, and gain some easy Backcountry skiing confidence. The two Intermediate loops that follow can be skied individually or even combined for greater challenge. Both loops start at the Jefferson Viewpoint.

Mount Jefferson Loop. (Map 33) From the Campground Junction east of Trillium Lake ski the Mud Creek Ridge road to the Jefferson Viewpoint. Here descend southward into the Telemark Hill clearcut and descend 0.7 mile and 350 feet to the Lower Ridge road. Turn right and ski this road back past the lower quarry to your starting point. About 3 feet of snow are needed to make the clearcut skiable and safe. This loop and round trip from the sno-park totals 7.9 miles.

High Divide Loop. (Map 33) This 10.8-mile round trip provides good exercise and gives you a chance to expand the loop to the Lostman Trail or take side trips in the southern basin. Elevation gain is just over 1,000 feet.

Ski to Jefferson Viewpoint and enter and descend partway the Telemark Hill clearcut, bearing left, however, to locate the Jefferson Viewpoint Cutoff Trail (unmarked), the start of which may be partially obscured by second growth. Ski this old logging road to the Lower Ridge road, then ski around Big Bend, over the high point of the High Divide road, and back to Jefferson Viewpoint. On the way, the top of Norse Hill will give you a view of the Clackamas high country, including High Rock and Signal Buttes.

LOSTMAN TRAIL AND LOOP

(Map 33) Some of the loveliest meadowlike skiing in the entire basin is on this 10.4-mile round-trip tour following both marked roads and off-road routes, with an elevation gain of just 990 feet, and an easy tour for Intermediate skiers. There are fine views of Mount Hood, Ghost Ridge, the Salmon

River valley, Frog Lake Buttes, and Wapinitia Pass. You will experience a sense of isolation on this superb tour.

Follow the Mud Creek Ridge road 0.6 mile beyond the Jefferson Viewpoint to the High Divide, the highest point on this part of the ridge. Here, the Lostman Trail is the obvious side road to the left (east). The trail shortly curves north and descends gently for 0.5 mile to a large, level clearcut overlooking the Salmon River valley. Turn right and ski south through connecting clearcuts and fringes of forest. Ultimately you will reach the High Divide road where you turn north and return to the Jefferson Viewpoint.

HIGHLINE CUTOFF TRAIL

(Map 33) The off-trail section of this 10.7-mile round trip is most interesting and scenic. Most of the tour is on marked, and often groomed, roads. This route is particularly suited to Intermediate skiers who want a little adventure in route finding. A beautiful meadow occupies a bench halfway along the trail, where there are good views of Hood and to the west. The Highline Cutoff provides a link with the lower end of the Valhalla Loop, with the Wapinitia Overlook area, and the end of the Salmon River road. This entire area is wonderful to explore when there is good snow and weather.

The most scenic approach to the trail is via Jefferson Viewpoint then along the High Divide road and around Big Bend. Just west of Big Bend look for a side road to the west along the bottom of a clearcut. This road leads to Asgard Meadow, an old clearcut that is hidden behind a screen of trees. But before you get that far, turn right where it starts to curve and take another side road and go right (north) into big timber. Go 200 yards and exit the old growth onto the Highline Cutoff, an area of clearcuts and meadows. Turn left then curve northward on this bench overlooking the Mud Creek valley and the Salmon River road below.

Descend to Salmon River road and turn right to return to the Trillium Lake area, or turn left to ski the Valhalla Loop, which adds only 1.8 miles to your return route, a small price to pay for the scenic rewards.

VALHALLA LOOP

(Map 33) If you want isolation, this 9.6-mile Advanced round trip from the sno-park should provide it. There are no long hills to climb but there is a long, almost unnoticeable descent to the far end of the loop, then a climb of 500 feet back to your starting point. Partly on unmarked roads and a large clearcut, this tour will satisfy a need for adventure and provide great views. Your first tour of this loop will always be your best as you work out its course. The best direction to ski the loop is clockwise.

Ski the Lower Ridge road from the Trillium Lake area to Quarry Junction, the northernmost point of the loop itself. Here you can go right onto

Snow-drifted bridge in area that is now totally clearcut (Photo: Steve Recken)

the Valhalla Trail road, but the best direction continues on the Lower Ridge road, then branches off onto the Salmon River road. Ahead along the way you will see a steep, rounded, and forested landmark hill. Just beyond this hill is a clearcut, rapidly regrowing. Here, look for an obscure, narrow road leaving the main road at an angle and heading west 300 yards down to the bottom of the clearcut and an old but sturdy bridge across Mud Creek. At 3,360 feet this is the lowest point of the loop.

Cross the creek and climb the moderately steep slopes to the west edge of the clearcut, then northward as the clearcut levels out. Rapidly growing trees in the clearcut are diminishing previous views. At the north end of the clearcut, enter forest and follow a road (Valhalla Trail) as it climbs past clearcuts before it descends to Quarry Junction.

Valhalla and Sherar Burn Road Connector. (No sketch map) Sometime in the future, the Forest Service plans to open a connector trail and Telemark route from near Fir Tree Campground (4,500 feet) on the Sherar Burn road (5.1 miles from the sno-park) down an 850-foot descent to the northern end of the Valhalla clearcut, using clearcuts at the bottom. The moderately steep slopes of the connector are forested with some openings. The connector will also serve as an access route to the road above and will complete a loop route.

SALMON RIVER ROAD

(Map 33) The 6.7 miles one way to the end of the Salmon River road take you to a remote, seldom-visited part of the basin. This Advanced tour is partly on unmarked roads, although several miles may be machine groomed. Elevation gained is 800 feet on the return trip.

Follow directions for the Valhalla Loop, but do not leave the Salmon River road and continue 1.6 miles to the large clearcuts at the end of the road where there are grand views of the surrounding ridges.

To ski a loop, climb the clearcuts northward to Wapinitia Overlook, then ski past Asgard Meadow and on up to Lower Ridge Road, about 1 mile from the end of the Salmon River road. From here, the best return is around Big Bend, then onto the Lostman Trail and back to the Trillium Lake area by way of the Mud Creek Ridge road.

WAPINITIA AND SALMON RIVER OVERLOOKS

(Map 33) A rocky outcrop high on the edge of the Salmon River at the very south end of the Trillium Basin offers grand views. For Advanced skiers, the 5.8-mile one-way ski tour from Snow Bunny, almost all on marked roads, with an elevation gain of only 600 feet, offers solitude where most skiers never visit.

Follow directions for Highline Cutoff Trail but continue around the curve and ski past Asgard Meadow and then 300 yards farther across a large, nearly level clearcut to an obvious knoll. Climb the knoll for views here at the Wapinitia Overlook.

SISU LOOP

(Map 33) The Sisu Loop is an Advanced 10.6-mile round-trip tour that suits its name well. *Sisu* is a Finnish word that is difficult to translate but means something akin to perseverance and fortitude. The tour is somewhat demanding but not really difficult, requiring some modest route finding, clearcut skiing, a stream crossing on logs, and hill climbing—requiring some determination but offering fine views and a sense of adventure. Much of the tour is on unmarked roads, and the elevation gain is 1,100 feet.

Ski to Quarry Junction and keep right at the junction, skiing the right branch, the Valhalla Trail road. Pass several clearcuts with views, and 1.3 miles from Quarry Junction reach the top of Finnlander Hill, recognized as the longest clearcut in view, now covered with second growth. The narrow, straight-sided clearcut descends gently to the edge of Mud Creek, 0.5 mile below the Valhalla Trail road. At the creek is a round, level meadow—in reality a summer marsh—an interesting place to explore.

Logs provide safe but exciting crossings of the narrow, shallow creek.

Use care here, and if you get wet feet, wring out your socks or better yet put on dry ones and keep going. Once across, ski up to the Salmon River road and turn left (east) to the foot of Highline Cutoff Hill. Do not ascend this clearcut, but from its lower, far corner ascend a narrow clearcut upward 0.5 mile to the Lower Ridge road. Here turn left to the Jefferson View Cutoff route to Jefferson Viewpoint and continue north to the campground junction east of Trillium Lake.

VEDA BUTTE

(Map 33) Veda (pronounced Vee-dah) is a compound word formed from two abbreviated first names. This Advanced tour of 5 miles one way climbs 1,700 feet to the top of the butte at 5,050 feet, where exceptional views will reward your efforts. The summit is reached after a long road tour on gentle grades followed by off-road travel on moderately steep slopes through scattered trees. Less adventuresome skiers need not go clear to the summit but will find fine views by climbing a short distance above the road. There is a 3-mile downhill run on the return trip along the Sherar Burn road.

Veda Butte is a high point on a massive ridge west of the Trillium Basin. Eureka Peak resides to the north on the ridge, and across Still Creek sits Multorpor Mountain near Government Camp.

Ski to the Westside Divide Junction west of Trillium Lake (see Trillium Lake Loop) and ski up the Sherar Burn road 1.6 miles to the Veda–Eureka saddle at 4,160 feet. From the saddle ski 1.4 miles to where the road finally eases off, becoming almost level. Here, climb above the road through immature trees. Beyond this point the road finally descends slightly, passing a small pond on the right.

Anywhere along here is a good place to start up off the road (4,470 feet). Ski up and northward, and climb 580 feet in 0.5 mile on a moderately steep ascending traverse to the summit, where you'll have a breathtaking view that can be improved by skiing southeast along the summit ridge for an excellent view of the Salmon River valley, and more views of the basin as if seen from an airplane. On the descent, the slopes above the pond are the steepest, whereas the open slopes northward are less steep.

The steep slopes below the summit should not be skied after heavy snowfall or during warm weather due to potential for avalanche danger. Do not ski above the road unless visibility and weather are good.

SHERAR BURN TO KINZEL LAKE

(Map 34) This 23.4-mile round-trip ski tour to Kinzel Lake on unmarked roads is a challenge even for Advanced skiers. The route is not difficult, but the distance is long and the cumulative elevation gain is 2,920 feet. This long road tour requires several elusive ingredients for success: good

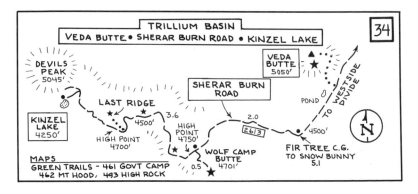

snow, good weather, and a good dose of determination. Some skiers turn back before reaching the lake and thereby miss the most scenic part of the tour, the last 4.5 miles. As you get farther out, there is a remarkable sense of solitude.

The route passes through forest with no views until near the high point, where a side trip to Wolf Camp Butte reveals a panoramic view. This spectacular spot, little more than an open sidehill, is 0.5 mile downhill and off the main ski route to Kinzel Lake and 7.6 miles from Snow Bunny. This is the site of a former fire lookout. The next and possibly more impressive viewpoint of the tour is only a short distance west of and downhill from the tour high point of 4,750 feet.

Ski the Sherar Burn road from the Westside Divide to Fir Tree Campground 5.1 miles from the sno-park. From here the Sherar Burn road rolls westward with long, tiring, but gentle ups and downs. To reach Wolf Camp Butte take an obscure side road to the left (south) from the main ski route, which here is a distinctive, straight lane through second growth, and about 100 yards east of the tour high point. Views range across the wide, deep, Salmon River valley to Mount Wilson, Wolf Peak, and High Rock, far to the south in the Clackamas high country.

Just beyond the high point the road turns and crosses a steep slope that will require caution if icy. From there (the 7.6-mile point) the road loses 400 feet, then gains it back as it climbs to Last Ridge. A short side trip here to the ridgecrest offers a view of Hood, and a wild scene of deep canyons, peaks, and ridges. A final descending traverse drops 450 feet to Kinzel Lake. The small lake is not really the goal of the tour—the goal is to complete the tour. The best time of year is spring, when all conditions are stable and days are longer, but when south-facing slopes may be icy.

Chapter 11

SALMON RIVER BASIN

The little-known Salmon River Basin extends from Barlow Pass on the east to Snow Bunny Sno-Park on the west. The east and west forks of the Salmon River run through the area while the main stream, a small creek, descends from near Timberline Lodge to join the two branches near the interchange of Highways 26 and 35. The Pioneer Woman's Grave on old Highway 35, now a scenic, snow-covered road leading to Barlow Pass, is in the eastern part of the small basin.

The main area, from the shallow basin to Snow Bunny, is characterized by generally level forests with a few gentle grades and a number of marshes and meadows hidden from view and just off the traveled trails and roads. The East Fork Salmon River (Upper Salmon Basin) contains a compact group of short roads reached by climbing through moderately steep forest from the lower areas of the basin.

Accessibility to some of the tours is hampered by Highway 35, which must be crossed on foot. In years of low snowfall this is no problem, but when roadside snowbanks are high some care is required. The three streams of the Salmon River segment the area, but crossings are managed on snow bridges, or at the highway edge where the streams run through culverts.

There is potential here for miles of marked loop trails suitable for Novice skiers, and the future will no doubt see a sno-park for trail development. At this writing the area has limited parking and few marked trails, although there are several easily followed unmarked tours that do not appear on Forest Service winter maps.

BEAVER MARSH AND PIONEER WOMAN'S GRAVE LOOP

(Map 29) This is an exceptional 2.5-mile loop tour, with less than 200 feet of elevation gain following both roads and trails suitable for Novice skiers. If there is sufficient snow, you can also explore a number of small meadows, open areas, and short skid roads from old logging days.

From the Pioneer Woman Sno-Park (not always plowed) just east of the Highway 26/35 interchange, 1.5 miles from Snow Bunny, ski along the snow-covered side road, which is a section of the former Highway 35 to Barlow Pass and is now open in summer as a scenic alternative. Follow this road 0.4 mile to where it starts to curve right, 100 yards before the Pioneer Woman's Grave site. Leave the road here and turn left onto a marked trail—the start

Springtime skiing in meadow

of the Beaver Marsh Loop—leading into the trees. At the road this trail is not obvious, but soon is easy to follow.

The trail twists through the open forest, shortly passing an obscure side road on the left, the pioneer Barlow Road route (a leg of the unmarked Pioneer South Loop). The marked loop, however, continues and eventually joins a logging road that heads to the right, up a gentle hill. Ski along this road eastward 0.8 mile to where it crosses a bridge. Here the loop enters a large clearcut, former site of a magnificent stand of ancient forest, logged in 1987—perhaps the finest stand of such trees on Mount Hood. Several examples still stand along the clearcut's edges.

The loop continues into another large clearcut to the south then shortly goes downhill and crosses a creek and becomes a narrow trail, paralleling closely the original Barlow Road just a few paces to the left. From the creek crossing it is 250 yards of winding, easy downhill trail to the small meadow across the road from the Pioneer Woman's Grave. You are now less than 100 yards from where you left the road to start the loop. In summer the grave appears as a large pile of smooth stream stones.

Historical Note: A number of forest fires have raged through this area and the Trillium Basin since the pioneer wagons passed through on the way to the Willamette Valley. Very few of the trees you now see were standing then to witness the passing wagons. The few remaining giant trees are some of the only witnesses left and should be preserved from logging, which threatens some sections of the area.

BUZZARD POINT TRAIL AND BARLOW ROAD LOOP

(Map 29) This 2.8-mile loop with one leg for Novice skiers and the other for Intermediate skiers, with an elevation gain and loss of 480 feet, offers everything from an easy marked road to unmarked forest skiing. Because of the steepness of Barlow Road, less experienced skiers should probably not attempt this leg of the loop, and for most skiers, the Barlow Road leg is best skied from bottom to top.

Barlow Road Trail. (Map 29) Starting from the Pioneer Woman's Grave, cross the small meadow opposite the snow mound of the grave site and enter thick forest. At first the Barlow Road route may not seem obvious as it is no longer marked by the Forest Service. In fact, the trail was abandoned as a ski trail due to the danger of deep snow holes made by water on the road. As the old road is a historic and cultural asset, the roadbed cannot be damaged by drainage ditches. In summer this route is called "Grave Trail."

The unmarked route continues through forest and soon parallels a large clearcut to the north, part of the Beaver Marsh Loop. Continue upward and the old road soon becomes obvious. As it climbs into old growth it passes another clearcut to the south, which climbs to join the Buzzard Point Trail (the old highway). Beyond here Barlow Road becomes steeper, makes several sharp turns in tunnel-like dense forest, and ends at the west edge of Barlow Pass Sno-Park.

Skiers who want to ski this route from Barlow Pass are advised that the unmarked Barlow Road Trail starts from the midpoint of the sno-park's west side, but the first 200 yards of the descent are steep and difficult, and skiing down the historic road is not recommended.

Buzzard Point Trail. (Map 29) Starting at the Pioneer Woman's Grave the 1.8-mile road is obvious, wide, and generally not interesting except for a view of Hood 0.5 mile from Barlow Pass Sno-Park, where a large clearcut climbs to the edge of the road. From Barlow Pass Sno-Park this trail starts at the sno-park's south end. Experienced skiers may want to ski down to the clearcut then ski it down to Barlow Road for a shorter loop. Although the Buzzard Point Trail road is gentle, if conditions are icy or crusty it should not be skied.

PIONEER ROAD LOOPS

(Map 29) Two short Novice loops (0.7 and 1.1 miles) on almost level terrain are available for those interested in exploring unmarked segments of Barlow Road. When a sno-park is constructed in the Salmon River Basin, these loops will no doubt become official, marked trails.

Park at the Pioneer Woman Sno-Park, a turnout just east of the Highway 26/35 interchange (not always plowed) and ski the old highway 0.4 mile to where the Beaver Marsh Loop starts. Enter the forest on the Beaver Marsh Loop and ski about 50 yards. To your left you will see a narrow, open way in the forest: this is the old Barlow Road. To your right is East Fork Creek and the deeply carved pioneer roadbed, where it forded the stream.

South Loop. (Map 29) Leave the Beaver Marsh Loop here and go left (north) on the old road as it winds for 400 yards to Highway 35 and across to the other side. Small wooden signs nailed to trees at the 7-foot level on both sides of the highway mark the route's crossing. To remain on the South Loop do not cross the highway here but turn right at the edge of the highway and ski east 50 yards to a snow-covered road leading into the woods. Follow this road about 350 yards to where blue markers on the right indicate the return leg of the loop to your starting point near the Pioneer Woman's Grave.

North Loop. (Map 29) Parts of this loop offer very different scenery from that of the South Loop. Crossing the highway twice, the loop is just over 1 mile long. To ski it, go to the Beaver Marsh Loop, ski the first 50 yards, then ski Barlow Road north to the highway (see South Loop), cross the highway, and follow obscure Barlow Road up a gentle slope through trees. After 170 yards, the trail turns left and in one straight line angles back to the highway through scattered trees and small openings.

You may experience some difficulty following the precise roadbed, for snow obscures it and the scattered trees do not outline the route well. On this last leg you may hear the creek clucking away out of sight on your right. Do not cross the creek, which parallels the old road for some distance. If you feel disoriented, do not fear: you cannot get lost here.

This loop eventually intersects the highway near the Salmon River culvert. Cross the highway to the small sno-park, then ski the old highway back to the start of the Beaver Marsh Loop to try the South Loop.

To expand this loop and explore the area north of Highway 35 there are numerous other short alternatives here to keep you busy for most of the day.

SALMON RIVER CLEARCUT

(Map 29) This unmarked road tour is only 1.2 miles round trip on almost level terrain, and ideal for Novice skiers. Numerous other side trips are possible. The area offers quiet forest, and a view of Ghost Ridge.

From the sno-park just east of the Highway 26/35 interchange ski along the north shoulder of the highway back to the interchange, where a snow-covered road leads north, curving through a former campground and then on to several small clearcuts. Ski 350 yards from the highway to a junction where roads go both east and west. The west branch goes to three small clearcuts, the first with a good view of Ghost Ridge. The road ends only 0.5 mile from the highway. The other branch goes east to a nearby clearcut, from where you can ski south into forest, connecting with a primitive road to form an interesting loop.

If you enjoy off-road skiing it is possible to ski to this area from Snow Bunny Sno-Park, although the forest is a bit tight in places. Most of this unmarked route is through open forest, but if you get too far from the highway you will run into marshes and slide alder thickets. Stay near the highway, and if possible ski two abandoned highway segments, both overgrown with alders. When you reach the West Fork, cross at the highway culvert.

UPPER SALMON BASIN

(Map 29) Although there are only 3 miles of roads here just west of Boy Scout Ridge, the area offers interesting, unmarked ski routes for Intermediate skiers. At this time there is a problem of access, as there is no marked ski route through the Salmon River Basin to these roads.

The roads lead to off-road skiing in scenic, small clearcuts and open forest that climb gently to the Yellowjacket Trail (see map). Down lower, a side road leads to a steep clearcut, the upper edge of which is only 80 yards from the top of Boy Scout Ridge and where skiing about 700 yards south along the ridgeside summer trail (if you can keep on it) will take you to Panorama Dome for the view. This is a compact area in which to explore and gain off-trail skills. To reach the roads here, see Pioneer Road Loops. Ski to the North Loop, then leave it and ski eastward 0.7 mile paralleling Highway 35, eventually climbing on a steep sidehill traverse that leads to a shallow basin and to the upper roads. Ski to the end of either and enter forest to find the nearby Yellowjacket Trail. The east road leads to the most scenic forest skiing. It is also possible from this area to ski eastward easily to the Boy Scout Ridge area on the Pacific Crest Trail (PCT), which cuts through from Boy Scout Ridge.

SALMON RIVER MEADOWS

(Map 35) Depending on snow cover in the beautiful meadows, this Novice-rated round trip could extend from 2 to 4 miles, with an elevation loss of 100 feet. Located only a short distance off the highway, this large meadow offers solitude in a deep basin surrounded by high, forested ridges.

The meadow is not visible from the highway and consequently is seldom visited. From the Highway 26/35 interchange drive south on High-

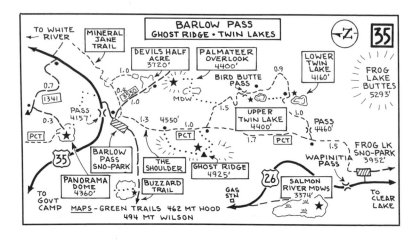

way 26 for 2.3 miles to a gas station, then another 0.4 mile to where the highway starts uphill. Park near the end of the west guardrail, where an obscure access road is located. Follow this road 0.5 mile down a gentle grade to the meadows.

Your success in exploring the meadows depends on the snow depth. The meadow's elevation is low, and in some winters there is a minimum of snow. The beauty of the large meadow, however, invites exploration. Over a mile long from north to south, the meadow is squeezed at both ends between the impressive, steep ridge to the south extending out from Wapinitia Pass, Ghost Ridge to the east, and Mud Creek Ridge on the west.

The winding banks of Ghost Creek on the meadow's east edge offer a lovely tour. To the north of the meadow the Eternal White Guardian is splendid in its white winter robe.

Chapter 12

FROG LAKE AND BLUE BOX PASS

A great deal of variety is offered here, from the demanding summit tour of Frog Lake Buttes with its sweeping views to the relatively gentle terrain of the Frog Lake area. The small turnout sno-park at Blue Box Pass offers road skiing that is less suitable to Novice skiers but which provides several fine views from Wapinitia Ridge clearcuts.

FROG LAKE

(Map 36) This area is 4.1 miles due south of the Highway 26/35 interchange. Most tours here are on generally easy terrain, follow roads, provide views, and are suitable for less-experienced skiers. All the tours in this area

Frost crystals on stream ice

start at Frog Lake Sno-Park (toilet available) at Wapinitia Pass.

This area is open to snowmobilers, but midweek skiers see few of them. Since this is snowmobile country, though, the roads are likely to be hard-packed and icy. Keep to the sides of your route to avoid speeders. This is their turf so respect their presence.

Frog Lake Loop. (Map 36) This scenic 1.4-mile loop to the lake follows unmarked roads and is a generally level route. The north end of the lake is wide and open, while the massive bulk of Frog Lake Buttes dominates the east shore. The lake's south end offers a view of Mount Hood in fair weather.

From the sno-park at 3,952 feet the lake is only 0.7 mile to the south. Here you have the choice of two routes, both easy. The first and less inter-esting follows Road 2610 south from the sno-park for 0.4 mile. Turn right onto a side road and descend a gentle hill to where the road branches. The left branch goes directly to the campground at the near end of the lake. The right branch goes straight ahead to the west side of the lake and then on to the far end. Either way it is a short distance to the north end of the lake.

For the most scenic approach to the lake, however, ski south from the sno-park and in only 100 yards angle right onto a lovely primitive road blocked by a snow mound. Ski this 0.4 mile to where it joins an abandoned highway section that leads gently down to the west shore of the lake. Link this route with the previous one to form a loop.

From the south end of the lake it is possible to ski southward through lovely forest on an unmarked route up a wide swale 0.6 mile to Blue Box Pass (see Wapinitia Ridge). Do not confuse this attractive route with the nearby abandoned highway section that also goes to the pass west of the swale.

Road 2610 Clearcuts. (Map 36) The distance to the clearcut viewpoints along the road varies from 1.5 to 3 miles depending on your interest. This is a tour for Novice skiers on a level road.

From the south end of Frog Lake Sno-Park ski south on Road 2610 past side roads leading to Frog Lake Buttes and to Frog Lake. Continue south through forest for 1.4 miles to where a side road leads down to a quarry. Do not take this road, but continue straight, traveling along the top edge of almost continuous shelterwood cuts that offer good views to the west. The finest view, however, is 3 miles from the sno-park, just after passing through a band of old-growth forest. Here there are grand views to Mount Wilson and Clear Lake Butte (lookout tower) and across miles of forest and low ridges. Beyond here the road descends and offers little of interest.

Frog Lake Buttes. (Map 36) This unrelenting climb of more than 1,300 feet over 3 miles of road to the summit is for strong Intermediate skiers or better. The fight against gravity to the top, then the almost uncontrollable dash down is enough to convince some skiers that there is truth in the old adage that once is enough.

From Frog Lake Sno-Park ski south on Road 2610 0.2 mile to the first road on the left. This is Road 220, which you follow to the summit, climbing moderately steep grades with no letup. There are few views on the way up,

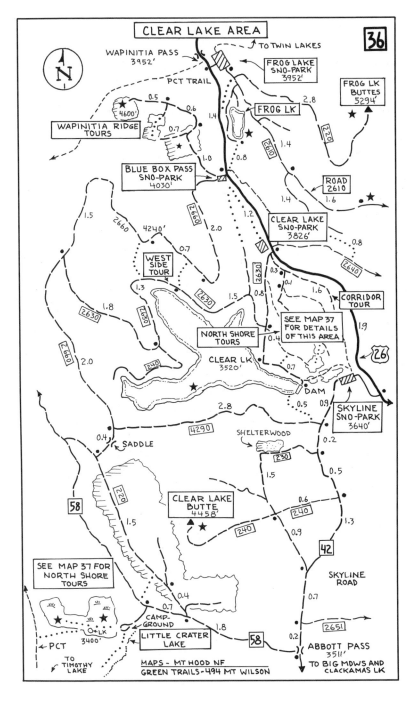

CLEAR LAKE AREA

36

TO TWIN LAKES

WAPINITIA PASS
3952'

FROG LAKE
SNO-PARK
3952'

FROG LK
BUTTES
5294'

PCT TRAIL

0.5

0.6

1.4

2.8

FROG LK

4600'

0.7

1.4

220

WAPINITIA RIDGE
TOURS

1.0

0.8

2610

BLUE BOX PASS
SNO-PARK
4030'

1.2

ROAD
2610

1.4

1.6

CLEAR LAKE
SNO-PARK
3826'

0.8

2640

1.5

2660

4240'

2.0

2660

0.7

WEST
SIDE
TOUR

2630

0.3

0.1

1.6

CORRIDOR
TOUR

1.3

1.5

0.8

2630

1.8

2630

2630

SEE MAP 37
FOR DETAILS
OF THIS AREA

1.9

26

2660

2.0

240

NORTH SHORE
TOURS

0.4

CLEAR LK
3520'

0.7

DAM

0.5

0.9

2.8

0.4

SADDLE

4290

SHELTERWOOD

230

SKYLINE
SNO-PARK
3640'

0.2

220

1.5

0.5

58

CLEAR LAKE
BUTTE
4458'

0.6

240

0.9

240

1.3

42

SKYLINE
ROAD

SEE MAP 37 FOR
NORTH SHORE
TOURS

0.7

0.4

LK
3400'

0.7

CAMP-
GROUND

1.8

58

0.2

2651

PCT

LITTLE CRATER
LAKE

ABBOTT PASS
3511'

TO
TIMOTHY
LAKE

MAPS - MT HOOD NF
GREEN TRAILS - 494 MT WILSON

TO BIG MDWS AND
CLACKAMAS LK

so the view of Hood from the summit plateau is well deserved.

The descent is often fast and difficult, especially if hardpacked or if snowmobile washboards are present. For most skiers the long descent is a thigh burner and not much fun, but for hardy skiers the speedy descent is almost unmatched. The descent is more than most skiers can comfortably control, and many falls are possible. It the road is hardpacked, ski elsewhere. If the snow is light, however, this is a great run. The road to the summit is closed to snowmobilers during the month of February.

BLUE BOX PASS TO WAPINITIA RIDGE

(Map 36) Several hillside clearcuts provide splendid views from the ridge west of Wapinitia Pass. From Blue Box Pass Sno-Park it is only 2.5 miles to the most distant views and an elevation gain of 600 feet. The unmarked roads are rated Intermediate, and there is off-road skiing through clearcuts to a high point of 4,600 feet. More adventuresome skiers may ski directly to this area by crossing the highway at Frog Lake Sno-Park and skiing the open forest westward, a distance of about 0.8 mile following in general the unmarked PCT.

At the Blue Box Pass parking turnout there is a Y-junction. The left fork goes to Clear Lake, and the right fork goes to Wapinitia Ridge. Ski the uphill, moderately steep branch 0.5 mile to the first clearcut for a view of Mounts Wilson and Jefferson. Exit the clearcut at its northeast corner and continue on the road 1.1 miles to the farthest clearcut, with a view of Hood. On your return, ski only 0.5 mile then turn right (southwest) on a road and enter the top of a long, southward-sloping clearcut. Ski 0.5 mile to its lower end with views of the Mutton Mountains near Kah-Nee-Ta. Then ski a road at the bottom eastward and back to the first clearcut you entered for a loop return.

Blue Box Pass Connector. (Map 36) Blue Box Pass is contiguous with and easily reached from the Frog Lake area but not yet connected by a marked trail. The area is serviced only by a small turnout parking area just 1.4 miles south by road from Frog Lake Sno-Park. Although it is only 1.1 miles from Clear Lake Sno-Park, there is no connecting trail at this time, so easiest access is from Frog Lake. Blue Box Pass is 5.5 miles south of the Highway 26/35 interchange.

If parking is not available at the small Blue Box Pass turnout, park at Frog Lake Sno-Park, ski to the lake's south end, then up an unmarked, forested swale south to Blue Box Pass, a distance of 1.7 miles.

Chapter 13

CLEAR LAKE AND
MOUNT WILSON

Nordic skiers have generally overlooked the Clear Lake Basin. New clearcuts and logging roads, however, offer an increasing variety of tours.

There have been three main reasons for lack of skiing interest in the area. First, its relatively low elevation means inconsistent snow depth and quality in some winters. Conversely, since the basin is situated slightly east of the heavier Cascade snowfall zone, it at times enjoys somewhat better weather, but less snow, than the often wet and stormy Government Camp area. A second reason skiers have avoided the area is that it is one of the two centers of snowmobile activity on Mount Hood (the other is Frog Lake) and there are no skiers-only trails in the entire area, a situation that hopefully will change. Yet a third reason may be that the Clear Lake Sno-Park is about 10 miles beyond Government Camp, over another pass, and until recently has had limited parking for skiers.

The Clear Lake Sno-Park, formerly a small turnout parking area, is being vastly enlarged and hopefully will be available for the 1994–1995 season. The increased size, however, will unfortunately attract snowmobilers to a part of the region lightly used by machines previously.

Skyline Sno-Park, the best access point for many of the longer ski tours south of Clear Lake, is a large sno-park with a shelter and toilets, and is located 2 miles farther east on Highway 26. The sno-park is heavily used by snowmobilers.

On a positive note, the Clear Lake area has many exceptional ski tours, most on gentle terrain, including the unique opportunity to ski the lake's long, wide shoreline. Clear Lake itself, with its scenic vistas, is the star attraction of the area. There are, however, many notable attractions for skiers south of Clear Lake itself: Clear Lake Butte, Little Crater Lake and its beautiful meadow, and massive, forested Mount Wilson towering over scenic Big Meadow.

Skyline Sno-Park leads to the lake's eastern end and the region south of the lake. Clear Lake Sno-Park gives access to many easy trails, and the north shore of the lake.

Recommended tours in the Clear Lake Basin are the Lakeshore Tour, Clear Lake Butte, and the North Shore Tours for skiers looking for short, nearly level terrain with old growth and views. If you plan on longer ski tours, contact the Bear Springs Ranger District for winter logging and road plowing information.

It is possible that Warm Springs Reservation lands may be closed to entry on a year-round basis in the future. If so, this may affect access to the

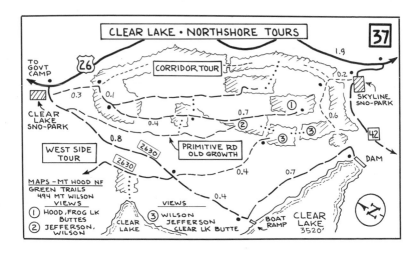

Mount Wilson and Big Meadows areas, although it is reported that Skyline Road (Road 42), which passes through the northwest corner of the reservation, would remain open to recreationists.

NORTH SHORE TOURS

(Maps 36 & 37) Near Clear Lake Sno-Park are several roads, on generally level terrain, passing through clearcuts that lead to views of the lake and skiing through old-growth forest. The shortest out-and-back tour is just under 2 miles. There are several loop opportunities that will be obvious from studying the map. This area is ideal for Novice skiers, although the roads are not marked for skiers.

From the sno-park cross the access road eastward and ski on a forest road 0.3 mile to a clearcut where you turn right and follow a road southeast across the clearcut 200 yards to where it forks. The right fork leads southeast in 0.4 mile to a large clearcut that is entered and crossed, then to a second clearcut that is entered for views of Mount Wilson, Mount Jefferson, and Clear Lake Butte. This clearcut connects with another farther on that gives access to a ski route from Skyline Sno-Park that leads to the Clear Lake dam and lakeshore road.

This North Shore area is worth exploring with its connecting roads and clearcuts that form loops and provide adventure as you probe the area's mysteries. In particular, a primitive road in old-growth forest, a rarity in the Clear Lake basin, parallels the road you skied to the viewpoint. See the map and search for it. The entire area is open to snowmobilers, but they are not a problem in this area. The Bear Springs Ranger District has been asked to make part or all of this a skiers-only area.

CORRIDOR TOUR

(Maps 36 & 37) From Clear Lake Sno-Park start out on the North Shore Tours and once through the first band of forest do not turn right but continue straight ahead. The tour proceeds through a narrow, ribbonlike clearcut that goes 1.6 miles to Skyline Sno-Park while losing less than 200 feet of elevation as it closely parallels Highway 26. This is also an excellent unmarked route for Novice skiers, and those wishing to form a long loop with North Shore roads and clearcuts.

LAKESHORE TOUR

(Map 36) Following unmarked roads to Clear Lake this tour is for Novice skiers who want to explore the lake area and enjoy the grand vistas along the shoreline. It is a 2.4-mile round trip to the lake, 3.8 miles round trip to the dam, and 7 miles around the lake following the shoreline. The elevation loss to the lake from the sno-park is 300 feet. In winter, Clear Lake is transformed from an unattractive scene into a snowy expanse of shorelines and distant views to the surrounding rolling, forested hills—truly a scenic gem.

From Clear Lake Sno-Park, follow Road 2630 1.2 miles to the shoreline boat ramp and campground, a gentle descent. The shore is wide and free of trees, offering a scenic tour regardless of direction. It is 0.7 mile to the dam at the lake's east end along either the road or shoreline. The north arm of the lake is especially lovely, and the tour around the lake is long but rewarding. Crossing inlet streams may offer small but surmountable problems, depending on snow depth.

Because of the lake's low elevation of 3,520 feet, lake ice is often not as solid as it may appear, particularly along the shorelines. Even if the ice appears safe, it is best to stay off the lake.

WESTSIDE TOUR

(Map 36) This 10-mile Intermediate round-trip tour along an unmarked road leads westward to the north end of the lake through heavy forest. Although it has no views to commend it, it is protected from weather.

From Clear Lake Sno-Park ski down Road 2630 0.8 mile then turn right (still on 2630) as it circles the north end of the lake to where it joins Road 240, a sheltered route, 3.6 miles from the sno-park. It is possible to reach the lakeshore from several points along this route.

CLEAR LAKE ACCESS FROM SKYLINE SNO-PARK

(Map 36) From the sno-park's west side near its entrance ski northwest into a large clearcut (south end of Corridor Tour), then downhill to its southwest corner and through tall timber onto an obscure, primitive road used by snowmobiles. Then enter tall second growth to the north shore road, and ski left as the road curves to the dam. From the sno-park to the north shore road is 0.8 mile, and the dam is only 200 yards farther. An alternative to this route from Clear Lake Sno-Park follows the Corridor Tour then goes down to the north shore road to complete a loop back to the starting point.

CLEAR LAKE BUTTE

(Map 36) The summit of Clear Lake Butte (4,458 feet) has a fire lookout and a sweeping view of the entire region. From Skyline Sno-Park it is a round trip of 10.8 miles on unmarked roads. The tour is rated Advanced, and the elevation gain is 900 feet.

From the sno-park ski south on Road 42 (Skyline Road), at first downhill followed by a short uphill to Road 230 1.1 miles from the sno-park. This is an obscure road that is missed by some skiers, but it is the shortest route to the top, although it is not shown on Forest Service maps. Once on the road it climbs into clearcut, shelterwood, and immature forest. Ski the road to the far end of a shelterwood area on your right below the road and turn left, continuing on the hard-to-follow road to a junction with the east-west road coming off the summit, the lower leg of which is also not shown on some maps. Turn and ski up this steepening road 1.5 miles from this last junction to the summit plateau. If you miss Road 230, continue south on Road 42 to the obvious, wide, and monotonous road that leads directly west to the summit.

In some winters Road 42 is plowed for winter logging. If so, drive as far as possible but do not block the road when you park.

LITTLE CRATER MEADOWS AND LAKE

(Map 36) This long, rolling Advanced tour on wide roads with no views goes one way 6.6 miles and loses 240 feet of elevation to reach the beautiful meadow, which will more than reward you for the monotonous approach route.

From Skyline Sno-Park ski south on Road 42 to a junction with Rd 58 3.8 miles south of the sno-park. Here turn right and ski 2.5 miles to a side road that leads west to the nearby meadows and a small lake.

Small, deep, crystal-clear Crater Lake, only 100 feet in diameter, is quite unusual. Located 300 yards from the campground and end of the road, it is protected from cattle by a rustic fence. The huge meadow, fringed by an undulating tree border, is inspiring. Mount Hood rises above the forest to the north.

To explore the meadow, ski north 100 yards from the lake, turn left, and ski into a long meadow extending westward. Here a beaver dam has created

Little Crater Lake in Clear Lake area with Mount Hood beyond

a large pond about 400 yards from the lake. The meadow and pond area turns northward and extend farther for more exploration.

The unmarked Timothy Lake Trail, part of the Pacific Crest Trail (PCT), can be found, with luck, only 300 yards from the lake in the old growth to the west, from where it is only 0.3 mile to Timothy Lake. Another route follows the edge of Crater Creek to the lake from the Little Crater Campground. You will see many otter tracks along here.

A loop return to the sno-park may be made by skiing Road 220 northward on the west side of Clear Lake Butte to Road 4290, thence east to Road 42. This route is 5.9 miles if you exit the campground road at Little Crater Meadow then cross Road 58. Here you enter forest and climb easily to join Road 220.

BIG MEADOWS

(Map 38) For strong Intermediate skiers the 14-mile round trip to the remarkable meadows on unmarked roads is a unique experience. Although there is an elevation loss of 190 feet, the rolling route demands little more than determination to complete.

Big Meadows are the largest meadows below timberline on Mount Hood and certainly the most perfect in several respects: wide, 2 miles long, curving out of view, and dominated by the majestic bulk of heavily forested Mount Wilson. The meadow is in a spectacular setting.

From Skyline Sno-Park ski south on Road 42 (Skyline Road) and ski 0.6 mile beyond the Road 58 turnoff to Little Crater Meadow, then turn off Road 42 onto Road 260. Opposite the first clearcut is a dense screen of trees concealing a lovely, circular pond. The road then curves and goes south past several clearcuts and over a low pass.

Big Meadows is 1.4 miles from Road 42 and is hidden from view by a narrow band of trees. A short side road through this band suddenly opens onto a magnificent scene—the wide, long meadow extending to the foot of Mount Wilson, which rises 2,000 feet in a smooth sweep of forest. As you ski along the edge of the meadow, the scene changes, providing a variety of impressions.

Although the meadow is 5.8 miles south of the sno-park, the tour may be much shorter if Road 42 is plowed for logging. Call the Bear Springs Ranger District to verify plowing.

BIG MEADOWS LOOP

(Map 38) A challenging alternative to skiing just to the meadow and back to your car, this 7-mile Intermediate–Advanced loop tour offers scenic variety and several miles of skiing on primitive roads, and adds only 4.3 miles to a straight-back return.

To ski the loop, ski south in the meadow then westward as it curves and narrows, squeezing you either into dense pine thickets or old growth, depending on your choice. Leave the meadow, ski north to a nearby primitive road, and turn left following it to Road 42. Turn south (left) 0.3 mile, then pick up a road on the right. This forest road climbs gently to a large clearcut area, eventually leading back on Road 270 to Road 42.

A snowmobile may have broken a track for you. Roads are gentle for the entire distance. Carry and use a Forest Service map as there are many side roads, some not appearing on the map. If snow is not deep, road signs will be visible.

CLACKAMAS LAKE HISTORIC RANGER STATION

(Map 38) Eight miles south of Skyline Sno-Park on Road 42, and near Big Meadows, is a historic group of Forest Service buildings. A rough log cabin was built here in 1906, followed by the present group of buildings in 1933–1934, which includes a beautiful District Ranger's residence, another residence, and equipment buildings. The Friends of Clackamas Lake Historic Ranger Station have undertaken to preserve the buildings constructed by

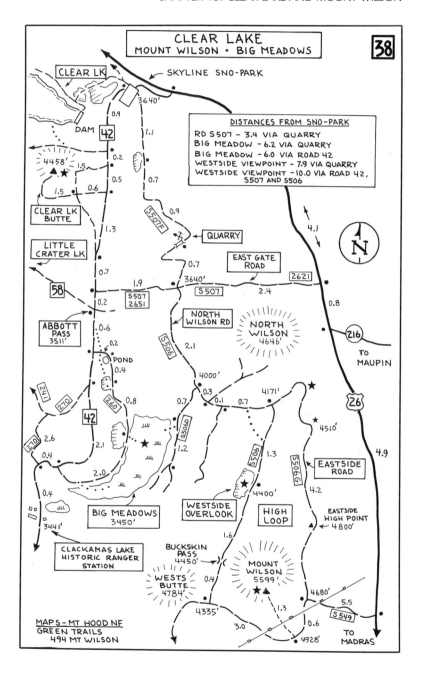

CLEAR LAKE
MOUNT WILSON • BIG MEADOWS

38

CLEAR LK

SKYLINE SNO-PARK

3640'

DAM 42

0.9

1.1

4458' 1.5

0.2

0.5

0.7

CLEAR LK BUTTE

1.5 0.6

1.3

LITTLE CRATER LK

58

S507F

0.9

QUARRY

EAST GATE ROAD

2621

DISTANCES FROM SNO-PARK
RD S507 – 3.4 VIA QUARRY
BIG MEADOW – 6.2 VIA QUARRY
BIG MEADOW – 6.0 VIA ROAD 42
WESTSIDE VIEWPOINT – 7.9 VIA QUARRY
WESTSIDE VIEWPOINT – 10.0 VIA ROAD 42,
    S507 AND S506

4.1

N

0.7

0.7

1.9

3640'

S507 2651

S507

2.4

0.8

0.2

216

TO MAUPIN

ABBOTT PASS 3511'

0.6

0.2

POND

0.4

NORTH WILSON RD

NORTH WILSON 4646'

S506

2.1

4000'

0.7

0.3

0.1

0.7

4171'

4510'

26

4.9

241

270

260

42

0.8

S506b

1.2

S506

1.3

S506G

EASTSIDE ROAD

270 2.6

0.4

2.1

2.0

EASTSIDE HIGH POINT 4800'

0.4

3441'

BIG MEADOWS 3450'

WESTSIDE OVERLOOK

4400'

HIGH LOOP

4.2

CLACKAMAS LAKE HISTORIC RANGER STATION

1.6

BUCKSKIN PASS 4450'

MOUNT WILSON 5599'

WESTS BUTTE 4784'

0.4

4680'

5.5

S549

4335'

3.0

1.3

0.6

TO MADRAS

4928'

MAPS – MT HOOD NF
GREEN TRAILS
494 MT WILSON

the Civilian Conservation Corps (CCC) and solicit membership through the Bear Springs Ranger District.

The group of buildings is near a small, marshy lake, and with good snow on Road 42 that is often groomed for snowmobilers this tour is not too long for many skiers. The entire Advanced route is rolling with no steep hills. The tour to the historic site can be combined with a Big Meadows visit.

MOUNT WILSON

(Map 38) Mount Wilson (5,599 feet) is a massive, heavily forested, gently rounded shield volcano 9 miles southeast of Clear Lake. It lies within the Warm Springs Indian Reservation. Although seemingly remote, there are direct ski routes. Skiing is essentially on roads as the forests are impenetrable. There are, however, many clearcuts that provide off-road opportunities. Although the mountain has three summits only the main summit is accessible and rewarding. Tours to the higher areas of Mount Wilson are the *piece de resistance* for adventurous skiers— offering distance, remoteness, a sense of adventure, and sweeping views in all directions.

The many roads of the area to the north and west are regularly groomed by heavy, special machinery from Skyline Sno-Park for snowmobiler use, an advantage to skiers: the packed roads make long-distance skiing easier. The mountain's summit is accessible from the east, the shortest route, and from Skyline Sno-Park to the north. Big Meadows, a marvelous, large meadow, lies at the west foot of Mount Wilson. The route to this meadow also provides access to Mount Wilson.

Although it is necessary to carry the Mount Hood National Forest map, it does not show the roads of the Mount Wilson area accurately, nor indeed does it show some roads at all. The Warm Springs Reservation road-numbering system is used in this book's map as Forest Service maps assign no numbers to the roads.

Mount Wilson Summit—Eastside Approach. (Map 38) Drive 4.9 miles on Highway 26 beyond its junction with Highway 216 to the obscure Beaver Butte Creek Road S-549. There is no sno-park, so carry a shovel to improve roadside parking. Park outside the fog line to be legal. The low elevation (2,800 feet) means shallow snow at the start. The elevation gain to the summit is 2,800 feet along a relatively easy-to-follow 7.4-mile one-way road system. Views from the summit are rewarding as this is the highest summit of the region.

The upward route, rated Advanced, passes many clearcuts and goes under a powerline three times. The route is obvious, if you are alert. Carry a map even though it may be essentially untrustworthy. The final 2.5 miles are the most rewarding as you climb through lovely forest, which diminishes in height as you gain elevation. The rounded summit is the site of a former lookout cabin. Views are panoramic.

Mount Wilson Summit—North Approach and Westside Overlook.
(Map 38) For this demanding 13.4-mile one-way Intermediate tour, with a
cumulative elevation gain of over 2,000 feet, park at Skyline Sno-Park. Go
to the northeast corner of the sno-park (in front of the log shelter) and ski
along road S-507F, usually groomed for snowmobilers.

Although the road passes through tedious forest, the route is direct, passes
several clearcuts with views, then descends steeply to cross Clear Creek,
the site of a quarry. Cross the creek, climb, and soon cross the East Gate
road (S-507). Here, 3.4 miles from the sno-park, the tour becomes more scenic as you toil gently upward on S-506 through many clearcuts and through
forest onto the west side of Mount Wilson. At 4,171 feet turn south and
follow S506 south 1.3 miles.

Here at 4,400 feet and 7.6 miles from the sno-park you reach a level section of the road at the top of a large clearcut. Here at the Westside Overlook
you have a grand, sweeping vista of miles of forest. Although occasionally
a monotonous tour, this view is a worthy reward. Timothy Lake, Big Meadows, and Hood are seen along with the distant Clackamas high country,
Devils Peak, and the neighboring Sherar Burn Ridge above the Trillium Basin. To the north are Bonney Butte, Lookout Mountain, and other features.

To continue your tour from the Westside Overlook on to the summit proceed on the rolling road 1.6 miles past clearcuts to Buckskin Pass, then down
0.4 mile to a junction. Turn left (east) and ski upward 3 miles to the final
junction. Here the old lookout road climbs 1.3 miles on a moderately steep
grade through alpine firs. The rounded summit is the site of a former fire
lookout. Attempt this tour only in favorable weather.

Mount Wilson—High Loop. (Map 38) The 11.1-mile loop, circling the
summit of Mount Wilson on roads, starts 6.6 miles from Skyline Sno-Park,
which makes this a very long tour of 24.3 miles. The tour is usually possible
only because of grooming for snowmobilers. The loop's low point is 4,171
feet, the high point is 4,928 feet, and the cumulative elevation gain for the
entire tour is about 1,900 feet.

Follow directions for Mount Wilson Summit—North Approach and ski
to the Road S-506/S-506G junction. Here at 4,171 feet go east up Road S-
506G. It turns southward, and 0.7 mile from the junction there is a fine view
of Hood where the road starts swinging around the east side of Mount Wilson. Another 0.7 mile takes you to a sweeping view of Lookout Mountain,
Grasshopper Butte, Hood, and others across a deep, forested valley. If time
is short for you, there is a good turnaround here at the best view of the tour.

To continue on the High Loop, enter heavy forest and climb southward
over a high point (4,800 feet), then descend to join the eastside road approach, then climb to 4,889 feet at the summit side road. From here, descend to Wests Butte and swing around onto the west side of the mountain
through many clearcuts to close the loop.

As with all long tours, carry a good repair kit, maps, compass, and clothing suitable for a range of conditions.

Chapter 14

BARLOW PASS

Barlow Pass, at 4,157-foot elevation, was the highest point reached by the first wagon road across the Oregon Cascades, portions of which remain to this day to be hiked and skied. This pass, located on Highway 35 between Snow Bunny and White River, is a great attraction for those seeking forest-trail skiing and areas that are not heavily used. Trails radiate from Barlow Pass in all directions, offering a variety of scenery and two outstanding viewpoints not far from the sno-park. Several of the trails provide fine forest skiing.

The principal trails are the Twin Lakes Trails to the south, Devils Half Acre to the east, Buzzard Point Trail to the west, and Panorama Dome-Boy Scout Ridge to the north. In addition, there is the Mineral Jane Trail, a connector to Barlow Ridge and White River. From the sno-park there is even an unmarked route directly onto historic Barlow Road to the west, and also to the east.

BUZZARD POINT TRAIL AND BARLOW ROAD LOOP

(Map 29) These trails starting from Barlow Pass Sno-Park are described in the Salmon River Basin chapter. Refer to that chapter as the area it describes is contiguous with several of the Barlow Pass trails. The Buzzard Point Trail is an easy road tour for Novice skiers, and provides a fine view of Hood only 0.5 mile from the sno-park.

TWIN LAKES TRAIL AND LOOP

(Map 35) This beautiful, marked forest trail is for Intermediate skiers who want a challenge. It is a 7.6-mile round trip to the upper lake, and 9.7 miles round trip on the loop that passes by both lakes. There is a cumulative elevation gain of 1,100 feet on the loop, and almost the same for the upper lake tour. If the snow is not good, the loop is tiring.

From the northeast corner of Barlow Pass Sno-Park climb the snow bank, go several yards, turn right (south), and ski through big timber along the Pacific Crest Trail (PCT). The trail climbs moderately to The Shoulder and then on to the nearby high point (4,550 feet) 1.3 miles from the trailhead.

At The Shoulder there is a brief view of Mount Hood and just off the trail a view down to Devils Half Acre and across to Barlow Ridge. The trail then descends gently along the east side of Ghost Ridge, and 2.3 miles from the trailhead is the junction of the PCT with the side trail to the Upper Twin Lake Trail.

The Upper Twin Lake Trail descends, levels out in old growth, then climbs through a small meadow and up two switchbacks to Bird Butte Pass at 4,500 feet. The trail then descends moderately through open forest for several hundred yards to the upper lake at 4,400 feet. The trail goes along the east shore to the south end where there is a view of the top of Hood.

The return trip is particularly exciting for most skiers from The Shoulder to the trailhead where an almost 1-mile hill demands control. As you pick up speed be concerned for other skiers ahead of you who are coming up the trail. Everyone loses control here in places, and there are many thrills and spills.

To ski the loop from the upper lake, follow the moderately steep trail down to the lower lake. This trail loop is best skied by Advanced skiers, who might enjoy the challenge of skiing an off-trail shortcut down the east side of the upper-lake outlet draw to the lower lake.

From the lower lake (see Frog Lake and Blue Box Pass chapter) ski up the draw 150 yards, turn left (west), and follow the loop trail over a low pass, then down to the PCT. Then follow the PCT north to Barlow Pass Sno-Park.

An alternative to these tours is to set up a car shuttle to Frog Lake Sno-Park, then ski from Barlow Pass to Frog Lake, thus shortening the tour and eliminating the descent from The Shoulder.

LOWER TWIN LAKE

(Map 35) This Intermediate ski tour on a 2.5-mile marked forest trail to the lake reaches a high point of 4,360 feet before descending to the lake. The elevation gain is 608 feet. The trail passes through impressive stands of hemlock trees to reach the beautiful, forested lake basin.

This is a good tour for advanced Novice or Intermediate skiers to test ability against a variety of moderate terrain challenges. Some route finding may be required. The heavy forest provides some shelter in case of stormy weather.

Locate the Pacific Crest Trail (PCT) at the north end of Frog Lake Sno-Park, then follow it as it winds gently upward through old-growth forest then through second growth. At 1.5 miles a side trail to Lower Twin Lake leaves the PCT at a right angle, climbing gently eastward for 100 yards to a pass at 4,460 feet.

From the pass make a long, gentle traverse downward, then turn sharply right and ski 150 yards to a point near the north shore of the lake. From here, the trail climbs to Upper Twin Lake (see Twin Lakes Trail earlier in this chapter). Leave the trail and descend an easy, short, but steep slope to the lake. If the lake is not solidly frozen, the west shore provides easy terrain for skiing and exploring. The lake is nestled in a deep, forested basin that offers ample scenic reward. It is possible to ski a loop trail to Upper Twin Lake then return on the PCT, a trip of just over 8 miles. A direct, but steeper, unmarked route from Lower Twin Lake to the upper lake follows the east side of a draw connecting the two lakes and is found back up the trail 150 yards on the return to the sno-park, at the right-angle turn to the left to the long traverse. Here, ski directly up 0.3 mile and climb only 240 feet to the upper lake.

GHOST RIDGE

(Map 35) This is the finest easily reached viewpoint on Mount Hood, requiring only a 4-mile round trip and a climb of 800 feet, the last 0.6 mile off-trail. The viewpoint is just off the Twin Lakes Trail and the reward is a panoramic view of the entire region.

From Barlow Pass Sno-Park ski the Twin Lakes Trail to The Shoulder, then continue on to the nearby high point of the trail. Leave the trail and enter dense, small trees to the west, quickly reaching an open slope (seen from The Shoulder if you skied up that trail). Climb this slope (4,800 feet) to its western edge for the best views. Continue to the top of the slope and climb moderately through forest, making your way through as best as possible

With the clouds on top of Ghost Ridge

where resistance is least. You will soon reach open slopes, then the top of Ghost Ridge, which is clear of trees. The view goes from Mounts Jefferson to Hood and sweeps across the entire Trillium Basin. You'll also see Mount Wilson and Broken Top far to the south. The lower-overlook slope is for Intermediate skiers, and the summit for strong Intermediates. The descent is not demanding if the snow is favorable.

PALMATEER OVERLOOK

(Map 35) This exceptional viewpoint near Barlow Pass is reached only with some effort, as off-trail Intermediate skiing is required. The top of the ridge is a 5.4-mile round trip with a cumulative elevation gain of 900 feet.

Ski the PCT south from Barlow Pass, over the high point, then down to the Upper Twin Lake Trail junction. Take the left fork and descend about 300 yards to old-growth forest. Stay on the trail and after about 150 yards through the old growth, the trail starts gently uphill through second growth. This is where the off-trail skiing begins.

At the edge of the old growth (and the 2-mile marker) turn left off the trail. Keeping left, traverse on an almost-level course through old growth. If you drop too far to the right you will encounter difficult slide alder thickets—if so, keep above the thickets. After 300 yards enter second-growth pines and firs. Contour where necessary to avoid problems, but head slightly downhill where possible and you will ski right into Palmateer Camp Meadows. Sounds difficult, but it is easy, and it is hard to get lost as all downhill directions lead into the meadows.

From the upper end of the meadows ski east and climb the low ridge, then continue up the narrow, tree-covered ridge, which soon widens and opens up. A moderately steep slope leads to the ultimate viewpoint at 4,400 feet. Several picturesque snags rule over this remarkable ridgecrest and viewpoint.

The view, to say the least, is spectacular. Devils Half Acre is far below, and the U-shaped Barlow Creek valley extends away for miles. The view of Hood is especially striking due to foreground ridges and hills that sweep grandly up to its vast snowfields. To stand here with the snow dropping off on all sides is indeed exciting.

Although the tour is quite easy, carry a map and compass and ski the tour only if you can leave a good track for your return.

DEVILS HALF ACRE LOOP

(Map 35) This Intermediate 2.5-mile marked loop starts with a road descent to a delightful meadow in the deep Barlow Creek valley and returns along a lovely forest trail, following the route of historic Barlow Road. The elevation loss to Devils Half Acre, the first leg of the loop, is 400 feet.

Sign at Barlow Pass

From the northeast corner of Barlow Pass Sno-Park descend Road 3530 in a southeasterly direction for 1 mile to Devils Half Acre. The road descends at a moderate grade as it winds its way through thick forest to the meadow, where Mount Hood can be seen.

On the way down the road you will notice a trail sign marking a branch trail to the left (north), the Mineral Jane Trail, which in summer is seen to be the heavily worn pioneer Barlow Road, descending to Devils Half Acre. The loop may also be skied downward in this direction, but you will find more difficult sections if you ski the loop clockwise. Skiing counterclockwise, down Road 3530, directly to Devils Half Acre, is the easiest direction.

However, if you choose to ski clockwise, down the old Barlow Road (to the left on the branch trail), be warned that the first 300 yards is quite steep, in fact nasty, and should not be skied if the snow is crusty or hardpacked. This side trail down the old road is called the Mineral Jane Trail, which continues on to Barlow Saddle and White River. Not far beyond the steep section the trail enters a small meadow, and this is where it goes left and climbs through forest to the north.

To ski the Devils Half Acre Loop, turn right (south) in the small meadow and follow trail markers as the trail enters beautiful old growth. There are three very short, moderately steep sections on the trail. It leaves the forest and enters a long side meadow that connects with the Devils Half Acre meadow. From the main meadow turn northwest and ski up Road 3530 to complete the loop.

BARLOW SADDLE AND WHITE RIVER CONNECTOR TRAILS

(Map 39) Barlow Saddle (4,000 feet) is a wide, clearcut saddle at the west base of Barlow Ridge. Boy Scout Ridge is west of the saddle across Highway 35. Occasionally it is possible to park at the Barlow Ridge road on Highway 35, but this is not dependable. If you park here, park outside the fog line, a legal way to park if you are not in a sno-park.

Barlow Saddle is the access point to Barlow Ridge, a scenic tour, and to the Boy Scout Ridge roads. Most skiers will ski the Mineral Jane Trail from either Barlow Pass or White River West Sno-Park to reach Barlow Saddle. Two interesting loops can be skied by using the Boy Scout Ridge trails.

Barlow Saddle will be the site, in the distant future, of a sno-park. A clearcut was planned and the timber removed at the site itself several years ago.

Mineral Jane Trail. (Map 39) This 3-mile marked Intermediate trail connects Barlow Pass with White River. From White River the trail continues on to Bennett Pass as the Mineral Jane Trail East.

From Barlow Pass Sno-Park descend the Devils Half Acre Trail 250 yards, then turn left onto the Mineral Jane Trail and down a difficult, often nasty,

Cornice at saddle on Barlow Ridge

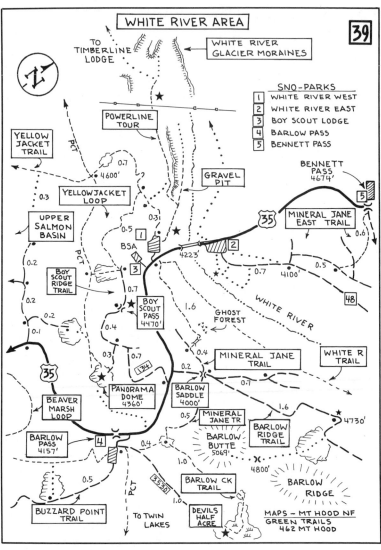

and steep section of the old Barlow Road to a small meadow. Go left and climb a forested hillside (a moderately steep descent in the opposite direction) to a series of clearcuts and road that leads to Barlow Saddle 0.9 mile from Barlow Pass. From Barlow Saddle the trail follows a road through a clearcut, then leaves the road to cross Mineral Creek, then climbs gently to the highway bridge at White River opposite White River West Sno-Park.

Mineral Jane Trail, dedicated in 1986, is a compound name recognizing both Mineral Creek and Jane Cox, a long-time skier who organized many friends to build a skier bridge and the trail that bears her name. The Barlow Ranger District directed the efforts of the volunteers and provided work tools and materials for the bridge.

BOY SCOUT RIDGE AND PANORAMA DOME

(Map 39) Boy Scout Ridge is a rolling, old-growth-forested, partially clearcut, wide ridge that extends from Barlow Pass northward about 2 miles. The northern half loses its ridgelike form as it merges into the wide, gentle slopes descending from the Timberline Lodge area where the Yellowjacket Trail crosses. The PCT, climbing from Barlow Pass and crossing Panorama Dome, goes north along the very west edge of the ridge and crosses the Yellowjacket Trail. The PCT is marked from the Dome, and just to the east a nearby road goes north from the Dome along the top of the ridge, crosses Boy Scout Pass, and dead-ends 0.7 mile north of the pass. At the pass, leave the road and climb open slopes eastward for fine views.

Panorama Dome and Boy Scout Ridge. (Map 39) This Intermediate 3-mile route is mostly marked, gains 270 feet, and extends from Barlow Pass to White River. The 0.5-mile section from Barlow Pass to Panorama Dome is not marked, and although the PCT traverses this short section it cannot be followed. From the entrance road to Barlow Pass Sno-Park walk down the highway east 100 yards, then climb upward onto the ridge making your way as best as possible through scattered openings, an awkward ascent of 200 feet to the open slope that is the Dome. It is a rounded slope that faces west and offers a 270-degree panorama, including Hood and the Trillium Basin.

A marked trail starts here and goes north along a road, through old growth, and crosses Boy Scout Pass (4,470 feet) to near the end of the ridgetop road. Here it turns left and splits, with one branch going to White River on a forest trail and the other branch climbing a short slope to join the PCT, which goes gently uphill to join the Yellowjacket Trail.

From Panorama Dome a marked trail goes north, to the left of the road, then descends northwestward and joins the PCT along the west side of the ridge, ultimately crossing the Yellowjacket Trail and going on to Timberline Lodge along an unmarked, seldom-skied route.

From Panorama Dome the road route goes 0.3 mile north to where a side road (Road 134) descends toward Highway 35 and Barlow Saddle, permitting a skiing loop with the Mineral Jane Trail and Barlow Pass.

Panorama Dome Loop. (Map 39) Starting from Barlow Pass this partially marked 2.8-mile Advanced loop takes you to a scenic viewpoint through old growth, on roads, and on forest trails, with some off-trail skiing. See the Panorama Dome description above, then ski to the Dome. Here, pick up the road (not the PCT) 0.3 mile to Road 134 and descend it to

Highway 35. Cross the highway, ski to Barlow Saddle, then return to the sno-park along the Mineral Jane Trail.

BARLOW RIDGE

(Map 39) This Intermediate tour can extend up to 2.8 miles one way and has an elevation gain of 730 feet. Strong Novices will make it with some difficulty, but the long descent will be very difficult if crusty. The tour follows a road that climbs gently up the north side of Barlow Ridge to a fine viewpoint of the White River valley, then continues on the level through several clearcuts to a dead end.

The tour is best started from Barlow Pass, the closest sno-park, for a round trip of 7.4 miles. Ski the Mineral Jane Trail to Barlow Saddle, then turn east onto the road that goes up the ridge. It soon forks, and the left forks dead-end in clearcuts with few rewards. Continue straight ahead climbing steadily and gently through old-growth hemlock and noble fir forest for 1.6 miles to the high point (4,730 feet), where the road makes a sharp turn, levels out, and passes the first clearcut.

At the high point on the shoulder of the curve there is an inspiring view of Mount Hood and the sprawling White River valley 1,000 feet below. You can see up the valley all the way to its head at the White River glacier and from there down along its deep, twisting course as it widens and flattens out. Covered with winter snow, the sand and gravel flats far below form interesting finger patterns groping downvalley.

Beyond the high-point curve there is a clearcut, now rapidly overgrowing, that leads to the scenic saddle between Barlow Ridge and Barlow Butte, a climb that will require some route finding. The summit of Barlow Ridge can be reached by steep climbing from several clearcuts farther east. The crest of Barlow Ridge is thickly forested and difficult to ski.

Barlow Butte. (Map 39) The summit of the butte (5,069 feet), best attempted by strong Intermediate skiers, is the site of a long-gone fire lookout. It is a 1,069-foot climb from Barlow Saddle, but has no views as it is forested. The summit is best reached by skiing to the high point (4,730 feet) of the road (see Barlow Ridge tour) then around the curve to the clearcut that climbs southwest to the saddle between the ridge and the butte. Locating the fine views at the saddle at 4,800 feet will require some route finding. From the road's high point it is 1 mile to the summit. From the saddle, it is a 300-foot climb to the summit, and the reward is the descent of the north or northwest sides down through open forest. The westside summer trail is direct and steep and brushy in places. It is not a recommended ascent or descent route.

Chapter 15

WHITE RIVER

This immensely popular area offers six different tours and access to two nearby touring areas. White River is located 7 miles east of Government Camp on Highway 35. There are two large sno-parks, one at either end of the White River bridge. A third, much smaller, sno-park just south of White River West Sno-Park is for visitors to the nearby year-round Boy Scouts of America lodge.

The main attractions of the area are open, gentle slopes above the highway bridge and a gravel quarry formerly known as The Bowl, but now called The Gravel Pit due to the extensive ongoing excavations that have destroyed the old bowl. The Pit entertains young and old, skilled and unskilled, and is usually crowded with skiers practicing and enjoying the slopes. It is one of the most popular and congested Nordic skiing areas on Mount Hood.

Another attraction of the White River area is the physical beauty of the wide, flat valley enclosed by impressive, forested ridges. Except for the Timberline Lodge area, White River is the only Nordic sports area where you need only step from your car to behold truly breathtaking scenery.

The downvalley view alone is worth the drive, with massive, forested Bennett Ridge and snowy-sided, tentlike Bonney Butte on the left and the rugged Barlow Ridge and Barlow Butte on the right. The lower valley drops impressively into distant, hazy depths, and cloud ghosts often writhe about the ridges and through the trees, imparting an ethereal touch to the scene. On special occasions, each successive tree-clad ridge is outlined by white mist, giving a powerful three-dimensional effect. Regardless of weather, even with the high ridgetops hidden in clouds, the downvalley view is ever changing and always splendid.

The view up the valley is also one of great beauty. The mighty guardian, Mount Hood, dominates the scene, with its intense whiteness bold against the sky. On occasion, lenticular clouds move about the summit or snow banners blow from the highest point. The valley itself, with its flat bottom and steeply tilted sides, leads the eye upward along the twisting, forest-edged corridor to the mountaintop. It is not surprising, then, that skiers are attracted time and again to this beautiful winter setting.

GRAVEL PIT TOUR

(Map 39) The Gravel Pit is the focus for many beginners. It is only a 1-mile round trip over gentle slopes for skiers along a marked ski trail or the paralleling quarry road along the edge of the White River. The elevation gain is a modest 100 feet.

To reach the Gravel Pit area, ski uphill 0.4 mile from White River West Sno-Park on the wide road on the north side of the sno-park, and follow the crowd. In summer this is a dusty area, but in winter it is transformed into a long, open ridge, offering slopes and practice areas for skiers of every skill level. It is not unusual for as many as 200 skiers to be in the area at any one time.

The other route follows the first 500 yards of the Yellowjacket Trail starting from the center of the sno-park's west end at a marked trailhead. This trail climbs through scattered lodgepole pines as it twists uphill to where it enters tall trees. Here, turn right and angle upward 200 yards through an open area to the top of the Gravel Pit ridge for a fine view of Hood. Drop down into the pit, or continue upward along the edge to ski up the White River on the bench above the valley floor.

On the way up to the Gravel Pit scattered trees and open areas provide good skiing and practice. The top of the Gravel Pit ridge is at 4,400 feet, a 200-foot climb from the sno-park. Rock removal from the quarry in recent years has considerably altered the shape of the area and will continue to narrow the scenic plateau above the quarry.

POWERLINE TOUR

(Map 39) This 3-mile unmarked round-trip tour climbs 380 feet following the "plateau" above the Gravel Pit, a tree-studded bench overlooking the White River. On the return, it offers a nice downhill run. Novices will struggle to get to the bench, and struggle on the final descent on the return, so this is a tour recommended for Intermediate skiers.

Ski to the Gravel Pit (see preceding tour) and climb the moderately steep ridge on the south edge. Then proceed up gentle slopes winding through scattered lodgepole pines. There are several trails here (none marked), all leading upward, so there is no way to lose the route. The overhead powerline, serving the Mount Hood Meadows Ski Area, is about 1 mile above the Gravel Pit. But continue a short distance farther to a fine off-trail viewpoint of the White River canyon. Most skiers turn around here and return, enjoying a fine downhill run.

From the high point above the powerline you may continue another 0.5 mile, climbing steadily through scattered pines to where the slope leads gently out onto the flats of the White River at 5,080 feet. (Up to here a low bluff prevents easy descent to the river flats). If adventuresome, cross the river on snow bridges, usually with no trouble, or by hopping rocks, and ski down the north side of the river to the highway, or just follow the obvious flats along the south side. The northside flats are always less crowded and more interesting. Be careful near the river, and stay off the steep south-facing slopes on the north side of the valley, which may be dangerous in warm weather.

WHITE RIVER GLACIER MORAINES

(Map 39) This superb tour for Intermediates takes you on a 4-mile round trip, with elevation gain of 980 feet, to the foot of giant moraines set in a wild scene of alpine solitude. The route follows the gentle snowfields along the flat bottom of the White River (or the Powerline Tour). On the return there is a long downhill run.

From White River West Sno-Park ski up the valley. Along the 2-mile ascent you will find the scenery almost overwhelming. The steep, snowy sidewalls and forested ridges enclosing the flat valley bottom are impressive as the valley appears to turn and twist endlessly upward. You will feel a strong sense of adventure as you approach the moraines, which resemble ridges in the bottom of the valley. The White River glacier has been receding for years, and its present snout is about 1.5 miles above this point. This is a fine place for a spring picnic lunch in the warm sunshine. One of the moraines is flat-topped and may be climbed for even better views. You will see Barlow Butte and Barlow Ridge, and to the south Mount Jefferson.

It is usually possible to cross the river on snow bridges if you have skied up the north side of the valley, but it may also be crossed on foot if necessary, by stepping on stones. Take great care, however, and use your poles for balance.

Near the moraines, you will see on the south side of the valley a short, almost bowl-like side valley. This is the route leading to or from Timberline Lodge, only a mile farther. (Before attempting these steep and potentially dangerous slopes, however, read the description for the Timberline Lodge to White River tour in Chapter 9.)

The lower valley is very safe, but beyond the 1-mile point the steep sidewalls to the north offer potential avalanche danger during or after heavy snowfall and in periods of warm weather. Stay off and away from the bottoms of these slopes.

YELLOWJACKET AND WHITE RIVER TRAILS LOOP

(Map 39) This 1.9-mile marked loop for Advanced skiers climbs about 300 feet and will challenge most skiers. The loop is composed by joining three separate trails, and is entirely through forest.

From White River West Sno-Park (at the center of the west end) find the Yellowjacket Trail sign and ski 500 yards uphill on the trail and enter forest. Ski to a nearby junction with the Boy Scout Ridge Trail. This is where the loop itself begins. Ski the Boy Scout Trail as it contours through forest on a sidehill for 0.5 mile. Near the road end on Boy Scout Ridge, the trail then turns westward in an opening and climbs 0.1 mile to join the Pacific Crest Trail (PCT), where it climbs gently to join the Yellowjacket Trail, which in turn is followed northward and back toward White River at first through a large meadow then forest to a final, moderately steep descent at the loop's end.

WHITE RIVER TO MINERAL JANE TO BARLOW SADDLE TO BOY SCOUT RIDGE LOOP

(Map 39) This 5-mile Advanced loop is partly marked and should present no problems in route finding. The loop gains 500 feet of elevation. From White River West Sno-Park follow directions for the Yellowjacket-White River Trails Loop, ski the Boy Scout Trail, but continue on Boy Scout Ridge along the road over Boy Scout Pass (4,470 feet), then descend Road 134 and cross the highway to the road leading east and down to nearby Barlow Saddle. Here turn north and ski the Mineral Jane Trail back to your starting point.

MINERAL JANE TRAIL TO BARLOW PASS

(Map 39) This Intermediate connector trail goes to Barlow Pass and gives access to Barlow Ridge and several loops. The north end of the trail starts across the highway from White River West Sno-Park, and the first 2 miles are a lovely ski experience. Explore off the trail into the ghost forest between the trail and the White River. Ski through these old, silver snags and join the White River Trail to form a return loop. (For details of the entire Mineral Jane Trail see Chapter 14.)

WHITE RIVER EAST AREA

(Map 39) Park at White River East Sno-Park, climb the snowbank, and ski east into a nearby, lovely area of scattered, small trees and small openings that offer perfect terrain for all skill levels. It is an area for just strolling on skis, but it is really best for setting up short practice loops, crossing dips and shallow gullies in places to make it more demanding and to test your skills—and to develop confidence on the changing terrain. When bored, reverse your direction and ski the loop the other way. Ski the dips and gullies at different angles. As the track gets used it gets better and faster, helping to improve your technique and confidence. When all this gets boring, just ski over to the edge of the White River for a peaceful and scenic experience away from the other skiers.

Mineral Jane Trail East to Bennett Pass. (Map 39) This 2-mile Intermediate trail, climbing 575 feet to Bennett Pass, follows Road 48, then logging roads, and finally a forest ski trail from White River East Sno-Park to Bennett Pass along a marked route. The upper end of the trail passes through beautiful old growth and along traces of an old wagon road.

The upper trail area was scheduled to be logged in 1988. Efforts by the author, Chris Shore of the Sierra Club, and the Sierra Club Legal Defense Fund halted, for the immediate future at least, the Fishhook Resell timber sale.

From White River East Sno-Park ski northeast down Road 48 0.7 mile, then turn uphill on a side road for 50 yards, then turn right onto another road and follow trail markers off the road into forest to Bennett Pass. The first 500 yards or so of Road 48, an uninteresting road to ski, may be bypassed by immediately entering the scattered trees west of Road 48 and skiing parallel to the road as far as possible.

WHITE RIVER TRAIL AND BARLOW CREEK PIONEER ROAD LOOP

(Map 39) Two trails go downriver, one from White River West Sno-Park and the other from Barlow Pass, and they join at Barlow Crossing about 8 miles to the east and 1,300 feet lower. These two can be joined to form a 19-mile loop, using the Mineral Jane Trail as a connector.

Or each of the long legs of the loop (White River Trail, or Barlow Creek Pioneer Road/Devils Half Acre) can be skied to connect with Highway 26, a one-way tour of about 15 miles. The last leg of this one-way tour follows Road 43 5.2 miles to meet Highway 26 just 2 miles south of Skyline Sno-Park.

Anyone skiing the loop, or the one-way out to the highway, should be an Advanced skier. Skiers just exploring the first few miles of each trail will find the trails easy (except the descent to Devils Half Acre) and suitable for Intermediate skiers.

The Barlow Creek Pioneer Road (via Devils Half Acre) is heavily forested beyond the meadow and follows the old, twisting, primitive road. There are no views below the meadow.

The White River Trail follows the open flats, then scattered trees and openings. The trail starts at the Mineral Jane trailhead across the highway from White River West Sno-Park.

These are long, tiring tours, so pick good snow conditions and be sure the snowline extends to Barlow Crossing at 3,000 feet, usually a matter of conjecture. Be prepared to stride diagonally most of the distance as the grades are very gentle.

Chapter 16

BENNETT PASS

Bennett Pass is the trailhead for a number of fine tours. Most are rated Intermediate or Advanced due to the distances, though Novice skiers often ski the first 2 miles of Bennett Ridge, which are not steep. At 4,674 feet, Bennett Pass is the highest highway pass on Mount Hood. It is situated on Highway 35 on the southeast side of Mount Hood 2.2 miles northeast of White River and just 200 yards south of the entrance to Mount Hood Meadows Ski Area. Bennett Pass is 9.7 miles east of Government Camp and 32 miles south of Hood River.

Bennett Pass, Hood River Meadows, and Pocket Creek are contiguous and are connected by trails that form interesting and sometimes long loops. Connector trails provide short, direct access routes between the ski areas. There is an interesting assortment of trail combinations from which to select a tour suitable to your skill level and your ambitions for the day.

The most popular trail in the area is the road tour along Bennett Ridge to the Terrible Traverse, 2.4 miles from the pass. Beyond the traverse, the tours are long and often demanding, earning a rating of Advanced even though the roads are seldom steep.

With more skiers on the trails each year, tracks are being pushed farther and farther. Distant objectives that were previously too far to break trail to are now becoming common goals.

The popularity of the area has created a parking problem as there is not room at the pass for a large sno-park. Carpool and park carefully so there is more room for others. If parking is filled, drive to Hood River Meadows 1 mile north, or to Teacup Lake or Clark Creek Sno-Park farther along. There is a toilet near the trailhead information board.

BENNETT RIDGE TRAIL

(Map 40) The trail starts at Bennett Pass Sno-Park and goes 2.4 miles to the Terrible Traverse along a splendid, rolling, forested ridge following a primitive road with an elevation gain of 380 feet. If you continue to Bonney Junction, 4.3 miles from the highway, the gain is 840 feet. For capable skiers, the trail goes on to Camp Windy or Bonney Butte. The trail's main attractions are the splendid old growth and occasional views. The high elevation of the ridge often ensures deeper and better snow conditions than in other areas.

The trail first climbs on the north side of the ridge, and after a mile crosses to the other side for a long, gentle descent. Along the way, and just 0.2 mile beyond the high point (which is 1.1 miles from the trailhead), a logging

*Clouds in White River valley with Barlow Ridge, Frog Lake Buttes,
and Mount Jefferson beyond*

road was built in 1991 along the north crest of the ridge paralleling for 0.4
mile the Bennett Ridge Trail. There are two narrow, steep clearcuts along
this side road that provide grand views of the East Fork Hood River valley,
Gunsight Ridge, Elk Mountain, and Lamberson Butte, and of Hood rising
serenely to the west. This short side trip is a must for all skiers on Bennett
Ridge. The clearcuts will lure Backcountry Telemark skiers as the north-
facing slopes will often have powder snow. But skiing these slopes requires considerable caution as several feet of snow are required to cover
obstacles.

In addition to the exceptional views from this side road, the broad saddle
at the foot of the S-turns also has had its north slopes logged, creating equally
good views of the region. For Novice skiers this saddle, 1.9 miles from the
trailhead, is a good place to rest then turn around. From here on the trail is
difficult for inexperienced skiers as the trail climbs and descends, generat-
ing many problems for those lacking downhill skiing skills. The S-turns
climb moderately to where two open sidehills provide views and favorite
rest and sunning spots for lunch breaks on clear days.

Within 200 yards the trail descends to Windy Saddle at the west foot of
the Terrible Traverse, which is a steep 180-yard-long sidehill traverse on the
north side of the ridge immediately under a snow-covered cliff. This notori-
ous place turns back many Novice skiers, who do not wish to cross what
appears to be a dangerous slope. In summer the Terrible Traverse is a narrow roadbed carved out of a rock face; in winter it appears as a steep,

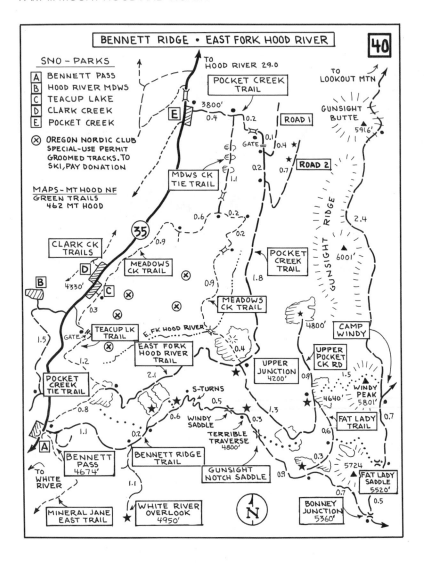

inclined snow shelf with intimidating slopes dropping off below.

In years of deep snowpack the Terrible Traverse is steeper than usual. It is always impressive, but few skiers have slipped here and there is no record of an injury. At times of deep, fresh snowfall, especially during or immediately after a storm, or during very warm weather, this slope could avalanche. An icy or crusty surface also increases the difficulty. Always be cautious here, and once you decide to cross on skis or on foot, proceed across rapidly.

At the east end of the Terrible Traverse there is a safe, level spot on which to rest. The platform offers grand views down the length of the East Fork Hood River valley, into upper Pocket Creek, and across to Gunsight Ridge and to Lookout Mountain, miles away to the northeast. Mount Hood and Elk Mountain are also seen.

The trail quickly passes through the prominent rock towers of Gunsight Notch, then descends 100 yards to Gunsight Notch Saddle before once again regaining the south side of the ridge for the rest of the way to Bonney Junction. On the way up there is easy access to the viewpoint on Fat Lady Trail and farther up there are two openings from which Frog Lake Buttes, Barlow Ridge, and Mount Jefferson may be seen in addition to the distant low peaks west of the Trillium Basin.

At Bonney Junction (5,360 feet), a forested saddle, roads lead to Camp Windy and Bonney Butte. From this junction, 1.6 miles from the Terrible Traverse, you can ski south to Bonney Butte or Bonney Meadows, or north to Camp Windy, Gunsight Ridge, Badger Butte, Badger Lake, and Grasshopper Point. You can even ski to Lookout Mountain, but this is best approached from the north.

White River Overlook. (Map 40) One mile from Bennett Pass, at a high point on the ridge, a logging road goes south, curving and remaining generally level, for over 1 mile, then climbing a steep hill. Ski to its end, and enter the forest to a natural hillside meadow with fine views of the White River valley, Bonney Butte to the left and Barlow Ridge on the right.

BONNEY BUTTE AND MEADOWS

(Maps 40 & 41) Site of a former fire lookout, the butte is 6 miles and a climb of 1,500 feet from Bennett Pass. The tour along primitive roads except for the last half mile or less is not steep and is rated Intermediate to Advanced. On a clear day the view is unrivaled in the Mount Hood area. You can see not only the Eastern Oregon desert, but also eight Cascade volcanoes. The view 2,500 feet down into the White River valley with Hood at its head is truly grand.

Follow the Bennett Ridge Trail (see preceding tour) to Bonney Junction 4.3 miles from the trailhead. Keep right and make a level traverse across the

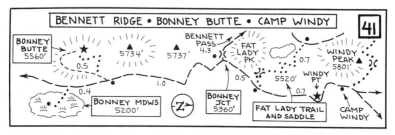

top of a clearing, climb through old growth to a shoulder, then descend southward through a beautiful forest of slender, pointed firs that is unique to the area.

The trail descends gently through the postcard scene of firs to Bonney Meadows, 1 mile south of the shoulder on a side road to the left. If you are headed up Bonney Butte, a long, low ridge, turn off to the right and either follow an old road to the south foot of the butte as it circles upward to the crest, or just ski through small, widely set firs to the top, a short 240-foot climb. On top there is an unobstructed view. You will see Broken Top, the Sisters, the tip of Three-Fingered Jack, Jefferson, Hood, and Adams. The return is a wonderful downhill glide from Bonney Junction, a bit fast at times but never intimidating.

CAMP WINDY

(Maps 40 & 41) Most of the 5 miles to Camp Windy are eventful and scenic with a gain of 726 feet. Camp Windy is located 1 mile northeast of Bonney Junction at the head of Boulder Creek. It is little more than several open slopes with scattered trees in a wide, gentle basin sloping eastward. From Camp Windy one road leads north along Gunsight Ridge and Lookout Mountain, and one leads northeast to Badger Butte, Badger Lake, and Grasshopper Point, site of a former fire lookout at the edge of the Cascade forest and eastern drylands.

Ski to Bonney Junction (see Bennett Ridge Trail). From there ski north through forest on a scenic route to Windy Point, a shoulder with unusual rock formations, and good views to the north and east. This breezy shoulder, often windpacked, is the logical end of the tour as Camp Windy just 0.4 mile farther has little more to offer unless you are skiing farther out Gunsight Ridge or plan to climb over the ridge and descend to upper Pocket Creek by way of the Windy Peak connector route.

The road junction at Camp Windy is not well defined if you are skiing farther. The Badger Lake/Grasshopper Point road descends gently from the junction and the Gunsight Ridge road climbs gently. The "camp" is well named, for exposed as it is to the east and south, it is often cold and windy.

Windy Peak (Point 5801). (Maps 40 & 41) As you ski past the gargoyle-like rocks at Windy Point, just south of Camp Windy, Windy Peak is the obvious high point on the ridge above Camp Windy. A 400-foot ascent from Camp Windy up open slopes is worth the effort as the view from the ridgetop is breathtaking. Mount Hood rises 7,000 feet above the East Fork Hood River valley below you. In addition, you will see Adams and many other features of the Cascades.

Windy Peak Traverse. (Map 40) This 1.5-mile off-trail tour from Camp Windy to Pocket Creek adds a new dimension to skiing the Camp Windy area and offers an alternative return to Bennett Pass for adventuresome skiers. It is a rugged, zigzagging descent from Windy Peak directly down 1,100 feet to the "Mount Adams view clearcut" on the upper Pocket Creek road.

From Camp Windy climb generally open slopes to the broad saddle just north of Windy Peak (Point 5801), then descend the west side down moderately steep forest, at times through forest that confines your movements. On your descent, if you miss the Mount Adams view clearcut, you cannot overshoot the road beyond because it is obvious, and it will lead you south to the clearcut.

BENNETT RIDGE AND POCKET CREEK LOOPS

(Map 40) The following four Advanced loops are suggested for skiers who are tired of skiing "out and back" and who want to add spice to their experiences by doing some "adventure skiing":
- Fat Lady Loop—via Fat Lady Trail/Fat Lady Saddle/Bonney Junction (2.2 miles)
- Terrible Traverse Loop—via Bennett Ridge/Fat Lady Trail/East Fork Trail/Pocket Creek Tie Trail (3.7 miles)
- Camp Windy Loop—via Bonney Junction/Windy Peak Traverse/Fat Lady Trail (4.3 miles)
- Camp Windy Loop—via East Fork Trail/Windy Peak Traverse/Bonney Junction/Bennett Ridge Trail (11.2 miles)

Chapter 17

EAST FORK HOOD RIVER REGION

The East Fork Hood River region encompasses a large area on the east side of Mount Hood located below both Mount Hood Meadows Ski Area and Bennett Ridge. The area, divided by Highway 35, extends 4 miles downhill to Pocket Creek Sno-Park and the Robinhood area. The East Fork basin of some 7 square miles contains 32 miles of ski trails. The area's complexity is best presented by describing the individual areas separately.

The East Fork Hood River flows through the center of the area, but is seldom seen except for three bridge crossings. Its tributary creeks are more visible to skiers since they are crossed several times on skier bridges.

The area includes two groomed-track systems—the Mount Hood Meadows Nordic Center, a fee-use area, and the Teacup Lake area trails, where a donation is requested. The miles of Teacup Lake groomed tracks operate on a donation-requested basis, and interestingly, its special-use area is completely surrounded by trails constructed by the Forest Service, for which there is no fee for use.

The numerous trails of this area are in the jurisdiction of the Hood River Ranger District, which deserves a great deal of appreciation from skiers for the wide diversity and many miles of trails constructed since the mid-1980s. Maintenance on an annual basis is beyond the ability and funding of the ranger district, so it depends on volunteers. But it takes many volunteers to replace markers, remove fallen trees, and cut brush. Please consider volunteering your services for even just one day to one of the ranger districts on Mount Hood, or elsewhere. You will find it a rewarding experience.

HOOD RIVER MEADOWS

(Map 42) Several trails and a Nordic Center are accessed from Hood River Meadows Sno-Park, reached by a turnoff on Highway 35 11 miles from Government Camp and 1.1 miles below and north of Bennett Pass. Most of the trails here are "out and back," but there is an outstanding 10-mile loop linking the area with Pocket Creek.

Nordic Center Groomed Tracks. (Map 42) The Mount Hood Meadows Nordic Center (lessons and rentals) is located in Hood River Meadows Sno-Park. Originally, the groomed tracks were only in the meadows and along the Sahalie Falls road. With the addition of miles of new groomed trails for the 1992–1993 season on both sides of the sno-park access road, it remains to be seen if the tracks in the meadows and the Sahalie Falls road will continue to be part of the fee-use system.

The presence of fee-use groomed tracks in these two locations may have

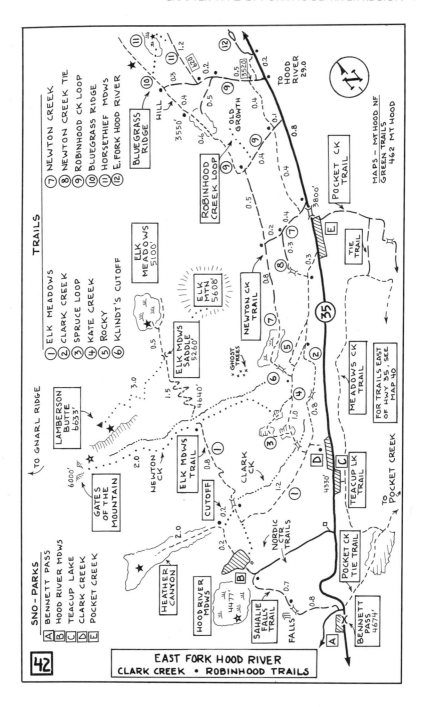

TRAILS

① ELK MEADOWS
② CLARK CREEK
③ SPRUCE LOOP
④ KATE CREEK
⑤ ROCKY
⑥ KLINDT'S CUTOFF

⑦ NEWTON CREEK
⑧ NEWTON CREEK TIE
⑨ ROBINHOOD CK LOOP
⑩ BLUEGRASS RIDGE
⑪ HORSETHIEF MDWS
⑫ E. FORK HOOD RIVER

MAPS – MT HOOD NF
GREEN TRAILS
462 MT HOOD

SNO-PARKS
A BENNETT PASS
B HOOD RIVER MDWS
C TEACUP LAKE
D CLARK CREEK
E POCKET CREEK

42

EAST FORK HOOD RIVER
CLARK CREEK • ROBINHOOD TRAILS

inhibited skiers from using them. It is legal to ski the meadows and the Sahalie Falls road (former Highway 35) if there are groomed tracks there as long as non-paying skiers stay off the groomed tracks.

The miles of groomed tracks start at the southeast corner of the sno-park and parallel the Clark Creek trail system from which they are screened by forest. Special "linear logging" sales were designed to open the forest for these groomed trails.

Hood River Meadows and Sahalie Falls. (Map 42) Hood River Meadows at 4,477 feet is situated in a beautiful, deep bowl formed by forested hills. It is a scenic jewel of the region. Both the meadow and the Sahalie Falls road are suitable for Novice skiers. The area routes are not marked. The falls are 1 mile from the sno-park and a climb of only 100 feet. The falls are viewed from a bridge on the road. By continuing beyond them, you will in 0.8 mile reach Bennett Pass.

The downhill ski-area chairlift near the large, circular meadow does not intrude on the quiet atmosphere of the meadow. The impressive east face of Hood, towering 6,700 feet above, is visible. The meadow and the forest edge offer an opportunity for exploring and the quiet contemplation of nature.

The Sahalie Falls Trail follows a portion of old Highway 35, now a scenic summer bypass road. From the opening to the meadows off the old highway, follow the road south as it climbs gently uphill past the falls, and then on to where it joins the access road to Mount Hood Meadows Ski Area on Highway 35 near Bennett Pass, 1.8 miles from the sno-park. This is an easy tour, and there is a pleasant, safe, downhill run on the return trip. The falls and the meadows may also be reached by skiing from Bennett Pass following the snow-covered scenic road.

HEATHER CANYON TRAIL

(Map 42) The unmarked Heather Canyon route is one of the most scenic on Hood, following beautiful, winding meadows uphill along Clark Creek. The 2.2-mile one-way Intermediate tour climbs 800 feet and offers a long downhill return run. The tour in the valley bottom is rated Intermediate. The entire route is used by alpine skiers descending from above, and the lower canyon, being narrower, demands particular alertness by Nordic skiers, who should ski along the edges of the run.

At Hood River Meadows Sno-Park climb the snow bank at the center of the north side and enter a wide lane into the forest. There is a sign here indicating the status of avalanche conditions along the upper part of the route. The trail soon turns left into the narrow canyon where it climbs gently but persistently up the enchanting valley contained by steep, forested ridges. About 2.2 miles from the sno-park the meadows end and you are standing at the lower end of the upper canyon, which is wide, impressive and immensely scenic. On the north a bare glacial moraine rises 650 feet, and on the south a massive ridge climbs steeply to the runs of the ski area. Here you are 800 feet above your starting point.

Farther on, the canyon can be dangerous, so use good judgment if you wish to continue climbing. A witness to the danger of the area is an avalanche gun emplacement far up to the left on the ridge. Heed the warning sign at the sno-park as well as one farther along the trail. Also use your common sense. If you know little about avalanches or snow structure, proceed no farther, even if the signs indicate the area is open. Instead, enjoy the long, euphoric run back to the trailhead.

Heather Canyon Cutoff. (Map 42) This pleasant, unmarked 0.2-mile cutoff leaves the Heather Canyon Trail 0.2 mile from the sno-park at the lower end of the narrow meadows. Go right (east) into the trees then climb to the right along the abrupt edge of an old streambank to the Elk Meadows Trail.

To ski from the Elk Meadows Trail to the Heather Canyon Trail, ski to the Clark Creek bridge (single log with railings) and turn uphill before crossing the bridge. The Heather Canyon Cutoff route follows near the creek's edge as it parallels the creek.

CLARK CREEK AND ROBINHOOD AREA

(Map 42) The many trails of this area starting from Clark Creek Sno-Park, and lower down from Pocket Creek Sno-Park, with both areas connected by trails, offer many loops and trail choices and some off-trail terrain. The Elk Meadows Trail leads uphill to several marvelous Backcountry tours. The Robinhood area, at an elevation of 3,550 feet, occasionally has minimal snow but is wonderfully scenic and is best reached from Pocket Creek Sno-Park. It offers several loops, all especially suited to less-experienced skiers.

Clark Creek Sno-Park is 1.5 miles below and north of Bennett Pass. Pocket Creek Sno-Park is 1.5 miles below Clark Creek Sno-Park toward the town of Hood River. There are toilets at both Clark Creek and Pocket Creek Sno-Parks.

Elk Meadows Trail. (Map 42) This 2-mile trail climbs 400 feet to Newton Creek below Elk Mountain, at first along a 1.2-mile built-for-skiing trail to the Clark Creek single-log bridge where it joins the summer Elk Meadows hiking trail. This trail is rated for Intermediate skier use, and provides easy access to several Backcountry routes that will be described later.

From Clark Creek Sno-Park ski a trail 150 yards to the junction where the Clark Creek Trail starts. Here turn left and ski uphill on moderate grades through old growth and always near but seldom in sight of Clark Creek. There is only one view of Hood along the trail until Newton Creek is reached.

The log bridge with railings at Clark Creek requires removal of skis for a safe crossing. Here also is where the 0.4-mile route joins from Hood River Meadows Sno-Park. Cross the bridge then enjoy several challenging, sudden dips and sharp turns. The "corkscrew," two tight turns on a steep, short

Carrying skis across Clark Creek bridge on Elk Meadows Trail

hill, is the scene of many spills and thrills. The return to the sno-park is aided by the subtle downhill of the trail. The trail ends for most skiers at Newton Creek, usually a difficult crossing—there is no maintained bridge here in the Mount Hood Wilderness area. Seasonal creek floods usually carry away logs used for crossing. The Newton Creek Trail from Pocket Creek Sno-Park formerly reached this place but has been discontinued due to trail maintenance problems with running water that made skiing difficult and unsafe.

Clark Creek Trail. (Map 42) From the trailhead at Clark Creek Sno-Park ski 150 yards to a trail junction and turn right onto the 1.8-mile trail that descends 400 feet to Pocket Creek Sno-Park. The Intermediate-rated trail passes through dense forest, a shallow draw, then across a bridge into more open forest following old skid roads. Mixed tree types and partial cutting allow for off-trail exploration. The trail passes a junction with the end of the Kate Creek Trail (forms a loop) and soon enters thick lodgepole pine stands. It makes several turns, then goes another 0.4 mile to the Newton Creek Tie Trail, which goes left, crosses the creek, then joins with the Newton Creek Trail (another loop) and the Robinhood trails. From the tie-trail ski 0.3 mile to Pocket Creek Sno-Park.

Kate Creek Trail. (Map 42) This interesting 1-mile trail forms an Intermediate-grade loop with the Clark Creek Trail and gives access to the Spruce Loop, a short side trip. Follow Elk Meadows Trail directions, turn left at the first junction, ski uphill 125 yards, and leave the trail at the Kate Creek Trail junction. Ski north on the trail and cross the creek to a short, sudden dropoff, the steepest move in all the trails of the area.

The trail then winds downhill through tall trees to join the Clark Creek Trail. Partway along the trail there is a side trail to Klindt's Cutoff, a bridge connector to the Newton Creek Trail, and farther along there is a junction with the Rocky Trail.

Rocky Trail. (Map 42) This 0.6-mile Intermediate side leg between the Kate Creek Trail and the Clark Creek Trail offers an additional challenge as it crosses a boulder-filled washout close to Newton Creek. It also offers another loop opportunity.

Spruce Loop. (Map 42) This 0.6-mile Intermediate trail off the Elk Meadows and Kate Creek Trails passes through several small clearcuts and is quite scenic. If you are interested in exploring off-trail you might consider skiing to the clearcut on the loop's north leg, entering the forest, and skiing uphill parallel to Newton Creek, usually 50 to 100 yards from the creek, to the Elk Meadows Trail near where it crosses Newton Creek. In the future, this route will probably become a ski trail, and it will form an interesting loop.

ELK MEADOWS, LAMBERSON BUTTE, AND ELK MOUNTAIN

(Map 42) As all three objectives are closely related and accessed by the same trail that leads into the Mount Hood Wilderness, they appear here in one group. Although these areas are all Backcountry tours demanding considerable determination but not exceptional skills, they should not be approached lightly. Be sure to have a good map. Ski climbers would be helpful but are not necessary.

For all three tours, ski to Newton Creek via the Elk Meadows Trail. Cross the creek, which may be easy or difficult, depending on snow depth and other factors, ski down along the creek 50 yards, then attempt to follow the unmarked summer hiking trail upward steeply as it zigzags to Elk Mountain Saddle at 5,260 feet. Here, the different routes diverge. It is 1.5 miles from Newton Creek to the wide, flat, forested saddle.

All three tours should be skied only in good weather. Take a map and compass, and have Backcountry experience. Do not ski in weather that will cover your return tracks. The small, but steep open slopes above Newton Creek may be dangerous during avalanche conditions as you struggle up the steep trail from the creek. Wilderness area ethics dictate not marking trails.

Elk Meadows. (Map 42) To find the meadows, the most popular objective, ski northeast and down from the saddle through gently sloping forest 0.5 mile to the large, scenic meadow where there is an exceptional view of Hood. From Clark Creek Sno-Park it is 4 miles to Elk Meadows.

Lamberson Butte. (Map 42) At 6,633 feet, the butte is 1,370 feet above the saddle and 2,400 feet above the sno-park on a demanding one-way route of 6.5 miles. The bare butte is the highest point on Gnarl Ridge and one of the finest viewpoints on Hood. The ridge is on Hood's east flank, and descends to Elk Mountain Saddle and Elk Mountain. From the saddle it is 3 miles to the top of the butte, a real battle with gravity on the last 2 miles, although the slopes are not steep.

From the saddle follow as well as possible the obscure summer hiking trail through open, then thick, stands of trees. As the route climbs you will find more and more open areas. The south edge of Gnarl Ridge drops off steeply into the Newton Creek canyon and will serve as the southern edge of your route, although you will in general as you get higher be working away from that side and around to the north side of the ridge. There are no landmarks, so just do your best. The route is not difficult or tricky.

From the top of Lamberson Butte there are sweeping views. The most impressive looks down 1,000 feet into Newton Creek and across to the enormous, bare moraine. The Newton Creek canyon is the route for the Gates of the Mountain tour. The east face of Hood rises impressively, and a fine panorama from Broken Top and Mount Jefferson to Adams and Rainier is awesome.

Elk Mountain. (Map 42) At 5,608 feet, this is the forested east end of the Lamberson Butte ridge. It is an elusive goal and the true summit may be difficult to find, so carry a map and compass for the view is worth the extra effort. From the saddle it is a frustrating 340-foot and 0.8-mile climb through at times very thick forest and dog-hair growth. The summer trail will probably be impossible to find or follow. Tree blazes may at first help, but they are usually at best hard to follow. Visit this area in summer to become familiar with the route. The summit is the site of a former fire lookout and the view is worth the struggle through dense forest. There are outstanding views across the deep East Fork valley to Lookout Mountain, Gunsight Ridge, and Bennett Ridge.

GATES OF THE MOUNTAIN

(Map 42) If you are looking for scenery on a monumental scale this Advanced tour should satisfy you. The ultimate goal is to reach the upper Newton Creek canyon, a distance of only 4 miles one way and a climb of 1,800 feet. The upper canyon is a wide, snow-filled, flat-bottomed valley with gigantic walls on both sides with Hood rising 6,000 feet at the very head of the canyon. The Gates of the Mountain are formed by two rocky buttresses that almost close off the upper canyon and form an impressive gateway to higher adventure. This upper valley, however, has great potential for avalanches once you are out of the forest and under the high, open walls and cliffs.

Ski the Elk Meadows Trail to Newton Creek. Do not cross the creek but enter the forest and parallel the creek on gentle grades for about 0.5 mile, occasionally scanning the creekbed for skiable terrain. As you get higher the creek bottom becomes skiable and it is followed on a twisting course upward into the great, wide valley below the cliffs of Gnarl Ridge and Lamberson Butte. Here is dramatic alpine scenery!

Do not attempt to ski up the bottom of Newton Creek from the usual crossing place of Elk Meadows Trail. The lower canyon is steep-walled and dangerous and the creek is not well bridged. Stay in the forest where in low-snow years tree wells may exasperate you. Depending on conditions, you may be alternating between forest travel and the streambed. Do not let minor obstacles deter you as the majestic basin is a worthy goal.

The upper canyon, as scenic as it is, is often crusty and wind-blown. If you venture near the "gates" the open steep slopes on both sides should be of concern. Gnarl Ridge can be ascended from here, and from through and beyond the "gates," but only under ideal, safe conditions.

NEWTON CREEK, ROBINHOOD CREEK, AND HORSETHIEF MEADOWS

(Map 42) This is a wonderful area for skiers seeking easy terrain and variety—old growth, skid roads, forest trails, and open areas all contribute to a sense of adventure for Novice skiers. There is also an uphill tour for great views, and a tour along the bank of the East Fork Hood River. For skiers wishing to develop route-finding skills, it is an area in which to use one's imagination, make decisions, and solve simple problems. The most-used point of access is Pocket Creek Sno-Park 3.3 miles north of Bennett Pass and 28.5 miles south of the town of Hood River.

Newton Creek Trail and Loop. (Map 42) This marked trail is only 1.4 miles long and rated Novice, but the best way to ski it is as a loop, skiing to its end, then crossing Newton Creek on a short connector called Klindt's Cutoff to the Kate Creek Trail. The Newton Creek Trail formerly extended an additional 1.2 miles to the Elk Meadows Trail crossing, but water drainage problems made the trail difficult and unsafe to ski. It was therefore abandoned. It may, however, eventually be replaced by a trail on the south side of Newton Creek from the Spruce Loop through beautiful forest to the Elk Meadows Trail crossing of Newton Creek. To enjoy beautiful views, do not hesitate to ski into the open areas and ghost forest above the trail's end and above Klindt's Cutoff to the Wilderness boundary. Here you will have grand views of Hood, and east to Gunsight Ridge and Bennett Ridge.

Upper Newton Creek with Mount Hood

To find the Newton Creek Trail from Pocket Creek Sno-Park, walk 150 yards north down Highway 35, crossing a bridge, to the trail signs west of the highway. Follow the trail as it winds gently uphill along the creek then on old skid roads through scenic forest. In about 0.6 mile you reach a wide, straight road that is followed uphill to its end in a meadow. Continue to Klindt's Cutoff. If you cross the creek here to Kate Creek Trail you will have a choice between the Newton Creek Short Loop and the Newton Creek Long Loop.

Newton Creek Short Loop. (Map 42) Cross the bridge, ski to and descend Kate Creek Trail and then the Clark Creek Trail for a loop length of 3 miles.

Newton Creek Long Loop. (Map 42) This splendid 10-mile loop is almost entirely on marked trails and is rated Intermediate, but is for strong skiers. The loop goes into the upper Pocket Creek area to follow the Pocket Creek road back to Pocket Creek Sno-Park on its final leg. A more challenging final leg can follow Meadows Creek Trail, the recommended route. This is a classic loop as it has great variety and interest and is easily accessible from several places. All this contributes to making it perhaps the best one-day loop on Mount Hood.

To ski the loop, follow directions for Newton Creek Trail, cross the bridge at Klindt's Cutoff, ski uphill on Kate Creek Trail, and then uphill on Elk Meadows Trail to the Clark Creek bridge. Here, turn left (south) and ski to Hood River Meadows Sno-Park. Remove your skis and walk to the snow-bank on the far side and ski to Hood River Meadows along the access road's shoulder. Ski up to Sahalie Falls (old Highway 35) and continue to Bennett Pass. Cross the highway, then ski down the Pocket Creek Tie Trail to the East Fork Trail, a wide road. Here you have three choices to complete the loop: ski the Teacup Lake Trail, ski east to the Meadows Creek Trail, or continue onto the Pocket Creek Trail, a wide, uninteresting road all the way back to Pocket Creek Sno-Park. Skiing the Meadows Creek Trail makes the loop 11 miles long.

Robinhood Creek Loop. (Map 42) Following primitive roads and narrow trails and passing through open forest and old clearcuts, this 3.9-mile loop (from sno-park) offers a variety of skiing experiences for Novices, but will appeal to all levels of experience. The loop's west leg, however, will be quite a challenge for most Novices as it has a short hill descending northward, which can be avoided by skiing the loop counterclockwise.

From Pocket Creek Sno-Park follow directions for the Newton Creek Trail and ski 0.6 mile to a wide road where you turn right and ski north 0.4 mile. Turn left, leave the road for a narrow ski trail, and pass through scrubby growth and old clearcuts. Continue along the very foot of Bluegrass Ridge (on Elk Mountain), then enter old growth, descend the moderate hill, and reach a wide road. Turn right for the next leg of the loop. The wide road also goes left and climbs along the side of Bluegrass Ridge for views.

To complete the loop, follow the wide road eastward for 0.9 mile, reenter forest by turning right onto a primitive road, then follow a trail through open forest to close the loop. The loop encloses a large area of old growth where there are several primitive roads for exploration.

Horsethief Meadows. (Map 42) Lying at the foot of Bluegrass Ridge, the long, narrow, attractive meadows are located 2 miles from Highway 35. The route is level and suitable for Novice skiers. The shortest approach is from a turnout on Highway 35 about 0.9 mile north on the highway from Pocket Creek Sno-Park near Robinhood Campground. Near here, Road 3520, a leg of Robinhood Creek Loop, goes northwest 0.7 mile to a level side road going north. This road goes through endless clearcuts, and 0.5 mile from Road 3520 an obscure side road to the left leads to a broken-down wood bridge that you may or may not be able to cross. If possible, cross and ski through a thin band of trees to the beautiful meadows that extend north for almost a mile, broken in places into segments. If you don't find the bridge, continue on the road for another 0.7 mile, passing through a beautiful, large meadowlike area of scattered, small pine trees with wonderful views of the ridges. The road makes a sharp bend and crosses a culvert, and this is where you ski off the road westward through a band of trees to the northern end of Horsethief Meadows. If there is sufficient snow depth, the meadows may also be reached by leaving the Bluegrass Ridge Trail early and descending northward to the meadows. The meadows may also be reached by skiing the Robinhood Creek Loop counterclockwise 1.5 miles to the very obscure side road leading to the broken-down bridge.

Bluegrass Ridge. (Map 42) From Pocket Creek Sno-Park it is 3.2 miles and a climb of 450 feet to the end of the Bluegrass Ridge Trail, in reality a rather wide, uninteresting road, but with fine views. Follow directions for Horsethief Meadows but continue on Road 3520 to the hillside where it starts climbing. Go as far as you want. Of course, the views of Lookout Mountain, Gunsight Ridge, and the valley below get better as you climb higher.

Old-Growth Tour. (Map 42) Ski out Road 3520 0.5 mile from Highway 35, turn left onto a side road, and follow this to the clearcuts of the Robinhood Creek Loop's west leg, or turn left off the road before you get this far and enter the old growth for some exploration. The area is being harvested a piece at a time, but it is level forest skiing and beautiful.

East Fork Hood River Trail. (Map 42) From Highway 35 ski into Robinhood Campground just north of Road 3520. Ski to the north end of the campground loop, then ski this Novice route onto a skid road that soon turns into a hiking trail along the very edge of the rapidly flowing river. After about a mile you will meet a crossroad. Turn left and ski west into scenic meadows. A primitive road paralleling the trail along the river offers variety and less restricted skiing. A foot of snow is required for this tour, which is rated Novice.

TEACUP LAKE AREA

(Map 40) Across Highway 35 from Clark Creek Sno-Park and 1.4 miles below Bennett Pass is Teacup Lake Sno-Park, which services not only the Oregon Nordic Club's groomed-track system (donation requested) but also two splendid trails that form two legs of a loop that completely circles the Nordic Club trail system. The lower and northern end of these trails is at Pocket Creek Sno-Park 1.8 miles down Highway 35 from Teacup Lake Sno-Park.

Teacup Lake Groomed Tracks. (Map 40) For years members of the Oregon Nordic Club, with many affiliate chapters around the state of Oregon, have dedicated thousands of hours of volunteer work to the construction of many miles of wide ski trails in this area. The trails are groomed on a regular basis, and the area is operated on a special-use permit from the Forest Service. For years the area operated as a private function for members who contributed time or donated to its maintenance. Although not accessible to the general public, it is open to all skiers for a suggested donation for use of the tracks. Several major Nordic ski races are held here annually, and the tracks are groomed for skating. The area is used for a youth ski-training program. The tracks go through forest on trails, follow roads, and cross lovely meadows. It is an interesting area to ski as it contains a wide variety of ski terrain. The groomed trails in the area are not described in this book.

Meadows Creek Trail. (Map 40) This 3.3-mile Intermediate trail starts at Teacup Lake Sno-Park and at first parallels Highway 35 northeast through beautiful forest, then swings southeast through scabby forest on skid roads (passing a side trail to Pocket Creek Sno-Park), and then takes a sharp turn to cross Meadows Creek. Now in attractive forest, the trail heads southward on a twisting course to a crossing of the East Fork Hood River. It finally reaches a huge clearcut that climbs moderately to the Upper Junction of Pocket Creek, directly under Bennett Ridge.

If, however, you skied up the Pocket Creek Trail to the Upper Junction and want to return on the Meadows Creek Trail, a low, obvious, rounded knoll at the bottom of the clearcut is your landmark for the trail's entry into forest. Ski past the west side of the knoll to find the marked trail.

Constructed in 1987 by the Hood River Ranger District, the trail is more interesting than many other trails of the area for its wide variety of terrain and significant length. The trail has a cumulative elevation gain of about 500 feet. There is a long, gentle descent of 450 feet in the first 1.5 miles from Teacup Lake Sno-Park.

The midpoint of the trail may also be reached from Pocket Creek Sno-Park by skiing 0.4 mile on the Pocket Creek Trail, then turning right onto a side road, the Meadows Creek Tie Trail. There is no particular advantage to the direction in which the Meadows Creek Trail is skied. An interesting 7-mile loop can be made with the Teacup Lake Trail.

Meadows Creek Tie Trail. (Map 40) This 1.1-mile connector trail takes off 0.4 mile from Pocket Creek Sno-Park, follows a level, wide road through a series of small clearcuts, crosses Clark Creek, and joins the Meadows Creek Trail.

Teacup Lake Trail. (Map 40) This 1.5-mile trail serves as a connector trail to the Upper Junction of Pocket Creek, and as one of three legs of a splendid 7-mile loop with the Meadows Creek Trail. Although rated Intermediate, it will be a challenge for any skier and difficult for weak Intermediate skiers as it has several sudden, twisting hills that require good control.

From the south end of Teacup Lake Sno-Park, ski the trail 300 yards to a road and follow it 120 yards. Near here you pass the Teacup Lake Groomed Tracks warming hut, where skiing these tracks starts. The trail then leaves the road and climbs a low rise through forest. The trail rolls along and crosses another road, then a bridge, on the East Fork Hood River, then goes through a "plantation" to join the East Fork Trail, a wide road to the Upper Junction 2.1 miles to the east. If you cross this "plantation" and then turn right (west), you will be on the Pocket Creek Tie Trail that climbs steeply through a clearcut, then forest, for 0.8 mile to Bennett Pass.

POCKET CREEK TRAILS

(Map 40) With its miles of gentle roads and many open views, Pocket Creek is popular with Novice skiers. Most skiers who visit here seek the open beauty of the upper basin, where an inspiring panorama unfolds. It is surprising then that few skiers explore beyond the Upper Junction at 4,200 feet, for not far above several outstanding viewpoints offer even finer vistas, including a view of Mount Adams, a peak usually seen only from the higher, more remote summits of the Mount Hood region. With timber harvest in recent years, an easier route has been opened from Bennett Ridge into the upper basin, which will attract skiers. In fact, recent logging and road building have opened up yet another loop, partly off-road and not marked, over Fat Lady Pass to the Camp Windy road across Gunsight Ridge.

Pocket Creek Trail. (Map 40) Although this is a Novice road tour of 2.7 miles one way on a wide, uninteresting road, the fine scenery and easy grades make this tour a popular, often crowded experience. Interestingly, the tour is in reality misnamed as the great majority of the area is in the East Fork Hood River valley, while only a very small part of the upper basin is occupied by Pocket Creek itself.

From Pocket Creek Sno-Park, 13 miles around Hood from Government Camp, ski east on the almost level road 0.6 mile to a bridge crossing of the East Fork. Cross the bridge and follow the road up the east side of the valley on a gentle climb through alternating forest and clearcuts to a road junction, hereafter referred to as the "Upper Junction," 2.7 miles from the trailhead.

At the Upper Junction there are two roads for further touring. The road going left (south), the upper Pocket Creek road, climbs gently beneath the Terrible Traverse (Bennett Ridge Trail) and curves eastward in a long U-

Shadows on Pocket Creek Trail

turn northward to the road end 2.2 miles from the Upper Junction. This road, the most scenic of Pocket Creek, climbs through a number of clearcuts with views of Hood and Adams, 60 miles north. The other road, the East Fork Hood River Trail, goes west 2.1 miles along a nearly level route.

The low elevation of the trailhead (3,800 feet) results some years in shallow snow, and early melting in spring, leaving a bare road at the lower end. If so, don't give up and drive away because it is usually worth hiking up the road to skiable snow. The upper basin normally has a deep snow pack that is protected from melting by the high ridges.

As an alternative approach to the upper basin in the spring, use one of the connector trails from Bennett Pass or Bennett Ridge (see Pocket Creek Tie Trail and Fat Lady Trail) to descend into the basin for often excellent late-season skiing. Remember, however, that in late season the snow in the forest is often rough, crusty, and dirty, with tree wells offering a challenge in places. For the rewards you will experience in the basin, the tour is probably worth such inconveniences. If necessary, walk through the difficult areas to better skiing.

Although the upper Pocket Creek road is usually quite safe, the slopes below and north of the Terrible Traverse are avalanche prone. Stay out of the clearcut immediately below the Terrible Traverse during and after heavy snowfall or during very warm weather.

Pocket Creek Tie Trail. (Map 40) This 0.8-mile trail connects Bennett Pass with Pocket Creek. Although marked at Bennett Pass the trailhead is not obvious. It is located down from the Bennett Ridge trailhead about 80 yards from where the tie trail dives into the forest. The trail requires strong Intermediate skills. It soon enters a large clearcut where a road is descended steeply to the East Fork Trail road and the Teacup Lake Trail junction.

East Fork Trail (Pocket Creek). (Map 40) Following a nearly level, wide road along the north base of Bennett Ridge, this east-west 2.1-mile trail serves as an important connector that allows several loops to be skied. At its west end the trail ends at a clearcut where two other trails join—Pocket Creek Tie Trail, descending 0.8 mile through forest from Bennett Pass, and the 1.5-mile Teacup Lake Trail coming from Teacup Lake Sno-Park. The East Fork Trail's east end joins with the Meadows Creek, Pocket Creek, and upper Pocket Creek trails.

Fat Lady Trail and Fat Lady Saddle. (Map 40) This unmarked trail is a 0.9-mile road from a clearcut in upper Pocket Creek to the ridgecrest beside the Bonney Junction road, where there are grand views of the East Fork valley, Hood, and Adams. Fat Lady Saddle (5,520 feet) is east of the trail and at the north foot of a pyramid-shaped high point on Gunsight Ridge at the head of Pocket Creek. It is reached through unmarked, old-growth forest.

The trail serves as a connector from upper Pocket Creek to the Bonney Junction road, and thereby forms two more loops for skiers seeking new terrain. One loop is over Fat Lady Saddle, to Bonney Junction, then down to reconnect with the upper end of the Fat Lady Trail. The other loop combines this trail with the Bonney Junction road, then goes downhill and off-trail, from Gunsight Notch Saddle to the upper Pocket Creek road.

Because the trail (a road) is very steep, the fine view at its upper end can be enjoyed more easily by anyone who skis across the Terrible Traverse then uphill 0.9 mile from Gunsight Notch Saddle to an obvious open area near the road. Leave the road, and ski 30 yards east through trees to the upper end of the Fat Lady Trail for the view.

To ski the Fat Lady Trail, from the Upper Junction ski upward 1.3 miles on the upper Pocket Creek road to the Mount Adams view clearcut at 4,640 feet, a gain of 440 feet. Here, a logging side road (Fat Lady Trail) turns off and climbs back up going southward, at first gently through the clearcut then steeply to its end, 0.9 mile from its start.

To reach Fat Lady Saddle and cross it to the Camp Windy road, ski the Fat Lady Trail 0.6 mile up from the Mount Adams view clearcut to where a steep snowfield appears through the trees to the left (east). This is a summer rock slide. Climb up the left side of the open slope and switchback up through the old growth to the 5,520-foot saddle, a climb of 620 feet from the bottom of the talus slope. The saddle is forested, flat, and descends easily to the nearby Camp Windy road.

"Fat Lady" is a name derived from having skied with a woman, up from Pocket Creek and over the saddle, years before there was a road into the area, through old growth, exploring, and locating the saddle that leads to the Camp Windy road. The woman, a strong skier, was in an advanced state of pregnancy.

Windy Peak Traverse (Camp Windy Connector). (Map 40) This 1.5-mile off-road unmarked ski route climbs 1,100 feet over Gunsight Ridge from the upper Pocket Creek road and descends 400 feet to Camp Windy, an area of open slopes at the head of Boulder Creek. This is a rugged, moderately steep tour entailing exploratory skiing through forest. The rewards are fine views from Windy Peak (Point 5801) and views from the Camp Windy area to the east. Another reward is the descent on open slopes to Camp Windy, then the return by way of Bonney Junction and the long downhill run to the Terrible Traverse.

To reach the connector from the Upper Junction ski up the upper Pocket Creek road, around the big bend into a large, rectangular clearcut. Climb to the top, northeast corner of the clearcut, enter forest, and zigzag upward to the flat, forested saddle north of Windy Peak.

Chapter 18

COOPER SPUR

Located high on the northeastern flank of Mount Hood, overlooking the deep, wide Hood River valley, the Cooper Spur area offers fine views particularly of the volcano itself, but also of the rolling ridgelands to the east and of the Columbia River Gorge and major volcanoes to the north.

Cooper Spur, a prominent buttress extending down from the summit ice, becomes broader and gentler downslope, where there are two principal touring areas. The higher and more difficult area centers on historic Cloud Cap Inn, which is located near timberline and is accessible only to skiers

North face of Mount Hood from near Cloud Cap Inn on Cooper Spur

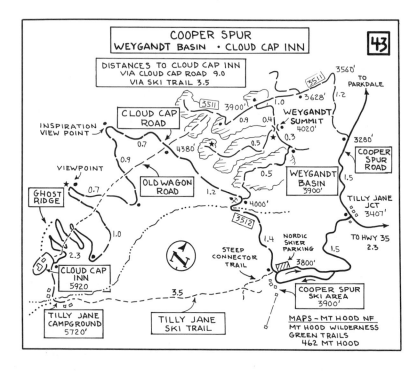

willing and able to undertake a long, rather tiring tour. The lower area is the rolling Weygandt Basin, which offers a wide range of road and clearcut skiing, almost all of it on gentle terrain.

If you are a Portland skier, you will find the distance to Cooper Spur is about 86 miles, regardless of whether you drive through Hood River or Government Camp. Depending on your approach, Drive Highway 35 either 23 miles south of Hood River or about 20 miles from Government Camp. Take a side road (old Highway 35) west to Cooper Spur Junction. Turn left and drive uphill to the ski area, 3.8 miles from Highway 35. Continue on the one-way road past the ski area and downhill for 150 yards to the Nordic skiers' sno-park, a wide spot in the road. The sno-park is located at the beginning of the winter road to Cloud Cap.

WEYGANDT BASIN

(Map 43) Only 2 miles from the Cooper Spur Ski Area lies the gentle Weygandt Basin, almost totally clearcut and providing a short but memorable unmarked tour. Although it is only a 5-mile round trip on roads, the tour will stretch a Novice skier to his or her limits. The elevation gain is a mere 200 feet that are not demanding, but the long, gentle hills will tax the skills of the inexperienced. Rewards that make this tour a special experience are the views of Hood towering far above, the upper Hood River valley spread out below, Mill Creek Buttes, and three major volcanoes.

Drive to the Nordic skiers' sno-park (see chapter introduction). Ski up the Cloud Cap road 1.4 miles to a small, clifflike quarry on the left side of the road. Opposite the quarry a road angles off to the right. Follow this road 0.8 mile to the basinlike clearcuts for fine views. The road continues over the north rim of the basin (Weygandt Summit, 4,020 feet) and descends 0.4 mile to Road 3511. This road goes 2.2 miles east and south downhill to the Parkdale-Cooper Spur road, the former Highway 35.

A short, interesting loop tour starts at Weygandt Summit and follows a logging road and continuous clearcuts west 0.5 mile up gentle grades to the edge of the forest. There, a view to the east includes Shellrock Mountain, Mill Creek Buttes, Dog River Butte (with snowpatch), and the partially hidden Lookout Mountain. By penetrating the forest 50 yards west, you can locate the old wagon road to Cloud Cap Inn. Going directly up this old road 0.5 mile brings you to the Cloud Cap road. In the other direction, skiing downhill on the old road brings you quickly to Road 3511 and a fine viewpoint, then along the road back to Weygandt Summit, a splendid short loop.

There should be at least 3 feet of snow cover for safe downhill skiing in the clearcuts. If visibility is limited, be sure to orient yourself. The area is a maze of roads and clearcuts, with no landmarks. It would be easy to become confused.

CLOUD CAP INN

(Map 43) There are two distinct ski routes to Cloud Cap Inn, and each climbs 2,120 feet to a high point of 5,920 feet. The Tilly Jane Ski Trail is 3.5 miles one way, and the Cloud Cap Inn road is 8.6 miles one way. The loop is 12 miles.

See the chapter introduction for directions to the sno-park. The Tilly Jane Ski Trail is the shortest route to Cloud Cap Inn, following the crest of a ridge on a wide-cut trail constructed many years ago for skiers prior to the Nordic skiing wave. The trail climbs vigorously and directly up—a real battle with gravity where ski climbers may be of help.

The tour to Cloud Cap Inn is a tiring trip, so be sure you are in good shape before attempting it. Carry survival gear, repair kit, maps, and compass. Descending the Tilly Jane Ski Trail, which was constructed during the days of heavier boots and skis, is not easy on light Nordic equipment, so many skiers select the road for the return to the sno-park.

The Nordic skiers' sno-park is reached by driving through the downhill ski area and down on the one-way road 150 yards. Just west of the small sno-park, on the left side of the Cloud Cap road, a 1-mile trail climbs steeply to join the main Tilly Jane Ski Trail. Although designed to steer Nordic skiers away from climbing the downhill ski hill to the ridgetop trail, this short connector trail is not recommended as a descent route unless you are a very competent skier.

Once on the ridgetop, ski the wide, easy-to-follow trail upward to the Tilly Jane Campground. It is a remorseless climb all the way on this route, but the road route is remorselessly longer.

At 5,720 feet, 0.6 mile below Cloud Cap Inn, the trail levels out and passes directly in front of two cabins on the left. The first is a two-story overnight shelter open to the public; the other is an old American Legion cookhouse with several wooden sleeping platforms. The first cabin is definitely the better one for overnighters. If you plan to spend the night, carry a ground sheet, pad, and sleeping bag. Because the cabin is heavily used, you should contact the Hood River Ranger District near Parkdale to confirm availability of space. If your name is not on the registry list, you may have to sleep out in the snow. If you sleep inside, prepare to be crowded.

After leaving the cabins, you soon cross a small ravine, passing two green cabins just above the trail. From there follow a roadbed to the main Cloud Cap road. Those wishing to continue to the vast, open slopes above timberline (sometimes windswept and crusty) should follow the left side of the ravine uphill. Those going to Cloud Cap Inn should follow the roadbed 200 yards to where it turns right. Leave the road here and climb left up a short, steep hillside to the inn, which is visible above.

The building just below and north of Cloud Cap Inn is the Snowshoe Club cabin, a historic, old, limited-membership social club. Both buildings are locked and not open to the public at any time, but the historic inn is worth a close inspection. The view from the inn, eastward across distant ridges to Lookout Mountain, and southwestward to the steep, impressive north face of Mount Hood, with its glaciers, is a superb reward for negotiating the tiring uphill trail. Eliot Glacier and Barrett Spur, a prominent buttress on Hood's north side, are just two of the many alpine features to be seen. St. Helens, Adams, and Rainier far to the north, across the Columbia River Gorge, are also seen.

There is off-trail skiing on Cooper Spur, above Cloud Cap Inn. In good weather, this area of huge open snowfields, moraines, and glaciers is the realization of the wilderness skier's wildest fantasy. You will not soon forget the wild scene of deep canyons, rugged ridges, and snowfields if you explore.

Most skiers descend to the trailhead by way of the Cloud Cap road, which offers a gentle grade all the way. If snow is favorable, however, you can bypass several long switchbacks by skiing down Ghost Ridge, a moderate descent, then joining the road at the second hairpin turn at 5,240 feet. To find the top of Ghost Ridge, a wide, open snow slope, ski toward the canyon from the northwest corner of the Snowshoe Club cabin. If the skiing is good on the descent of the ridge you can easily overshoot the second hairpin, so be alert and watch for the obvious road cut on your right as you descend. Another shortcut descends the old wagon road, formerly called Telephone Line Trail.

Historical Note: Cloud Cap Inn, built in 1889 as a mountain resort, is a rustic, one-story log building, which originally was held down by cables and had an observation deck on the roof. Guests arrived in Hood River by train and then rode horse coach or wagon to the inn the same day. The Weygandts, father and son, worked as mountaineering guides here for many years. The inn closed in 1940. It was purchased by the Forest Service, and is now used by the Hood River Crag Rats alpine club as a base for mountain rescue operations.

OLD WAGON ROAD

(Map 43) This 2-mile unmarked route descends 1,540 feet from Cloud Cap Inn and is used as a shortcut downward, cutting through the zigzags of the Cloud Cap road. It descends in a generally straight line, steep near the upper end, moderate in the last two sections.

The trail starts about 50 yards northeast of the Snowshoe Club cabin just below Cloud Cap Inn. The start is not obvious, but if you miss it, just ski down the road and pick up the trail where it crosses each section of the road. To be marked in the future, the crossings are not easily located at this time. Most skiers prefer to ski down Ghost Ridge to the second of four hairpin turns from the top, then follow the road until choosing to ski the old wagon road. Once on it, it is easy to follow.

The trail, an exciting descent full of thrills and spills even for the best skier, cuts off about 4 miles from the total road distance. The upper parts of the old road are rated Advanced. The lower two sections, which cut off about 1.5 miles, are Intermediate.

Be prepared for sudden falls and surprises. Do not ski the trail unless the snow is favorable. If you descend too far you will cross the last section of the Cloud Cap road without knowing it and end up on a logging road in Weygandt Basin. This error would ultimately put you several miles below Cooper Spur Ski Area and your sno-park unless you select the correct route back through Weygandt Basin to the Cloud Cap road.

Chapter 19

CLINGER SPRING AND BROOKS MEADOW

East of Cooper Spur, across the Hood River valley, lies the high, rolling, forested Clinger Spring area. Clinger Spring (4,200 feet) is little more than a point on the map (the spring is not even visible in winter), but it is the departure point for a number of tours. Although the terrain is easy for Intermediate skiers, the long distances of some tours earn them an Advanced rating. Clinger Spring itself is 1,000 feet above and 3.6 miles from Highway 35. There are no marked trails or roads in the entire area.

All tours in this area are reached by skiing (or driving) uphill on Road 44 from Highway 35. The snowline is seldom as low as the highway (3,280 feet) so it is usually possible to drive up Road 44. Unless plowed, the road is never drivable beyond a road cut at 3,840 feet, 1.6 miles from the highway. There, the road makes a sharp bend on the ridgecrest and enters shady north slopes where the snow gathers all winter. Because snowmobilers occasionally use the area, do not block the road when you park at the snowline. Road 44 winds gently uphill from Highway 35 past several good views.

The entire region is crisscrossed with many roads and a few trails, offering great potential for cross-country skiing. It is, however, an area where prior familiarity will ensure greater confidence and success while skiing. Therefore, you may want to explore the Clinger Spring country in summer—by car, on bike, or on foot—when flowering meadows and beautiful forests await you.

Road 4410 leads south to Lookout Mountain, an immense, forested volcanic peak, the highest point east of Mount Hood, a long but rewarding goal. The summit is a spectacular viewpoint, as is High Prairie on the peak's west shoulder.

Although round-trip distances are often given from Highway 35, they may be shorter, depending on the snowline. If you record the distance from Highway 35 to the snowline, you can adjust guidebook distances to determine the actual skiing distances.

Regarding maps, be advised that at this time USGS maps do not show roads correctly in several places, and show a long-gone guard station in Brooks Meadow. This guidebook's maps are accurate. Construction of new logging roads and new junctions requires careful map reading and interpretation.

CLINGER RIDGE

(Map 44) This Intermediate road tour of 10.2 miles round trip from Highway 35 gains a total of 960 feet and reaches a high point of 4,200 feet.

Ski up Road 44 to Clinger Spring. The first side road you encounter to the north is Road 620, the Clinger Ridge road. It goes north through clearcuts and drops gently, losing 300 feet in 1.5 miles, where it ends at 3,900 feet at a view of the upper Hood River valley, St. Helens, Adams, Rainier, and the two summits of Mill Creek Buttes. Dog River Butte is just across the steep, narrow valley to the east.

VOLCANO VIEW

(Map 44) A 10-mile Intermediate round trip on roads leads to a scenic 4,600-foot viewpoint. The short side trip from Road 44 into shelterwood cuts provides views of Hood, St. Helens, Adams, Dog River Butte, and the Mill Creek Buttes.

Ski past Clinger Spring about 200 yards and turn right (uphill) onto Road 4410, the Lookout Mountain road. Ski upward past the first side road, then follow a wide, obvious turn to the east to arrive at a level junction at 0.8 mile. The Lookout Mountain road cuts back at a reverse angle, reaching Horkelia Meadow in 0.6 mile. For the best views, however, ski east from the level junction for 0.4 mile to the viewpoint. Beyond here the road is not interesting. From the viewpoint, 1.4 miles from Clinger Spring, it is possible to ski straight downhill through clearcuts to Road 44.

SURVEYOR TRAIL

(Map 44) This scenic, primitive road goes 1.5 miles from Clinger Spring to Brooks Meadow with little elevation gain to a high point of 4,280 feet. The old road goes both west and east from Clinger Spring, closely paralleling and offering an interesting Intermediate alternative to skiing on the generally uninteresting Road 44. The westward segment goes downhill 0.8 mile to a steep, open hillside leading up to Road 44. Beyond there the route is blocked by fallen trees. The Surveyor Trail is the original road from the Hood River valley to Brooks Meadow. Later, Road 44 was built for "resource extraction."

The eastward section of the old road starts at Clinger Spring just a few yards from Road 44, enters forest, and soon reaches a clearing with a view of Adams. After another 0.5 mile a larger clearcut offers a view of Hood. Later, the trail joins Road 44 briefly, then reenters the forest and crosses Cooks Meadow just 500 yards south of Brooks Meadow. Near Brooks Meadow the trail intersects with another primitive, obscure road, the Aqueduct Road, which circles around Dog River Butte. On the Surveyor Trail the only route-

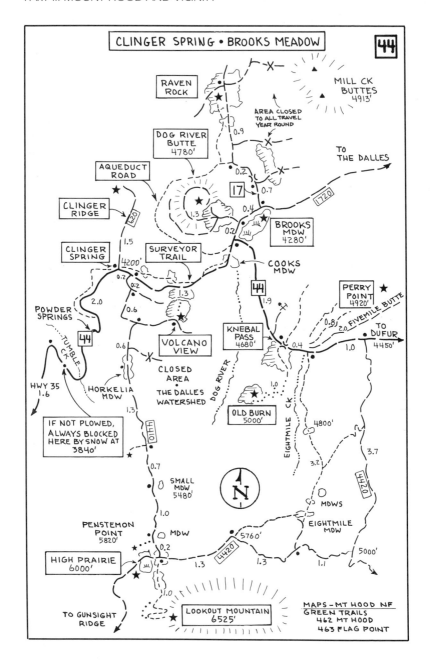

CLINGER SPRING • BROOKS MEADOW

44

finding problem might be in the second clearcut where the trail exits the clearcut in the far upper corner.

BROOKS MEADOW

(Map 44) The Intermediate tour to this beautiful half-mile meadow is 10.2 miles round trip with an elevation gain of 960 feet to the high point of 4,280 feet. There are several interesting side tours from Brooks Meadow.

From Clinger Spring continue on Road 44 1.5 miles, or better yet ski the more interesting Surveyor Trail to the Road 44/1720 junction. Enter the trees straight ahead to locate nearby Brooks Meadow. For the best view of Hood ski to the far end of the meadow.

From Brooks Meadow there are tours to the top of Dog River Butte, around the butte on the Aqueduct Road, and south to Knebal Pass. All offer scenic rewards and a hint of adventure. All the roads of the area are easy to follow, but maps are important to the winter traveler in this area where there are many roads and few landmarks.

AQUEDUCT LOOP

(Map 44) Starting just south of Brooks Meadow, this 4.2-mile Intermediate loop circles Dog River Butte in a clockwise direction, offering an interesting alternative route to Raven Rock. The loop follows a primitive road that once served as a maintenance route for the long-abandoned wooden water-pipe aqueduct for The Dalles watershed. Since the aqueduct was a gravity-flow underground pipe, the road, which is always just above, rolls along gently, neither climbing nor descending significantly. This route is part of the Forest Service Surveyor Trail 688, a combination of roads and trails.

To locate the start of the loop, go to the junction of Roads 44 and 1720 at the south end of Brooks Meadow. Ski 200 yards south on Road 44, enter forest to the right (west), and locate the primitive road, which may take a few minutes. Follow it as it circles the butte through solid forest. At 1 mile there is a short, exciting downhill with a good runout. There are no views at this time from the old road, but future logging may change this. At 2.7 miles from the start of the old road, a side route leads to Raven Rock.

To complete the loop, ski to Road 17 which is followed southward over a high point, Raven Pass, then along the west side of Brooks meadow 1.5 miles from the end of the old road to the junction of Roads 44/1720.

There are few of the old, primitive roads left in our woods today. Most have been widened, straightened, graded, and often paved for efficient log hauling. The original character of these wonderful roads has been lost to both the summer explorer and the skier.

DOG RIVER BUTTE

(Map 44) Climbing 540 feet from Brooks Meadow, this 2.6-mile Intermediate round trip reaches a high point of 4,780 feet with views over Eastern Oregon. The most interesting route of the several roads on the butte is the spiral road tour to the summit.

From the junction of Roads 44/1720 just south of Brooks Meadow, follow 1720, then take the first side road north of the junction, a distance of 350 yards. Enter the forest to the left and ski into a large, old clearcut where the road divides. Take the center road and follow its spiral route upward to the summit, where you will be at the top of the large, old clearcut you crossed below. The view is sweeping, from Lookout Mountain to the Mill Creek Buttes, and on a clear day to the vast flatlands of Eastern Oregon stretching out to the horizon.

RAVEN ROCK

(Map 44) This Advanced 4.8-mile round trip from Brooks Meadow crosses the low Raven Pass and drops to Raven Rock in a large clearcut where there are fine views, perhaps the best of the area. From Brooks Meadow ski up Road 17 1.1 miles to Raven Pass where a side road to the right (east) leads to a clearcut with a view of St. Helens, Adams, and Rainier. This side road is closed to further travel as it enters The Dalles watershed. Return to Road 17 and ski downhill northward 1.1 miles to Raven Rock, a prominent outcrop. Here there are sweeping views of the Hood River valley and St. Helens. The towering presence of Hood dominates the scene.

The prominent twin Mill Creek Buttes are just to the northeast. Unfortunately, the area east of Road 17 is closed to any travel, summer or winter, because Road 17 is the western boundary of The Dalles Watershed. The closure reduces potential fire damage to and prevents human contamination of the watershed. Please observe the closure. Road 17 continues to Shellrock Mountain along an unrewarding route.

OLD BURN AND KNEBAL PASS

(Map 44) This tour, just over 16 miles round trip from the highway and with an elevation gain of 1,720 feet, will appeal to Advanced skiers seeking a challenging, scenic tour with some route finding. The goal is a hillside viewpoint where a forest fire many years ago cleared a large area, now rapidly regrowing. A 1.1-mile off-trail route climbs to the area from Knebal Pass.

Knebal Pass. (Map 44) This 4,680-foot pass lies 1.9 miles southeast of Brooks Meadow (and 7 miles from Highway 35) on Road 44, a gentle climb of 440 feet. The pass, just a high point on the forest road, is the source of three interesting destinations: the Old Burn, Perry Point, and Fivemile Butte. Each of these tours is challenging in its own way and offers good views.

To find the Old Burn, ski to Knebal Pass (see Brooks Meadow) where a short side road to the right leads into a large cut-over area. Ski 0.4 mile to the southeast corner of the area to where an obvious open, natural corridor leads up gentle slopes. Follow this to a meadowlike hillside with scattered stands of trees. As you climb, start circling south then southwest.

As the clearings get smaller and the lodgepole thicker, continue upward where possible through openings. (If you veer too far south you will hit an impenetrable wall of dog-hair growth.) Eventually you will be climbing westward on moderate slopes. As the grade levels out at 5,000 feet you arrive at the Old Burn, with grand views of the east face of Hood, St. Helens, Mount Defiance above the Gorge, nearby Dog River Butte below Defiance, Mill Creek Buttes, Rainier, and Adams. Ski to the far west end of the Old Burn 1 mile from Knebal Pass for the best views.

The descent is fast and offers Telemark skiing around the clumps of trees. The future will unfortunately see a road from Knebal Pass pushed uphill behind the Old Burn for logging to the south. That road will provide less adventurous skiing than that described here.

Perry Point and Fivemile Butte. (Map 44) The outstanding views from both of these high points at the eastern edge of the Cascades will not disappoint you, although both tours are long. Both are rated Advanced—the Perry Point tour is 6.2 miles and the Fivemile Butte tour is 8.6 miles, both round trips and from Brooks Meadow, with elevation gains of up to 700 feet. Both are unmarked routes.

See Old Burn and Knebal Pass for initial directions. For both tours, ski east 0.4 mile downhill from Knebal Pass to an obvious side road on the left (north) side of Road 44.

Perry Point. (Map 44) Take the side road on the left (north) side of Road 44, which immediately turns and goes to Fivemile Butte, but leave it quickly and climb into a nearby opening. Turn right (east) and climb through a meadow into forest following a primitive road. Continue through clearings and forest to sidehill meadows with great views south and east. Go to the far end of the ridge (1.2 miles from Knebal Pass), where you will enjoy the beauty of the craggy, snow-drifted narrow point with weathered, twisted pines. It is a wild place with views for miles.

Fivemile Butte. (Map 44) Leave Road 44 at the side road described above, then almost immediately turn east and follow the 2-mile road to the fire lookout. It is an easy route with a climb to the final, flat ridge. Two side roads to the left on the way up should be ignored. You'll see wheat fields, the Klickitat Hills beyond The Dalles, and Mount Adams.

The lookout is available for rental. Call the Barlow Ranger District in Dufur for details.

Hoar frost crystals

LOOKOUT MOUNTAIN

(Map 44) This 6,525-foot summit is the highest point east of Mount Hood, and the views are panoramic on this Backcountry 18.8-mile round-trip unmarked tour from Highway 35. The elevation gain is 3,245 feet. The length and isolation of the tour make this a wilderness tour even though it follows roads most of the way. The tour is best done in late winter, early spring, or after periods of stable weather, when the snow is more consolidated and weather more predictable.

Ski past Clinger Spring and follow Road 4410 for 5.8 miles to the summit. Follow instructions for the Volcano View tour, then ski to Horkelia Meadow from the upper end of which you will see St. Helens. The road now is lovely and primitive and will hopefully remain so unless Forest Service "resource extraction" justifies widening and straightening, which would be a great loss. A better viewpoint 1.4 miles above Horkelia offers an exceptional view of Hood.

Continue up to High Prairie, a large meadow at 6,000 feet just below Lookout Mountain. Note your return route as you head upward through a maze of meadows, then bear right to the open west shoulder of the summit ridge. On a good day the summit view is spectacular. The deep Badger Creek valley and wilderness lie below, five major volcanoes are visible, and the Bennett Pass area and a large chunk of Eastern Oregon are all evident, making for a memorable experience worth the long haul.

If you do not have time to go to the summit, ski to the west edge of High Prairie for remarkable views that in themselves are worth the trip.

Part III
THE CLACKAMAS HIGH COUNTRY

The Clackamas high country, just south of Mount Hood, is characterized by high ridges—some of which are open and skiable—above deep, forested valleys. You can easily explore the area using logging and forest roads that penetrate the valleys and follow some of the ridgetops.

Compared to the Mount Hood area, the Clackamas is not heavily visited by winter recreationists, and a sense of isolation pervades most tours. The ski tours described in this chapter are the best in the Clackamas, although there are many other roads and areas to explore. Due to the absence of sno-parks, there are no marked ski routes in the entire area.

Skiing amidst old-growth mountain hemlock

Chapter 20

THE CLACKAMAS HIGH COUNTRY

To reach the Clackamas high country drive to Estacada, a small town in the Cascade foothills. The town is about 40 miles from Portland via the town of Sandy on Highway 26, and then about 32 miles via Highways 212 and 224. From Estacada continue on Highway 224 for 26 miles to the Ripplebrook Ranger Station, the starting point for all tour descriptions. The road is winding and scenic as it closely follows the Clackamas River through a deep, and often narrow, gorge.

Highway 224 is plowed only as far as the Ripplebrook Ranger Station at 1,500-foot elevation, although there is seldom snow this low. How far you drive beyond there depends on the snowline, which in an average winter fluctuates between 2,000 and 3,000 feet. All parking is roadside. In general, roads are well maintained, are not steep, and present no unusual driving hazards under normal winter conditions.

When parking your car at the snowline do not block access to the road beyond, as others may want to pass. Few snowmobilers use the area. Select your parking spot with care as heavy snowfall during your tour may isolate you and your car far from help.

Because trails and roads in the Clackamas are not marked for Nordic skiing, be sure to carry a Forest Service map. A USGS or Green Trails map, of course, is always a requirement when skiing off-road routes. Maps will not only contribute to your pleasure here, but also to your safety.

Distances given in the tour descriptions are for average winter snow levels. In mid-winter, however, when the snowline is usually low, long distances often make the high country inaccessible to day skiers. For those days of unexpected low snowline conditions that prevent you from achieving ambitious goals, three ski tours are described here that are easily accessible—Harriet Lake, scenic Oak Grove Butte, and the lower Cache Meadow road, all near the Ripplebrook Ranger Station.

For most skiers spring and unusual midwinter periods of high snowlines are the best times to visit the Clackamas. When the snowline is higher, some roads may even be plowed for logging, making some trips that much shorter. Spring is especially fine because the days are longer and snow is consolidated, and the weather more predictable. For snowline and road information call the Ripplebrook Ranger Station during office hours.

HARRIET LAKE

(Map 45) This Novice tour of 7 miles round trip or less climbs only 300 feet and follows a road. The lake at 2,100 feet is the high point of the tour. If

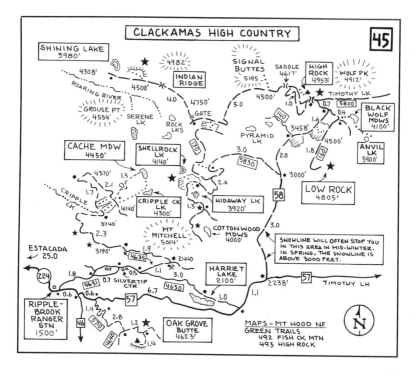

you cannot drive beyond Ripplebrook due to low snow, Lake Harriet is a good consolation prize. Nestled in a narrow, forested valley, the lake and dam provide an easy destination.

Drive to Ripplebrook. Turn left onto the road beside the ranger station and drive uphill 2.5 miles to the Silver Tip Work Center, the end of winter snowplowing. Park here. Ski Road 4630 into the trees and past Road 4635 along a winding route to the lake. You pass one fine view of a distant valley behind you. This is a pleasant tour through nice forest. See Cache Meadow tour for an alternative tour in this area.

CACHE MEADOW AND CRIPPLE CREEK LAKE

(Map 45) This Intermediate to Advanced tour features a road with great views and a summer trail leading through heavy timber and open areas to beautiful Cache Meadow. You can ski a loop from the meadow by returning to the road by way of Cripple Creek Lake. Until this summer trail is marked, the off-road portion is rated Advanced due to the route finding required. The distance will depend on the snowline and will range from 8 to 12 miles round trip with an elevation gain of up to 2,000 feet. The high point of the tour is Cache Meadow at 4,450 feet.

Drive to Silver Tip Work Center (see Harriet Lake), where winter road plowing ends. Follow Road 4631 for 0.5 mile and turn left onto Road 4635, and ski or drive 1.1 mile to a Y-junction at a small quarry. Take the left fork (Road 4635) and climb gently for 4.2 miles to Cripple Creek. On the way you have many views to the left, and about a mile beyond the Mount Mitchell trailhead there is a remarkable vista of the deep Clackamas River valley and the high, imposing ridges beyond. When free of snow, this road provides numerous places for turning around or parking.

At Cripple Creek, in a curve of the road, you have three choices for reaching the summer trail, which begins directly above you where the road again crosses Cripple Creek. First, you can continue on the road for 3.8 miles. Or, for your second and third choices, you can cut off about 2.5 miles by climbing either of two clearcuts, snow depth allowing. The first clearcut, just beyond the creek, has a steep cat road at its far end. Climb to the top of the clearcut, entering forest for a short distance before emerging on the upper road, where you turn right a short distance to the creek. It is a 400-foot climb to the upper road. For the second clearcut, go 200 yards beyond the first one, then climb steep rock slides to a clearcut that extends all the way up to the upper road.

The summer trailhead is near the left or west bank of Cripple Creek. About 200 feet into the woods, the trail forks. The right fork, marked by unblazed, orange-painted trees, goes to Cripple Creek Lake, about a mile up gentle slopes through dense trees. Take the left fork, which is marked by blazes only. It is hard to follow in winter. The 1.5-mile trail is very beautiful, leading to a small lake and generally following a string of long, narrow openings and meadows above the lake. For the last few hundred yards the trail goes through old-growth forest before dropping gently into the northwest corner of Cache Meadow. There is another lovely meadow to the left, and the old, dilapidated shelter may still stand across the meadow on the southeast side.

From the meadow follow the creek flowing south to Cripple Creek Lake 0.5 mile away. If there are still orange-painted trees at the southwest corner of the lake, these can be followed to the road. The route is primitive, and the close-set trees do not offer good skiing. The trail always parallels the north bank of the outlet creek, which is easy to follow.

The trail is so beautiful that it is worth the trouble to locate and follow. Considering the configuration of the terrain and the location of the creek, it is hard to imagine anyone being lost for very long. Carry a map and compass.

OAK GROVE BUTTE

(Map 45) Site of a former fire lookout, the 4,624-foot summit offers grand views. The Intermediate to Advanced tour up the north side of the butte—

of up to 13 miles round trip and an elevation gain of almost 3,000 feet—is a prime objective at any time of winter. However, it is particularly rewarding during periods of low snowline when you cannot drive to the higher and more distant tours of the Clackamas.

The dirt and gravel road that winds its way to the summit starts at 1,640 feet and 1.2 miles from the Ripplebrook Ranger Station. From the ranger station drive 0.6 mile to a junction with Road 46, then go left onto Road 57 and drive 0.6 mile to Road 5710, a side road that climbs 6.8 miles to the summit. Drive up this road as far as possible.

There are no views until 1.4 miles from Road 57, at a clearcut at 2,240 feet, where you'll see Whale Head peak and other high ridges to the west. Another 2.5 miles gives a good view of the Clackamas River valley. Farther up, a view of Hood appears, then 5.4 miles from Road 57 the road forks in a regrowing clearcut. The left branch goes 0.4 mile to a good view, and the other branch goes 1.1 miles to the summit, the last 500 yards being quite steep up the east side of the summit. From the top you will see Hood (High Rock is just to its left), Olallie Butte, Jefferson, Whale Head, the Collawash River valley, and many other features.

HIGH ROCK

(Map 45) The sweeping view from the rocky summit is a fair reward even for the long trip in winter. And in spring the tour may be much shorter. Several major volcanoes are visible across the many high ridges that rise out of the deep valleys surrounding the peak. Round trip will range from 10 to 14 miles on this Intermediate to Advanced tour. At the most, the elevation gain will be 2,700 feet, and the high point of 4,953 feet is the summit of High Rock.

From the Ripplebrook Ranger Station continue on the main road for 0.6 mile to a junction. Turn left onto Road 57 and follow it 8.4 miles to a junction with Road 58. At 2,238 feet, this is where the snowline often stops cars in winter 8.5 miles from the summit.

Drive Road 58 as far as possible. When you park, do not block access to the road beyond. Continue on skis. At Road 5830, the road to Hidaway Lake, you are 3 miles from the Road 57/58 junction. Another 2 miles brings you to Road 140, which leads to Pyramid Lake, a difficult, off-road tour not described here. Occasional clearcuts in this deep valley offer views.

Continue up the gently ascending road past two huge clearcuts on the right. Partway up the second clearcut, there are good views. Ski all the way up the second clearcut for a shortcut route to Low Rock. Come to another clearcut at the junction with Road 160 on the right. The route continues along the main road as it curves to the left and enters forest. In summer the road is paved this far. It starts climbing more steeply to the pass just southeast of the summit, where Hood first comes into view and where Wolf Peak rises nearby. At that point, Road 58 from Clear and Timothy Lakes joins from the east. Continue up the main road and at a fork go right to circle around the south and west sides of High Rock. At the saddle (4,617 feet) on the west side of the peak, ski a narrow, moderately steep road to a point just under the summit from where it is an easy walk to the top.

From the summit there is a spectacular view in all directions. To the west are the open slopes of Indian Ridge and the peaks of the Sentinel Buttes, which can be reached by road skiing. The deep Roaring River valley lies just below. All the familiar areas near Hood are seen—Veda Butte, Trillium Basin, Ghost Ridge, Lookout Mountain, and others, including Barlow Ridge and Bonney Butte and other old friends. Of course Hood is there, and farther north, Adams, and before the 1980 explosion, St. Helens was visible.

On this tour, a long way from your car, carry a full pack, all the basic essentials including a repair kit, and warm clothing for the summit.

LOW ROCK

(Map 45) The summit of this high, broad ridge is only 2 miles south of High Rock. In spite of its unassuming name, Low Rock offers a dramatic, panoramic view that rivals some of the best views of the area. Like all Clackamas tours, it can be short or up to 12 miles round trip with a gain of 2,600 feet to its 4,805-foot high point. With a small amount of Backcountry bravado (and experience) it is possible to ski without difficulty from Low Rock down to Anvil Lake and Black Wolf Meadow for a loop return.

Follow directions toward High Rock. Turn right onto Road 160 just 2 miles from the top of High Rock and follow the road through a clearcut into forest, and past the Black Wolf Meadows trailhead. Continue through forest as the road curves and climbs gently southward, paralleling Road 58 far below, which can be seen from the top of a huge, steep clearcut. This clearcut, covering some 650 vertical feet, offers a good shortcut to Low Rock from Road 58. There are wide views, which include Hood, from the top of the clearcut.

The road reenters forest and climbs to a large, plateaulike summit clearcut. For the best view climb an unusual, low rock formation, which also serves as a good windbreak on cold days. The view is unexpected and contrasts with that from High Rock, which features deep valleys in every direction. On Low Rock you look across the open summit plateau to distant peaks and ridges ringing the entire horizon. Signal Buttes are prominent to the northwest, and the dome of Adams is visible to the side of the buttes. To the south, Jefferson and Olallie Butte seem close, and Three Fingered Jack appears as a small spire. To the east is a good view of Timothy Lake and the undulating forest that extends in an unbroken carpet to the summit of massive Mount Wilson beyond the lake. This is a scene of grand scale.

Low Rock, Clackamas high country

BLACK WOLF MEADOWS AND ANVIL LAKE

(Map 45) This attractive meadow at 4,100 feet is 2 miles southeast of High Rock and may be as much as 12 to 14 miles round trip from the snowline, or much shorter in spring. Elevation gain may be 2,000 feet. This is an Intermediate tour, but Advanced if over 12 miles. From the summer trailhead a short trail goes through level forest, and although unmarked, the meadow is easily located.

Follow directions toward High Rock. Turn right onto Road 160 and climb a clearcut. About 200 yards beyond the upper end of the clearcut the road curves right and at 0.4 mile from Road 58 passes a side road on the left. The summer trailhead is about 150 feet before this side road.

The trail heads eastward through open timber. Few trees are blazed, and the summer path is not obvious. The terrain is level, however, and by going straight ahead you reach the meadow in 0.5 mile. In spring there are many melted areas and tree wells in the forest, but persevere. The half-mile-long meadow is crescent-shaped and scenic. The summer trail passes along the west side, marked by 5-foot poles.

At the south end, where the meadow narrows, the trail enters forest to the right and parallels a small creek flowing southward to Anvil Lake. The forest is magnificent old growth. The route begins on the level but soon starts a gentle descent, crossing the creek and continuing through tall timber. About 0.7 mile from the meadow, a side trail abruptly turns off to the small lake, only 100 yards west. If the trail is obscure, just follow the creek directly to the lake, which is rimmed by marshes and forest.

HIDAWAY LAKE AND SHELLROCK LAKE

(Map 45) These two forest-rimmed lakes offer serene winter beauty, and the 1-mile tour between them is very scenic. The tour up the gentle, wide valley to the lakes has many open places and numerous views. The return trip is a long downhill run. The round trip may reach 16 miles, but could be much shorter, and elevation gain may reach 1,800 feet to the high point of 4,140 feet at Shellrock Lake.

From Road 58 it is 5.6 miles to Hidaway Lake. Follow directions toward High Rock, but turn left (west) onto Road 5830. The road descends gently for 0.8 mile before climbing up the valley. At 0.3 mile from the lake is a junction. The side road on the left goes directly to the lake. The main road continues 0.5 mile to a clearcut between Hidaway and Shellrock lakes.

From Hidaway Lake there are two routes to Shellrock Lake, a recommended side trip. Ski along the north shore of Hidaway to the outlet stream on the north side. Ski into beautiful, snow-covered marshes and meadows that line the outlet stream to the clearcut between the two lakes. Cross Road 5830, which passes through the clearcut and makes a good shortcut route back to Hidaway Lake junction, 0.5 mile below.

To reach Shellrock Lake, which is only 100 vertical feet above the road at the bottom of the clearcut, ski northward across the center of the open hillside. Do not climb too high, but enter the forest at the north side of the clearcut and proceed 300 yards to the lake. The flat east shore is the best place to appreciate the lake's steep-walled confinement and sense of isolation.

Another particularly interesting side trip near Hidaway Lake follows a scenic logging road and offers a splendid view of Jefferson and Three

Fingered Jack. Ski to the clearcut between Hidaway and Shellrock Lakes and follow the road as it heads west and then south around the Hidaway basin. The road climbs gently for 1.3 miles to a wide saddle (4,460 feet) in a clearcut, from where the volcanoes are visible across Shellrock Creek Canyon.

Meltback of the snowline in spring and plowing for spring logging make some of these tours very accessible. Call the Ripplebrook Ranger Station for road and snow information.

INDIAN RIDGE

(Map 45) This unusual Advanced tour of up to 20 miles round trip from Road 58 is a high-snowline or late-season tour that climbs 1,750 feet. The tour route follows a primitive road along a high ridge extending in an erratic westerly direction for 9 miles from High Rock to Shining Lake. The road stays close to the 4,700-foot level, passing a number of exceptional viewpoints from which eight Northwest volcanoes are visible. This is a rare tour that is not only very rewarding but also very challenging.

Ski or drive to Road 5830 (3,000 feet)—the Hidaway Lake road (see Hidaway Lake-Shellrock Lake). Follow Road 5830 for 3 miles to the West Fork Shellrock Creek crossing (3,500 feet). Leave the road and ascend open timber east of the creek into a clearcut and to Road 130. Follow the road 1.8 miles to a long, steep, narrow, natural clearing above the road. Climb this to the top at its east end, then through a dense stand of small trees to the Indian Ridge road, a climb of 400 vertical feet from Road 130.

Turn left on this road and ski a short distance to a Y-junction. To the south you can see Jefferson, Three Fingered Jack, and the North and Middle Sisters. At the Y-junction, take the right-hand road, which seems to disappear in scattered trees. Keep skiing northward and the road immediately becomes obvious. After 0.5 mile some splendid views open up to the east and north of Hood, to Signal Buttes, and down Cougar Creek to the deep Roaring River valley.

Enclosed by small trees, the road soon passes to the left of a high point and reaches another saddle with more views, this time including the Rock Lakes, Jefferson, St. Helens, Rainier, Adams, and the impressive nearby ridges projecting northward, one of which is a goal for today.

The road continues, again passing another high point on its left, then dropping almost imperceptibly for a mile or so. It travels monotonously through dense tunnels of trees, but after a mile a small break appears in the trees to the right. Climb this roadside opening to survey your next move.

A half mile northwest you can see a flat spur extending north from the ridge: this is your goal. Ski down the road several hundred yards and then cut north into the dense thicket of trees. (If you ski too far down the road, you will have extra dog-hair through which to struggle.) You soon pop out at the edge of the spur. Follow the rim through beautiful, open, almost level terrain to the north end of the spur. This is the logical trip destination as the views are splendid. To continue along the road means getting trapped on a rapidly descending course with no views. The High Rock ski tour route may be used to reach Indian Ridge, but would add 3 miles to the one-way distance.

Part IV
THE SANTIAM REGION

The entire length of the Oregon Cascades, some 300 miles from the Columbia River to the California border, is crossed in only eight places by year-round highways. Seven of the Cascade crossings offer magnificent cross-country skiing, and much credit must be given to the U.S. Forest Service for building extensive trail systems in all these areas.

The Willamette National Forest and Deschutes National Forest share jurisdiction of the Santiam Pass area—the Willamette, to the west of the Cascade crest, and the Deschutes to the east. Skiers should own both area maps for general orientation. Santiam Pass is 135 miles from Portland, 88 from Salem, 86 from Eugene, and 41 from Bend.

For simplicity, the vast area east and west of Santiam Pass, including the pass, is presented here in two chapters: Santiam West, the areas approaching the pass from both Salem and Eugene; Santiam Pass, the Cascade crest area, and the east slope extending to Black Butte near the town of Sisters. The combined areas extend 20 miles east to west, and for Santiam West alone some 45 miles north to south.

On the Cascade crest near the pass are two wilderness areas, the Mount Jefferson and the Mount Washington. All trails in these areas are summer trails and are not marked for skiing due to wilderness ethics. These areas are therefore Backcountry areas and will be treated only lightly in this book. If you ski in either of these two areas, be sure to have the appropriate wilderness maps. These maps and the "Santiam Pass Winter Recreation" map by Imus Geographics showing the marked trails of the area are available from the U.S. Forest Service and map outlets.

Chapter 21

SANTIAM WEST

(Map 46) Extending some 45 miles southward along the west side of the Cascade Mountains crest from Mount Jefferson to the White Branch of the McKenzie River are several ski trail systems and individual ski tours often overlooked in the rush to drive to higher elevations at Santiam Pass.

Most of the trails of the Santiam West area have in normal winters excellent ski conditions. Indeed, many are passed up due to lack of familiarity. The variety and scenic rewards of this area rival the best of any other area.

The many miles of ski tours at Santiam Pass itself are treated in a separate section and are not part of the Santiam West section, although several trails go from one area to the other.

JEFFERSON PARK

(No sketch map) Jefferson Park is an idyllic parkland at the north foot of craggy Mount Jefferson. The mountain rises steeply from the level meadowlands of the park. One of Oregon's most scenic one-day Backcountry ski tours, this is a 12-mile or more round trip gaining up to 3,000 feet to a high of 6,200 feet. The safest and easiest route into Jeff Park, as it is called, is via summer trail 3375. The other access to Jeff Park is the one climbers use, up the Whitewater Creek road, then the Sentinel Hills Trail, a longer and, in places, dangerously steep route.

From Salem drive east on Highway 22 47.5 miles to Detroit and turn left (north) onto Road 46 and drive 11.2 miles, passing the Breitenbush Resort entrance, to Road 4685. Follow 4685 4.7 miles to a road bend where Trail 3375 starts at 3,100 feet. Follow the trail 6 miles to the northwest rim of Jeff

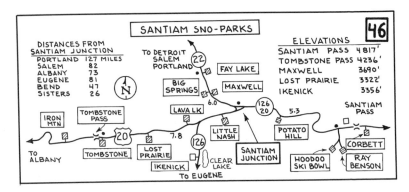

Park, which lies only 200 feet below you, an easy descent. Mount Jefferson rises gloriously beyond.

This route is best done in springtime when it is possible to drive to the trailhead; you may find it necessary to carry your skis to the snowline. In the upper reaches, the trail will be lost, but the route through mostly open country is obvious, usually staying fairly near the edge of the valley of the South Breitenbush River to your right.

SOUTH BREITENBUSH GORGE TRAIL 3366

(No sketch map) This route is rated Intermediate, with up to 4 miles round trip, a starting elevation of 2,500 feet, and an elevation gain of 300 feet. The trail, through old-growth hemlock and Douglas fir, is a reward in itself, or a consolation prize if weather and snow are not favorable for the Jeff Park tour. The trail is not marked for skiing, but is fairly easy to follow. Gentle to moderate grades predominate and only one short, steep grade across a gully may be a problem. You will pass a narrow, rocky gorge with a raging stream. Exercise caution at its edge. The ancient forest stands toward the eastern end of the 2-mile trail.

From Road 46, drive or ski east on 4685 0.5 mile (see Jefferson Park route) to a trail signpost. At first the trail is level, then it climbs moderately and twists along a hillside. The gorge is 1 mile from the trailhead, 50 yards below the trail, and the only place you will be near the

Northside view of Mount Jefferson from upper end of South Breitenbush summer trail to Jefferson Park (Photo: Nancy Chapman)

river that parallels the trail. The trail, always close to 4685, climbs steadily from west to east and rejoins the road at its far end.

ELK LAKE AND GOLD BUTTE LOOKOUT

(Map 47) The lake at 3,720 feet lies in a basin at the south foot of Battle Ax Mountain and offers an easy, scenic ski tour suitable for Intermediate

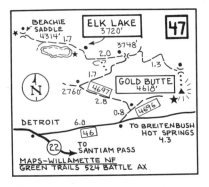

BEACHIE SADDLE 4314' 1.7
ELK LAKE 3720' **47**
3748'
2.0
1.3
1.7
N
2760 4697
GOLD BUTTE 4618'
2.8
0.8 4696
DETROIT 6.0
46 TO BREITENBUSH HOT SPRINGS 4.3
22 TO SANTIAM PASS
MAPS—WILLAMETTE NF
GREEN TRAILS 524 BATTLE AX

skiers with a 6-mile round trip and elevation gain of 1,000 feet, all depending on the snowline. Gold Butte at 4,618 feet, however, is a demanding, short climb, but the views of Jefferson and the region are spectacular.

Follow driving directions for Jefferson Park and then drive 6 miles from Highway 22 on Road 46, turning left onto Road 4696. In 0.8 mile make another left onto 4697. Continue climbing 2.8 miles on the one-lane road (many turnouts) to a junction/switchback at 2,800 feet, then 1.7 miles to Dunlap Saddle at 3,748 feet. This is the end of driving unless the snowline is lower.

Ski west over easy terrain 2 miles to the lake. The road continues along the lake's north side, climbing 1.7 miles and passing a dangerous avalanche chute halfway, to Beachie Saddle (4,314 feet) for more views. For the rugged, a 1,200-foot climb on foot, northeastward to the top of Battle Ax, is possible. There is scenic camping at Dunlap Saddle and at the west end of the lake in a meadow, which is reached by a road descending from the northside road to Beachie Saddle.

For a more accessible view, from Dunlap Saddle follow a steep, primitive road southeast 1.3 miles, then a steep trail to the Gold Butte summit fire-lookout cabin at 4,618 feet, a climb of 900 feet from the saddle.

PAMELIA LAKE

(Map 48) A steep-sided valley at the west foot of Mount Jefferson contains this long, narrow lake at 3,884 feet. The tour could be up to 12 miles round trip with a gain of up to 1,580 feet. The Intermediate, unmarked route at first follows a wide road, then a summer trail through cathedral-like forest. The scenic rewards are not as great as those of the Elk Lake tour. Access to higher country from the lake is limited to the Pacific Crest Trail (PCT), which crosses steep, dangerous terrain.

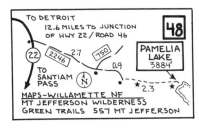

TO DETROIT
12.6 MILES TO JUNCTION OF HWY 22 / ROAD 46
48
22 2246 2.7
750
PAMELIA LAKE 3884'
0.9
TO SANTIAM PASS N
2.3
MAPS—WILLAMETTE NF
MT JEFFERSON WILDERNESS
GREEN TRAILS 557 MT JEFFERSON

From Detroit (see Jefferson Park) continue on Highway 22 12.6 miles to Road 2246, the Pamelia Lake road, at 2,300 feet. As Doug Newman said in *Oregon Ski Tours*, long out of print, "snow level, forever fluctuating, is the final distance maker" on this tour. From Highway 22 it is 5.9 miles to the lake, of which the forest trail is 2.3 miles. The lake is 1,584 feet above the highway. The first 1.5 miles of the forest trail follow fairly closely to the north side of Pamelia Creek, but for the remainder of the distance to the lake, the creek actually is underground.

Be wary of skiing on lake ice anywhere, and always stay away from inlet and outlet areas. The best view of Jefferson is from the west shore if you can ski there on the lake. The only other view is 1 mile below the start of the forest trail.

COFFIN MOUNTAIN

(Map 49) A high ridge on a road near the top of Coffin Mountain at 5,771 feet may be the most accessible viewpoint of the Central Cascades in winter. Depending on snowline, this Intermediate tour may reach up to 12 miles round trip with a gain of 1,700 feet. Located south of Detroit Lake and west of Highway 22 and Mount Jefferson, the view includes all the volcanoes between Hood and the Three Sisters. Jefferson stands directly east only 11 miles across the North Santiam River valley. The tour should be rated Advanced for distance, but the roads are easy to follow, and you may be able to drive several miles to the snowline.

From the village of Idanha drive 13.9 miles toward Santiam Pass on Highway 22 and turn west onto Road 11 (3,208 feet), a paved, two-lane road, for 4.1 miles to Road 1168 (4,000 feet), a gravel road. The paved road climbs steadily on moderate grades through forest with few views. Road 1168 climbs through clearcuts and second growth 1.7 miles to an open saddle with views of Three Fingered Jack, Mount Washington, and the Sisters. Ski west from the saddle to a second saddle and continue, now eastward, to a wide bend on an open, clearcut ridge, the high point of the tour at 4,900 feet and 1.5 miles from the first saddle. This high point is 7.3 miles from Highway 22.

The view from this road bend is marvelous, and includes the summit of Coffin Mountain and the fire lookout 1.5 miles north and 1,300 feet higher. If time permits, ski 0.9 mile on a gentle descent across open, steep hillsides to the saddle at the foot of the final, bare ridge to the fire lookout. Here the summer trail climbs 1,600 feet on south-facing open slopes to the final, almost-level forested ridge to the lookout. This last 1.5 miles to the summit is best left to Backcountry skiers.

FAY LAKE

(Map 50) Although the lake is small and fringed by forest, and not a particular reward, the primitive road to it is lovely. The 6-mile round-trip tour on marked roads gains only

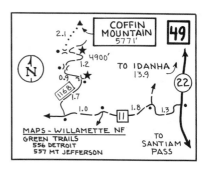

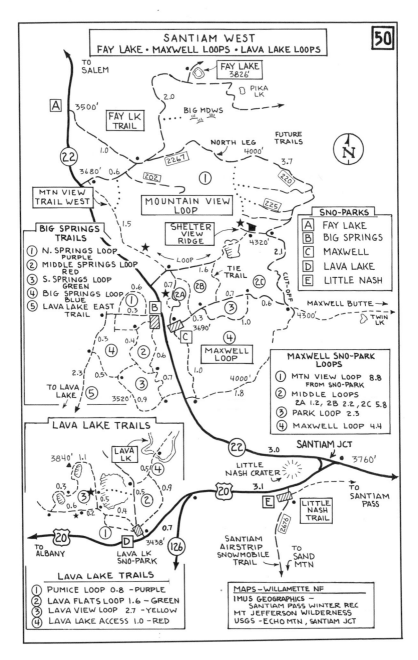

400 feet to a high point of 3,826 feet, and it is rated Novice to Intermediate. The area also offers opportunities for off-trail exploring into nearby Big

Meadows, and borders Maxwell Sno-Park ski-trail system for more opportunities. The Maxwell system is accessible from the same parking area.

Drive 25.2 miles from Detroit toward Santiam Pass on Highway 22 to the Fay Lake trailhead. From the junction of highways 22/20 the trailhead is 6 miles north. There is limited parking available. It is 3 miles farther (south) by highway to Maxwell Sno-Park, and there are connecting ski trails.

Park at Road 2267, the Fay Lake trailhead, and ski 1 mile to a Y-junction. Go left, briefly downhill to level terrain and 0.4 mile to some peeled pole fences (Duffy trailhead to Eight Lakes Basin). Continue on the winding road 0.2 mile to a crossing of the culvert containing the headwaters of the North Santiam River. For a sidetrip here, follow off-trail the north side of the river eastward 200 yards to the edge of the Big Meadows area.

For Fay Lake ski north from the culvert 1.4 miles on the road through thick forest and shelterwoods, up a moderately steep but short hill then level road to the lake. If you are exploring, ski up the Pika Lake road about a mile for an overview of the Big Meadows area. This road will eventually be a marked route.

BIG SPRINGS TRAILS

(Map 50) The superb variety of marked ski trails here will suit every skier, regardless of skill level or aggression quotient. The large area is serviced by two sno-parks, on opposite sides of the highway and only 300 yards apart. Big Springs Sno-Park west of the highway serves generally easy trails, while Maxwell Sno-Park serves both easy and demanding trails that climb to high viewpoints. Both areas use logging roads, many being primitive routes. Widespread clearcutting has created many views.

Big Springs area has over 9 miles of marked trails and loops, with the option to ski 3.5 miles to the Lava Lake ski-trail system to the southwest. Maxwell has over 15 miles of marked ski trails with miles more of open hills and roads to explore. These areas are 76 miles from Salem, 83 from Eugene, and only 9 miles below and northwest of Santiam Pass. Both sno-parks are at 3,700 feet.

Note: The Imus Geographics map uses letters to designate junctions. This book's sketch maps do not.

The four principal loops (see maps), suitable for Novice skiers, are well marked and identified by colors with alphabet letters (see Imus Geographics map) indicating trail junctions. Elevation gains and losses are minimal on all loops.

Loop 1: North Springs Loop. (Map 50) The 1.2-mile loop starts from the west side of the sno-park and goes through both forest and clearcuts. A snowmobile corridor cuts across the center of the loop. The south leg hugs the edge of a clearcut from the west end of which views of Maxwell Butte and Three Fingered Jack can be seen. The north leg goes through ancient forest.

Loop 2: Middle Springs Loop. (Map 50) Starting from the south edge of the sno-park the 1.6-mile loop shares its north leg with Loop 1, and passes through ancient forest and clearcuts but provides more variety of terrain.

Loop 3: South Springs Loop. (Map 50) Ski south 0.6 mile from the sno-park to join the 2.1-mile-long loop. The loop has great variety, but its south and southwest legs are on wide, rolling, uninteresting roads. There is a view from its lowest point. The Maxwell trail system across the highway is easily reached from the south leg by walking 200 yards south on the highway.

Loop 4: Big Springs Loop. (Map 50) This 3.7-mile loop follows the trails on the outside legs of Loops 2 and 3, but here only its 1.8-mile northern loop (Junctions H, G, D, C, B—see Imus Geographics map) is mentioned here. This loop is very interesting, mostly on primitive roads (west, southwest legs) crossing varied terrain with a brief view of the North and Middle Sisters, of a lava flow, and of Three Fingered Jack. There is old growth on its west side.

LAVA LAKE EAST ACCESS TRAIL

(Map 50) Go west from the sno-park following the south leg of Loop 1, then descend gently on a primitive road through beautiful forest. In 3 miles (Intermediate rating) reach Lava Lake, usually a dry lakebed. The last mile passes through scenic, open lava flows with scattered stands of trees. To connect with the Lava Lake trail system, ski 0.5 mile across the south end of the lake and climb a steep bank through trees on the southwest side to pick up the marked trail that goes to Lava Lake Sno-Park.

MAXWELL SNO-PARK TRAILS

Mountain View Trail West. (Map 50) This is the most scenic, easy trail of the area for skiers not wanting to climb long distances but wanting the most variety and scenery for a modest investment. The trail goes 2.2 miles north from the sno-park and connects with the Fay Lake Trail for longer distance skiing. This trail is the west leg of the Mountain View Loop and begins at Maxwell Sno-Park.

Proceeding north through magnificent old growth, the trail enters meadows at the foot of a dome-shaped hill with a view of Three Fingered Jack. Your choice is to ski west around the hill, through forest, or to climb around the east side of the dome on open slopes, rejoining the alternative beyond as you descend to large flats northward. The trail at 0.7 mile then meets the Mountain View Loop for the first time, swings west, crosses and climbs through huge open hillsides, enters forest, and finally ends at the north leg of the Mountain View Loop 2.2 miles from the sno-park.

For more adventure, enter the large east-west clearcut at the trail's north end, ski to the clearcut's eastern end, then climb on Road 202 into the hills at the center of the loop. Make your way back, your choice. Or from the base of 202, ski to the Y-junction (see Fay Lake) and ski on to Fay Lake, a total of 4.8 miles one way from your car.

Mountain View Loop. (Map 50) Aptly named, this 8.8-mile loop for strong Intermediate skiers, with a vertical gain of 520 feet, is the most scenic and challenging ski tour of the area. The loop offers numerous opportunities for shortcuts, off-trail routes, and Telemark skiing as it climbs to Shelter View Ridge, surrounded by open slopes. The future will see more tie and connector trails in this area as it is ideally suited to a complex of trails. From the long, narrow, open Shelter View Ridge you can see Three Fingered Jack, Mount Washington, all three Sisters, and the tip of Mount Jefferson. The loop itself travels the perimeter of a huge clearcut of several square miles of rolling, hilly terrain—truly a spectacular ski tour.

If your downhill skills are not great, ski the loop counterclockwise as the south leg is fairly steep, and the north leg will offer a long, gentle descent. The Mountain View Tie Trail is the most direct access to the loop and Shelter View Ridge.

The loop itself is reached by skiing north from the sno-park along the Mountain View Trail (west leg), then skiing east and up the loop's south leg to a clearcut. The route crosses to the clearcut's northeast corner, through more forest, then to the edge of forest for a look across a basin to the Shelter View Ridge. This route to the ridge is 2.3 miles.

Take time to enjoy the view of five Cascade volcanoes, then ski east on the ridge to the forest, actually the boundary of the Mount Jefferson Wilderness, then turn north on a road to continue on the loop. Turning south puts you on the Maxwell Cutoff Trail.

Near the west foot of the loop's north leg you will be near the Y-junction of the Fay Lake Trail. Near here turn left into a long east-west clearcut that goes almost to the highway. This clearcut is part of the north leg. A shortcut climbs to the top of the clearcut, where you can ski through a fringe of trees to pick up the loop farther south. If you stay in the clearcut on the north leg, it eventually turns south near the highway, which it will parallel through continuous clearcuts divided only by screens of forest, a beautiful ski route.

Middle Loops. (Map 50) These three short loops near the sno-park are formed by legs of both the Mountain View and Maxwell Loops and the Maxwell Cutoff Trail. The generally level terrain of 2A and 2B makes them good choices for Novice skiers, while Loop 2C is for experienced skiers as it climbs eastward and loops northward to Shelter View Ridge, the most scenic site of the region (see Mountain View Loop).

Loop 2A. (Map 50) Just 1.2 miles long, the loop uses legs of other loops to form a pleasant, easy, level route.

Loop 2B. (Map 50) This loop of 2.2 miles is a bit more demanding for Novices with some easy uphill and downhill.

Loop 2C. (Map 50) This 5.8-mile loop, the Maxwell Cutoff Loop, is for strong, experienced skiers looking for a challenge and a direct route to some of the finest views and skiing of the area. From the sno-park, ski east up the

Maxwell Loop north leg, climb 650 feet to the Maxwell Cutoff Trail, then turn northward to Shelter View Ridge. Ski the south leg of the Mountain View Loop to return, descending some moderately steep hills.

Park Loop. (Map 50) For strong Intermediate skiers, this 2.3-mile loop climbs east of the sno-park 0.3 mile to the loop trailhead to the right. It follows a road up into a steep clearcut. Exit the clearcut near its top, go briefly through forest to the Maxwell Loop Trail (north leg), turn left, and descend it to return. Downhill skills are useful. This north leg of Maxwell Loop is the lower end of the Maxwell Butte Trail 3391 that climbs steeply past Fawn Lake in 5 miles of relentless uphill to the summit of Maxwell Butte at 6,229 feet.

Maxwell Loop. (Map 50) Least interesting of the loops, this 4.4-mile route climbs up the Park Loop trails to the Maxwell Cutoff Trail, the loop's high point 610 feet above the sno-park. Here turn south and ski 0.3 mile on a contour to a clearcut, descend 200 yards to a primitive road in the forest edge, and follow this south and down as it loops back to the sno-park. Leave the old growth and ski across rolling terrain in a large clearcut with rapidly growing pine stands to the sno-park.

LAVA LAKE TRAILS

(Map 50) The Lava Lake trail system totals only 5.5 miles, but it is truly a small, splendid jewel in the Santiam West crown of outstanding areas. You will see more volcanoes, six in all, than you will from any other trail system of the Santiam Pass area. In addition there is a variety of terrain and inspiring groves of old-growth giants. Lava Lake Sno-Park is 3.8 miles west of the Highway 22/20 junction and 0.7 mile west of the Highway 20/126 junction.

Note: The Imus Geographics map uses colors and letters to designate trails and junctions. This book's sketch map does not.

Pumice Loop. (Map 50) This Novice 0.8-mile loop (purple markers) starts at the west side of the sno-park, follows a road bordered by old growth, then turns north and returns through a clearcut. There is little climbing, and there are views from the clearcut.

Lava Flats Loop. (Map 50) To ski this Novice 2.5-mile loop (green markers), ski east from the sno-park into forest and follow the trail through noble stands of ancient groves for 0.9 mile over rolling terrain. The trail joins the Lava Lake Access Trail (red markers) and turns left for 0.2 mile through second growth to join a road that leads back to the sno-park. The road is shared with machine users. The huge clearcut climbing west above the road invites exploring and offers increasingly better views the higher you climb. From the road itself you will see Jefferson and Three Fingered Jack.

Lava View Loop. (Map 50) This 2.7-mile loop (yellow markers) for Intermediate skiers climbs 600 feet and uses the Pumice Loop initially for 0.4 mile, then a short connector trail through old growth. Although described as a view loop, and there are several good views, the most notable feature is the old-growth forest. The views may all be enjoyed by skiing only the near south and east legs 1 mile from the sno-park for panoramic scenes.

Ski to junction A from the sno-park on the Pumice Loop and then to the Pumice Loop's far west end, turn left, and go 0.1 mile through old growth to the loop itself. Here you have a choice: ski clockwise or counterclockwise, depending on time available. For a short 0.5-mile tour to the grandest view of the area, ski counterclockwise onto the east leg through old growth and out onto a huge clearcut for the view of six volcanoes. To ski the loop clockwise, go 0.2 mile to a view of the Three Sisters and Mount Washington at a road that you then follow 0.6 mile before turning uphill (north) at junction C. In 0.3 mile you leave the last clearcut and enter deep, virgin forest. The high point of the loop, a 600-foot climb from the sno-park, is at a long, narrow clearcut. Ski to the end, turn right, enter second growth at the edge of tall timber, ski to the grand viewpoint, then reenter forest to complete the loop.

Lava Lake Access Trail. (Map 50) To ski the 1 mile (red markers) to the large meadowlike Lava Lake, ski north from the sno-park on the wide road, shared with snowmobilers (west leg of Lava Flats Loop), or better yet ski the Lava Flats Loop east leg through wonderful old growth to meet the access trail. At junction E turn right for 0.3 mile onto a narrow, ever-steepening trail to Lava Lake. A final, short, steep pitch takes you to the open meadow area. Across the way 0.5 mile is the Big Springs "Lava Lake East Access Trail" that joins the two trail systems.

LITTLE NASH, SAND MOUNTAIN, POTATO HILL, AND LOST LAKE

(Maps 50 & 51) Two sno-parks access 5.2 miles of marked ski trails with 4.5 miles more and a shelter planned for the future. Little Nash Sno-Park at 3,760 feet is 0.8 mile west of Santiam Junction (Highways 22/20), and Potato Hill Sno-Park at 4,120 feet is 1.3 miles east of the junction.

Little Nash Trail. (Map 50) At 3,760 feet, this is a good ski tour for Novice skiers. The almost-level, marked 1.1-mile trail follows a logging road to and past the Santiam airstrip through second-growth forest. A 2-mile loop is proposed for south of the airstrip.

Sand Mountain. (Maps 50 & 51) The sno-park gives access to Road 2676, the Santiam Airstrip Trail, a snowmobile route. It follows roughly the 4,000-foot contour 2.5 miles south, then turns east and joins the Old Santiam Wagon Road to a 4,560-foot pass north of Sand Mountain. The summit of Sand Mountain, 5,459 feet, is reached by a road on the northeast side. In 1990 a new fire-lookout cabin was built on the south summit after a lightning strike burned the former lookout. The summit has a 400-foot-deep cinder crater and exceptional views. Sand Mountain is 6 miles one way from both the Little Nash and the Ray Benson Sno-Parks, the latter requiring less elevation gain.

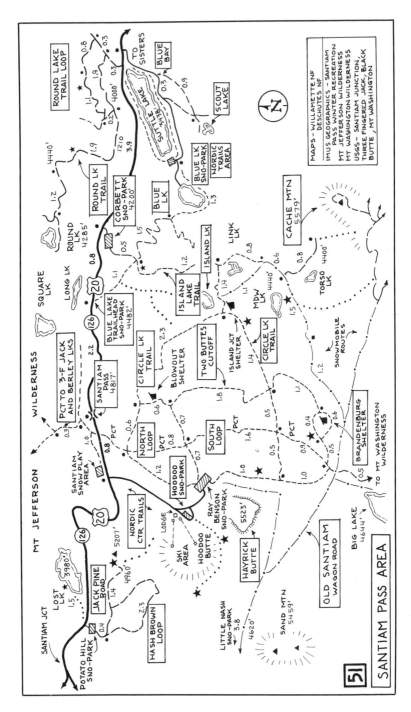

SANTIAM PASS AREA

Jack Pine Road Trail. (Map 51) The Jack Pine Road Trail, a very scenic climb of over 800 feet in 1.8 miles, is the principal attraction from Potato Hill Sno-Park (4,120 feet). For strong Intermediate skiers, the road climbs vigorously 1.8 miles up moderately steep grades from old growth into rapidly reestablishing second growth. The road ends at a fine view of Jefferson, Three Fingered Jack, and the bare, double cones of Sand Mountain. The first views, 0.7 mile from the sno-park, are of Mount Washington and the Three Sisters.

The Hash Brown Loop starts where it leaves the Jack Pine Road Trail 0.4 mile from the sno-park, descends gently through tall forest, levels, then climbs assertively to 4,640 feet, where it rejoins the Jack Pine Road Trail. A shelter is proposed for this area at 4,400 feet.

Lost Lake. (Map 51) The beautiful lake at 3,980 feet is 1.5 miles east of Potato Hill Sno-Park and north of the highway.

Cross the highway and ski east along the north side onto a road leading down to the lake. The lake, visible from the highway, has a wide shoreline and open stands of firs and cottonwoods along the north shore. There are no notable views, but the wide, forested basin is beautiful. Hogg Rock rises to the southeast.

TOMBSTONE PASS TRAILS

(Map 52) Several short but scenic ski tours at this 4,236-foot pass provide variety and views worthy of a side trip to the area. The pass is 63 miles east of Albany on Highway 20 and 11 miles west of the Highway 22/20 junction.

Civil (Iron Mountain) Tour. (Map 52) A short road for Intermediate skiers on the west side of Iron Mountain leads 2.1 miles to a switchback at 4,340 feet with dramatic views. The road continues steeply 0.5 mile to its end, where the summer trail to the summit lookout starts. This steep, final half mile is too steep to ski, as are the upper slopes of the peak, and there are no better views than at the switchback below.

To start the ski tour to the switchback, drive 1.5 miles west of Tombstone Pass to the Iron Mountain road. The road climbs steadily, gaining 560 feet to the switchback, the end of the scenic tour. The view is worth the uphill

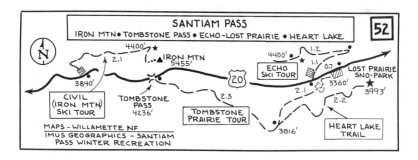

grind. The first 0.6 mile from the highway parking area is moderately steep to a junction where the route turns eastward. There is a marvelous view here of Iron Mountain, Echo Mountain, and the Three Sisters. From here to the switchback the climb is gentle to moderate. A side road, 0.6 mile above the first turn, offers more views that make it worth skiing north. Share this tour with snowmobilers.

Lost Prairie and Heart Lake. (Map 52) This ski tour for Intermediate skiers is essentially one trail with a side leg. Skiing to its eastern end will reward you with wonderful views. The 4.5-mile marked trail is best started from Lost Prairie Sno-Park (3,360 feet) as you will have a downhill return. If you start from the pass, the tour, following a road, descends 520 feet in 2 miles. The trail name, Heart Lake, is deceiving as the lake is inaccessible and hidden 880 feet above the trail in forest.

Start skiing at Lost Prairie Sno-Park, going west on a marked route through a meadow, enter forest, go 200 yards, then turn left and cross Hackleman Creek in 150 yards. The wide trail through old growth enters and climbs a steep clearcut 0.3 mile from the creek. In 0.1 mile meet an uninteresting road through large clearcuts. After 2.1 miles and at 460 feet above the sno-park join you will reach the Tombstone Pass and Heart Lake Trails, both roads.

Turn left (east) and follow the narrower, winding road 2.2 miles to its end in a large clearcut. On the way out, there are marvelous views across the deep valley and of Jefferson and Three Fingered Jack. Skiing out into the final clearcut beyond the end of the road provides superior views.

This Heart Lake Trail is a road carved from the steep mountainside. Where steep clearcuts descend to the road, be wary of snow conditions in years of heavy snowfall.

Echo Ski Tour. (Map 52) Closed to snowmobilers, this moderately climbing road is located 0.7 mile west of Lost Prairie Sno-Park. The road climbs 800 feet in 2.8 miles through thick forest with no views except of Mount Washington near the upper end. This route is not as rewarding as the Heart Lake Trail.

Tombstone Prairie Trail. (Map 52) Starting from Tombstone Pass, the trail follows a descending road 2.3 miles eastward through old growth and drops 520 feet to the Heart Lake Trail junction above Lost Prairie. There are good views along the Tombstone Prairie Trail.

IKENICK AND FISH LAKE

(Map 53) Ikenick (Isaac Nickerson) Sno-Park at 3,280 feet is 6.4 miles south of the Santiam Junction (Highways 20/22). There are two marked Novice loops through heavily logged areas with many views.

Prairie View Loop. (Map 53) The 5.7-mile Novice loop climbs 300 feet, its east leg following a road, the west leg mostly through clearcuts, and the south leg (from the sno-park westward) along a 1.3-mile shared route with snowmobilers. There are, however, good views of Three Fingered Jack and

Day-use shelter on Brandenburg Butte, one of several shelters in Santiam Pass area

Mount Washington, and a fine, framed view of the Three Sisters 0.9 miles west of the sno-park. The extension trail going 2 miles to Highway 20 from the north end of the loop is uninteresting. There are off-trail routes to Fish Lake and the Old Santiam Wagon Road. Smith Prairie appears on some maps of this area, but its existence is clearly apocryphal, so clearcuts will have to stand in its place.

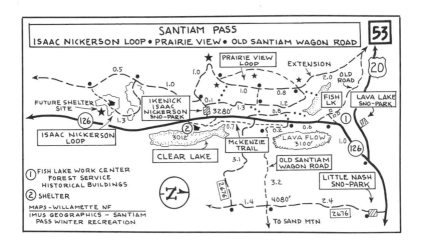

From the sno-park, ski the south leg as it climbs gently through open areas to several viewpoints. The loop turns northward through extensive open areas for more good views. Complete the loop by descending to the east leg and returning to the sno-park.

Isaac Nickerson Loop. (Map 53) Ski 0.1 mile west from the sno-park to start the 3.8-mile Novice loop, and follow up gentle grades along a road 1 mile south to a left turn, climb a clearcut, enter forest, and loop southward to a viewpoint. This is the site for a future shelter, and it features a beautifully framed view of the Sisters over a steep, forested canyon. Continue on the loop, reenter forest, then a clearcut to the road. Turn north to return to the sno-park.

Clear Lake. (Map 53) The long, narrow lake at 3,012 feet, opposite the sno-park, is hemmed in by a lava flow and old growth. There are no obvious ski routes, but it is possible to ski the area.

Park at Ikenick Sno-Park and hike 100 yards north on the highway, then ski 0.5 mile east down the road to the lake. The west shore is steep and unskiable. An abandoned road crosses the access road halfway to the lake. Ski this (rated Novice) northward as it parallels the McKenzie River Trail.

North of the lake's resort cabins the lake becomes a marsh, skiable some winters, with several beaver dams. The summer trail to the footbridge starts at the cabins. Cross the footbridge that leads to an eastside trail to the lava flow. Climb a steep pitch or two through old growth to the lava flow. Snow depth is often inadequate at this elevation.

Do not ski on this lake at any time. A current flows through it, and if there is ice, it is very dangerous.

Fish Lake and Old Santiam Wagon Road. (Map 53) This interesting area is worth a visit, with a variety of skiing experiences available. If turnout parking is not possible, park at Ikenick Sno-Park and ski north on the east leg of the Prairie View Loop. Ski about 1.3 miles, enter forest to the east, find a primitive road, and ski this north to Fish Lake and access to all the routes.

Fish Lake. (Map 53) There are no marked trails here at this time, but it is a Novice area worth exploring. The 1-mile-long "lake" west of the highway north of Ikenick Sno-Park is often dry in summer. Nearby is the Fish Lake Work Center, a group of historic Forest Service buildings from which mule trains left on work trips.

The Old Santiam Wagon Road, built in the 1860s, and a toll road until 1914, goes through the area past the log cabins and 150 yards farther, past a pioneer grave on the right. Continue west on the old road uphill through old growth to join the Prairie View Extension Trail near Highway 20.

Old Santiam Wagon Road. (Map 53) To locate the old road east of the highway, ski south from Fish Lake along the highway's west side about 400 yards, cross the highway, and locate the summer parking lot for the McKenzie

River Trail (to Clear Lake). From the parking lot in the lava flows ski south then southeast through the lava flows 400 yards, then turn east to follow the Old Santiam Wagon Road with difficulty (Intermediate rating).

Ski uphill through scattered old growth along the twisting route 3.4 miles and a thousand vertical feet to a junction with Road 2676, a snowmobile route coming south from Little Nash Sno-Park 2.4 miles north. Road 2676 goes south, then turns west shortly and parallels the Old Road, an easy escape route if you are stressed by route finding.

The old road, after crossing 2676, goes east past Sand Mountain and on to and past the south side of Cache Mountain, a popular snowmobile route.

INDIAN RIDGE

(Map 54) This remarkable viewpoint (5,405 feet), a fire lookout on a flat-topped bare ridge, offers sweeping views of the Cascade Range. Although at a modest elevation, the views are equal to those from Frissell Point—stunning!—perhaps, even, the best of many outstanding viewpoints of the Cascade Range, and one to which you can ski with relative safety and ease.

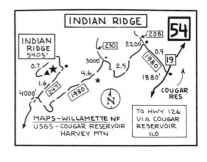

Indian Ridge stands near the west edge of the Three Sisters Wilderness and looks down on French Pete Valley, famed for its old growth, and saved from logging by legal action. From Road 19 at 1,880 feet to the summit is 9.6 miles, part of which may be drivable, depending on the snowline elevation. This is a trip best done in springtime.

Drive east from Eugene on Highway 126 through Blue River to Forest Road 19, 45 miles from Interstate 5. Drive south on 19 3 miles to the Cougar Reservoir dam, and continue around the west side of the reservoir and beyond. Eight miles south of the dam turn west onto Road 1980 (1,880 feet) and drive or ski up this road, which circles to the upper end of a spectacular deep valley, then climbs along an east-facing mountainside with airy dropoffs. The first 3.4 miles to side road 230 is winding and not interesting, but the tour soon becomes rewarding.

The road is wide and safe, but as with any Backcountry trip exercise caution, especially in deep-snow years. The summit view includes all the major volcanoes from Hood south to Diamond Peak, a sweep of some 125 miles.

The junction of Road 19 with Highway 126 from Eugene is about 27 miles southwest of the Highway 126/22 junction near Santiam Pass.

FRISSELL POINT

(Map 55) For Advanced skiers, this 3,000-foot climb on logging roads for up to 8 miles one way on the east side of Frissell Point leads to dramatic views of rugged valleys, cliffs, and near-vertical buttresses.

Located 18 miles west of North Sister, Road 2650, the ski route, starts at Highway 126 2.5 miles north of the Highway 126/242 junction, and 20 miles south of the Highway 20/22 junction near Santiam Pass. Starting at 1,600 feet, Road 2650 may be below the snowline. Drive as far as possible up the one-lane gravel surface with many turnouts.

At 3,000 feet, 3.2 miles from the highway, you will encounter two side roads, each worth a detour of 400 yards for views. The first, Road 613, skirts a clearcut, enters old forest, descends gently, and ends with grand views. Just beyond, Road 620, also on the right, offers equally fine views. The next mile up is steep as you cross open areas, traversing the vast, wrinkled mountainside.

You will be stunned by the scenery 6 miles from the highway—wild scenes of crags and isolated stands of old trees on rocky crests paint a dramatic scene similar to one of Thomas Moran's famous early Western paintings. Another 3.2 miles takes you to a junction north of the peak where a road goes north along the long, narrow ridgecrest.

Reaching the topmost ridgecrest 9.2 miles from the highway is unimportant. The wild scenery of the incredibly broken east face of Frissell Point is more than enough reward.

MARYS PEAK

(Map 56) An outlier of the Coast Range, Marys Peak (4,097 feet) lies 25 miles west of I-5 and appears as a solitary skyline landmark west of Albany, Oregon. Marys Peak is the highest point of the Oregon Coast Range from the Columbia River to Southern Oregon. The distance to the summit from Highway 34 at its base is 9.2 miles by road, then off-road 0.7 mile to the very summit, a climb of 2,867 feet. The snow is seldom as low as the highway, however, and even with a low snowline, you will usually be able to drive

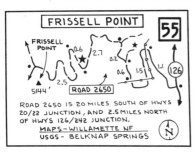

several miles up the peak on the two-lane, paved road. The long, heavily forested south ridge of the peak climbs gently northward to the open summit.

Select fair weather for this scenic Novice–Intermediate tour and for the panoramic views from the summit meadow area. You will see eight Cascade volcanoes from Hood to Diamond Peak near Willamette Pass.

Reportedly, even Mount Rainier can be seen.

From Albany, 72 miles south of Portland and 44 miles north of Eugene, drive west on Highway 20 11 miles to Corvallis and continue west to Philomath, then 9.4 miles west on Highway 34 to a low Coast Range summit (1,230 feet)

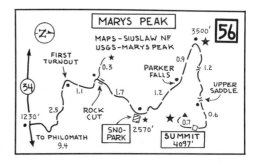

26 miles west of I-5. From Portland, the most scenic—but slower—highway route is Highway 99-W through McMinnville, Monmouth, and beautiful, rolling farm country.

At the highway summit, leave the highway and start up the Marys Peak road. Drive to the snowline. Views start 2.5 miles from the highway, and 0.5 mile farther the first view of the summit is seen. After another 0.6 mile, a side road goes west 0.3 mile just before a rock cut to grand views of the Coast Range. The road soon descends briefly into old growth, then climbs and at 2,570 feet reaches a large parking area 5.3 miles from the highway with good views over the Willamette Valley and the Cascade Range.

The summer hiking trail to the summit, the East Ridge Trail, starts at this parking area and climbs the east side of the ridge. The trail is not marked, not easily followed, and not recommended.

Continue up the road past Parker Falls. At 7.4 miles and 3,500 feet there are views worth the trip. Ski through two minor saddles. At 9.2 miles the road ends at a parking area in a huge hillside meadow that climbs 340 feet and 0.7 mile to the open summit. If you do not ski to the top, ski east of the parking area for the best views of the Willamette Valley and the Cascades.

Although snowmobilers are not permitted on the peak, four-wheel-drive vehicles can use the road legally, which is unfortunate as wheel ruts can be a problem for skiers. For information regarding the area and snowline, call the Alsea Ranger District, Siuslaw National Forest (503-487-5811) during office hours.

Chapter 22

SANTIAM PASS

At 4,817 feet, Santiam Pass receives heavy snowfall and offers downhill skiing at Hoodoo Ski Bowl and cross-country skiing across miles of ideal terrain. The pass area is a vast, rolling plateau with several volcanic buttes scattered about, including impressive, cliff-topped Hayrick Butte, a landmark. Some 11 square miles are laced by marked ski trails passing through forests, across meadows, and around several small lakes.

In addition to the ski-trail areas, there are 6 square miles of open terrain going west to Sand Mountain, crossed by snowmobile routes but also open to skiers. The scenery is impressive. Mount Jefferson, Three Fingered Jack, and Mount Washington are the three highest peaks seen from the area. Square-topped Hayrick Butte rising 700 feet above the plateau and Cache Mountain at the eastern edge make skiing here a scenic experience.

Nine square miles of the plateau are almost totally without trees due to the 1967 Airstrip Burn, a forest fire of huge dimensions. Only a few silver snags remain as evidence.

Of the four sno-parks in the pass area, Ray Benson Sno-Park gives access to most of the ski trails. It is reached from the Highway 20/126 exit to Hoodoo Ski Bowl by driving 0.3 mile past the Ski Bowl entrance to the combined skier-snowmobiler sno-park.

SANTIAM PASS SKI TRAILS

(Map 51) There are three unique but connected areas of marked ski trails—the North Loop, 4.6 miles of trails; the South Loop, 11.3 miles of trails; and the Eastside Trails, 12 miles of trails, some shared with machines. Each area has a three-sided log shelter. The Eastside Trails are also accessible, most directly from Corbett Sno-Park (4,200 feet), which is located 3.8 miles east of the Hoodoo Ski Bowl access road and east of Santiam Pass on the highway. A Nordic Center with groomed tracks operates from the downhill ski-area lodge.

Nordic Center Trails. (Map 51) There are 5 miles of groomed ski tracks north of the downhill ski-lodge area. The trails are on level terrain and are ideally suited for Novice skiers. There is a trail-use fee, and the center offers ski rentals.

North Loop. (Map 51) For Intermediate skiers, the 4.6 miles of trails have several short, abrupt, and difficult ascents and descents. The trails are mostly through forest.

From Ray Benson Sno-Park ski northwest (clockwise) through mixed forest to the north leg, which follows the old Hogg railroad grade. Ski past the North Blowout Shelter (near a shallow cinder crater), then swing back to the sno-park on the south leg, which is also the north leg of the South Loop. This 1.4-mile section is quite hilly and difficult for inexperienced skiers.

The marked Pacific Crest Trail (PCT) passes through the center of the loop and follows a fairly rugged and narrow 0.8 mile through thick forest.

South Loop. (Map 51) The 11.3 miles of this loop are suitable for Novice skiers, although the small hills of the east leg will be intimidating for inexperienced skiers. Outstanding features of the loop include gentle terrain and magnificent vistas from vast, open areas.

Start skiing from the sno-park's west side and ski the west leg, which lies directly under the cliffs of Hayrick Butte. The trail crosses flats and goes down a gentle hill or two that take you into the sweeping, wide-open spaces of the Airstrip Burn. Both east and west legs eventually reach and climb the bare slopes of Brandenburg Butte (4,888 feet), where an open log shelter sitting on the east side provides a fine view of Mount Washington and massive, forested Cache Mountain. Brandenburg Butte, although not high and steep, is not suited for Novice skiers.

The South Loop-Circle Lake Trail crosses the South Loop from east to west, cutting it into a shorter loop for Novices, thus avoiding the climb of Brandenburg Butte. The PCT, little used here, cuts the loop from south to north and adds 2.5 miles included in the total of 11.3 miles of trails for the South Loop system.

Eastside Trails. (Map 51) Among the 12.6 miles included in the total of 11.3 miles of marked trails that cross this eastside area, the 3.7 miles of the Circle Lake Trail are closed to machines. This beautiful trail is the most used of the Eastside Trails and has many rewards.

Circle Lake Trail. (Map 51) Rated Intermediate, this trail is east of the busy North and South Loops and offers a sense of isolation. The trail starts at the northeast corner of the North Loop and is best reached by skiing the west and north legs of the North Loop.

The trail passes through lovely forest, meadows, and alongside a small lake or two, often not noticed when the snow is deep. A section of open forest glades follows and leads to a junction with the Fireline Loop Trail, a machine route that goes through the loops to the sno-park. At the junction, turn southwest and ski 100 yards on the Circle Lake Trail and then to the off-trail knoll where the Island Junction Shelter is sited. There is a grand view here of North Sister and Mount Washington. From the shelter, ski the trail southwest as it climbs to join the South Loop. The trail passes along the edge of the Airstrip Burn with almost continuous views.

Two Buttes Cutoff Trail. (Map 51) This 1.8-mile segment of the east leg of the South Loop is a hilly, twisting route best suited for strong Intermediate skiers who will find it challenging. The trail climbs, contours, descends the sides of two small cinder cones. If you are less experienced, ski this section from south to north.

Hayrick Butte Loop and Hoodoo Butte Plateau. (Map 51) Although

Hoodoo Butte's eastern slopes contain a busy downhill ski area of chairlifts and scurrying alpine skiers, a plateau at 5,000 feet on the butte's west side provides isolation and marvelous views. The area is not marked for cross-country skiers at this time and will be best enjoyed by strong Intermediate skiers.

To circle Hayrick Butte, park as far south as possible in Hoodoo Sno-Park, then on skis aim for the low pass to the south between the two buttes, scarcely a half mile distant. Spectacular cliffs to the east dominate the narrow valley leading to the pass. At the pass, enjoy a view of Big Lake and Mount Washington to the south.

To circle Hayrick Butte, a 4-mile loop, follow along the pass's contour and descend moderate slopes to the open flats of the Airstrip Burn, then turn east to join the South Loop. It is possible to ski to your car by staying close to the base of Hayrick Butte.

To reach the Hoodoo Butte Plateau west of Hoodoo Butte—the most desirable objective from the pass—ski southwest, climbing gently from the pass along a roadbed on the steep sidehill for 0.5 mile. As you turn more westward, views will slowly unfold. The plateau extends west and northwest, undulating and eventually dipping to meet the open areas of the burn and leading to the Sand Mountain area and the Old Santiam Wagon Road.

There are views of Mount Washington and Big Lake at its foot, and Three Sisters (South Sister just peering around the Middle's shoulder). Sand Mountain is the double-summited white butte. Farther around you'll see Jefferson, Three Fingered Jack, and many other highpoints and ridges.

The plateau edge is steep, but there are numerous places to descend to the burn if you are going to Sand Mountain or elsewhere. Ski this route and the burn only in good weather. On bad days, ski the marked trails.

SANTIAM EAST AND CORBETT SNO-PARK TRAILS

(Map 51) Across Santiam Pass 3.8 miles east of the Hoodoo Ski Bowl access road is Corbett Sno-Park at 4,200 feet. The trail leading from the sno-park is used by machines and must be shared by all users. The trail, which follows a road, leads to all the Eastside ski routes.

The little-known Blue Lake Trailhead Sno-Park at 4,482 feet is located 1 mile from Corbett Sno-Park toward Santiam Pass. At this time it serves little purpose except for off-trail skiing south of the highway, and for Backcountry skiers entering the Mount Jefferson Wilderness north of the highway. The marked trail from this sno-park at this time goes only downhill to the Island Lake Trail. Future plans include another connector trail from the sno-park to the Circle Lake Trail.

From Corbett Sno-Park ski along the road (the Island Lake Trail) past two views east to Black Butte, a massive, symmetrical, forested volcanic cone. Save your film for the second view. At 1.7 miles the Island Lake Trail turns west and goes uphill through scattered old growth past Island Lake (north) and in 1.4 miles joins the Circle Lake Trail.

If you do not turn west and ski uphill at 1.7 miles, go straight ahead (south) along the road for great views. At 2.7 miles along the winding road you'll have your first view of Mount Washington rising impressively to a pointed summit. Keep going for an even more dramatic view. There are several small lakes west of you, but these are not seen from the trail. At about 3 miles Meadow Lake, with a low bluff on its north side, is nearby. At 3.4 miles the road narrows into tight jackpine forest, and from here on you must make your own route. At 4.3 miles you find yourself on a rolling plateau, open in all directions with views of Three Fingered Jack, Mount Washington, Cache Mountain, Hayrick Butte, and only 0.8 mile to Brandenburg Butte with its eastside shelter. Be adventuresome: ski west and north to intercept other trails and form a loop.

SUTTLE LAKE, BLUE LAKE, AND ROUND LAKE

(Map 51) Downhill and east of Corbett Sno-Park 3.9 miles the area contains several Forest Service ski trails and a Nordic Center with a groomed-track system. Although lower in elevation than Santiam Pass, there is often sufficient snow for good skiing. The trails in the Suttle Lake-Blue Lake area offer a different skiing experience from those at Santiam Pass, where there is more variety and greater scenic values.

Suttle Lake. (Map 51) Suttle Lake, 1.5 miles long, is located 7.7 miles east of the Hoodoo Ski Area entrance. The lake sits at an elevation (3,438 feet) that does not have consistent snow depth, but with a foot of snow or more the marked around-the-lake 3.2-mile trail can be enjoyed. Although it follows an uninteresting road for 0.6 mile, neighboring Scout Lake is a scenic jewel and a worthwhile goal.

A sno-park is plowed at the west end of Suttle Lake near Blue Lake, an adjoining, smaller lake. Both the north shore and south shore marked ski trails start from the sno-park. Other plowing for parking may be available depending on conditions.

Northshore Trail. (Map 51) Best left for Intermediate skiers, the trail is narrow, often poised on a steep bank, and has many sudden, short dips and turns with which a Novice would have problems. The benefits of this trail are the forest skiing and views of Cache Mountain and Mount Washington. Black Butte is visible from the lake's west end.

Southshore Trail. (Map 51) This trail also necessitates a few moves difficult for Novices, but it is more user-friendly than the Northshore Trail. The east end is particularly tricky in places and may be hard to follow in places. The terrain generally becomes easier as it follows a trail and goes through campgrounds. Novices should ski it with caution. About 1 mile along the trail, skiing eastward, a marked side trail leads upward, crosses the lake's plowed access road, then follows a road to Scout Lake.

Scout Lake. (Map 51) A 1.8-mile Novice loop to Scout Lake touches the Southshore Trail in two places. If you start your tour from the west end of Suttle Lake, it is necessary to ski 1.1 miles to the beginning of the loop (total distance to lake and back is 4 miles). It may, however, be possible to park closer to the loop. The loop's north leg is the Southshore Trail, then the loop climbs from the Southshore Campground and crosses the plowed access road. It then climbs 0.6 mile on the Scout Lake road. The return leg of the loop follows an old road eastward to the Blue Bay Campground.

The small lake's shoreline is wide and open, and ponderosa pines add a unique beauty. The lake is ringed by forest and there are no mountain views, but the special beauty of the setting is reward in itself.

Blue Lake Nordic Center. (Map 51) Overnight accommodations lure many skiers to the long-established resort at the beautiful small lake west of Suttle Lake and 2.2 miles from Highway 20/126 using the Suttle Lake road. Up to 14 miles of trails are groomed and a fee is charged.

Round Lake Trails. (Map 51) Round Lake, an uninteresting lake with a view of Three Fingered Jack, is at 4,285 feet. Two trails near Suttle Lake and across the highway lead to good views of Jefferson and Three Fingered Jack, and to the forest-ringed lake. Total one-way length from Highway 20 for this Novice-Intermediate tour is 5.5 miles with a cumulative elevation gain of 1,500 feet.

Drive to the Suttle Lake access road and park where possible, usually at the west end of Suttle Lake at the sno-park (see Suttle Lake). Ski to and cross Highway 20 at the unplowed summer entrance to the lake's north shore picnic area. Behind a pile of boulders across the highway is the trail leading into forest to the Round Lake Trails. Ski 0.3 mile uphill to Road 1210, the main road that goes to Round Lake. The wide road climbs gently 3.8 miles to its high point at 4,440 feet and views of Jefferson, Three Fingered Jack, and Black Butte.

There is also a view of the Three Sisters before the high point. From here, in a large clearcut, the road descends 1.2 miles to a junction. Go straight 0.2 mile and turn left to the nearby lake.

Round Lake Trail Loop. (Map 51) The most scenic and interesting route to the upper views on Road 1210 is the north leg of the 4.3-mile loop. The loop is partly formed by its 1.9-mile south leg on Road 1210. The north leg is a primitive road, has a view of Jefferson only 1.4 miles from the highway, and is scenically much more interesting.

To ski the loop, ski up from the highway 0.3 mile, then turn right (east) and descend Road 1210 0.3 mile. Turn left onto a narrow road (the loop's north leg) that becomes more narrow, twisting, and scenic as it climbs westward to rejoin Road 1210 in 2.1 miles. It is possible to ski up or down a large clearcut that crosses the loop (see map).

If there is little or no snow near Suttle Lake but you want to ski the Round Lake Trail Loop, drive 0.9 mile south of the Suttle Lake access road, turn left onto Road 12, drive north 0.9 mile to Road 1210, then drive up 1210 to the snowline. Do not drive the Loop's north leg— it is narrow and has no turnouts.

Blue Lake Trail. (Map 51) This Intermediate 3.9-mile trail is not heavily used and is normally skied with a car shuttle. Starting at Blue Lake Trailhead Sno-Park, 1 mile west of Corbett Sno-Park, the trail goes downhill 1.1 miles where it crosses the Island Lake Trail from Corbett Sno-Park (0.5 mile from the sno-park). The Blue Lake Trail then continues east, following moderately steep logging roads downhill through clearcuts for 1.5 miles. It then joins the final 1.3-mile trail section to Blue Lake for a total elevation loss of 1,000 feet. Be sure snow extends all the way down to Blue Lake, or you may wind up carrying your skis at the bottom end.

CAMP SHERMAN, BLACK BUTTE, AND SISTERS

(Map 57) Camp Sherman, a quiet resort village at the north foot of Black Butte, the landmark forested volcanic cone, has several flat-land ski trails, marked and unmarked through ponderosa forests. The elevation of 2,960 feet does not allow for consistent snow depth, but when there is skiable snow it is a unique and lovely place to visit, and its overnight accommodations are the closest to Santiam Pass, some 13 miles to the west.

The small town of Sisters, 12 miles south of Camp Sherman, gives access to interesting skiing at higher elevations where there are marked trails, views, and access to spectacular backcountry near Three Creek Lake and Broken Top Mountain.

Camp Sherman and Black Butte. (Map 57) A quiet resort village of some 200 souls, Camp Sherman sits 12 miles north of Sisters in a beautiful ponderosa forest. There are nine resort facilities offering a wide range of accommodations. The area is primarily Forest Service land, but there are many

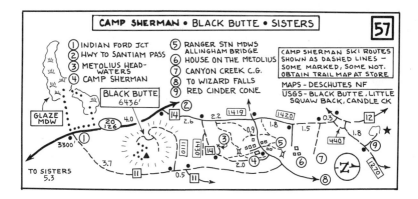

summer cabins clustered along the edge of the beautiful Metolius River, which flows through the center of the area and is fed by giant springs. Ten Forest Service campgrounds along the river offer scenic ski-touring routes, together with several marked ski trails. Black Butte sweeps upward from near Camp Sherman, rising 3,000 feet above the Metolius valley.

Camp Sherman Ski Trails. (Map 57) In addition to two existing ski trails, the Forest Service plans more for both biking and skiing. The terrain is level in all directions and ideal for Novices. The trails parallel the Metolius River, cross meadows, and go through campgrounds and stands of old-growth ponderosa pines.

The only marked ski trail at this time starts at the store and post office and goes south paralleling a summer-home road, crosses a bridge, and heads into ponderosa forest. At the bridge, an alternative marked route remains on the east bank and continues south through campgrounds and beautiful forest. Ultimately this route leads to the headwater springs of the Metolius River only 2.5 miles south of the village near the foot of Black Butte. With adequate snow depth, there are miles of open forest to ski right from the center of the village.

Another ski route, unmarked, goes north on the east side of the river through summer homes then campgrounds to the Allingham bridge, where you cross to the west to Ranger Station Meadows and ski back through the long, beautiful meadows, then past summer cabins.

Metolius River Headwaters. (Map 57) You can take another route to the headwaters, less interesting than the Camp Sherman ski trail that parallels the river southward from the store. Park at the Y-junction and ski 1.5 miles along wide, unplowed Road 14 eastward. The Y is 2.8 miles from Camp Sherman on the access road to the highway and Sisters, and 2.6 miles from the highway. Ski Road 14 eastward along the base of Black Butte, then turn into the summer parking area for the final 400 yards on the walkway to the viewing area of the springs that form the Metolius River headwaters and to where you will also see Jefferson across a meadow.

Red Cinder Cone. (Map 57) This small, undistinguished cone rises only 650 feet above the flat Metolius valley but offers sweeping views of the Cascades. This is the best viewpoint within miles of Camp Sherman except for slopes high on the west side of Black Butte. This is an ideal 6.3-mile ski tour for Novice-Intermediate skiers, measured from the store. The road is usually plowed, however, 2.4 miles to the House on the Metolius, a resort lodge, making the tour that much shorter.

Drive north on Road 1420 to the end of plowing and park off the road. Carry a shovel to improve parking and do not block the private drive or Road 1420. Ski north on the road past the Canyon Creek Campground road to Road 440 (to the right), which connects with Road 1270 and goes to the cinder cone. The cinder cone serves as a quarry for red cinders for road surfaces. If you miss wide Road 440 you will quickly reach Road 12, which you can follow a short distance to Road 1270. There are two side roads to the quarry—take the second one and ski 0.3 mile to the top of the cinder butte. If you ski to the west side, the view sweeps from Green Ridge on the east past Black Butte to Broken Top, the Three Sisters, Mount Washington, Three Fingered Jack, and Jefferson.

Black Butte. (Map 57) A massive, symmetrical, forested volcanic cone at 6,436 feet, the butte is one of Central Oregon's most visible landmarks. Rising over 3,000 feet above and north of the town of Sisters, it lures a few adventuresome skiers for the panoramic views from the summit. The ascent is Advanced–Backcountry, and from the spiraling road it is still a steep and difficult 2-mile, 1,600-foot climb to the top following the summer hiking trail. Due to the thick, impenetrable forests on its sides, and the very steep slopes, the road is the only practical route to the summit trail. Do not be deceived by the open stands of ponderosa pines below—these soon change to thick, brushy slopes.

The best route starts with a drive to the Indian Ford–Road 11 junction with Highway 20/126, 5.3 miles north of the town of Sisters. Proceed on paved Road 11 to Road 1110. Drive up 1110 as far as possible and proceed on skis to the end of the road (4,800 feet) where the summer foot trail starts. From here the summer trail climbs northward moderately, then switchbacks for the final, long traverse that increases in steepness. About a mile above the road, the trail breaks out into the open for the remainder of the climb. Ski climbers are recommended.

Glaze Meadow. (Map 57) This mile-long, crescent-shaped meadow is located southwest of Black Butte and west of Highway 20/126. Rated Intermediate, the tour is 3 miles round trip through forest and open areas. There are views of Cascade volcanoes and of nearby Black Butte towering far above.

Drive to Indian Ford junction with Highways 20/126 (see Black Butte) 2.1 miles south of the Black Butte Ranch entrance and 5.3 miles north of Sisters. At the junction with unplowed Road 11, park and cross the highway to the west side and ski west into the forest on skid roads to Glaze Meadow.

Another route proceeds north along the west side of the highway 0.9 mile to what maps call Black Butte Swamp. This large open area is where you turn west, traverse through a band of forest, and enter the east end of Glaze Meadow.

Three Creek Loops and Snow Creek Trail. (Map 58) South of the town of Sisters are several trails and loops, and a skiers' shelter with a view. Two short loops—Warren's and Nancy's Loops—along with the Three Creek Lake and Snow Creek Trails total 9.5 miles of skier-only routes ranging from Intermediate to Advanced in difficulty.

To reach the trails from the small town of Sisters (3,184 feet), 22 miles northwest of Bend, turn south onto Elm Street, which becomes Road 16 south of town. Continue south on Road 16. At 5 miles the road climbs a ridge with fine views. At 11 miles reach Upper Three Creek Sno-Park. From the sno-park ski a few yards south up Road 16 past the gate and turn right onto the Three Creek Lake Trail. This trail leads to all the loops and trails of the area.

Three Creek Trail. (Map 58) This Intermediate trail leads in 6 miles to Three Creek Lake in a 1,200-foot climb along a primitive road for most of the way. At 0.7 mile, after a demanding short ascent, the trail meets Warren's Loop, then 1.3 miles later passes near the Jefferson View Shelter in a large clearcut. The trail at first climbs through ponderosa pines, then jackpine for most of the remainder to where it rejoins Road 16 2 miles below the lake. Your first view of the imposing Tam McArthur Rim rising above the lake is from Trapper Meadows, 1.5 miles below the lake.

Warren's and Nancy's Loops. (Map 58) Each of these two Novice–Intermediate loops is just under 2 miles in length, and they share a mutual leg. The north leg of Warren's Loop is the most scenic of all the legs, passing through varied forest, shelterwoods, and clearcuts. The loops and trails offer occasional views of Jefferson and North Sister. The two loops, of course, are popular as they are near the sno-park, and their east and west legs form part of the Three Creek and Snow Creek Trails. The shelter with its views is only 0.6 mile above Nancy's Loop, the upper loop. From the sno-park ski up the Three Creek Trial 0.7 mile to Warren's Loop. Nancy's Loop is 0.5 mile farther. The loops are named for retired Forest Service employees Warren and Nancy Seaward, who live in Sisters and conceived of the trail system and did much of the scouting and construction.

Snow Creek Trail. (Map 58) An adventuresome Intermediate return to the sno-park is by way of the Snow Creek Trail, starting near Trapper Meadow (also known as Three Creek Meadow). It follows the summer Park Meadow Trail, at first an old road. It leaves Road 16, goes west paralleling a historic irrigation canal, following the mostly level, primitive road to a pumice desert at 1.1 miles, then descends steeply on a forest trail 0.8 mile to a right turn at Snow Creek.

Then it descends northward on moderate grades through beautiful, scattered meadows in a narrow valley, climbs a short ridge with ponderosas, and descends along the west legs of both Warren's and Nancy's Loops, ending at the sno-park.

Three Creek Lake and Tam McArthur Rim. (Map 58) Exceptional views

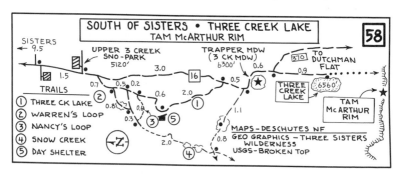

are the rewards for the tour into Three Creek Lake. If conditions are good, the tour to the rim above the lake provides views of nine major Cascade peaks, with panoramic views of the entire region and its rolling forests and countless cinder cones and buttes. See directions for Three Creek Lake Trail for route description.

This is an Advanced tour climbing 1,440 feet to the lake, and 2,180 feet to the top of the rim at 7,300 feet. The trail is marked to the lake and is a 12-mile round trip from the sno-park. From the lake to the upper rim is 3 miles one way.

From where the Three Creek Trail rejoins Road 16 after 4 miles, ski up the road as it winds through Mountain Hemlock then reaches Trapper Meadow with the first view of Tam McArthur Rim. The view is impressive: rimrock cliffs, large cornices, snow bowls, and rolling open slopes. From the meadow ski 1.5 miles uphill to the lake through open areas and forest (the summer campground). From the lake it is possible to explore the snow benches above for better views of the volcanoes to the north, or ski 1 mile westward to Little Three Creek Lake.

The best tour from the lake, however, climbs to the east end of the rim (7,300 feet), from which you can see volcanoes from Adams to Broken Top lined up in an inspiring array of forms and heights. The best route from the lake is along the moderate, tree-covered ridge immediately to the east. A more challenging route leaves the southwest shore and climbs through forest, over consecutive snow benches, and across small basins to the crest. The route is considerably east of a prominent rock buttress on the rim.

From the rimcrest follow gentle, vast snowfields through scattered stands of alpine trees. At 7,800 feet, a flat ridge northeast of Broken Top offers the finest views of the entire area, including the great snow basins at the north foot of Broken Top, and the Three Sisters all rising over a mile from their bases. From the lake it is about 3 miles to this viewpoint, which can also be reached from Dutchman Flat 8 miles to the south (see Three Creek Lake and Tam McArthur Rim).

Cross-District Trail to Dutchman Flat. (Map 58) This 17-mile partly unmarked route from Upper Three Creek Sno-Park to Dutchman Flat, a snowmobile trail, may be of interest to some skiers. The Advanced–Backcountry route requires a car shuttle and follows Road 370. The skiing distance includes using the cross-country ski trails at either end. The distance is sno-park to sno-park, and the cumulative elevation gain is 2,600 feet.

From Trapper Meadow (see map) ski up Road 370 through scattered and then dense, scrubby jackpine, then mountain hemlock before the road breaks out into the magnificent, open slopes of Ball Butte. Along the way, the road descends into Tumalo Creek (turn right at a junction) then climbs through Happy Valley to the open slopes east of Broken Top at 6,880 feet and above Dutchman Flat for the final descent on the marked trails to Dutchman Flat Nordic Sno-Park.

McKENZIE PASS LAVA FIELDS

(Map 59) This scenic tour takes you to the very crest of the Cascades at McKenzie Pass on an Advanced, 12.4-mile round trip on an unmarked road with an elevation gain of 1,284 feet to a high point of 5,324 feet. You will enjoy unusual lava-flow scenery and views of nearby North Sister, Mount Washington, Three Fingered Jack, and Jefferson.

From the town of Sisters, 22 miles northwest of Bend, drive 8.4 miles west on Highway 242 to the snow gate—or as far as possible, depending on the snowline. McKenzie Pass and Highway 242 are not plowed in winter and remain closed until late spring.

Follow the road through forest as it climbs gently toward the pass. Three miles from the snow gate, at Windy Point (4,909 feet), the first views of Mounts Jefferson and Washington appear. The road is fairly obvious as you near the pass, cutting through shallow valleys in the lava flow, which covers the area for miles. At the pass a small, unusual stone building—an observatory for summer tourists—sits on a prominent point on the south side of the road. Although the pass is the official end of this tour, you can explore in many directions across the immense lava fields and cinder cones.

North and Middle Sisters from McKenzie Pass

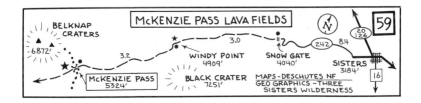

The view from the pass is outstanding, across vast snowfields to the solitary, high volcanic peaks of the Central Cascades. This tour is particularly enjoyable in the spring, when the snow is consolidated and the weather more stable and predictable. In bad weather the pass area offers serious route-finding problems. This is not a tour for days when snow is falling and blowing.

Historical Note: The John Craig Memorial Cross-Country Ski Race and Tour are held along this route each year in April to commemorate the memory of John Craig, who carried mail on skis across McKenzie Pass in the late 1800s. Like Snowshoe Thompson of California legend, John Craig made many remarkable trips across the pass before dying in a winter blizzard. The race and tour are sponsored by the Oregon Nordic Club, a cross-country skiing club with several chapters throughout the state. There are usually several hundred participants each year for this interesting and historic event.

OTHER SANTIAM PASS TOURS

Cache Mountain. (Map 51) The forested, massive bulk of Cache Mountain (5,579 feet) is a prominent landmark southeast of the Santiam Pass area. It is not often climbed because it is so far from the sno-parks. The summit is the site of a former fire lookout. The tour is rated Backcountry, is up to 16 miles round trip, and has an elevation gain of a modest 1,500 feet. Distances to the summit (and elevations gains) are 8.5 miles from Ray Benson Sno-Park (1,000 feet), 7 miles from Corbett Sno-Park (1,500 feet), and 9.6 miles (east route) from Highway 20 (2,300 feet).

The most obvious route to the top of Cache Mountain is from Ray Benson Sno-Park, by way of the South Loop then on past Brandenburg Butte and onto the Old Santiam Wagon Road, a popular snowmobile route that goes around the south side of Cache Mountain, called the Cross-District Trail by machine users. A series of roads climbs the south side of the mountain with one going to the very summit.

From Corbett Sno-Park ski out the Island Lake Trail south 3.1 miles to Road 800. Ski this road 0.8 mile to its end, climb the clearcut above, then travel through forest to the 5,080-foot saddle east of Little Cache Mountain, then up to the top.

Hoodoo to McKenzie Pass Traverse. (Map 51) This 22-mile Backcountry tour from Ray Benson Sno-Park to the snow gate west of the town of Sisters is a spectacular trip. Views from the vast lava fields south of Mount Washington around Belknap Crater are dramatic. The cumulative elevation gain is 2,000 feet. The route attempts to follow the PCT, but route-finding skills are necessary. Ski this trip only when snow conditions are good, before tree wells are formed, and when there is sufficient snow depth to cover the lava flows.

From Ray Benson Sno-Park ski 2.5 miles to a road on the east shore of Big Lake often used by snowmobilers, then ski through the camp buildings along the shore. Ski out the south side and angle up to find the PCT, not always easy to locate. Climb steadily as you ski south but stay below 5,600 feet. The route crosses many minor ridges and gullies. Six miles south of Big Lake you reach the lava fields. Climb to the 5,540-foot saddle between Belknap Crater and Mount Washington, then follow the contour around Belknap's east side, maintaining elevation then descending to McKenzie Pass. From the pass to the snow gate is 6.2 miles.

If Big Lake is frozen safely, you can ski across to the southeast side and climb to the PCT.

Santiam Pass Wilderness Areas. (No sketch map) Two designated wilderness areas border the Santiam Pass cross-country ski area—Mount Jefferson Wilderness to the north just across the highway, and Mount Washington Wilderness south of Big Lake. Of the two, because of easy access, Mount Jefferson Wilderness receives more regular visits by Backcountry skiers.

Other than blazes on trees, usually under snow, there are no marked trails for winter travel, and few signs, a result of the modern wilderness ethic. Here you are totally on your own with your skills, map, and compass. Most people either ski the PCT north, climbing the south slopes of Three Fingered Jack, or ski to the Berley Lakes basin between Three Fingered Jack and Maxwell Butte.

The PCT is not particularly interesting for the first 2 miles as there are few views. Beyond 3 miles it crosses very steep slopes high on the mountain's west side and is not recommended. On the descent, the PCT is narrow, twisting, and difficult.

For Berley Lakes, follow the PCT about 1.4 miles, then branch off to the northwest on the Berley Lakes Trail. The lakes lie in a wide, open basin about 2.5 miles north of Highway 20/126 at 4,800 to 5,200 feet, but the total trail distance is closer to 4 miles.

To locate the PCT trailhead, drive to the Santiam Snow Play Area parking lot on the north side of the highway just east of the Hoodoo Ski Bowl access road. From the sno-park ski east paralleling the highway 1 mile to the PCT trailhead parking area (not plowed in winter), then ski the PCT 0.3 mile to its first junction, with the Square Lake Trail. Go north 1 mile to the next junction and go left for the Berley Lakes, or go right for the PCT. Maxwell Butte can be climbed from Berley Lakes, or from Maxwell Sno-Park on Highway 22 west of the butte.

Part V
THE CENTRAL CASCADES

Skiers from all over Oregon and from out of state are attracted to the beauty of this region and the variety of skiing. Ranging from groomed trails and many miles of marked trails to exceptional backcountry skiing in the Cascade crest forests and wilderness areas, the choices seem limitless. Magnificent major volcanoes and their vast, high snowfields dominate the skiing areas.

Author and wife in lower crater, Broken Top beyond (Photo: Ruth Warbington)

Chapter 23

THE BEND AREA

The Bend, Santiam Pass, McKenzie Pass, and Sisters areas of Oregon contain the most concentrated collection of high-quality cross-country ski trails in the state. Once judged by all as the unrivaled cross-country ski-trails area of Oregon, the Bend area now faces stiff competition from the Santiam Pass area where extensive, well-planned trail systems have been built by the Forest Service in several locations. Skiers outside of Oregon have increasingly recognized the high-quality skiing in the Bend area, and some experts reasonably foresee Bend developing into the finest Nordic skiing center in the United States (if indeed it is not already). Bend's advantages include its higher elevation and its proximity to the nearby town of Bend with its profusion of overnight accommodations for skiers, primarily fueled by the growth and popularity of the Mount Bachelor downhill ski area.

Skiers of all skill levels find a bewildering variety of trails from which to select. They range from beautifully marked and groomed trails to untracked backcountry tours. The Bend area also has consistent snow depth, and experiences more favorable weather and snow conditions and enjoys a longer snow season than ski areas on the western slopes of the Cascades. Finally, the unusual natural beauty of the region is a great attraction—sagebrush desert, low-elevation pine woods, alpine old-growth forests, and the incomparable volcanoes of the High Cascades.

The town of Bend, located at 3,500 feet in the high desert of Central Oregon, is the focus for most travel in the area. To reach Bend from Portland drive Highway 26 through Government Camp and southeastward through the Warm Springs Indian Reservation to Madras, on Highway 97. Then follow Highway 97 south to Bend. Total distance: 160 miles. From the Willamette Valley skiers can drive Highways 22, 20, or 126 to Santiam Pass, then across the pass and down to Bend on Highway 20.

Most of the Bend area tours described are west of Bend along and at the end of snow-blocked Highway 46, better known as Century Drive or the Cascade Lakes Highway. In winter this highway ends 22 miles west of Bend, near the Mount Bachelor Ski Area. A short road continues to West Village Sno-Park, which provides direct access to the Nordic Sports Center and its excellent groomed-track system. Skiers not using the groomed-track system should park at Dutchman Flat Nordic Sno-Park.

Weekend accommodations in Bend are often tight and reservations are recommended. For information on local accommodations call or write the Bend Chamber of Commerce, 63085 N. Highway 97, Bend, Oregon 97701,

503-382-3221. Overnight parking is permitted at Mount Bachelor sno-parks, but check first with the night watchperson or information desk. A shuttle bus transports skiers from Bend to the ski area for a fee, serving only Mount Bachelor customers, alpine and Nordic, and going directly to the West Village parking area. The bus does not stop at sno-parks en route. The bus may be boarded behind the Mount Bachelor corporate offices on Century Drive just beyond all the ski shops.

Nordic trails in the Bend area are built and maintained by volunteers from the Oregon Nordic Club, Central Oregon Chapter, in cooperation with the U.S. Forest Service (USFS). In addition, the volunteers maintain and stock wood for the shelters. Please use wood sparingly. Your cooperation is essential to keep these facilities available in the future for public use. Pack out all trash, discourage vandalism, and encourage others to do the same. The following areas are specifically closed to dogs: Dutchman Flat, Vista Butte, Swampy Lakes, and the Meissner Trails. However, dogs are permitted, with a free permit from the Bend USFS office, if they are in harness and then only on groomed snowmobile trails. The reason for the restrictions is the problem with dog droppings, the damage caused by dogs to ski tracks, and the heavy use of trails by skiers. Dogs are permitted, but not encouraged, on the Edison Butte trails. Owners are required to remove their dogs' excrement. If the privilege is abused, the Edison Butte area will be closed to dogs.

There are many miles of groomed snowmobile trails in the Central Oregon area, some passing through cross-country ski areas. Be alert at trail crossings. If you ski on snowmobile trails, ski to the right and allow the machines to pass on the left. Many square miles are closed to snow machines and are for the exclusive use of "quiet users." All wilderness areas are closed to machine use including the Three Sisters Wilderness, Mount Washington Wilderness, and Mount Jefferson Wilderness.

With the heavy skier and snowmobiler use of trails in Oregon there are inevitable conflicts. The Forest Service has done its best to separate the two groups, and to reduce conflicts through education. Please try to not ski on snowmobile routes, and if you do, ski to the edge of the trail for your own safety and to permit passage of snowmobilers, to whom these routes are dedicated. In some areas there are shared-use corridors such as Cascade Lakes Highway/Century Drive toward Todd and Sparks Lakes and Road 370 going past Todd Lake and Big Meadow to the Moon Mountain flats. Areas closed to snowmobilers include Ball Butte, Broken Top, and the areas south of Century Drive and west of and north of Road 370.

The shelters in all the Bend skiing areas are maintained by volunteers of the Oregon Nordic Club, Central Oregon Chapter. Your cooperation is essential in keeping these shelters available for public use in the future. Again, please use wood sparingly, discourage vandalism, and encourage others to do the same. Dogs and motorized vehicles are not permitted on these trails, nor on any ski trails north of Century Drive.

MOUNT BACHELOR NORDIC SPORTS CENTER

(Map 60) At an elevation of 6,400 feet, the 30 miles of groomed tracks for both classic and skating styles are usually in good skiing condition. The many loops and trails, for every level of skill, extend westward from the West Village parking area where the Nordic Center lodge is located. The perfectly set double tracks for side-by-side skiing provide a fine skiing experience. A fee is charged for use of the groomed trails. The Nordic Center has a ski school and rents equipment.

FOREST AND MEADOW TOURS

Dutchman Flat Connector. (Map 60) This Novice trail links Dutchman Flat Nordic Sno-Park with all the other trails of the area. From the sno-park the trail enters the large meadow, or flat, where poles along the east edge mark the way northward. The trail forks twice in the meadow. The first fork leads left (west) to the Todd Lake Trail and the Common Corridor to the Nordic Center. The second fork leads right (east) to the Big Meadow and Swampy Lakes Trails.

This Novice trail extends for 1.2 miles and ends where it meets both Century Drive and the end of the Common Corridor Trail. (See the following description.)

Common Corridor Trail. (Map 60) This 0.4-mile Intermediate connector trail links the Mount Bachelor parking area and the Nordic Center with Dutchman Flat. Although it crosses the center's trail complex, the Common Corridor is a free route. After descending a moderate slope from the Nordic Center it goes around the east side of a cinder cone (the Old Maid), then through a small valley to snow-covered Century Drive, where signs will guide you to the destination of your choice.

Todd Lake Trail. (Map 60) This 7-mile round-trip trail will challenge Novices who are in good condition. The trail offers both forest and meadow skiing while following a scenic road most of the way. Todd Lake, at 6,120 feet, is set in a steep-walled cirque with the jagged summits of Broken Top rising above the far rim.

From Dutchman Flat Nordic Sno-Park ski north into the meadow, take the first trail fork to the left, and proceed to the Century Drive junction with the Todd Lake Trail. The marked trail descends a long, moderate road grade, then follows along scenic meadowlike areas paralleling the curving foot of a ridge to the right. The trail eventually curves left, then goes down a short, curving turn before leaving the road. It turns right, into trees, suddenly emerging into a large, beautiful meadow. The north end of this meadow is only 250 yards from the south end of the lake.

To reach the lake, cross Road 370 and follow the lake access road up a gentle grade to the lower end of the scenic basin. If you follow the snowmobile route

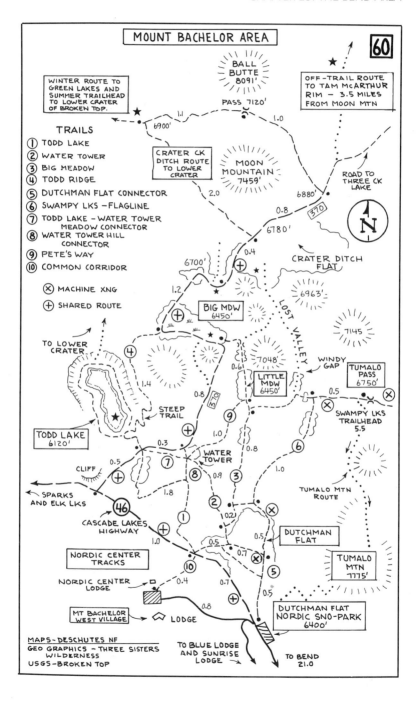

MOUNT BACHELOR AREA

60

BALL BUTTE 8091'

PASS 7120'

WINTER ROUTE TO GREEN LAKES AND SUMMER TRAILHEAD TO LOWER CRATER OF BROKEN TOP.

OFF-TRAIL ROUTE TO TAM McARTHUR RIM – 3.5 MILES FROM MOON MTN

TRAILS

① TODD LAKE
② WATER TOWER
③ BIG MEADOW
④ TODD RIDGE
⑤ DUTCHMAN FLAT CONNECTOR
⑥ SWAMPY LKS – FLAGLINE
⑦ TODD LAKE – WATER TOWER MEADOW CONNECTOR
⑧ WATER TOWER HILL CONNECTOR
⑨ PETE'S WAY
⑩ COMMON CORRIDOR

Ⓧ MACHINE XNG
⊕ SHARED ROUTE

CRATER CK DITCH ROUTE TO LOWER CRATER

MOON MOUNTAIN 7459'

ROAD TO THREE CK LAKE

6900'

1.1

1.0

6880'

370

0.8

6780'

2.0

0.4

6700'

CRATER DITCH FLAT

6963'

N

1.2

BIG MDW 6450'

TO LOWER CRATER

④

1.4

7145'

7048'

LOST VALLEY

WINDY GAP

TUMALO PASS 6750'

0.6

LITTLE MDW 6450'

STEEP TRAIL

0.8

370

⑨

0.5

Ⓧ

SWAMPY LKS TRAILHEAD 5.5

TODD LAKE 6120'

⊕

1.0

0.8

⑥

0.3

WATER TOWER

0.5

CLIFF

⊕

⑦

⑧

0.9

③

1.0

1.0

TUMALO MTN ROUTE

SPARKS AND ELK LKS

1.8

②

0.2

Ⓧ

CASCADE LAKES HIGHWAY

46

⊕

①

0.5

0.7

Ⓧ

0.5

DUTCHMAN FLAT

TUMALO MTN 7775'

1.0

NORDIC CENTER TRACKS

⑩

0.5

⑤

NORDIC CENTER LODGE

0.4

0.7

0.5

MT BACHELOR WEST VILLAGE

◇ LODGE

0.8

DUTCHMAN FLAT NORDIC SNO-PARK 6400'

MAPS – DESCHUTES NF
GEO GRAPHICS – THREE SISTERS WILDERNESS
USGS – BROKEN TOP

TO BLUE LODGE AND SUNRISE LODGE

TO BEND 21.0

along Century Drive, turn right onto Road 370 at a meadow below a prominent cliff.

To ski around the lake, go clockwise and stay off the ice. By climbing the slopes at the far end of the lake it is possible to reach Broken Top's lower crater by skiing north through open forest and scattered meadows.

Big Meadow Trail. (Map 60) This Intermediate 2.7-mile one-way trail leads gently upward from Dutchman Flat to Big Meadow through magnificent stands of old-growth mountain hemlock to a beautiful, large meadow nestled between ridges. From Dutchman Flat Nordic Sno-Park follow the trail northward for 0.5 mile, then turn left toward Century Drive. Turn right at the next junction, ski north toward the forest, then make another right onto the Big Meadow Trail, with picturesque forest scenes at every turn. The trail climbs steadily but gently, and in 2.2 miles from the sno-park it enters Little Meadow, where you can see South Sister, Broken Top, and Mount Bachelor. Both Pete's Way and Swampy Lakes Trails exit from this meadow. Ski upward to Big Meadow where you have a number of opportunities to continue farther or return, perhaps by the Todd Lake Loop, by Pete's Way, or some other way.

Water Tower Trail. (Map 60) To ski this Intermediate, 0.9-mile one-way trail, start at Dutchman Flat Nordic Sno-Park and head toward the Big Meadow Trail, but go straight onto the Water Tower Connector Trail at first through lodgepole pine forest then hemlock. The trail leads to Water Tower Meadow and provides another route to Todd Lake, as well as the chance to ski several short loops. This is a beautiful connector trail that athletic Novices will have little trouble with.

Todd Lake to Water Tower Meadow Connector. (Map 60) This Intermediate tour stretches 0.9 mile one way. From the large meadow just below Todd Lake take the curving Road 370 uphill to the Water Tower Meadow east of the road. At the south edge of the meadow is the monolithic black cylinder, an anomaly in the area. To avoid using the road, which is a snowmobile route, start at the Todd Lake access road and ski uphill 50 yards to a trail going to the right that parallels the road to the water tower.

Water Tower Hill Connector. (Map 60) This is a 0.1-mile Advanced connector from the Todd Lake Trail and climbs very steeply to the Water Tower. In reverse, it demands considerable skill to descend the 100-yard-long hill. The trail is found 50 yards south of the water tower.

Pete's Way. (Map 60) If you are headed for Big Meadow from either Todd Lake or the Water Tower Meadow, this Intermediate 1-mile trail offers an alternative to skiing Road 370. From the north end of Water Tower Meadow enter forest and ski to Little Meadow.

Todd Ridge Trail. (Map 60) This Advanced 1.4-mile trail permits a loop return to or from Big Meadow and is best skied from the bottom (south) uphill to the top (north) due to the moderately steep hillside traverses and switchbacks. The trail starts at the west end of Big Meadow, enters a fine stand of big trees, then circles a small butte with a view of Broken Top, then descends 350 feet along a route only enjoyable for those with strong downhill skills. If you are skiing the easiest way, from the bottom to the top, the trail starts near the south end of Todd Lake.

Swampy Lakes and Flagline Trails. (Map 60) Climbing over Tumalo Pass from Dutchman Flat, this Intermediate, 8-mile one-way trail with a car shuttle offers much variety and some splendid downhill gliding. The trail is well marked, and the old-growth forest at Tumalo Pass is beautiful. The trail climbs 350 feet to a 6,750-foot pass, then descends 1,170 feet (cumulative).

From Dutchman Flat Nordic Sno-Park, ski the trail north along the east edge of the open flat, then enter old growth to the trail that connects Little Meadow with Tumalo Pass. Turn right (east) here 2 miles from the sno-park, and ski 0.5 mile to the flat pass through alternating open swales and small meadows, where the forest becomes almost enchanting. If you do not have time to ski the full distance to Swampy Lakes, at least ski to Tumalo Pass.

At first the trail goes through primeval forest then a transition zone to the denser lodgepole pine woods of the lower trail. Several right-angle turns and a couple of short, steep hillside traverses add interest to the tour. The last mile to the Swampy Lakes Shelter is less attractive, passing through dense stands of pines, but features a widely cleared trail with many long, smooth downhill runs, the best of the entire route. From the Swampy Lakes Shelter cross the open flat, climb the ridge, and descend to the sno-park where your car shuttle is waiting.

This is essentially a midwinter tour when there are fewer tree wells and when snow is generally better. West of the Swampy Lakes Shelter you will pass a trail leading to Vista Butte, an excellent alternative route on which to complete the tour with a grand view from the top of the butte.

If the snow is heavy or there is no broken track ahead, this can be a very tiring tour. Stem turning and step-turn skills are helpful. If you miss a trail marker, back up and find the trail at the last marker. There are long, nearly level stretches, so pick good snow for this tour.

Lost Valley Off-Trail Route. (Map 60) This exceptionally scenic tour on both marked and unmarked routes for Intermediate skiers from Little Meadow to Crater Ditch Flat is gentle in grade and gives direct access to the Moon Mountain area. There is a 380-foot gain to a high point of 6,780 feet.

From the lower end of Little Meadow ski east and uphill on the Swampy Lakes Trail through a sinuous meadow to the large meadow at its head. Leave the trail and bear north into the east arm of the meadow, following almost continuous meadows, somewhere along here passing through Windy Gap and along the east side of a low, forested ridge. You will eventually reach Crater Ditch Flat, a huge, level meadow at the southeast foot of Moon Mountain. The route has no real landmarks so ski it in good weather, and don't be surprised if you see a snowmobile. To ski a loop, return by way of Big Meadow.

Broken Top Crater. (Map 60) At 9,175 feet, Broken Top Mountain with its jagged outline is one of the major volcanoes of Oregon. It also bears two small glaciers under near-vertical cliffs. The Intermediate to Advanced tour is up to 10 miles round trip, of which 4 miles are on a marked trail. The tour gains 500 feet to a high point of 6,900 feet.

Although the north side areas above timberline lure a few Backcountry skiers from Three Creek Lake, the lower crater on its south side is easily reached from Dutchman Flat Nordic Sno-Park by way of Big Meadow Trail, then to the west end of Big Meadow and up the road to a blufftop view-point. Cross the road, ski through trees into a large meadow, then ski across the flats to the base of Moon Mountain and along the very foot of the butte on the Crater Creek Ditch around to the west side and into the lower crater. The ditch route follows the top of a manmade irrigation ditch built at the turn of the century to carry water eastward. The ditch is obvious and appears as a narrow road.

The lower crater is a wide, rolling, open valley that also serves as an alternative route to Tam McArthur Rim up the crater valley bottom and across the saddle on the north side of Ball Butte. Skiing higher than 7,500 feet in the crater will expose you to avalanche danger from the mountain's steep south ridge, an area that has seen huge slab avalanches. In spring, there is danger of rocks crashing down into the crater from the rotten cliffs.

BACKCOUNTRY TOURS

Tam McArthur Rim. (Map 60) Just 2 miles east of the jagged summit of Broken Top is the flat-topped, broad ridge of Tam McArthur Rim, which affords extensive views up and down the Cascade Range. Some think this is the most spectacular viewpoint of any ski tour in Oregon. For a description of the northern approach to the rim, see Three Creek Lake and Tam McArthur Rim.

The tour to Tam McArthur Rim is an Advanced, 16-mile round trip that climbs 1,400 feet to a high point of 7,800 feet. Only the lower half of the tour is on marked trails.

From Dutchman Flat Sno-Park ski to the base of Moon Mountain (see Broken Top Crater), then ski around the east side of both Moon Mountain and Ball Butte. From Moon Mountain to the rim is all open country. From the rim the views are dramatic. You'll see Hood, Adams, Jefferson, Three Sisters, and of course the sky-piercing outline of Broken Top. The precipitous north face of Broken Top falls in a complexity of colored cliffs to the small glacier far below, from where the timberline meadows slowly blend into sweeping forested expanses spreading northward. On a clear day the scene is breathtaking.

Spring is the best time to do this tour, and it is often skiable into June. Do not undertake this tour unless the weather is good. The route would be impossible in a whiteout. Carry a map, compass, repair kit, and survival gear.

Historical Note: The rim is named for Lewis A. "Tam" McArthur, writer, newspaper reporter, and member of the Oregon Geographic Board. He is the well-known author of *Oregon Geographic Names*, a definitive listing and analysis of Oregon place names.

Green Lakes. (Map 60) The three lakes lying in a 6,500-foot saddle between South Sister and Broken Top are reachable along a 10-mile one-way tour for the Backcountry skier. The many ups and downs of the wrinkled slopes along the route add up to a cumulative elevation gain of 1,500 feet. The route is not marked.

From the lower crater (see Broken Top Crater) ski westward near the 6,800-foot contour across both open and forested slopes. The route via the summer trail up Fall Creek from Sparks Lake—requiring a loss of elevation from Dutchman Flat—then the climb to the lakes is also 10 miles but over 2,000 feet of elevation gain. Look at a postcard view of Broken Top to familiarize yourself with the terrain before you go, and do the trip only in good weather.

Sparks Lake. (Map 61) Beautiful lake, meadow, and swamp areas lie in a 1-mile-wide basin with a high forested ridge to the west and Mount Bachelor to the east. It is a very scenic 10-mile round-trip tour for Advanced skiers. South Sister and Broken Top looming to the north dominate the tour.

From Dutchman Flat Nordic Sno-Park ski west on the Todd Lake Trail or Century Drive (Cascade Lakes Highway), a snowmobile route, and descend about 1,000 feet to Sparks Lake in 3.9 miles. Ski the east shoreline 1.5 miles south for the finest views from a peninsula just north of a memorial area for the late Ray Atkeson, noted Oregon photographer.

Moraine Lake. (Map 61) Sitting in a shallow, treeless bowl at 6,450 feet at the very foot of South Sister, the lake is a distant Backcountry goal some 8 miles from Dutchman Flat Nordic Sno-Park. Ski as for Sparks Lake, then from Sparks Lake go another 1.5 miles on Century Drive. Turn uphill at the Devils Garden and ski up the east edge of a large lava flow that shows clearly on the USGS map just east of Devils Hill. Climb almost 1,000 feet along the uneven foot of the lava flow to a saddle at the top of the lower lava flow. Ski 1 mile northwest through forest from the saddle to Moraine Lake. If time allows climb the broad, open ridge 350 feet to its top west of the lake for marvelous views of the area. The fascinating Rock Mesa, an almost round lava flow over a mile across, lies below to the west. To visit this geological

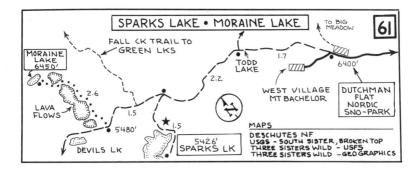

curiosity, descend through steep old growth to the level meadows that surround the lava flow. From the high ridge it is only 0.5 mile down to the Rock Mesa.

SWAMPY LAKES

(Map 62) This unique Nordic ski-trail complex is located north of Century Drive and 16 miles west of Bend. There are five primary trail loops ranging in length from 2 to 8 miles and a total of about 25 miles of skiing trails in 6 square miles. The terrain consists of gentle, rolling forest land, with several meadows and clearcuts and two high points for views. The skiing is on marked, well-designed trails and roads. Trail junctions are clearly signed with trail names, destinations, and distances. The Virginia Meissner Trails system to the east is connected to the Swampy Lakes Trails in several places.

Most tours start at Swampy Lakes Sno-Park, although Meissner Sno-Park 2 miles to the east may also be used. Vista Butte Sno-Park 2.7 miles to the west near the Sunriver road junction, with space for only a few cars, services the far west end of the Swampy Lakes area trail system. Four open-sided log shelters with stoves provide comfortable tour goals and lunch spots. Although the tours do not abound with viewpoints, the natural beauty of the area and the high quality of the skiing trails provide more than adequate compensation.

The Swede Ridge tour is the longest and the most demanding in terms of skiing skills, and in this respect it is similar to the Vista Butte trails, although a strong Intermediate skier would have few problems. The trail loop to the Emil Nordeen Shelter has a number of views on the south leg, and the shelter offers a view of Newberry Crater. The loop tour to the Swampy Lakes Shelter is often crowded and for this reason has been designated a one-way loop to be skied clockwise. The tops of Vista Butte and Telemark Hill offer views. Maps of the trail system are usually available at the trailhead. As the trail system is complex you should carry a map with you to better plan your skiing, although there are directional signs everywhere. The trails are closed to dogs and snowmobilers.

Beginner Loop. (Map 62) This beautiful 1.4-mile Novice trail climbs easily through lodgepole forest, then turns and returns to the starting point down a long, gentle hill. From Swampy Lakes Sno-Park ski the Swampy Lakes Trail toward Swampy Lakes Shelter as it travels through scattered pines and openings. In about 0.4 mile turn left at a trail junction and continue across a low divide through lovely forest. The trail then descends gently, and joins the Ridge Loop, where you turn left. The next 0.5 mile is a wonderful rolling downhill run. This loop is designated to be skied counterclockwise.

Ridge Loop. (Map 62) This 3-mile loop is best suited to Intermediate skills and is designated to be skied in a counterclockwise direction. The high point is 6,140 feet, and there is an elevation gain of 340 feet. Traveling entirely through forest, this is an interesting and challenging trail. From the

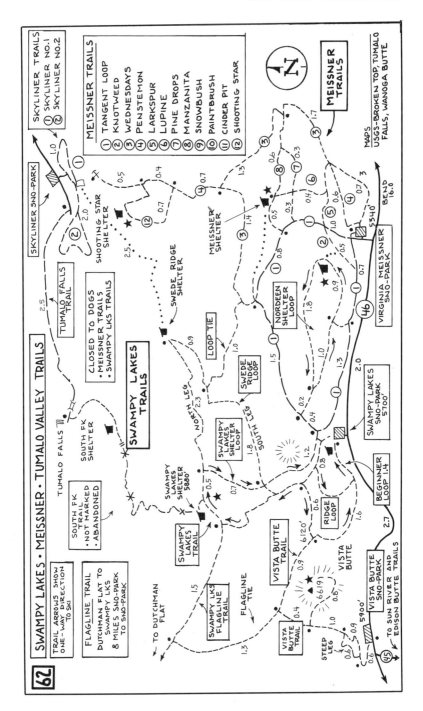

sno-park ski the Swampy Lakes Trail toward the Swampy Lakes Shelter, and in 0.8 mile turn left onto the Ridge Loop, which also leads to the Vista Butte Trail. The trail climbs a moderately steep sidehill, then passes a short side trail with a view of Broken Top. The trail continues climbing, passes the Vista Butte Trail junction, then descends southward and turns eastward to join the Beginner Loop to the sno-park.

Swampy Lakes Shelter Loop. (Map 62) Rated Novice–Intermediate, this 4.4-mile loop will tax some skiers, although there is only a 160-foot elevation gain. This loop, the most popular in the area, has been designated a one-way trail, to be skied clockwise to minimize the problem of skier congestion. Starting at the Swampy Lake Sno-Park, the loop goes through open stands of lodgepole pines, climbing a low divide then descending along the west end of the Swampy Lakes flats. The shelter sits on the north side of the wide meadow and 100 yards into the trees. From the shelter return to the meadow and ski east almost to the far end, where you turn south, continuing on the Swampy Lakes Shelter Loop Trail. Climb gently through pines, cross a divide, then descend to the trailhead.

Emil Nordeen Shelter Loop. (Map 62) The highlights of this Intermediate 4.9-mile round trip are the scenic route through several clearcuts and the blufftop setting of the shelter, which provides sweeping views to the east of rolling forests, volcanic cones, and the city of Bend. To the southeast is Newberry Crater, a massive, gently rounded feature. This tour may begin from either Swampy Lakes Sno-Park or Meissner Sno-Park just below and east.

From Swampy Lakes Sno-Park ski east on the Tangent Loop Trail that goes uphill and northeast 0.4 mile to meet the Nordeen Loop Trail to the shelter. (The other leg of the Tangent Loop Trail goes downhill eastward and parallels the highway.) Ski 0.2 mile to where the actual shelter loop begins. The loop is designated for one-way skiing in a counterclockwise direction. The south leg of the loop goes through pine forest, as well as several scenic clearcuts, the easternmost one follows a gently rolling, open ridgetop. The trail then enters forest and winds its way to the shelter site.

Historical Note: The shelter is named for Emil Nordeen, a Bend resident from Sweden, who skied and raced cross-country in the 1920s and 1930s. He was also a climber and a member of the first-ascent party on Three Fingered Jack.

Swede Ridge Shelter Loop. (Map 62) This is a long, Intermediate loop of 8.7 miles with a total elevation gain of 460 feet. If the snow is not good, it is a tiring trip. It is the longest, most challenging loop of the area, partly on trails and partly on roads. Ski first to the Swampy Lakes Shelter, then ski east to Swede Ridge Loop Trail, then through forest, some sidehills, and descending traverses that require care if the snow is fast. You eventually arrive at a clearcut, and the shelter is at its northeast corner in the trees.

To return, descend the clearcut near the shelter, skiing to its far end where you meet a road. Follow the road briefly to where the Loop Tie Trail joins and follow the Swede Ridge Loop's south leg as it crosses a divide and

Swampy Lakes Shelter

meets the Swampy Lakes Loop, which goes south to the sno-park on a wide snow-covered road.

Vista Butte. (Map 62) Not as long as the Swede Ridge Shelter Loop but a bit more demanding, the Vista Butte Trail skied from Swampy Lakes Sno-Park will give Intermediate skiers a workout. It is 7 miles round trip with a gain of 920 feet. There is a shorter access to the scenic top of the butte from Vista Butte Sno-Park, however, that reduces the round-trip distance to 4.6 miles and the elevation gain to 720 feet.

The summit of the 6,619-foot butte on the western edge of the Swampy Lakes area is a wide, windy snow ridge and the finest viewpoint of the area. The sweeping scene includes desert, wide expanses of forest, Mount Bachelor, Tumalo Mountain, Broken Top, Ball Butte, Tam McArthur Rim, and Newberry Crater to the southeast. Swampy Lakes Meadow appears far below with the Tumalo valley as a backdrop.

The most direct route is from the Vista Butte Sno-Park 2.7 miles west of Swampy Lakes Sno-Park and near the junction of the highway with the road to Sunriver. Ski up the trail from the sno-park. At 0.4 mile it makes a

Vista Butte summit, Swampy Lakes area

turn, and in 0.2 mile the trail forks. The shortest leg is to the left (north), but it is steeper than the other leg. The south leg of this short loop is the one recommended for your return as it is less steep. Both of these short legs (0.6 and 0.9 mile) join above and the trail continues 1 mile to Bruce's Ball Park, where the trail to the summit of the butte goes to the right. The final climb follows a road partway, then goes up the open ridge to the top.

The other route to the summit starts at Swampy Lakes Sno-Park and at first follows the Swampy Lakes Shelter Trail, turns left onto Ridge Loop and climbs to the Butte Trail, following it to Bruce's Ball Park, where the side trail to the summit goes to the left. See Ridge Loop description.

MEISSNER TRAILS

(Map 62) Named for Virginia Meissner, a popular cross-country ski-trip leader and instructor, and long-time resident of Bend, the sno-park and trails are a testament to her contribution to the sport in Central Oregon. Virginia Meissner passed away in 1990.

Virginia Meissner Sno-Park is located 16 miles from Bend, and at 5,340-foot elevation it is 200 feet below Swampy Lakes Sno-Park, and at the lower level of dependable snow. The area is characterized by rolling, gentle terrain ideally suited to Novice skiers, and almost all of the 17 miles of marked ski trails can be skied by inexperienced skiers. There is a minimal amount of vertical elevation gain in the area, and depending on what trails and in which directions you happen to go, it will not exceed 300 feet. There is some old-growth fir forest, much lodgepole pine, and some beautiful, old ponderosa "yellowbellies" or "punkin" pines. The trails are mostly on primitive roads.

The Meissner Shelter is located on a low ridge 1.5 miles north of the sno-park with good views in several directions. A second shelter is planned for the future. It will be called the Shooting Star Shelter and will be 3.7 miles by trails to east then north from the Meissner Shelter. A shorter new trail is planned. If you haven't yet guessed, the trails are named for one of the loves of Virginia Meissner's life—wildflowers. The entire area invites off-trail exploration and is perfect for the skier who wants to develop off-trail skills and confidence.

Dogs and motorized vehicles are not permitted on these Novice trails, nor on any trails north of Century Drive.

Tangent Loop Trail. (Map 62) This is the main trail of the area. Going south to north from the sno-park, it follows a wide, uninteresting road, but it does give direct access to the Meissner Shelter and to several side trails. If followed to its end, it will take you to Swampy Lakes Sno-Park. It also turns and goes west from Meissner Sno-Park to the same destination, forming a long, uninteresting loop.

Knotweed Trail. (Map 62) Passing through meadows and old-growth ponderosa pines, this beautiful trail travels along the foot of the steep ridge on the top of which is located the Emil Nordeen Shelter. To find Knotweed, ski north 0.1 mile from the sno-park, then turn west (left) onto the south leg of the Tangent Loop Trail. Ski this 200 yards west, then turn right onto the Knotweed Trail, which then goes north only 0.5 mile before it again meets the Tangent Loop, and where you can cross to ski east on the Larkspur Trail, or turn left onto the Tangent Loop to ski to the Meissner Shelter. There are so many interesting loop opportunities here that exploring them will be limited only by your time and energy reserves. The low ridge on which the shelter sits offers views of Tam McArthur Rim, Broken Top, Tumalo Mountain, Paulina Peak, Newberry Crater, and the Bend area.

Wednesdays Trail. (Map 62) Named for Virginia's midweek ski tours, this trail is 3.7 miles long and gives access to other trails. The trail goes east from the sno-park and forms a pleasant 1.3-mile loop with the Penstemon Trail, particularly good for Novices starting on their skiing careers.

TUMALO VALLEY SKI TRAILS

(Map 62) The Tumalo Creek valley 10 miles west of downtown Bend provides a scenically unique ski tour. There are several ski trails in the area, but the 2.5-mile trail to Tumalo Falls is the most rewarding. The valley, at 4,800 feet, is too low to always have sufficient snow to ski, but when it does, the area is worth a visit.

Skiing here is a fresh alternative to battling the heavy traffic toward Mount Bachelor, even though the widening of the highway beyond the Sunriver road junction has improved the rush-hour commute for skiers to Mount Bachelor.

The Tumalo valley was denuded by the 1979 Bridge Creek fire, and many silver snags, called "buckskins," bear mute testimony to the holocaust. The valley is flat-bottomed with ridges on either side, and the Skyliner Lodge, home of skiing at Bend before Mount Bachelor, is near the sno-park.

From downtown Bend drive to the riverside park and cross the Galveston Street bridge across the Deschutes River, one of two driving routes to Mount Bachelor. However, continue straight west as the street name changes to Skyliner Road. The sno-park is 10 miles from downtown.

Tumalo Falls. (Map 62) From near the sno-park, ski north down a hill (Novice rating) to a bridge crossing Tumalo Creek, then turn left onto the 2.5-mile almost level road that parallels the creek up the open valley. A stand of tall firs appears at the head of the valley where you cross a bridge and turn 100 yards uphill to the falls, climbing for best views.

South Fork Trail. (Map 62) This 4.2-mile trail to Swampy Lakes Shelter is no longer marked nor recommended as a ski route due to the steepness and narrowness that made it difficult to ski safely.

Skyliner Trails Nos. 1 and 2. (Map 62) Both trails begin at the Skyliner Snow Play Hill near the sno-park and provide short tours. Trail No. 1, a 1-mile loop, goes eastward, turns, and returns for a loop across easy terrain. Trail No. 2 requires more skills as it heads westward on a road for 1 mile then returns traversing northeast along a ridge in the Bridge Creek area. The triangular-shaped loop is 2 miles long and requires low-level Intermediate skills.

Sno-park permits are not required at the Skyliner Snow Play Hill area trailhead. An obscure, unmarked, primitive road a short distance up the play hill enters the forest to the west and can be followed up the ridge on moderate grades 2.5 miles to reach the Swede Ridge Shelter. The trail passes through forest including ponderosa pines, and may require some modest route finding near its upper end.

Historical Note: The Skyliner Snow Play Hill area was the first downhill ski area of Central Oregon.

EDISON BUTTE TRAILS

(Map 63) This 20-mile marked trail system opened in 1986 and 1987 and is a significant addition to the ski trails of Oregon. The unique nature of the area includes roughly sculptured lava flows, lodgepole pine forests, and giant ponderosa pine trees, all giving the compact area a flavor not found elsewhere in the Northwest.

The trail system is reached by driving from Bend toward Mount Bachelor past Swampy Lakes to the junction with Road 45 (to Sunriver) 18 miles from Bend. Drive south 4 miles on Road 45 to Edison Butte Sno-Park. From Sunriver it is 8.3 miles to the Old-Growth trailhead (lower chain-up area) at the lower end of the trail system, and another 4.3 miles to Edison Butte Sno-Park.

The Edison Butte trail system includes three main trails with numerous

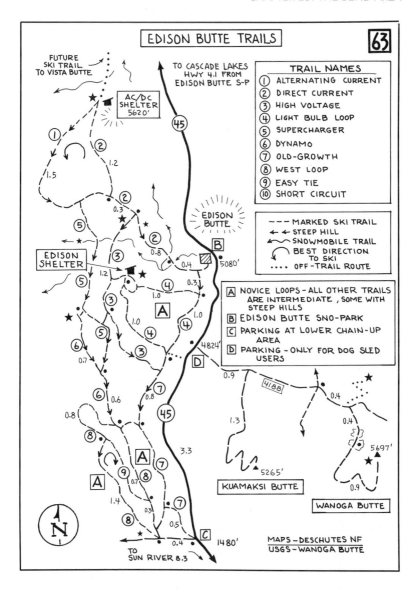

EDISON BUTTE TRAILS 63

FUTURE SKI TRAIL To Vista Butte

TO CASCADE LAKES HWY 4.1 FROM EDISON BUTTE S-P

AC/DC SHELTER 5620'

EDISON BUTTE

EDISON SHELTER

TRAIL NAMES

① ALTERNATING CURRENT
② DIRECT CURRENT
③ HIGH VOLTAGE
④ LIGHT BULB LOOP
⑤ SUPERCHARGER
⑥ DYNAMO
⑦ OLD-GROWTH
⑧ WEST LOOP
⑨ EASY TIE
⑩ SHORT CIRCUIT

--- MARKED SKI TRAIL
◄ ◄ STEEP HILL
SNOWMOBILE TRAIL
BEST DIRECTION TO SKI
.... OFF-TRAIL ROUTE

Ⓐ NOVICE LOOPS – ALL OTHER TRAILS ARE INTERMEDIATE, SOME WITH STEEP HILLS
Ⓑ EDISON BUTTE SNO-PARK
Ⓒ PARKING AT LOWER CHAIN-UP AREA
Ⓓ PARKING – ONLY FOR DOG SLED USERS

5080'
4824'
4188
5265'
KUAMAKSI BUTTE
5697'
WANOGA BUTTE

MAPS – DESCHUTES NF
USGS – WANOGA BUTTE

1480'
TO SUN RIVER 8.3

connectors that form many loops. This guidebook's map of the trails, necessarily drawn in a simplified manner, does not give the slightest hint of the rambling nature of the trails. Designed to take maximum advantage of the rolling terrain and changing forest types, the trails offer unusual variety and constantly changing directions, which provide an exciting skiing experience. Although there are few distant views, there is a new forest scene around every turn.

At this time, the trails extend 5 miles north to south, and 1.5 miles east to west at the widest. Edison Butte Sno-Park is at 5,080-foot elevation, and the trails descend 600 feet from the north end to the south end.

Old-Growth, High Voltage, and Dynamo Trails—the three principal trails in this area—join others and converge at the lower end, where there is usually less snow depth and where in some years the skiing may be spotty. If you ski the trails downhill to the Old-Growth trailhead, at the bottom of all the trails, a car shuttle is recommended.

Although there is a snowmobile corridor from Edison Butte Sno-Park westward through the trail system, crossing several trails, it does not cause a problem. The snowmobilers go miles west to play, but skiers must always remain alert when crossing any snowmobile corridor.

There are two shelters in the trail system. The Edison Shelter is 1.3 miles from Edison Butte Sno-Park, and the AC/DC Shelter is 2.7 miles from the sno-park at the northern end of the trail system.

In the future, the Forest Service will no doubt fine-tune the trail system by adding and eliminating some trails. It is likely that a 4-mile access trail will be built from Vista Butte Sno-Park to the AC/DC Shelter at the north end of the trail system.

Novice Trails. (Map 63) Most of the Edison Butte trails require Intermediate-level skiing skills, with occasional hills that are more difficult, and a problem for many skiers. That makes the area more exciting, of course. Beginners should ski the 5 miles of lower-loop trails that start at the Old-Growth Trailhead. This is an area of gentle, large meadows, beautiful ponderosa yellowbelly pines, and ideal trails for less-skilled skiers not seeking an aggressive learning experience.

If a Novice insists on skiing at the northern end of the trails, then the 3-mile Light Bulb Loop south of Edison Butte Sno-Park is the safest answer to that urge, although the west leg will be very challenging. Unfortunately, the first 0.3 mile from the sno-park to the loop is really too steep for Novices and should be bypassed if possible. An easier connector will probably be built in the future.

Other Trails. (Map 63) Most other trails are of Intermediate level with several hills (marked with arrowheads on the sketch map) that will challenge a strong Intermediate skier. If the snow is hardpacked or crusty, do not ski down these hills—for safety, plan your route to ski up. (Because of hills, all skiers should ski two loops counterclockwise, and these are marked with curved directional arrows on the sketch map.)

There are so many trails in the Edison Butte area that attempting to describe each would be meaningless. Let it be said that the variety and natural beauty of the area and its rolling, twisting trails guarantee to keep the average skier more than fascinated. The number of loops that can be skied here is limited only by your familiarity with the area and your imagination. The mix of lodgepole pine forests, ponderosa yellowbelly pines, stands of old growth, and open meadows makes an area unique to the Bend ski-trail systems.

The Edison ice cave is not shown on the map as it is the home of the endangered Townsend long-eared bat. If you find yourself in this area, do not enter the cave or disturb the area in any way. A snowmobile route was eliminated here to protect the bat population.

Dogs are permitted in the Edison Butte area on trails, but their presence is discouraged. If you must ski with your dog on ski trails, be aware that dogs damage ski tracks and cause problems with Novice skiers on the same track. Pick up your dog's droppings and carry the waste out of the area. Evidence of abuse of the basic rules by dog owners will threaten future access of dogs to the trails.

WANOGA BUTTE

(Map 63) East of the Edison Butte trails is a volcanic cinder cone with a fire-lookout tower on its summit. Views from the summit are excellent, and it is reported that Mount Shasta, about 200 miles south, can be seen. To ski to the butte, descend the east leg of Light Bulb Loop 1.3 miles to its lower end, turn east onto an unmarked, obscure road, and ski the short distance to Road 45. Cross the highway, ski north to Road 4188 (1 mile below Edison Butte Sno-Park), and ski east 1.7 miles to the lookout road. It angles off to the southeast, passes through several meadows, then climbs in earnest the 430 feet to the top, 1.3 miles off Road 4188.

If you don't have time to go to the summit, climb a clearcut north of the junction with the lookout road for views. An alternative unmarked ski route from the sno-park crosses the highway and goes around the base of Edison Butte itself through both open and thick lodgepole forest to Road 4188. All routes in the area are used by snowmobilers.

Kuamaksi Butte. (Map 63) This butte is lower and closer than Wanoga Butte, and there are views from its summit. Follow directions for Wanoga Butte but ski only 0.5 mile east of Road 45, then turn south on the Kuamaksi Butte road for 1.3 miles to the summit (5,265 feet), a climb of 440 feet.

Note: Parking at Road 4188 off Road 45 is restricted to dog-sled users. This turnout is not available to skiers. If you ski to either Wanoga or Kuamaksi Buttes, park at Edison Butte Sno-Park.

Chapter 24

NEWBERRY CRATER

Known variously as Mount Newberry or Newberry Caldera, but most commonly referred to as Newberry Crater, this massive shield volcano is 30 miles in diameter and has a central crater 5 miles across. High walls on three sides of the crater surround a flat floor that contains two large lakes, Paulina and East lakes. The crater also contains several lava flows, one of which is geologically unique and provides an unusual ski tour. In addition, there are several other tours of the crater and rim.

Newberry National Volcanic Monument, established in 1990, is America's newest monument. Containing the caldera, its surrounding rim, and many miles of volcanic lands to the north, it reaches to Cascade Lakes Highway west of Bend.

Although Central Oregon is dominated by many volcanoes and countless cinder cones, Newberry is second only to Crater Lake in size. Both were formed by the collapse of much higher tops. Newberry's size creates its own weather, receiving more snow than the surrounding area. Two mountains, one on the north rim and one on the south, reach almost 8,000 feet. The road to Paulina Lake Resort, on the west shore of Paulina Lake, is not plowed in winter and is usually not open until late May. Skiing is often good into May after the road is plowed to the lakes.

Future plans include more cross-country ski trails, including around Paulina Lake and to East Lake, several day shelters, and perhaps a sno-park 2 miles closer to the crater.

To reach Newberry Crater drive 23 miles south on Highway 97 from Bend, then drive 10 miles on the Paulina Lake road to Ten-Mile Sno-Park. From here it is 3.5 miles by ski trail to Paulina Lake and the year-round resort lodge and cabins.

All the roads of the region are open to snowmobilers, including the road to the very summit of Paulina Peak and the summer trail to the top of North Paulina Peak across the caldera on the north rim. The only trails for exclusive use of skiers at this time are two from Ten-Mile Sno-Park and one on the south shore of Paulina Lake. There are plans for more in the future.

Historical Note: Paulina Lake and Paulina Peak are named after the Snake Indian chief who was a skillful antagonist of the immigrants who invaded and settled in his Central and Eastern Oregon territory.

TRAILS TO THE CRATER

(Map 64) Two marked Intermediate ski trails from the Ten-Mile Sno-Park lead uphill to the Paulina Lake Resort area on Paulina Lake's west shore,

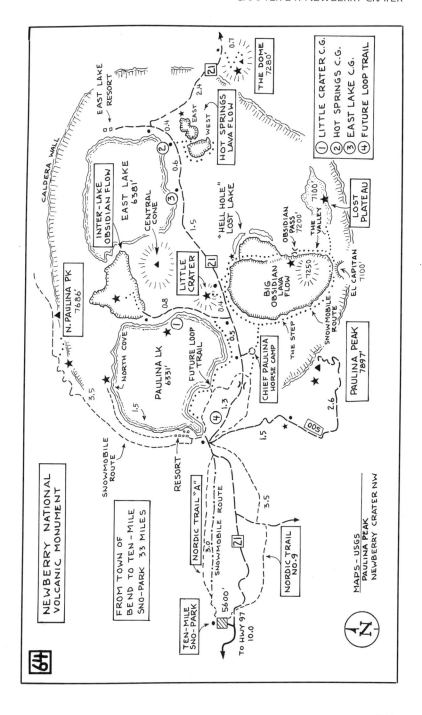

where you access all the trails and ski routes of the area, and to the road to the top of Paulina Peak. The elevation gain to the crater is 730 feet from Ten-Mile Sno-Park.

Nordic Trail No. 9. (Map 64) Rated Novice–Intermediate, this 3.5-mile marked trail starts from the southeast corner of the Ten-Mile Sno-Park. It crosses the Paulina Lake road and the snowmobile route, and follows a route upward south of the road to the crater through forest and open areas with views of Paulina Peak and the Cascades. Although slightly longer, this trail is the easier and more scenic of the two from the sno-park.

Nordic Trail A. (Map 64) This marked 3-mile trail is less interesting and scenic than Nordic Trail No. 9, but it is more direct. It starts from the sno-park's northeast corner and parallels a nearby snowmobile route along a powerline. The trail follows the powerline a short distance, then goes to the far eastern end of the first clearcut, then into forest. Near the top it reenters the powerline route. The trail's proximity to Paulina Creek is appealing.

PAULINA PEAK

(Map 64) For views at Newberry, this Intermediate tour cannot be surpassed. It is an easy, gentle ascent of 4.1 miles from the lake and an elevation gain of 1,570 feet, following a wide road all the way to the top. Views range from Shasta to Hood, and down to the two lakes in the crater. If skiing from Ten-Mile Sno-Park, add 3.5 miles and 730 feet of elevation gain.

From the Paulina Lake outlet dam, just south of the resort, ski south and up Road 500 to the summit at 7,897 feet. First views are at 1.5 miles from the lake, and thereafter are continuous as the route climbs easily around the south side of the peak. The Cascade volcanoes are all visible, as are the entire caldera, the two lakes, the unusual Big Obsidian Lava Flow east and below the summit, many of the 200 cinder cones surrounding Newberry, Fort Rock to the east, and the Ochoco Mountains to the northeast. It is a spectacular view, worth the long grind to the top.

LAKE TRAIL

(Map 64) Starting from the north end of the Paulina Lake Resort, this 1.5-mile Intermediate trail follows the summer hiking trail along the west and north shorelines to the North Cove Campground, a hikers' camping area. The trail offers wonderful views across the lake to the caldera walls and Paulina Peak. In the future, it will circle the lake, a distance of 5.8 miles.

SOUTH LAKESHORE TRAIL

(Map 64) Following the shoreline from the bridge at Paulina Lake's outlet stream near the resort, the proposed Novice trail goes eastward 2.5 miles to the campground on the lake's east shore. This trail gives easy access to the Big Obsidian Lava Flow by skiing south up the road leading into the campground from the road going to East Lake. At this time, the official name for this trail has not been established.

NORTH PAULINA PEAK

(Map 64) This 7,686-foot peak, a high point on the caldera's north rim, is infrequently visited by skiers for two reasons: it is a snowmobile route, and Paulina Peak on the south rim is higher, easier to reach, and has more views. Of course, viewing from the north rim gives a totally different perspective of the entire caldera, and this makes it rewarding.

The route is 3.5 miles one way and climbs 1,400 feet. The demanding course should be skied only by Advanced to Backcountry skiers. From near the outlet-stream bridge near the resort turn left (west) up a short road that turns north. This is the beginning of the snowmobile route up the north rim and your route to several fine views. The first 0.5 mile is along a primitive road with screened views of the lake. At 1.5 miles there is a view of the entire lake and Paulina Peak. At 3 miles the trail zigzags where the snowmobile route goes straight up. Go right here (south) into old growth to a view of East Lake. The trail leaves the rim, cuts back into lodgepole, then returns to the rim at the bottom of a long, uphill open slope with great views. Beyond the views you will find thick forest to the top and no views, which makes this place, at about 7,500 feet, a good turnaround point.

BIG OBSIDIAN LAVA FLOW

(Map 64) The unmarked 4.5-mile Advanced route around the Big Flow is quite remarkable. Although there are several fine views as you circle the flow, the main interest is the unique experience of skiing along the edge of the flow between forest and lava. This ski tour is best done in late spring after the road has been plowed to the Paulina Lake Resort, or better yet all the way to East Lake Resort.

If not plowed, the Big Flow is 2.2 miles from the resort area and 5.7 miles from Ten-Mile Sno-Park, from where the elevation gain would be 1,600 feet at Obsidian Pass. In addition, the loop around the flow itself is 4.5 miles, with a gain of 700 feet from its lower edge.

From the Paulina Lake Resort ski the South Lakeshore ski route or the Paulina Lake road (toward East Lake) to the foot of the obvious, open, 100-foot-high face of the flow beside the road. If your time is limited, ski to the left around the east side to a nearby saddle, a short, steep climb. Here you will see the Hell Hole, a crescent-shaped pond also called Lost Lake, below you at the foot of the curving lava-flow face. If it is frozen, descend and ski along its edge if you want to explore. The slopes on either side are too steep

Big Obsidian Lava Flow, Lost Plateau (beyond), *and south caldera rim* (right), *seen from summit of Paulina Peak*

to ski, but always be careful of skiing on ice. The long pond's name originates from its sulfur smell.

Further exploration from the saddle may lead you up onto the steep face of the flow, which leads to the relatively flat surface of the lower, east lobe, the route of the Big Flow loop. If you have time to do the entire loop, turn right at the base of the flow near the road and ski along the edge westward then southward; it soon becomes a moat or narrow valley between forest and lava. You soon reach a steep, 300-foot climb on the west side called The Step. At its top, the grade returns to moderate, and the moat becomes sinuous and scenic. An occasional backward glance reveals views of Paulina Lake.

At El Capitan, a vertical wall blocking the moat, scramble easily around the base of the cliff to almost level progress at 7,100 feet. As you turn northward, enter a deep, beautiful snow valley. The fringe of trees on the east edge is the access to the Lost Plateau, a half-mile, level pumice desert. At the head of the valley is Obsidian Pass (7,200 feet), the high point of the loop, with a fine view of the entire caldera and the lakes. This is a good turnaround point for less-experienced skiers.

From the pass, the route drops steeply 300 feet, levels out, then takes another breathtaking drop into the south end of the Hell Hole. To complete the loop, at the bottom of the first drop traverse steeply onto the top of the east lava lobe for a direct route to the saddle at the north end of the crescent-shaped Hell Hole.

Lost Plateau. (Map 64) To visit this pumice desert at 7,100 feet, ski to Obsidian Pass from either direction around the Big Flow, and from the pass enter lodgepole pines to the southeast and ski 100 yards. The pumice desert is at the very foot of the caldera wall, rising dramatically 500 feet to the crater rim. There is a good view of Paulina Peak from here.

HORSE CAMP CONNECTOR

(Map 64) The summertime horse camp is located 0.9 mile west of the foot of Big Obsidian Flow and provides a shortcut to the flow's west side. From the Paulina Lake Resort, ski the Paulina Lake road east 1.3 miles to the access road to the horse camp. Ski to the rear of the horse-camp area and find the obscure horse trail that follows a primitive road 0.5 mile east through lodgepole pine forest to the Big Flow. Future ski trails will no doubt make all this easier.

LITTLE CRATER

(Map 64) Opposite and just north across the Paulina Lake road from the Big Obsidian Lava Flow is Little Crater. It is a 150-foot climb to its partially forested summit ridge and open slopes where good views of the Big Flow and the caldera rim are enjoyed.

INTER-LAKE OBSIDIAN FLOW

(Map 64) The climb to the lava flow between the two caldera lakes starts 2.6 miles from the Paulina Lake Resort. This tour is for strong Intermediate skiers who enjoy off-trail skiing. From the lake's shoreline the off-trail route climbs up to 600 feet above the lake. Ski the lake's south shore or the Paulina Lake road to the Little Crater Campground on Paulina Lake's east shore, then ski to the far north end of the campground 0.8 mile from the Paulina Lake road. Enter forest and climb 600 yards to reach the edge of the lava flow. Follow its south edge eastward to a low pass, then ski onto the flow for views. If possible, ski across rugged lava surface to the flow's upper west edge for the best views. The lava flow extends from lake to lake.

HOT SPRINGS LAVA FLOW

(Map 64) In the spring when the road to East Lake is plowed, or if you are staying at the Paulina Lake Resort, this ski tour is worth considering. The Hot Springs Lava Flow is located south of East Lake immediately above the Hot Springs Campground, which is beside and south of the Paulina Lake road. The campground is 4.3 miles from Paulina Lake Resort. Two small but disconnected lava flows offer interesting exploration and views from their uphill sides. Each lava flow is a 1-mile climb of 350 feet from the road, and is best suited to strong Intermediate skiers who enjoy off-trail skiing.

Ski to the Hot Springs Campground and then to the meadow in the rear. Gentle grades climb around the west side of the west lobe, the larger of the two lobes. In 1 mile you will reach the upper back side for a view of East Lake, the north rim of the caldera, Paulina Peak, and Central Cone, the large cone between the lakes. It is possible to circle the west lobe, and to ski on its surface.

The smaller east lobe has a steeper, rougher, unskiable surface, but it can also be circled, and its upper back side provides a grand view. As you circle, the east side leads to a powerline route that can be followed down to the campground. It is 2 miles to ski both lobes in one loop. If time is short, ski 0.3 mile up between the two lobes and turn left to the top of the east lobe for the views, and return downhill around the west side of the west lobe.

THE DOME

(Map 64) This large cinder cone lies southeast of East Lake near the caldera's rim. A road leads to it, and from its treeless, flat, U-shaped 7,280-foot summit there are wonderful views.

Ski 0.4 mile past Hot Springs Campground and turn east onto the China Hat road. Ski uphill 2.4 miles to a 7,000-foot pass, then climb the steep side of the partially forested cone. In particular, views to the east and south are exceptional. The Dome is a 900-foot climb above East Lake. If you are skiing the east lobe of the Hot Springs Lava Flow, there is an obscure horse trail from the east side of the lobe with steep sections through thick lodgepole pine forest to the China Hat road.

Chapter 25

WILLAMETTE PASS

For Oregon skiers whose skiing experience has been limited to the Cascades of northern Oregon and southern Washington, Willamette Pass may come as a scenic surprise. The region is heavily forested with little sign at this time of logging. But the greatest impact may come from seeing endless, rugged, forested ridges, buttes, and volcanic cones in all directions. For northern Oregon skiers, accustomed to the splendid isolation of the three major volcanoes, rising from lowlands seldom averaging more than 4,000 feet, the contrast is exciting. It is indeed a spectacular area that must be explored on a number of trips to fully appreciate its uniqueness. Another unique aspect is the three large lakes—Waldo, Odell, and Crescent—each over a mile wide and several miles long. Most ski trails are above 4,800 feet, and the skiing area extends some 20 miles from west to east with seven distinct trail systems to explore. And for the Backcountry skier there is Waldo Lake and the Diamond Peak Wilderness, both relatively easy to visit on one-day tours over moderate terrain.

Willamette Pass, at 5,128 feet, is 185 miles from Portland via Interstate 5 and 227 miles via Government Camp and Bend. The pass is 70 miles southwest of Bend, and 67 miles southeast of Eugene. Four sno-parks service the ski trails.

WESTVIEW LOOPS AND PENGRA PASS

(Maps 65 & 66) An unusual geological situation has placed two mountain passes almost beside each other. Willamette Pass carries Highway 58 and is the site of the downhill ski area on Eagle Peak. The second, Pengra Pass, named for a pioneer, lies barely higher and less than 2 miles southwest. Under this pass, an almost 1-mile-long train tunnel passes. A number of trails radiate from Pengra Pass, some on roads and some on forest trails.

Westview Loops. (Maps 65 & 66) A series of short, connected trails for Intermediate skiers between the two passes offers great variety and access to the Diamond Peak Wilderness. The most popular access is from Gold Lake Sno-Park (5,000 feet) located 0.6 mile west of Willamette Pass and on the south side of the highway. The sno-park also serves the trail system north of the highway.

The Westview Loops are mostly forest trails and culminate at the top of a butte (5,428 feet) with a good but restricted view of Diamond Peak. There is a shelter on the butte's west slope with views. The Pacific Crest Trail (PCT) also accesses the trail system, starting at Willamette Pass just east and across

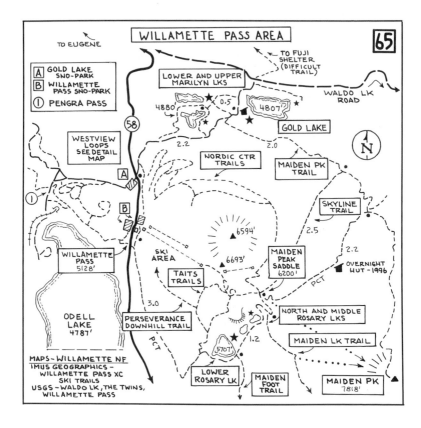

the highway from the ski area. A first visit to this area can be confusing due to the numerous choices and many short trails, so carry a ski-trails map. Imus Geographics's "Willamette Pass XC Ski Trails" map covers the entire region.

To reach the trails, ski from the far end of Gold Lake Sno-Park along a wide, uninteresting road 0.3 mile to where one of the trails climbs the hill to the left, the most direct route to the Westview Shelter. By continuing on the road another 0.5 mile you reach The Triangle, three short road segments forming a triangle from which several ski trails depart. Another Westview trail leaves from the triangle's east leg. Other than exploring the

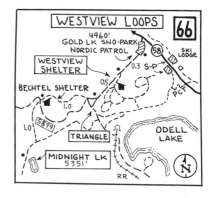

several short loops on the butte, it is possible to complete a 3.5-mile loop that circles the entire area by skiing from Pengra Pass on the PCT to Willamette Pass, crossing the highway, then skiing a trail north of the highway to the Gold Lake Trail, then crossing the highway again to the snopark. The PCT segment is through old-growth forest.

Bechtel Creek Trail. (Maps 65 & 66) From Gold Lake Sno-Park ski 0.8 mile to The Triangle (see Westview Loops), then ski west on a road that soon becomes a trail and climbs to the Bechtel Shelter (5,120 feet) 1.8 mile from the snopark. To ski a loop, climb above the shelter to Road 5899 and ski a mile back to The Triangle. This loop is an easy Intermediate, marked route.

Midnight Lake, Diamond Peak Wilderness, and Yoran Lake. (Maps 65 & 66) At 5,351 feet, Midnight Lake is a moderate 1-mile climb through forest and meadows from the Bechtel Creek Trail, and 1.7 miles from The Triangle. This is a pleasant ski tour for strong Intermediate skiers, and gives access to the Diamond Peak Wilderness along the unmarked PCT to Blue-Haired Lady Lake (5,840 feet), called Hidden Lake on some maps. The lake fills the bottom of a shallow basin and can easily be missed. Ski another 0.7 mile to Yoran Lake south of the PCT at 6,000 feet, which is recognized by a low cliff along its east shore and an island with a group of trees at its north end. At this time, the trail to Midnight Lake is marked for skiers with natural-wood diamonds. Do not ski on any lake surfaces here as they are often dangerously soft, but look deceptively safe.

There are many loop opportunities here for the experienced Backcountry skier who carries a map and compass and who uses good judgment. The lower ends of both the Yoran Lake and Trapper Creek Trails are steep in case you are planning a tour in that direction. The trails of this area are not easy to follow in winter, and special skills are necessary here. (See Diamond Peak later in this chapter.)

Shelter Cove. (Maps 65 & 66) Starting from The Triangle at Pengra Pass ski southeast on a moderately steep, narrow road downhill 0.5 mile to the railroad tracks near the tunnel's east portal. Cross the tracks with great care as several trains each day roar past here, and you will not hear them until they are very close. When across the tracks, pick up the marked ski trail in forest, which leads in 1 mile to the peninsula in Odell Lake, where there is a trail loop. The peninsula is 2.5 miles from Willamette Pass via the PCT, and 2 miles from Gold Lake Sno-Park. The elevation loss from Pengra Pass is 400 feet. Skiing on or along the tracks may coat your ski bases with oil—and is also a dangerous practice.

Willamette Pass to Gold Lake Trail. (Maps 65 & 66) This 1-mile trail leaves from the west end of Willamette Pass Sno-Park west of the ski lodge to link with Gold Lake Trail and Sno-Park. The trail passes through old growth and in one place along a "common corridor" shared with the Nordic Center groomed-trail system. The west end of this connector may be a difficult descent for some skiers. A fee is charged for skiing on the groomed tracks, and cross-country ski rentals are available at the lodge.

GOLD LAKE AND MARILYN LAKES

(Maps 65 & 66) This is certainly the finest system of short marked trails for the Novice skier anywhere in the region, except perhaps for the groomed trails at the Odell Lake Resort, which, however, lack the scenic beauty of the Marilyn Lakes. The compact area has three lakes with several wonderful views. Several short, steep hills will cause some anxiety for Novices, but in general it is easy, rolling terrain. The area's natural beauty means that it will always be crowded on weekends.

From Gold Lake Sno-Park 0.6 mile west of Willamette Pass, cross the highway and follow a primitive, winding road with gentle ups and downs 2.2 miles to Gold Lake. Along the way you will pass side trails into the Marilyn Lakes—Upper and Lower—both are gems to be explored. The first access trail is recommended to Novice skiers, while the second is a steep descent off the Gold Lake road. There is a good view of Diamond Peak from the north end of Lower Marilyn Lake.

There is a beautiful, old, three-sided log shelter at the south end of Gold Lake just off the road. A sleeping platform will accommodate four persons.

Ski 200 yards from the shelter down to the campground at Gold Lake's south shore for a view of the lake basin. It is usually not safe to ski on any of the three lakes. Be safe and stay off. It is possible to ski Gold Lake's west shore trail to the lake's north end for views. The scenic bog and swamp area at the north end is often not skiable.

ROSARY LAKES

(Map 65) The three lakes are very scenic, dominated by cliffs to the west. The marked Intermediate ski trail follows the PCT 3 miles from Willamette Pass, starting behind the Department of Highways shed just east of the lodge area. The trail climbs steadily through old growth on a moderate grade to the largest of the lakes, then continues on to the upper two lakes. Lower Rosary Lake, also known as South Rosary or Ethel, is at 5,707 feet, a 580-foot climb from the trailhead. The trail continues to climb to the upper lake with a vertical of 400 feet from South Rosary to the Maiden Peak Saddle at 6,200 feet.

TAITS TRAILS

(Map 65) You can find a 2-mile Intermediate–Advanced loop and two shorter ones on a forested plateau at 6,200 feet near the top of Eagle Peak and above the Rosary Lakes. They may be reached by skiing 4.2 miles to the Maiden Peak Saddle by way of the Rosary Lakes Trail, or by a one-way chairlift ride at the ski area (be sure to have runaway straps on your skis). From the top of the chairlift, there is a fairly steep 0.5-mile drop to Taits

Trails. To return from Taits Trails, accomplished skiers can descend the downhill ski area's Perseverance Trail from the southwest side of the main Taits Trail, or descend a steep trail to just below South Rosary where it joins the main trail.

MAIDEN PEAK

(Map 65) A massive volcanic cone, at 7,818 feet Maiden Peak attracts few casual skiers as it is essentially a serious ascent for experienced Backcountry skiers. The Maiden Peak Trail starts near Gold Lake, but this is a longer, more demanding route than skiing the Rosary Lakes Trail to the Maiden Lake Trail, a route totaling 7 miles one way with a climb of 2,700 feet to the summit.

Once on the Maiden Lake Trail, ski east about 1.2 miles to the 6,400-foot contour, then leave the trail and head for the summit. Be wary of snow conditions and cornices near the top. On the descent don't count on the Maiden Lake Trail, your return route, as a catch line—it is easy to miss it and continue down below it. If you descend a fall-line path you may wind up too far east, so use a compass course to retrace your upward route. A direct route from the Rosary Lakes to Maiden Peak is hard to navigate and not recommended. An overnight shelter is being built near the PCT northwest of Maiden Peak.

MAIDEN LAKE TRAIL

(Map 65) The lake at 6,400 feet does not attract many skiers so don't count on a broken track. The Advanced trail goes 3 miles eastward from the PCT north of the Rosary Lakes and passes through open forest to reach the small lake.

SALT CREEK FALLS AREA

(Map 67) Salt Creek Falls Sno-Park, the first sno-park after leaving Eugene, is 20 miles southeast of Oakridge. At 4,080 feet, it does not have

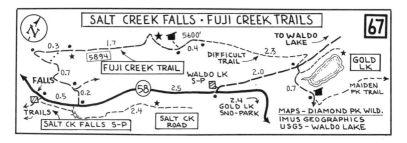

consistent snow depth. The sno-park also serves as the access to the Fuji Creek Trail.

Salt Creek Falls. (Map 67) The 286-foot falls are only 150 yards from the sno-park. A 3-mile trail system, primarily on roads and suitable for Novice skiers, is located southwest of the sno-park where a forest trail leads to the trail system.

Salt Creek Road. (Map 67) This is a varied ski tour that will tax some Novice skiers, but the rewards at the trail end are worthwhile for those who do not mind road skiing. At first, the marked trail goes east through the campground then into forest up a short, steep rise.

Ski 0.5 mile to a road, turn right, cross a bridge, and continue on the road, which changes from a wide, monotonous route to a winding primitive road with scattered meadows about 2 miles from the sno-park.

For access to the Fuji Creek Trail, turn left when you reach the road 0.5 mile from Salt Creek Sno-Park, and cross the highway to the Fuji Creek road, your route to the Fuji Shelter area.

Fuji Creek Trail. (Map 67) Although this Intermediate ski route follows a road and offers no significant challenge, it nevertheless offers some of the finest views of the Willamette Pass region. Such rewards are rarely found for such a modest expenditure of energy. The trip to the Fuji Shelter, near the end of the road, involves 1,400 feet of elevation gain and 4 miles of travel. The shelter has been carefully located at the top of a clearcut, above the road, for the best possible views.

See the Salt Creek Road description for access to the Fuji Creek Trail. Cross the highway and go east a few paces to Road 5894, your route up. The road climbs steadily at a moderately steep angle. At 1.2 miles you'll have your first views, which get better as you climb. The shelter is located at the top of the next-to-the-last clearcut. From the road end, a marked forest trail continues and descends in 2 miles to the Waldo Lake road, where it goes past the south end of Gold Lake. By this route, the Fuji Shelter is 5.6 miles from Gold Lake Sno-Park with an elevation gain of 600 feet.

The Fuji Shelter has a barrel stove, sleeping loft, and remarkable views across the deep, forested Salt Creek valley to Diamond Peak rising impressively only 8 miles to the south. Maiden Peak, Lakeview Mountain, Crater Butte, and even Mount Thielsen are in sight.

The night scene from the shelter is unique. Far below, you'll hear the eastbound, multi-engined freight trains laboring slowly upward with a roar, and the lighted passenger trains climbing only slightly faster with their trails of passenger car lights. Westbound trains break the darkness with great piercing beams of oscillating light that rotate across the valley. The night experience is memorable.

Off-trail travel north of the shelter is tempting, but safe only with compass and map. Fuji Mountain summit has huge, dangerous cornices, and the area below the peak is difficult to travel, with many low bluffs and steep gullies.

The route from Salt Creek Falls Sno-Park is best left to strong Intermediate skiers. The ski route to the shelter from Gold Lake is rated Backcountry. Do not ski either route if conditions are not good.

The rolling pond-dotted area north of the Fuji Shelter will see some 11 miles of marked ski trails added in the future. A 2-mile trail from the Fuji Shelter will access a future shelter on the south shore of Lower Island Lake. Another access trail into the area will start at the Waldo Lake road and follow an existing marked trail to the Fuji Shelter. This access trail is easily reached from the end of the Gold Lake Trail. The setting for these future trails is confusing to ski as there are few landmarks. Until the marked trails are completed, it should be visited only by experienced backcountry skiers.

WALDO LAKE

(Map 68) Located in the Waldo Lake Wilderness, Waldo Lake is the second-largest freshwater lake in Oregon and one of the purest in the world. It is 9 miles to the lake from Gold Lake Sno-Park. To the shelter at the lake's

Wind-blown old ski tracks

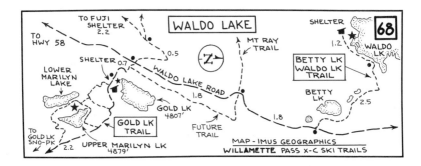

south end it is 10.2 miles and a cumulative elevation gain of 1,000 feet. This is a trip for strong, experienced skiers. Although a marked ski trail goes all the way, Backcountry experience is recommended.

Starting at Gold Lake Sno-Park, the route proceeds to Gold Lake, then along a tie trail to the Waldo Lake road (a snowmobile route) that you follow 3.6 miles to the marked Betty Lake-Waldo Lake Trail.

From the Waldo Lake road it is 2.5 miles to the lakeshore. At first, the trail climbs moderately through beautiful open forest to Betty Lake, levels, then ascends and passes Howkum Lake as it continues through open forest. It then descends to Waldo Lake Trail No. 3590, which is seldom more than 50 feet from the lake. If the lake is well frozen, ski along the lakeshore for an easier 1.2-mile route to the shelter at the south edge of South Waldo Meadows. The shelter, surrounded by tall, pointed firs, is 300 yards from the lake, which is out of sight. Saddle-summited Mount Ray south of the lake is a prominent landmark.

MAKLAKS LOOPS AND MAIDEN FOOT TRAIL

(Map 69) There are two Maklaks loops totaling 8 miles, mostly on logging roads. The trailhead is on the Davis Lake road just south of the Odell Lake Resort entrance 4.6 miles south of Willamette Pass. The 3-mile Maiden Foot Trail connects the loops with the PCT near the north end of lower Rosary Lake, a 900-foot climb. All are rated Novice.

ODELL LAKE RESORT AND CRESCENT LAKE TRAIL

(Map 69) Odell Lake Resort at the south end of Odell Lake and 5 miles south of Willamette Pass has a remarkable 8-mile groomed-trail system for which a fee is charged. The trails were beautifully designed by an Olympic skier to lead through thick lodgepole pine forest and are a pleasure for skiers of all levels.

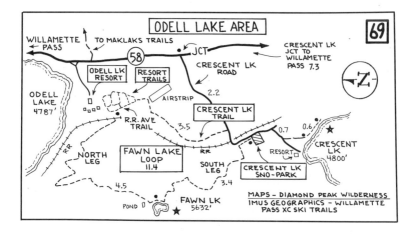

One of the two Fawn Lake trailheads is across the railroad tracks not far from the resort lodge. To locate it, ski out Railroad Avenue Trail 0.3 mile from the lodge, cross the tracks, and search the forest edge for the small sign marking the start of the hiking trail to the lake. See Fawn Lake description.

The parking at Odell Lake Resort is private and reserved for resort patrons. However, if you are not a guest, parking is permitted for a modest per-person charge when skiing the Fawn Lake Trail. If you pay to ski the track system, parking is free.

Crescent Lake Flats Trail. (Map 69) Connecting the Odell Lake Resort trails to Crescent Lake, this perfectly level 3.5-mile Novice trail is not marked outside the resort's groomed tracks, but its route is obvious as it follows a road that is seldom more than 100 yards from the railroad tracks.

From the south end of the groomed tracks follow open areas to the north end of an airstrip. Cross the end of it and bear right into the forest and onto an obvious, winding, primitive road that leads to the Crescent Lake access road. Turn right, cross the tracks, and the Fawn Lake trailhead is in front of you. Crescent Lake Sno-Park is 0.3 mile to your left. See the Fawn Lake description for warnings about skiing on or near the railroad tracks.

Crescent Lake Shoreline. (Map 69) The views from the easily accessible shoreline make it worth the inevitable association with snowmobilers that makes Crescent Lake a hornet's nest of activity. Drive to Crescent Lake Sno-Park (see Fawn Lake) and ski or walk 0.4 mile south on the road leading to the Crescent Lake resort area. Here, ski a snow-covered road to the left (the resort is out of sight beyond) 0.3 mile to the lake's shoreline, not far east of the resort. Ski east on this road as it parallels the lakeside for 0.6 mile, or ski the lakeshore. There is a special view of Cowhorn, Mount Thielsen, and Mount Scott on Crater Lake's east side. The view of Crescent Lake is terrific. If you are staying at the Odell Lake Resort, Crescent Lake is only 4 miles away along the Crescent Lake Flats Trail, an unmarked, easy-to-follow route paralleling the railroad tracks and described in the Odell Lake Resort description.

FAWN LAKE

(Map 69) At 5,632 feet, Fawn Lake is a lovely spot nestled in the forest, and although there are few views this is an interesting forest ski tour by either of the summer hiking trails marked for skiers. The trails are not heavily used and provide isolation and a good Backcountry experience for competent Intermediate skiers or better who carry backcountry gear.

The Fawn Lake trails were included in the enlargement of the Diamond Peak Wilderness several years ago. The standard blue diamonds for marking winter ski trails are being removed and replaced with wooden diamonds that more closely meet a standard for natural appearance. These new markers will not always be easy to see. Such marking is unusual as trails in wilderness areas are seldom marked.

From Crescent Lake Sno-Park it is 3.4 miles to the lake, and 4.5 miles from the Odell Lake Resort, with an elevation gain of 1,000 feet by either route. Skied as a loop, the distance is 11.4 miles.

Crescent Lake Sno-Park is 2.2 miles from Highway 58. From the sno-park follow trail markers as the trail parallels the access road 0.3 mile, then turns uphill following an old roadbed for 0.7 mile. Turn right onto the forest trail for the final 2.4 miles to the lake. At first through old growth and ponderosa pines, the trail then levels and enters jackpine forest, winding about with ups and downs until you reach the lake. Ski to the east shore for a view of Lakeview Mountain to the west. Although the trail is marked, don't count on it being easy to follow.

To ski the north leg of the loop to the lake, see Odell Lake Resort directions to the Fawn Lake trailhead. Once on the trail, it goes through jackpine as it climbs moderately westward almost paralleling the railroad tracks. At 2 miles old-growth firs are entered and the trail climbs, zigzags on steep sidehills, then levels out for more jackpine. Continue to the pond with a view of Lakeview Mountain 0.3 mile below the lake.

Be extremely careful crossing the railroad tracks. The trains pass very rapidly and, surprisingly, are not heard until almost upon you. Do not ski on the railroad tracks! In addition to the obvious dangers, you might also pick up oil on your ski bases, which will affect skiing and is difficult to remove.

ODELL BUTTE AND LITTLE ODELL BUTTE

(Map 70) At 7,032 feet, Odell Butte is a landmark volcanic cone rising 2,200 feet above Highway 58. East of Crescent Lake, the upper reaches of the butte offer a grand view of the region: both Crescent and Odell Lakes, Diamond Peak, and the Willamette Pass area with its many ridges and cones.

Drive 12.6 miles southeast on Highway 58 to a turnout parking place on the east side of the highway. From here, Road 5815, a wide logging road, climbs moderately steep grades for 5.3 miles to the summit lookout. The first mile delivers a view to the south, but the best view is from a hairpin turn at 6,480 feet, 0.8 mile from the top. The view is even better than from the Fuji Creek Road trail shelter. If possible, climb to the very sum-

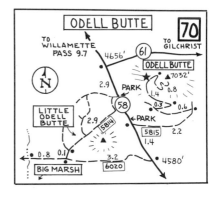

mit for views north. If you are lucky you will see Mount Shasta, the Three Sisters, Jefferson, and many others.

Little Odell Butte and Big Marsh. (Map 70) This small butte is located 3 miles southwest of Odell Butte across Highway 58 and offers an amazing 18 miles of trails, almost all following roads through jackpine forest and clearcuts. There are some views, and the terrain is gentle to rolling and suitable for Novice skiers.

The trailhead is 1.6 miles south of the Road 61/Gilchrist cutoff highway. Look for the chain-up area and park off the highway on the west shoulder. Walk south on the highway a short distance to Road 5814, the main access to the area. Ski the trails off Road 5814, which follow primitive roads and are more interesting than Road 5814 itself. The Little Odell Butte area is unfortunately not particularly interesting.

Road 6020, an east-to-west forest road south of the butte, is often plowed for railroad access and maintenance. If so, it is narrow, so allow passage on the road when parking. This road is located 1.4 miles south on Highway 58 from the recommended parking for Odell Butte. If you ski or drive Road 6020, it is 3.2 miles from Highway 58 to the junction of 6020 with 5814 coming south from the chain-up area.

From this junction, continue west 0.3 mile on 6020 for a view of Diamond Peak, and another 0.5 mile to Big Marsh Creek. Turn south and ski along the beautiful creek to Big Marsh, a vast meadow area, unfortunately frequented by snowmobilers. The beauty and isolation of Big Marsh justify mixing with other users if they are present. Big Marsh is the main attraction of this little-visited Little Odell Butte area.

DIAMOND PEAK

(Map 71) The climb to the summit of Diamond Peak (8,744 feet) is a serious undertaking. The peak and its surrounding high country are for Backcountry skiers, and the unmarked routes push toward 16 miles round trip. Spring is the best season for this tour, and for the other interesting

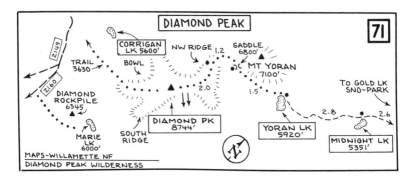

tours on Diamond Peak's west side. The best time to visit the west side of the Diamond Peak Wilderness is when the snow has consolidated and the snowline is higher and roads drivable to higher elevations. All the tours here require strong navigational skills and good weather. Wannabes need not apply here, and should learn off-trail skills on easier subjects before exploring this remote area.

From Oakridge, on Highway 58 on the way to Willamette Pass, drive south on Road 21 past Hills Creek Lake (a reservoir) about 30 miles to Road 2149, the Pioneer Gulch area at 3,100 feet. Drive up 2149 as far as possible, and at 3.2 miles Road 2160 joins from the south. Ski up 2160 about 0.6 mile to summer trail 3630, which will take you up to Trail 3699. Leave the trail, enter the forest, and ski northeast to meet the southwest ridge of Diamond Peak, which joins the south ridge at 7,800 feet.

On the way up minor ridges from the south may force you onto the main ridge. The ridge is not steep, but climbing skins are suggested. If snow is firm and stable, the huge bowl north of the southwest ridge may entice you as a route to the summit. The bowl is best approached from 6,000 feet or so, and, if safe, is an excellent descent route. The "safeness" of snow, however, on slopes over 30 degrees in angle, and in all bowls, is difficult to ascertain. Big avalanches occur in the bowls on the peak. If in doubt, use ridges and stay out of bowls. If crossing a bowl, always cross at its bottom.

Northside Route. (Map 71) From Willamette Pass it is over 10 miles and a climb of 3,700 feet to the Diamond Peak summit. From Gold Lake Sno-Park ski to Midnight Lake, then beyond and across the open snowfields above timberline. Ski to the northwest ridge of Diamond Peak and ascend this to the long summit ridge, which narrows as you ski, and climb southward to the highest point. The northwest ridge is recommended over any eastside route. The eastside bowls are steep and made dangerous by deeper snow deposits at higher elevations. Once you are back down to the base, the long ski run out in good snow is almost all gentle gliding except for the final 2 miles.

Corrigan Lake. (Map 71) This lake is a pleasant consolation tour on the west side if your primary goal is Diamond Peak but snow conditions or

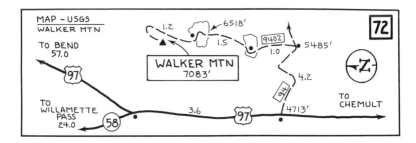

distances thwart your success. Ski summer trail 3654 from Road 2149 through old growth to the lake at 5,600 feet. You will want a good map and compass as you may not find or be able to stay on the trail.

Diamond Rockpile and Marie Lake. (Map 71) With a road most of the way up, Diamond Rockpile offers fine views. Ski up Road 2160 and try to find summer trail 3632, about 2.5 miles from Road 2149, or just take a direct line through the forest. There are some steep places to ski, and you'll need navigational skills and the wilderness map showing up-to-date trails and topographical features. If you are looking for a less-demanding tour than elusive forest trails allow, just continue skiing up Road 2149 to the summit ridge of nearby Bear Mountain and splendid views at 6,000 feet.

WALKER MOUNTAIN

(Map 72) An imposing, solitary butte, Walker Mountain (7,083 feet) offers an interesting road tour (rated Advanced) of up to 12 miles round trip to the fire lookout on the summit. Elevation gain is up to 2,000 feet. Located southeast of the Highway 58/97 junction 24 miles south of Willamette Pass, the long, ridgelike peak is a landmark.

From the 58/97 junction drive 3.6 miles south on Highway 97 and turn east onto Road 94 (4,713 feet). Follow this wide, graveled road 4.2 miles, at first crossing flats for 2 miles, then climbing moderately to Road 9402 at 5,485 feet.

Road 9402 will take you to the summit, climbing the long south ridge 3.7 miles to the fire lookout on top. It is a narrow, primitive dirt road that is best not driven if it is wet. If necessary carry skis to the snowline. One mile from Road 94 you will skirt the top of a clearcut, and at 2.5 miles you turn left in another clearcut at 6,518 feet where it levels briefly. At 0.4 mile from the top the road makes a sharp turn to the flat summit.

Views to the south and west are unrestricted—Mount Shasta, Mount McLoughlin, Crater Lake rim, Mount Thielsen, Diamond Peak, and minor volcanic cones in profusion. A historic one-room stone cabin residence still stands on the summit. Obviously, as on many tours where roads are not plowed in winter, the best time for this tour is in the spring when the snowline is higher.

Chapter 26

DIAMOND LAKE

At 5,183 feet, Diamond Lake is the centerpiece of a splendid mountain basin some 8 miles wide and 22 miles from north to south. The Cascade Range crestline and spirelike Mount Thielsen (9,182 feet) form the rugged eastern wall and Mount Bailey (8,363 feet) forms the western wall of the basin. On the south, the north rim of Crater Lake encloses the basin, and to the distant north the Umpqua River headwaters and Lemolo Lake lie partially enclosed by high, forested ridges. Diamond Lake itself is 2 miles wide and over 3 miles long.

Most of the skiing is done around the south shore, along its eastern shore, and the most adventuresome along the west-facing slopes of the Cascade crest. Skiing ranges from flat-land Novice tours to Backcountry skiing—a wide range to suit all tastes.

Lodging is available at Diamond Lake Resort, Lemolo Lake Resort, and Union Creek Lodge 24 miles southwest of Diamond Lake. Driving distances to Diamond Lake include the following:

- From Portland via I-5 and Roseburg: 259 miles
- From Portland via I-5 and Willamette Pass: 240 miles
- From Eugene via Willamette Pass: 130 miles
- From Eugene via Roseburg: 148 miles
- From Bend: 97 miles
- From Roseburg: 79 miles
- From Medford: 83 miles

Four sno-parks service the many trails. Howlock Sno-Park is located on the access road to the Diamond Lake Resort. Thielsen Sno-Park is on Highway 138, 2.7 miles south of the resort access road. South Diamond Sno-Park is at the southeast corner of the lake off Highway 230 and 0.2 mile from Highway 138. To the southwest of this sno-park 2.8 miles on Highway 230 is Three Lakes Sno-Park, which services the Silent Creek-Mount Bailey area.

NORTH SHORE AND RESORT AREA

(No sketch map) Due to proximity to the resort on Diamond Lake's northeast shore, this area is popular with skiers. Several trails leaving the resort area are suitable for Novices, and there is also access to the Howlock Mountain Trail, which ascends the west slopes of Mount Thielsen.

NORDIC CENTER TRAILS

(No sketch map) A cross-country ski-rental shop is located at the resort, and several miles of double-track groomed Novice trails are maintained at no charge to the public. The tracks, which include a skating track, are along the east side of the lake.

ROUND-THE-LAKE LOOP

(No sketch map) An 11.5-mile Intermediate ski trail circles the lake following a summer bicycle trail. The trail is closed in winter to machine use. On the lake's west side, where summer cabins exist, the trail climbs gently up and through forest away from the lake and above the many cabins. Otherwise, the loop is close to the lakeshore.

VISTA TRAIL

(No sketch map) Sometimes called the North Diamond Trail, the Vista Trail starts behind the motel units northeast of the resort. The trail follows westward near the lakeshore along a summer bicycle trail for 1.5 miles, and, as the name implies, there are many views. Of course, you'll have great views of the lake, Mount Bailey, and Mount Thielsen, and to the south the north rim of Crater Lake. Nearly level, the trail is suitable for Novices, but in some years may not have sufficient snow.

NORTH CRATER TRAIL AND EAST LAKESHORE

(Map 73) The little-used North Crater Trail follows a summer hiking trail south from Howlock Sno-Park through forest and well back from the lake's shore. This Novice–Intermediate trail goes over 7 miles south and southeast to connect with the Pacific Crest Trail (PCT). It climbs 600 feet in the last 4 miles after leaving the lake area. Most skiers prefer to ski along the east shore near the lake following roads through the campgrounds, although the route is often used by snowmobilers.

HOWLOCK MOUNTAIN, MOUNT THIELSEN, AND SPRUCE RIDGE TRAILS

(Map 73) The Mount Thielsen Wilderness covers almost 90 square miles east of Diamond Lake and includes miles of forest that sweep up the west slopes of the Cascade crest to Mount Thielsen and the rugged lower points

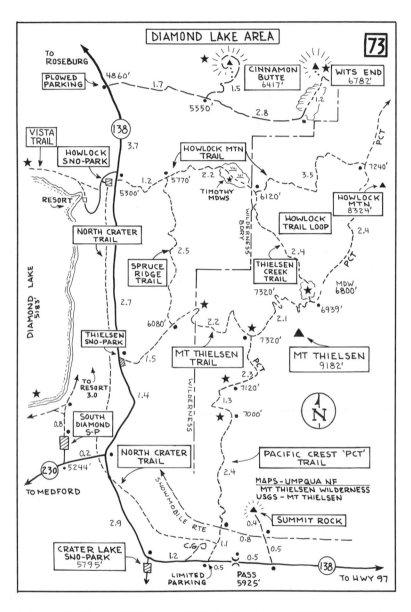

to the north. Howlock Mountain (8,324 feet) and Mount Thielsen (9,182 feet) are the highest points on the long Sawtooth Ridge of the Cascade crest, and are unattainable by skiers. The area is covered with dense lodgepole pine (jackpine) forests at lower elevations, then firs and hemlocks up higher, both of which are not suitable for off-trail skiing. Regardless of how inviting off-trail may appear at the lower elevations, be aware that if you leave the trails you will have problems where least expected, and waste time and energy.

The Howlock and Thielsen trails are more suited for Backcountry skiers as the trails are not marked and not always obvious. Views are infrequent until you get higher.

For the average skier seeking good exercise, variety, and scenery, the south shore trails and Howlock Mountain Trail are recommended, as are the Cinnamon Butte and Wits End tours.

Howlock Mountain Trail. (Map 73) For Intermediate skiers, this 3.4-mile one-way trail eventually leads to views and provides a wilderness experience on an unmarked trail. From Howlock Sno-Park on the Diamond Lake Resort access road, ski up the trail and through a tunnel under the highway. Ski 1.2 miles through viewless jackpine and second growth to the Spruce Ridge Trail. Even if you plan to turn south onto that trail, at least keep going up the Howlock Trail a mile or so to see the beautiful, long Timothy Meadows area with views. The farther up you ski toward the PCT, the more challenging it will be to stay on the trail. If you are challenged, however, to go beyond the meadows, continue up to the meadow at the head of Thielsen Creek following the west leg of the Howlock Trail loop. The meadow has a striking view of Matterhorn-like Thielsen rising 2,500 feet above.

Spruce Ridge Trail. (Map 73) The value of this Intermediate marked trail, which has only a few views, is that it provides a loop trail by connecting with the Mount Thielsen Trail. Ski up the Howlock Mountain Trail 1.2 miles, then turn south onto the Spruce Ridge Trail and ski its 2.5 miles as it twists and rolls along climbing slowly southward. If you are skiing a loop, be aware that after skiing down the Thielsen Trail and reaching the highway, you will have a 0.4-mile descent through untrailed forest to reach the east shore trail to complete the 10-mile loop.

Mount Thielsen Trail. (Map 73) The trailhead is at Thielsen Sno-Park on Highway 138, 2.7 miles south of the Diamond Lake Resort access road. From the east shore trails there is no marked trail or access to this trailhead. From the sno-park the trail climbs moderately, then more steeply, 1.5 miles to the Spruce Ridge Trail. Continue up the Mount Thielsen Trail another 0.5 mile to a switchback with a fine view of the mountain. The end of this trail, 3.7 miles from the sno-park, takes you to 7,320 feet, a climb of 2,000 feet, the highest point of all the trails on Mount Thielsen and a magnificent viewpoint.

CINNAMON BUTTE AND WITS END

(Map 73) Although these two viewpoints are Intermediate road tours, the views are stunning. The distance to the fire lookout on Cinnamon Butte (6,417 feet) is 3.2 miles with a vertical gain of 1,600 feet. For Wits End, farther up the same road, it is 5.7 miles from the highway and a gain of 1,982 feet to the 6,782-foot ridgetop. If you combine the two into a one-day tour, which is reasonable if the snow is favorable, you will have a skiing Grand

Looking south from near Wits End to Mount Thielsen

Slam with total round-trip distance of 14.4 miles and accumulated elevation gain of 2,850 feet.

The small trailhead parking area is on Highway 138, 3.7 miles north of the Diamond Lake Resort access road. From the parking area, ski uphill on the wide, monotonous, viewless road. A fleeting glimpse of the lookout will be the only view for a while. At 1.7 miles turn left off the road onto a moderately steep, primitive road that gets steeper as you climb. The sidehill above the road is steep, so be attentive to snow conditions as you continue to the summit of Cinnamon Butte.

You'll see Thielsen, Lemolo Lake, the upper Umpqua valley, Bailey, Diamond Peak, Cowhorn (Windigo Pass to its right), Diamond Lake, and the Crater Lake rim. This is today's best view by far, but Wits End is worth going on to. On the descent, ski down the steep east side from the summit, if the snow is good, for a shortcut and some excitement.

To reach Wits End, continue up the main road, passing one view on the way to a huge north-south clearcut 4.5 miles from the parking area. Climb diagonally to its northeast corner, enter mountain hemlock forest, and follow a road to where it turns east and drops. Remain on the ridge, leave the road, and climb the ridge northward 200 yards for the best views. You'll see the Three Sisters, Mount Bachelor, and Broken Top in addition to the view from Cinnamon Butte.

As you ascend the final, huge clearcut to Wits End, mark mentally where you entered the clearcut. It is easy to descend this clearcut so fast that you may overshoot your uphill road and waste a lot of time being temporarily "lost" in the forest and figuring out where you are and want to be.

PACIFIC CREST NATIONAL SCENIC TRAIL (PCT)

(Map 73) For the adventuresome Backcountry skier, this is the most scenic, most demanding trail of the region—6 miles and a cumulative elevation gain of 2,000 feet to the junction with the Mount Thielsen Trail. The trail climbs to open areas, 4 miles north of the trailhead on Highway 138, where there are extensive views from bowls and ridgecrests. The unmarked trail is not easy to follow, and a compass and topo map should be carried.

At the Mount Thielsen Trail junction, the view goes north to the Three Sisters and sweeps west and south to Crater Lake. If you don't make it this far, the view at 3.5 miles may be your reward, and only another mile northward, around the nose of a prominent ridge, reveals Mount Thielsen up close.

From the high point at the Mount Thielsen Trail junction, the PCT continues north, descends, crosses a ridge, switchbacks several times, then generally contours to the Howlock Mountain Trail 11.6 miles from the trailhead. If familiar with the Thielsen or Howlock Trails, you can descend these, then ski back on the North Crater Trail, or car shuttle.

Summit Rock. (Map 73) Although only an unpretentious basalt knob, there is nevertheless a good view to be enjoyed from Summit Rock. A 0.9-mile road tour leads to the top of the area quarry.

Drive 1 mile east of the PCT trailhead (0.5 east of the pass) to start the tour, or ski in on the PCT, and turn east on the snowmobile trail to intersect the Summit Rock road. There is a 340-foot elevation gain.

CRATER LAKE—NORTH RIM

(Map 73) The beauty of Crater Lake in winter attracts many skiers, although Oregon's only national park is a long distance from centers of population. In winter, the only access is from the south side to the south rim, which is described elsewhere in this guidebook. For visitors to the Diamond Lake area, the north rim is accessible and is a good alternative to driving about 60 miles around the west side on Highway 230 to reach the south rim.

The Intermediate–Advanced ski tour to the north rim from the Diamond Lake side is 9 miles one way on a snow-covered road (shared with snowmobilers) with an elevation gain of 1,400 feet. From Crater Lake Sno-Park (5,795 feet) 7 miles south of the Diamond Lake Resort access road, 14.5 miles west of Highway 97, or 2.9 miles south of the Highway 230/138 junction, follow the obvious, wide, straight road south. Although the first 7 miles are quite monotonous except for the crossing of a wide, flat pumice desert, the remaining 2 miles climb through stands of alpine firs and vast open snowfields with good views to the north. The view from the north rim at 7,253 feet overlooking Llao Bay a thousand feet below and across to the miles of snow-covered crater walls is, to say the least, remarkable. The lake is 5 miles across and there are 18 miles of cliff bands and crater walls to study. You will see Shasta, McLoughlin, Scott, Diamond Peak, Thielsen, and Bailey.

The tour is best done in the springtime, but be prepared for an unmerciful sun. Wear a sunhat and apply sunscreen often.

The return to the sno-park is tiring—the last 5 miles or so are almost level—but the views of the incredible lake and crater make it a memorable day.

SOUTH SHORE TRAILS

(Map 74) The south shore area is relatively open and extends over 2 miles east to west over almost totally level terrain where numerous public-use areas exist in summer. The round-the-lake road passes through here and you share the area with snowmobilers. A marked ski trail goes north then west from South Diamond Sno-Park to Silent Creek, then along the creek to Three Lakes Sno-Park, a total distance of 4.3 miles one way. The south shore can also be reached by skiing 3 miles along the east shore from the resort area.

Along the shoreline are wonderful views of Thielsen, Bailey, and the lake itself. Do not venture onto the lake ice. The areas near Silent Creek and the southeast corner of the lake are particularly dangerous throughout the winter.

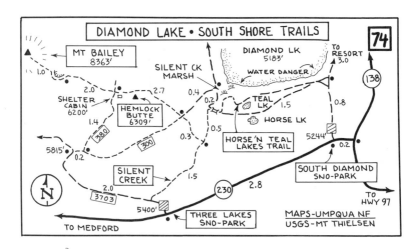

Horse 'N Teal Trail. (Map 74) From South Diamond Sno-Park on Highway 230, 0.2 mile west of Highway 138, ski north on a wide road 0.8 mile, then turn left. Follow trail markers or just ski along the south lakeshore. The route's western end passes the north side of Teal Lake, winds around, and turns south to cross the bridge over Silent Creek on the round-the-lake road. Off-trail skiing onto the Silent Creek marsh, or 400 yards southeast to Horse Lake from Teal Lake, is possible. It is 2.3 miles from the sno-park to the Silent Creek bridge.

Silent Creek Trail. (Map 74) This is a lovely 4-mile round-trip Novice trail through forest. From Three Lakes Sno-Park on Highway 230, 2.8 miles west of Highway 138/230 junction, ski 100 yards up road 3703 (a snowmobile route to Mount Bailey) and turn right onto the Silent Creek Trail. Ski 1 mile through forest before encountering the beautiful, spring-fed creek. At 1.5 miles pass the Mount Bailey Trail junction, then cross the creek on a road bridge and follow the east side of the creek to the lake if desired. After crossing the bridge you will encounter the South Shore or Horse 'N Teal Trail, which leads east to South Diamond Sno-Park 2.3 miles from the bridge.

Mount Bailey and Hemlock Butte. (Map 74) The gently rounded, massive volcano on Diamond Lake's west shore is an impressive sight. Rising almost 3,200 feet above the lake, the summit (8,363 feet) is a steep, demanding climb (13 miles round trip), only for experienced Backcountry skiers. However, Hemlock Butte (6,309 feet) along the route is 3 miles below the summit and a reward in itself. Just beyond Hemlock Butte, an open area—only an 800-foot climb above Silent Creek—provides good views of the region.

From the Silent Creek Trail take the Mount Bailey Trail at 1.5 miles from the sno-park, and ski upward through lodgepole pine forest around the north side of Hemlock Butte to open areas for views. This is near where an old forest road, 380, intersects the trail. A large A-frame cabin sits 250 yards east of the Road 380 junction with the Mount Bailey Trail. The cabin is available through the Forest Service for overnight trips.

The trail, marked to this point, steepens for the remaining 3 miles, going up switchbacks between the east-facing bowl to the north and one to the south. Circle left around a crater below a false summit. Continue steeply up the narrowing ridge to the summit. The ascent requires ski climbers and caution on the steep, windblown, and intimidating final 2 miles above timberline.

There are two other routes to Hemlock Butte and the summit. The first proceeds from South Diamond Sno-Park. Ski the south shore, cross the Silent Creek bridge, turn right, go 0.2 mile on the road, turn left onto Road 300 (a snowmobile route), and follow this 0.4 mile to the Mount Bailey Trail.

The other route is from Three Lakes Sno-Park. Follow Road 3703 west for 2 miles, turn right onto Road 300, then go up Road 380 to intersect the summit trail west of Hemlock Butte. Road 380 continues northward into the huge basin on the mountain's east side, but there is avalanche danger here. The Road 3703/300/380 route combined with the Mount Bailey Trail offers a loop tour if you don't mind sharing with snowmobilers on the roads.

Chapter 27

CRATER LAKE NATIONAL PARK

Crater Lake National Park, Oregon's only national park, may very well be the most unusual ski area in the state—imagine standing on a thousand-foot cliff and looking across a 5-mile lake contained by miles of ramparts and peaks! Located in Southern Oregon on the crest of the Cascades, the lake receives enormous amounts of snow, and there are often fifteen or more feet left on the ground in June from a cumulative snowfall of over 500 inches in a season. This means, of course, a lot of stormy weather, but when the weather is good, it is a magnificent place to be. The lake and its imposing caldera walls are one of America's great natural treasures.

For skiing there are vast, tilted parklands, rolling meadows with dense islands of mountain hemlock trees, and away from the crater rim forests of firs and lodgepole pines. There are 25 miles of marked ski trails in the park. They are not, however, all mentioned here—only the more popular trails and unique areas of the park are described.

Below the crater rim are a number of trails through forest and meadows, some to viewpoints. The lower trails are particularly welcome during periods of adverse weather when winter storms are rendering the open, windy areas of the rim unskiable. The rim area should be skied only when there is good visibility. The miles of crater rim are dangerous during periods of reduced visibility.

There is a growing interest in the 30-mile round-the-lake ski tour that follows the Rim Road and requires two or three days. For skiers not interested in such effort, there are easy tours along the crater rim to wonderful viewpoints.

There are no overnight lodgings available in the park. The closest resort facilities are at Union Creek Resort (west), Fort Klamath Lodge (south), and Diamond Lake Resort (north). The closest ski trails outside the park are at Union Creek to the west and at Diamond Lake to the north.

Winter access to Crater Lake National Park is limited to the south side, where the only plowed road into the park goes to the Rim Village on the south rim. The park's other entrance is not open in winter, but that road is used by snowmobilers, who are restricted to the road and allowed to go only as far as the north rim. Skiing access to Crater Lake's north rim follows the snowmobile route and is described in the chapter on Diamond Lake trails.

Winter visitors are encouraged to call Park Headquarters before visiting for road and weather information (days: 503-594-2211, nights: 503-594-2811). Another reason to call is that the road to the rim is occasionally blocked by snow for short periods of time.

Backcountry ski permits are required of all skiers camping overnight and can be obtained only at Park Headquarters during office hours seven days per week. Permits are not available by telephone or by mail. All campers must check in upon return.

Distances to the south rim of Crater Lake National Park include the following:

- From Portland via Bend: 300 miles
- From Portland via Willamette Pass: 287 miles
- From Portland via Medford: 347 miles
- From Klamath Falls: 57 miles
- From Bend: 145 miles
- From Eugene via Willamette Pass: 175 miles
- From Eugene via Medford: 237 miles

WIZARD ISLAND OVERLOOK TRAIL

(Map 75) The caldera rim west of Rim Village at 7,000 feet is the most popular area to ski in favorable weather. Rim Village, which is 3.4 miles by road above Park Headquarters, has parking, restrooms, and a restaurant. There are numerous places to enjoy stunning views of the legendary blue lake 1,000 feet below and of the caldera walls that frame the magnificent scene.

The ski trail west from Rim Village is marked and suitable for Novice skiers. The trail follows the Rim Road along rolling, open terrain spotted with beautiful stands of ancient mountain hemlock and fir. From the rim, the terrain slopes gently away and down to fir and dense lodgepole pine forests. The skiing and scenery along the trail are outstanding.

For the closest view of Wizard Island, a partly forested volcanic cone rising 800 feet out of the lake, ski to the 7,172-foot saddle between Discovery Point and The Watchman, almost 3 miles from Rim Village.

The saddle is at the foot of The Watchman, a prominent point on the west rim. The traverse around The Watchman's west ridge to its north side is steep and often icy, hardpacked, and dangerous. Site of a summer lookout, it is best climbed from the north side. Under some conditions the slopes of The Watchman may pose avalanche danger.

It is easy to become disoriented and lost on the rolling slopes of this area in poor visibility. Ski only with good visibility.

HEMLOCK TRAIL

(Map 75) This 1.6-mile marked loop for Novice to Intermediate skiers starts at the east end of the Rim Village parking area. The trail traverses east toward the lodge (closed in winter), then turns south, loops westward, and

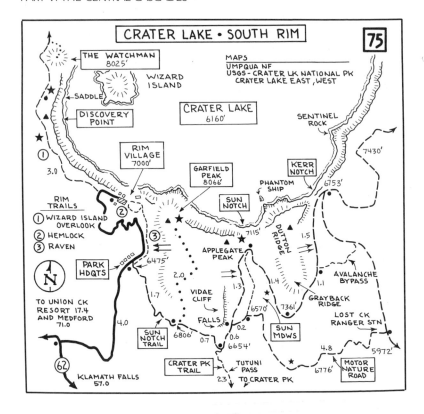

climbs back up to the trailhead. The trail passes through beautiful glades, parklands, and open areas. There are hills to play on and views to the Klamath Basin to the south.

If you are an explorer, ski into the saddle east of the lodge, then climb 200 yards or more eastward for a superb view of the lake, Mount Thielsen to the north, and Mount Shasta and its twin, Shastina, to the south over the Klamath Basin.

RAVEN, SUN NOTCH, AND CRATER PEAK TRAILS

(Map 75) These trails connect with each other and offer great scenic rewards whether you are trying to escape the winds or weather at the rim or just looking for a beautiful area to enjoy.

Raven Trail. (Map 75) Ski Hemlock Trail east to near the lodge, then follow Raven Trail signs as this trail goes farther east then turns downhill toward Park Headquarters. Raven is rated Intermediate to Advanced, and

Wizard Island and Crater Lake caldera viewed from Wizard Island Overlook Trail (Photo: Nancy Chapman)

descends 1 mile and 625 feet to its end at the Sun Notch trailhead at the Park Headquarters parking lot. Raven is fast, twisting, and steep in places, and after leaving the forest it crosses several avalanche paths that descend off Castle Crest Ridge, which rises to the east.

Sun Notch Trail. (Map 75) Sun Notch, a deep gash in the caldera wall east of Park Headquarters, is a spectacular place with a view 1,000 feet down to the lake. From the Rim Road you climb 400 yards up through old-growth forest to the Crater Lake viewpoint below the impressive Applegate cliffs. The 4.3-mile trail to this magic place is rated for Novice to Intermediate skiers, although Novices are going to find it fairly demanding.

Of course, there are distant views and a lot of scenery along the way to Sun Notch to reward you even if you don't ski the full distance. Because of open-slope traverses under steep sidehills that occasionally avalanche along the Rim Road, which is the marked ski-trail route, there is a safe bypass route. Check first with Park Headquarters for snow and avalanche conditions.

To ski the Sun Notch Trail, it is best to start from Park Headquarters, although you can ski from Rim Village down to the Sun Notch trailhead. From the parking area at Park Headquarters (6,475 feet) ski east 1.7 miles to the trail's high point after an initial descent then the long climb of over 400 feet. Continue on the Rim Road 0.7 mile to Crater Peak Trail, which goes off to the south. Stay on the Rim Road as it turns toward Sun Notch, and in 0.6

mile reach Vidae Falls and Motor Nature Road to the right.

If the Rim Road to Sun Notch, now only 1.3 miles from Vidae Falls and a 600-foot climb away, is safe, follow the road. If unsafe, ski down the Motor Nature Trail 400 yards to Sun Meadows, then turn left and ski uphill along the east side of the meadows to avoid avalanche runout on the way to Sun Notch at 7,115 feet.

Motor Nature Trail. (Map 75) This road from Vidae Falls to Lost Creek (5 miles) is used at times of avalanche danger on the Sun Notch and Kerr Notch routes where both the Vidae Cliffs and Dutton Ridge cliffs expose the Rim Road to danger. The Motor Nature Trail, sometimes called the Grayback Trail, follows an old, winding road, one-way in summer, that climbs as it rounds the lower end of Dutton Ridge (here called Grayback Ridge) on steep, open slopes, then drops to Lost Creek on its 5-mile, Intermediate-rated course from its start at Vidae Falls and Sun Meadows. From its high point on the ridge, the old road drops 800 feet to Lost Creek. From here the bypass route climbs 800 feet up the valley on the Pinnacles road 3 miles to Kerr Notch. The bypass route is 2.7 miles longer than following the Rim Road, but much safer most of the winter.

If you are at Sun Notch and want to ski to Kerr Notch, it is 4 miles, climbing steadily around Dutton Ridge then descending 600 feet to Kerr Notch.

Crater Peak. (Map 75) This high cinder cone at 7,265 feet is 4.7 miles from Park Headquarters and has a cumulative elevation gain of 1,600 feet round trip. The access route follows the Sun Notch Trail 2.4 miles, then the marked route turns south off the Rim Road and becomes an Advanced ski tour following an old road 1 mile downhill to Tutuni Pass at 6,500 feet. Near the pass the trail disappears in the snow and you make your way as best you can up a very steep 765 feet to the summit crater rim for panoramic views. The summit is about 2.3 miles from the Rim Road (see Sun Notch Trail).

GARFIELD PEAK

(Map 75) Garfield is the high peak immediately east of and above the lodge on the south rim of Crater Lake. The summer trail up the peak's precipitous west face to the 8,066-foot summit is far too steep and dangerous for winter travel, however the moderate south slopes of Garfield peak are a dream trip for the experienced Backcountry skier. Ski east on the Sun Notch Trail 1.7 miles to its high point at 6,806 feet. Here, leave the road and climb through forest, then parklands, and finally open meadows to the 7,750-foot caldera rim at the lower saddle between Garfield Peak and Applegate Peak. The 2 miles up from the Sun Notch Trail are demanding but not difficult. The total one-way mileage is 3.7 miles with a gain of 1,400 feet, and the views are outstanding.

CRATER LAKE RIM TRAIL

(Map 75) The roughly 30 miles around the lake following the Rim Road can be done in a day by strong skiers under perfect conditions—and with luck. All three factors rarely coincide, so don't try it. Instead, plan on two or three days. The route is not marked so you must have a compass and map, survival gear, repair kit, tent, and suitable clothing for all types of weather. The best time of year is spring, and there is good snow into late May.

In order to do this tour, you must personally register for a permit with Park Headquarters during office hours. Headquarters is open seven days a week. You will be advised of snow and avalanche conditions if they exist and places along the route that merit your concern.

The normal direction to ski the rim is clockwise, starting at Rim Village rather than at Park Headquarters. In this direction you will end your tour at Park Headquarters, 625 feet lower than the rim. Having your car waiting for you here will save you time and energy.

The Rim Road is not always easy to follow. Although other tracks may be ahead of you, do not count on those tracks being on your route! The northeast side of the loop is the most demanding in terms of route finding. In bad weather, the loop is very difficult and route finding almost impossible. Ski the loop only in favorable weather.

For additional information see descriptions of Wizard Island Overlook Trail, Raven Trail, and Sun Notch Trail.

Historical Note: In 1967 John Day and Bill Pruitt of Central Point, Oregon, accompanied by three members of the Italian national cross-country ski team, skied around Crater Lake in eight hours, a feat never repeated. The Italian racers later said they felt they could do the loop in less than four hours with ideal conditions!

Bill Pruitt has skied the loop many times, including twice at night. Starting after dark on full-moon nights, he completed the loop both times in ten hours.

Chapter 28

THE OCHOCO MOUNTAINS

The Ochoco Mountains of Central Oregon cover a vast area of gentle, rolling, forested high country northeast of the town of Prineville. The region has only three summits with sweeping views, unfortunately accessible only to more experienced skiers. The classic ski tour of the region is to the top of Lookout Mountain, the highest peak of the Ochocos, with superb views.

There is only one sno-park at this time in the entire range, located on Highway 26, 28 miles northeast of Prineville at Ochoco Summit where the highway crosses the mountains and descends toward Mitchell and John Day. This sno-park services an extensive trail system of loops called Bandit Springs Trails. The 14 miles of marked trails pass through stands of yellowbellies, the ponderosa pine found throughout the region. The complex trail system is the result of countless hours volunteered by Prineville skiers working with the Forest Service. As Highway 26 is the only plowed road through the Ochocos, emphasis on trail expansion will be placed on the Bandit Springs area. Crystal Creek near Bandit Springs has several scenic tours and is the access route to some wonderful, easy Backcountry skiing.

A number of very good ski tours for adventurous skiers are found in other parts of the Ochocos, but access is limited by the snowline or improved when roads are plowed for winter logging. If your skiing plans call for skiing off roads other than Highway 26, call the Forest Service during business hours for information on which roads might be plowed and general road and snow conditions. Weekends are usually the only safe time to drive logging roads due to heavy truck traffic. Unfortunately, the ski tour to Lookout Mountain is not always available to skiers as access depends on winter logging and road plowing, or a high snowline.

Although there are few viewpoints like those in the Cascades, the natural beauty of the area's open, eastside forests, meadows, and gentle terrain are ample rewards and offer unique experiences for skiers from the Cascades.

OCHOCO SUMMIT AND BANDIT SPRINGS

(Map 76) Skiing from Highway 26 is the obvious choice for most skiers who are not Backcountry types and who are looking for easy, safe, recreational skiing. For these skiers, Bandit Springs marked trails are the answer, or for more adventurous skiing, the Crystal Creek–Grant Meadows area may appeal. If you are at Bandit Springs and want to ski to a high viewpoint, a high

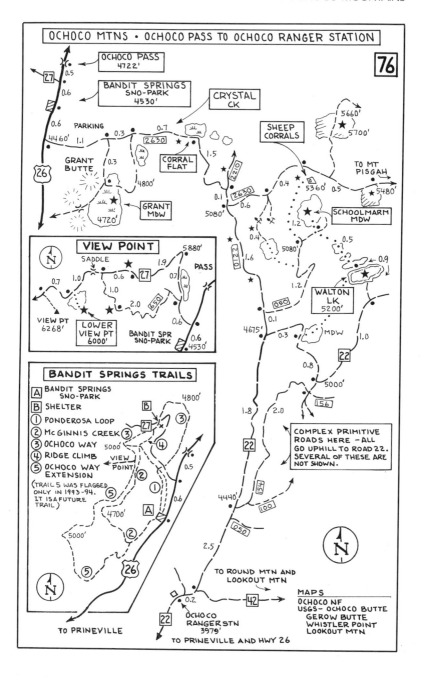

ridge west of the marked trails, reached by a winding, hillside-hugging primitive road, may attract you to the ridgetop called View Point Butte.

Bandit Springs Sno-Park, 1 mile south of Ochoco Summit, and 28 miles from Prineville, is situated at 4,530 feet at a rest stop with toilet facilities.

The 9 miles of marked trails are for both Novice and Intermediate skiers, and there are 5 additional miles of flagged trails, ultimately to be improved and marked. A shelter hut is located near the north end of the trail system just over 2 miles from the sno-park.

Ponderosa Loop. (Map 76) This short 1.4-mile-long, narrow loop has two legs that closely parallel each other and the nearby highway. It is suitable for Novice–Intermediate skiers and offers the best of the area. The east leg is uphill and more challenging, so if you are not a confident skier, ski this first to avoid returning along its tricky, numerous turns and little ups and downs. To ski the east leg first, climb the low ridge behind the restrooms and follow the trail markers along the ridgecrest, passing through forest and small openings. At a large opening at the north end the loop doubles back, going through Ponderosa pines and many small, lovely meadows to a long meadow nestled between low ridges, and you are suddenly back at the sno-park.

McGinnis Creek Loop. (Map 76) This beautiful 4.2-mile Intermediate loop has great variety. Ski either of the Ponderosa Loop legs north to the loop's end, then follow a trail northwest climbing three short zigzags up moderate grades, then through attractive meadows. Road 27 parallels closely to the north, a route that may also be used for the View Point Butte tour.

The trail reaches Road 650, a minor forest road (the preferred route up to View Point Butte) 1.5 miles from the sno-park, and follows this road 0.5 mile to where it plunges off onto a trail to the left. This is the high elevation of the loop. The trail sidehills here as it descends to a junction of old logging roads. Go right along one on a generally level course. The trail (road) turns down at McGinnis Creek past cliffs and creekside meadows along the loop's south leg.

Turning, the loop heads back to the sno-park 0.8 mile away through second growth along a forest trail with many ups and downs. Ski across a large meadow to end the loop, which is best skied counterclockwise to utilize long, gentle downhills.

Ochoco Way. (Map 76) This challenging 3.5-mile Intermediate/Advanced trail starts at the north end of Ponderosa Loop, crosses Road 27 and a small bridge, turns right, and climbs steeply to an undulating bench following a road as it loops back, recrosses Road 27, then reaches the shelter hut. The trail continues to a high of 5,000 feet, then descends to the McGinnis Loop.

Ridge Climb. (Map 76) This short Intermediate–Advanced 0.5-mile trail involves a steep climb, from near the shelter hut, to the north end of the McGinnis Loop.

Ochoco Way Extension. (Map 76) This Intermediate–Advanced 5-mile trail is presently flagged but not yet marked with blue diamonds, the standard trail marker. The trail starts at the west end of Ochoco Way, then more or less parallels the west leg of the McGinnis Loop, generally following the 5,000-foot contour. The flagged trail extends a mile southwest beyond the farthest leg of the McGinnis Loop, then swings around to join the McGinnis Loop.

View Point Butte. (Map 76) There are actually two summits on this ridge. The higher, at 6,268 feet and 5.7 miles from the sno-park, lies 1.1 miles beyond and 268 feet higher than the lower, first summit. Each has a fine view, but the higher is even better if you have the time and energy to go the extra distance. From the sno-park it is a 1,470-foot climb to the lower viewpoint. There are two routes to the saddle below the two summits: Road 27 is wide and scenic, and Road 650, a narrow, primitive road, is possibly even more scenic. The two can be combined to ski a loop.

The tour is rated for a strong Intermediate skier, and although it is not marked the route is quite obvious and easy to follow. This tour leads to the highest, most easily reached viewpoints of the Ochocos. The views are not panoramic, but they are rewarding because the tours themselves are interesting.

Start at Bandit Springs Sno-Park and ski the Ponderosa Loop to its upper end. Here you have a choice: continue on the trail to the McGinnis Creek Loop to Road 650 and follow the primitive road to the high saddle below the ridgetop, or ski onto Road 27 and follow it upward to the saddle, only 0.2 mile longer to the saddle.

From the McGinnis Creek Loop ski onto Road 650 and stay on it as it narrows and climbs 2 miles to a remarkable viewpoint as it hugs the steep hillside. At every stride uphill, the view gets better down into the deepening Marks Creek valley up which Highway 26 travels to cross Ochoco Summit.

Continue another 1 mile to the ridgetop saddle. Here turn left, enter old growth, and ski to a large, hillside meadow. The road continues 1.1 miles to the higher summit. To ski to the lower summit, stay on the road, cross a hillside meadow along the road, and go 200 yards to a long snowslope where you climb 350 feet to the top of the Lower View Point at 6,000 feet with grand views. If you still have time and energy, descend the snowslope and continue 0.7 mile through forest as the road climbs to open areas where you leave the road and ski east to the upper viewpoint, prosaically called View Point.

On your way back to the sno-park you have the choice of two routes, each going to the sno-park. At the wide saddle at the top of Road 650, called Grant Spring, go straight ahead north and stay on Road 27 for views north that you did not have on Road 650 on your ascent. The views are quite dramatic toward Stephenson Mountain with its unique horizontal red cliffs. At 0.6 mile from Grant Spring saddle leave Road 27 for the alternate loop (stay on Road 27 for a direct return) and climb a low rise to the right through mountain mahogany trees for the views to the south. Near the bottom of Road 27 rejoin the Bandit Springs trails.

Road 650 does not appear on the Ochoco National Forest map, but it is on the transportation map for the Prineville Ranger District.

CRYSTAL CREEK VALLEY AND GRANT MEADOWS

(Map 76) This enchanting small valley is perfect for Novice skiers. The road up the valley starts 0.6 mile below Bandit Springs Sno-Park and is identified by a large meadow with a giant boulder sitting near the highway. The area is used by snowmobilers, but don't let this turn you back, for this area has many rewards. Crystal Creek is also an access route for longer Backcountry tours to the Sheep Corrals area and Walton Lake.

Park at Crystal Creek, cross the wide meadow, and enter the little valley. At 1.1 miles look for a side valley to the south, which leads to the extensive Grant Meadows. Explore, then turn east from the meadow following a road through open areas as it swings back to Crystal Creek. Ski up the creek to Corral Flat, the last of the valley-bottom meadows. Another 1.5 miles winding upward lead to a junction with Road 2210. At the junction, ski north 200 yards for a good view of View Point Butte.

Continue 0.1 mile to the junction of 2630 and 2210. Follow 2630 1 mile eastward to the Sheep Corrals in parklands. Proceed off-trail 1.7 miles southward, through gorgeous meadows and yellowbellies and Schoolmarm Meadow, over gentle terrain to Walton Lake. This is an area of unbounded off-trail skiing through meadows and open forest.

Walton Lake and the Sheep Corrals. (Map 76) For the less-experienced Backcountry skier or the Advanced skier looking for more adventure, this is an area to explore to develop skills and confidence. The terrain is gentle, and once at your objective, most routes head downhill back to the trailhead. You will see few if any skiers, and perhaps an occasional snowmobiler. The area is characterized by shallow valleys and draws, large meadows, and marvelous parklands of ponderosas and other trees.

From Highway 26 via Crystal Creek to the Sheep Corrals is 4.7 miles and a gain of 900 feet. From the Ochoco Ranger Station, the end of plowing, it is 6.1 miles to Walton Lake and a gain of 1,720 feet. The lake and the Sheep Corrals are about 1.7 miles apart with only a 200-foot climb from the lake to the corrals. The road may be plowed for winter logging, however, so check with the Big Summit Ranger District for current status and snowline.

Crystal Creek Route to Sheep Corrals. (Map 76) First see the Crystal Creek Valley description, then ski up Crystal Creek 3.6 miles to the junction with Road 2210, ski south 200 yards to another junction, and then ski east 1 mile on Road 2630 to the Sheep Corrals at 5,360 feet. Two viewpoints near the corrals are worth the skiing. Reach the first by skiing off-road northeast from the corrals or skiing a side road (see map) to a clearcut just 0.5 mile from the corrals. Climb to the top of the clearcut for the best views to the west. To reach the other viewpoint, ski 0.5 mile on the road east of the corrals to a large meadow and a view south. Another side trip from the corrals leads south about 0.5 mile down gentle grades through meadows and parklands to Schoolmarm Meadow. This meadow is identified by a lone "schoolmarm" tree, two trunks joined together at the base and leaning apart.

From this meadow it is possible to ski to Walton Lake, although from here it will take some easy route finding. By skiing south, a bit west, and then eastward through alternating meadows and forest across gently descending terrain, you will find the lake 1.7 miles below the corrals. In reverse, skiing north to the corrals, you will find the route finding easier. Once at Walton Lake, a popular campground in summer surrounded by remarkable parklands of yellowbellies, you can ski a loop back to the 2210/2630 junction by skiing out the access road to the lake to Road 22 then downhill to Road 2210, a descent of 525 feet in elevation. Follow 2210 northward through a gorgeous valley of continuous meadows and parklands back to Crystal Creek. This loop from the corrals totals 6.7 miles, plus distance out Crystal Creek.

Ochoco Ranger Station to Walton Lake. (Map 76) Seventeen miles west of Prineville on Highway 26 is a junction with Road 22. Take Road 22 and drive 8 miles to the Ochoco Ranger Station, the end of winter plowing. This is also the driving route to Lookout Mountain. From the ranger station, drive as far as possible on Road 22. Side Road 100, a primitive road to the east, is 2.5 miles from the Road 42 junction just beyond the ranger station. Ski up Road 100 passing through a tight, winding canyon that opens into parklands, and 2.1 miles farther up rejoins Road 22. Turn right and ski northeast 1 mile to the 0.5-mile access road to the lake. Ski through heavy forest into the parklands surrounding the lake. The route is rated Intermediate–Advanced.

To ski to the Sheep Corrals, circle the lake to its north side and enter a thin band of forest into an east-west narrow meadow. Ski to its west end and find a primitive road that you follow into meadows and to Schoolmarm Meadow 0.5 mile below the corrals.

LOOKOUT MOUNTAIN

(Maps 76 & 77) Home of a herd of wild horses and antelope in summer, Lookout Mountain is the highest point of the Ochoco Mountains, and the

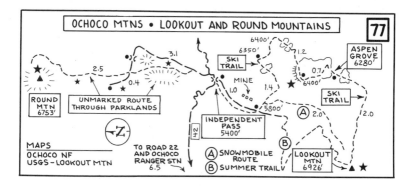

premier viewpoint of the region. Round Mountain, its neighbor 5 miles north, offers almost equal views, and both are reached from Independent Pass 6.5 miles above the Ochoco Ranger Station. The ranger station is 25 miles northeast of Prineville, first 17 miles on Highway 26, then 8 on Road 22, which is plowed in winter to the ranger station. From the ranger station, Road 42 is just 0.2 mile beyond and goes east up a narrow, deep canyon that holds snow. Road 42 to the pass is open in winter only when plowed for winter logging, and in some winters is not plowed at all.

Efforts to gain wilderness status for Lookout Mountain failed due to multiple-use priorities and pressure from snowmobile interests. The mountain is characterized by historic mining, roads—one to the very summit but closed to summer vehicles—dense forests, sagebrush plateaus, and stands of aspen trees—a unique area, indeed.

There are two routes to the summit. The snowmobile route that follows an old road totals 3 miles from Independent Pass at Road 42. The summer trail, marked for skiing, is 6.5 miles and although longer is much more scenic and is the recommended route. The former is moderately steep, and the latter is seldom more than moderate in grade. From the pass, the elevation gain is 1,500 feet, but add 200 feet for a drop to the large aspen grove along the summer trail that is marked for skiing.

The marked ski trail starts at Independent Pass (5,400 feet) and climbs the low ridge immediately to the right of the mine road to the Independent Mine 0.7 mile above the pass. The road may be skied, and it eventually joins the ski trail. Where the ski trail passes a stand of small aspens, look to the west for a meadow and a view of Mount Jefferson. Continue 0.3 mile to the summer trailhead at 5,800 feet. The marked ski trail goes east here through old growth to a meadow over a mile out, climbs steeply up a shoulder, and at 2 miles from the summer trailhead emerges onto a sagebrush prairie with views to the north and east.

The trail turns westward, crossing the plateau through meadows and reaching the edge of a bluff from which there is a view of Round Mountain. Follow trail markers on posts gently downhill across the prairie 0.7 mile to a grove of large aspens. Even if you don't have time to go farther, explore this beautiful shallow valley and grove.

From the grove climb south then west 2 miles to the summit where you will be awed by the sight of ten major volcanoes from St. Helens (barely) to Broken Top. This is impressive, but your main impression may be the vast scale of seemingly endless forests rolling to the horizon. Big Summit Prairie, below and east with its roughly 20 square miles of pastureland, and the Maury Mountains, low-lying to the south across the Crooked River, are also major features of the panorama.

Although the ski ascent of Lookout Mountain is never steep, less-experienced skiers should be cautious as it is a long tour. Do not attempt it in anything but good weather and visibility. A quick descent can be made via the snowmobile route, which enters scrubby forest about a mile below the

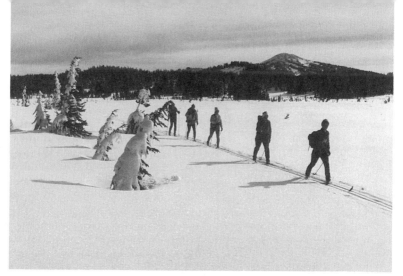

On ski trail to top of Lookout Mountain; Round Mountain beyond to right

summit and descends on an increasingly steep grade. To find the snowmobile route from the bottom, ski out 400 yards on the marked trail from the summer trailhead and turn right onto a road in the forest.

ROUND MOUNTAIN

(Maps 76 & 77) The rounded, bare 6,753-foot summit of Round Mountain has views comparable to Lookout Mountain, but the trail from Independent Pass is not marked and the upper slopes are steeper. The 6.8 miles from the pass and the 1,400-foot elevation gain are for skiers with strong Backcountry skills, although there are no dangerous slopes nor difficult route finding.

From Independent Pass at 5,400 feet (see Lookout Mountain description) you have two options for the first 3 miles or so: to follow an uninteresting but direct road or to ski along the ridge to its left, west of the road where the summer trail goes. The road starts just east of the pass, goes north, crosses a pass at 3.5 miles, then continues 0.4 mile to its end. There are views of the Cascades along the last section. The other option is definitely more pleasing.

From Independent Pass ski out the road and quickly gain the ridge. Ski along the ridge and enter yellowbelly parklands, cross meadows, and traverse the slopes on the east side of the ridge (along the summer trail) to eventually connect with the road at the pass. Continue along the last 0.4 mile to the end of the road on the west side of the ridge. From here, ski onto the ridge, eventually reaching ponderosa parklands, then start climbing in earnest through meadows, circling eastward while climbing to eventually connect with the four-wheel-drive road just below the summit, where you will find a relay station and marvelous views. On the descent, be wary of skiing into several barbed-wire fences that may be hidden by snow on the upper south-facing slopes.

DERR MEADOWS AND CAMP WATSON POINT

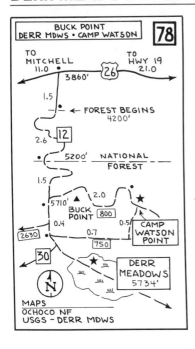

(Map 78) If you are driving between Prineville and John Day and have several hours to explore beautiful meadows, try this Novice–Intermediate road tour, which goes up to 11 miles round trip with a climb of up to 1,900 feet, depending on the snowline. From Highway 26 (3,860 feet), about 11 miles east of the small village of Mitchell and 21 miles west of the Highway 19/26 junction, drive south on Road 12 as it climbs gently then moderately 1.5 miles through sagebrush to the forest edge, then another 2.6 miles to the Ochoco National Forest boundary.

The one-lane road with many turnouts continues upward, and at 5 miles from the highway there is a fine view north of desert hills and rolling mountains, a view worth the tour—but keep going to the first meadow 5.6 miles from the highway. Just 0.3 mile before the meadow at a cattleguard is a primitive road to the east—this is Road 800, which winds through forest 2 miles to Camp Watson Point, where there is a view to the north. To ski a loop return to Road 12, ski south 0.5 mile, and join Road 750. Go west 0.7 mile on Road 750 to join Road 12 just 0.4 mile from Road 800, where you started the loop.

If you do not explore Road 800 or Road 750, explore the first meadow (5,755 feet) south of Road 800, the most scenic of the string of large meadows that descend gently southward into Derr Meadows. Buck Point (5,835 feet) is hidden somewhere in thick forest with no views and is not a goal.

MAURY MOUNTAINS

(Map 79) Some 30 miles southeast of Prineville, the Maury Mountains, a forested, gently rolling range, extend only 18 miles from east to west. The featureless, tree-covered summits, all near 6,000 feet, rise 2,500 feet above the wide Crooked River valley to the north. Small valleys, cattle ranches, and roads penetrate the range, giving access for winter recreation. One road runs along the entire crest of the range, but only one road crossing the range from north to south is plowed in winter. This is Road 16, which goes up Sherwood Creek from the Crooked River and descends the south slope of the range via Klootchman Creek on Road 1640. At Sherwood Saddle (5,260

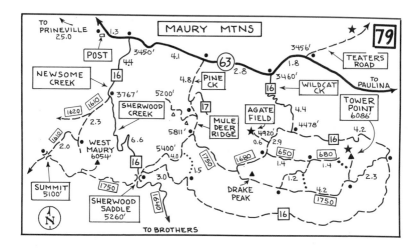

feet) where the road crests the range, Road 16 turns and goes east along the crest and eventually turns north near the east end, where it circles Tower Point then descends to the Crooked River.

There are three areas of the Maurys with skiing opportunities, and all are reached by roads from the Crooked River valley. Although Tower Point—at the east end of the range where there is a fire lookout tower—is not the highest summit, it may be the most scenic. The other two areas are Sherwood Saddle and Mule Deer Ridge.

To the north of the Crooked River, across from the east end of the Maurys, Teaters Road descends from the Ochocos over miles of open grasslands on south-facing slopes, a remarkably beautiful area.

To reach the Crooked River valley from Prineville to ski the Maurys, drive Highway 380 25 miles over scenic desert highlands then down a canyon to the "town" of Post, just a small store and a couple of houses near the western end of the range. There are no gasoline stations past Prineville.

Sherwood Saddle. (Map 79) From Post, drive east 1.3 miles to Road 16, which traverses the range over Sherwood Saddle (5,260 feet) and is plowed in winter across the mountains. From the Crooked River drive 11 miles to the saddle, where side roads go east and west through both forest and open areas. Where there are views you will see south to Paulina Peak and Newberry Crater, a large segment of the Cascade Range, the Ochocos to the north, and Lookout Mountain's long, snowy crest. Most ski touring in the Maurys is done from Sherwood Saddle due to plowed access. From the saddle, the most scenic route follows Road 1750 northeast to several ridgetop saddles. There are good views along this road.

Skiing west on Road 1750 (Novice–Intermediate rating) from the saddle also provides far-ranging views. East of the saddle, it is possible to ski a 7.7-mile loop (see map) by connecting Roads 1750 and 16 and skiing a primitive road. Heavy forests cover most of the area, but there are viewpoints.

Tower Point. (Map 79) Site of a fire-lookout tower, this 6,086-foot summit is located at the east end of the Maurys, and may be the most interesting ski tour in the area (Advanced rating), although the roads are not plowed.

From Post drive 8.2 miles east to Road 16 (3,460 feet) at Wildcat Creek. Drive up Road 16 as far as possible. The last house is 4.2 miles from the highway, and just beyond is a junction where you turn west onto Road 1680. Drive or ski 2.9 miles and turn southeast onto Road 650. Another 1.4 miles brings you to a dead-end road that leads 1.4 miles to a large clearcut, visible from the Crooked River valley and situated just below Tower Point. From the clearcut climb steep slopes and intersect the lookout road as it approaches the top on the peak's south side.

From the Crooked River this route is just over 9 miles, but the road will probably be plowed to the last house. Two other routes to Tower Point are 12 and 16 miles one way and not as open or scenic.

If you study a Forest Service map you will notice this book's map is more detailed. If you want more detail, obtain a transportation map of the area, available by writing to the appropriate ranger district.

If time does not allow for the Tower Point tour, but you want to see the area, refer to the sketch map and ski to the agate field. Ski 1.5 miles west from the junction of Roads 16 and 1680, then take a 0.6-mile descending side road to open sagebrush hillsides with excellent views northward over the Crooked River valley.

Mule Deer Ridge. (Map 79) This open grassy ridge descending from a high, forested point of 6,096 feet drops northward to Mule Deer Spring at 5,200 feet and offers several four-wheel-drive roads for Intermediate skiers to explore.

From Post drive east 5.4 miles to Road 17 and drive up this road 3 miles to the National Forest boundary. Continue about 2.5 miles to an obscure side road to the west. Follow this road to where you can leave it to climb the ridge to the west.

Another way to visit this ridge is by skiing from Sherwood Saddle 4 miles northeast on Road 1750. A steep descent on a primitive road goes down Mule Deer Ridge through forest to connect with Road 17.

Teaters Road and Sheep Rock Creek. (Map 79) The vast, gently sloping grasslands north of the Crooked River offer endless opportunities for open-country skiing when there is sufficient snow. Follow directions for Tower Point, but drive 1.8 miles east of Road 16 to Teaters Road, a gravel road that is followed up a beautiful, narrow, almost treeless valley with meadows and flat pastures. After several miles it opens up to rolling, sagebrush hills, then, farther up, to miles of grassy hillsides sweeping down the southern flank of the Ochoco Mountains. Sheep Rock, a prominent landmark of dark rock, forms a solitary outcrop. Five miles from the highway the sweeping vistas will take your breath away, but ski even farther up for the greatest views across the Crooked River valley to the Maurys and to the east.

Part VI
EASTERN OREGON

Most skiers are not familiar with the eastern areas of Oregon, where not only scenic and historical rewards will greet you, but where you will also have the opportunity to feel nostalgia for the Old West. Time seems to have changed the forests and valleys of Eastern Oregon very little. The high-desert sagebrush plateaus, grass-covered hills, rocky canyons, beautiful valleys, extensive forests, and stunning panoramas all provide exciting experiences as you drive eastward from the Cascades into this large, little-populated region of the state. Once experienced, the charm and relaxed atmosphere of the small towns and the magnificent scenery will draw you back time and time again.

From lower Dixie Butte saddle; Dixie Butte summit to left,
Vinegar Hill ridge in distance

Chapter 29

THE JOHN DAY REGION

(Map 80) There are unique scenic and skiing opportunities to be had in the mountains near John Day and neighboring Prairie City, and each of these small towns is a suitable base of operations. There are few skiers here and few snowmobilers, although many miles of roads are groomed each winter for the machines. There are few marked trails for skiers, and this is certainly part of the experience—feeling a sense of self-reliance and at times a great sense of isolation, feelings not often associated with skiing in the Cascades. This chapter covers a wide range of ski tours, from valley-bottom routes for times when the high country is not accessible due to low snowline and unplowed roads, to long Backcountry trips, to marvelous high viewpoints.

The largest town of the area is John Day with barely 2,000 people. Prairie City is just to the east, and the two towns lie in an extraordinary valley with wide ranchlands and a mountain wall over 30 miles long ranging along its south side. The nearby Strawberry Mountains crest at 9,000 feet, and several summits reach 7,000 feet. To the west lie the Aldrich Mountains above the town of Dayville.

Few roads penetrate the mountain ranges. The backsides, their south slopes, are gentle, descending in places to large, shallow basins and rolling plateaus bordered by forested ridges. The only transmountain road open all winter is Highway 395 going south to Burns from John Day. Several major forest roads go into high valleys, but it is an unfortunate reality that they are not always plowed, unless plowed for winter logging.

In spite of this, there is more than enough skiing every winter to keep the average skier busy for many days. Preplan your trip by calling the Forest

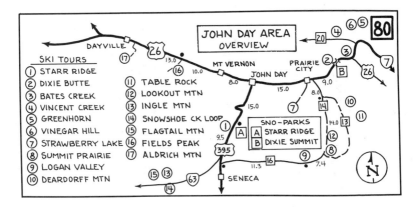

326

Service for road information off the main highways. Offices are open week-days only.

Although there are several places for the casual skier to enjoy, such as Dixie Butte—a must for every skier—many of the other outstanding view-points are remote, but well worth your best effort. The most prominent are described here, and although remote, none are difficult or dangerous and few are more than 6 miles one way, although all require some elevation gain.

The community of winter sportspeople in the small towns of Eastern Oregon is closeknit. Each group is small and tolerant of the other's inter-ests. There is therefore not the conflict between skiers and machines that occasionally boils forth in the crowded Cascades. There are few areas closed to snowmobilers except for wilderness areas. Some of the best ski routes are also traveled by machines, so be grateful for a broken trail.

From Portland, it is a toss-up whether driving the Mount Hood–Madras–Prineville–Highway 26 route (the fastest route) is preferable to driving up the Columbia River Gorge and taking the Biggs–Condon–Dayville route. Either way it is about 275 miles to John Day. The Condon route, however, is more scenic, particularly if you drive the Kimberly–Monument–Long Creek road. Either way, there are several passes to cross so be prepared to drive on snow. From Eugene, Albany, and Salem the distance to John Day via Santiam Pass is almost the same as from Portland.

Carry tire chains (in addition to studs) and a shovel. You might even talk to snowmobilers in town for road information when you have your plans made, and of course call the Forest Service so you will have alternative op-portunities. One plan may fail, and it is helpful to know more about other roads and ski tours in the general area. If you do not, you could lose half a day and have to drive extra miles. This area is not like the Cascades, where there are many sno-parks and alternatives and where you can make last-minute changes to ski other trails.

Most routes in the John Day area follow roads. All these roads do not appear on the Malheur National Forest map, although they appear on maps in this guidebook. Transportation maps are important for this area, and are obtainable from the Forest Service.

Driving to ski routes will at times intimidate you and require special confidence. Almost all the roads are well-maintained paved or graveled for-est routes. Having chains is important but you probably won't need them often. Your shovel will help you improve a parking situation. You will find the roads are not narrow, steep, or dangerous. Use judgment, and you will be rewarded by these special ski routes and the unique beauty of the John Day forests and mountains.

Weather in the region is more stable than in the Cascades although big storms occasionally hit. Be prepared for all eventualities, and particularly for colder temperatures than the Cascades. Sometimes just spare socks pulled over ski boots (cut out for bindings) will prevent cold feet. Carry thick mit-tens and overmitts, windpants, and a down jacket in addition to the usual windbreaker. A repair kit is absolutely essential on all tours, where you will seldom see other skiers. Be entirely self-sufficient, and confident. This is the key to continuing on to your goal.

STARR RIDGE

(Map 81) You may have driven many miles for high adventure in the John Day area, and after reading some of the more demanding trail descriptions you may feel that Starr Ridge, located only 15 miles south of John Day on Highway 395, is not a high priority for you. However, you will find some good, short tours on this high, rolling ridge. The ridge is forested, logged in places, with a few views, and offers skiing through old-growth ponderosa yellowbellies. Locals enjoy skiing here due to its proximity to town, but midweek you will seldom see anyone.

Park at Starr Summit (5,152 feet). In the future you may be able to park over the summit at Road 333. All the skiing is rated Novice, unless you are going for distance.

East of Highway 395. (Map 81) Road 196 is the primary ski route on the long ridge east of the summit, called Slaughter Ridge by the locals and commemorating a time when deer and elk were abundant. Start at the summit and ski past the old ski hill and a cabin and along the contour around the base to the south to join the new ridge road access. The road, used by snowmobilers, climbs gently east through old-growth ponderosa pines and areas of selective sylvan butchering (so, perhaps, "Slaughter Ridge" fits even today). About 2 miles out where the road turns briefly north

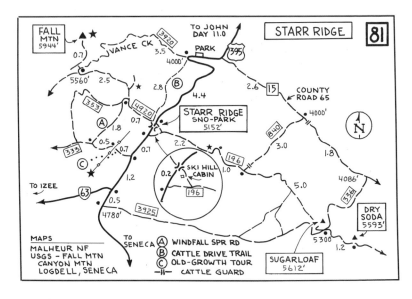

toward Canyon Mountain above John Day, take a spur to the left 200 yards for the view.

One popular local tour requires a car shuttle. First drive about 11 miles from John Day on Highway 395, turn left onto plowed Road 15 (County Road 65), and drive 2.6 miles to Road 840, just before a cattleguard. Park the first car where Road 840 comes off the north side of Slaughter Ridge. Then drive to the sno-park at Starr Summit and ski out the ridge 3.2 miles, then onto 840 for a wonderful 3-mile downhill run to Road 15. Drive back up to the summit to retrieve the second car.

Dry Soda Lookout. (Map 81) This 5,593-foot butte is located on Road 196 about 9.4 miles southeast of Starr Summit. Ski out Road 196 over rolling terrain. The lookout site offers splendid views of the Strawberry Range only 8 miles northeast. A car shuttle can be used on this route by driving up Road 15 (see previous trail description) to Sugarloaf Gulch Road (Road 336), approximately 4.5 miles from Highway 395.

Another approach to Dry Soda, but longer and more scenic, is by way of Road 3925, which goes east along the south side of Slaughter Ridge. From Starr Summit, drive south toward Seneca 2.6 miles to Road 3925. Ski this road 12 miles to the lookout, with a cumulative elevation gain of only 1,000 feet.

West of Highway 395. (Map 81) There are two prime objectives on this side of the summit. The first is Fall Mountain (5,944 feet) with its relay station and fine views. From the highway summit, ski Road 4920 3.9 miles to the mountain with a cumulative elevation gain of 1,000 feet.

Another popular tour follows Road 4920 0.7 mile to the Windfall Springs road junction. If you go just another 100 yards, ski a side road north for some views. From the Windfall Springs junction, ski gentle slopes southward downhill 1.8 miles through big trees that may be cut in the future. This road connects with Road 333 for a 1.2-mile leg east to Highway 395. For a car shuttle, Road 333 is only 0.9 mile south of the summit. The route can also be skied by parking at Road 333.

Another short tour from the turnout on Road 333 proceeds west 0.7 mile, then turns left and goes downhill on gentle grades, then under power-lines and enters old-growth groves of big ponderosa "punkins" in the Starr Creek area near the level of Bear Valley, a vast, open basin south of Slaughter Ridge.

Cattle Drive Trail. (Map 81) The Cattle Drive route is the westside ski route closest to Starr Summit. It follows abandoned Road 875 (South Fork Vance Creek), a primitive road descending from the summit northward. Until recent years, large herds of cattle were driven over the summit and down this old road and, amazingly, right down the main street of Canyon City just south of John Day. Starting at the summit the route makes a rousing, fast descent of 2.8 miles to the hairpin turn on Highway 395 where there is a turnout for a car shuttle.

The other descent to the same hairpin on 395 makes use of Road 3920 from Fall Mountain for 3.5 miles. The ridges between these two routes are not connected by any roads but are skiable with sufficient snow. Both descents to roads below require some eastside bushwhacking at their bottoms.

DIXIE BUTTE

(Map 82) Dixie Butte (7,592 feet) is a massive, long, forested butte projecting northward from Highway 26 east of John Day. The area is a scenic must for all skiers to the John Day area, regardless of skill level. The one-way 4.7-mile trail is marked. If you go the final steep mile to the summit lookout tower, a climb of 2,340 feet from the sno-park, the view will be panoramic. Otherwise, there are good rewarding views lower down.

Drive to Dixie Summit Sno-Park (5,251 feet) 22 miles east of John Day (60 miles from Baker City), or to the small sno-park 0.2 mile above the highway at the ski area. From Dixie Summit Sno-Park, follow Road 2610, the marked ski route, past the ski area, and in 0.5 mile pass minor side roads. Near here, an old road goes westward, initiating a 3-mile unmarked loop (possibly to be marked in the future) that joins a lower road.

After a mile on the main trail, there are views through ponderosa pines of the Strawberry Range and the John Day valley. At 1.9 miles the road levels and to the right is an obscure side road that climbs easily to a close-by saddle and view east to the Elkhorn Range. From this off-trail viewpoint, continue through forest northward and rejoin the main road where it crosses to the ridge's east side.

The trail climbs through old growth and makes two hairpin turns with many views to the south and east of the Elkhorns. You'll soon reach a level meadow in a saddle at the 6,800-foot timberline, a climb of 1,550 feet from the highway. From here the road gets steep and climbs around the bare butte's east side. You may stay at the meadow for the scenic feast, or take your skis off for the final climb to the top if the snow is hard and wind-packed. Vinegar Hill and the Indian Rock Scenic Area to the north are just part of the panorama. Take a map to identify the points in all directions.

Lower Road Loops. (Map 82) Road 096 starting at Dixie Summit Sno-Park and following contours for miles along the west side of Dixie Butte ridge offers a number of possibilities for both Novice and off-road skiers. Study this guidebook's map then use your imagination to form loops with the main trail on the ridgetop. The map shows dotted, off-road routes for Intermediate skiers looking for adventure. Just skiing out the road, however, takes you past several good viewpoints.

A 3-mile loop (unmarked at this time) is best skied counterclockwise to enjoy the descent off the ridgetop trail. Leave the main trail about 0.6 mile above the sno-park and ski an obscure road cutting back to the southwest. Follow this as best as possible through forest, scattered openings, and downhill to Road 096. For the first-time visitor to Dixie Butte, the main trail is the most rewarding route. If boredom sets in after that, ski off the ridge to the lower road to explore and ski a loop. Of course, for an enjoyable exploration there has to be sufficient snow depth to cover brush and obstacles.

BATES AND VINCENT CREEKS

(Maps 83 & 84) These two, short, low-elevation ski tours are scenic alternatives to driving longer distances. Although neither is marked, both are suitable for Novice skiers and will be enjoyed by any skill level for their scenic attributes. The two tours are located only 6 and 9 miles beyond (north-

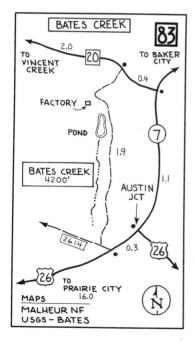

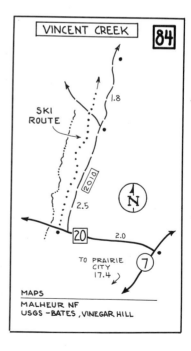

east of) Dixie Summit and parking must be made as best you can. One foot of snow or more makes these two routes skiable. The tours start at 4,200 feet and 4,000 feet respectively.

Bates Creek. (Map 83) From Dixie Summit, 10 miles east of Prairie City, drive northeast 6.1 miles to Bates Creek road (Road 2614). Here you are 0.3 mile from the junction of Highways 26 and 7. Park at Road 2614 and ski west to the first side road to the right (not shown on National Forest map) and ski the level road along the scenic creek's east bank 1.9 miles past a pond and an abandoned factory at the far end. The tour ends at Road 20. The tour is delightful as it follows the meandering stream, and there are views.

Vincent Creek. (Map 84) Located 2.4 miles west of Highway 7 on Road 20, this beautiful, small creek valley goes north, climbing gently from Road 20 as it parallels Road 2010, the road to Vinegar Hill. Park 0.1 mile beyond Road 2010 at the creek itself, and ski up the east side of the creek, at first passing through an uninteresting area. You will soon be in a scenic, forested valley, and an old roadbed can be followed up gentle grades. Valley-bottom skiing ends 4 miles from Road 20, but skiing can continue on Road 2010 if desired.

GREENHORN AND VINEGAR HILL

(Map 85) The site of a flourishing gold-mining settlement of hundreds of miners, there is little left of Greenhorn except a few caved-in log cabins and several private summer cabins. The road tour is a scenic 6.8 miles one way, and climbs 1,500 feet.

Although there are two roads to Greenhorn, Road 1035—primitive, narrow, and winding, but not steep—is shorter and vastly more scenic. This road leaves Highway 7 about 0.5 mile east of Tipton Summit (not well marked), which is 7 miles east of the Highway 7 and Road 20 junction east of Dixie Butte. If you are driving from Baker City, you will pass Whitney, a ghost town in a large meadow, and continue about 6 miles west to Road 1035.

From Highway 7 drive as far up Road 1035 as possible. You will encounter scattered meadows, and at 1.8 miles there are views of Vinegar Hill to the west. The road rolls along then descends gently to the mile-long Howards Meadow near McNamee

GREENHORN

85

TO VINEGAR HILL

2.2

1.9

GREENHORN
6540'

5000'

1.4

1042

N

HOWARDS MDW

8.3

3.5

1035

5040'

7

0.5

TIPTON SUMMIT

TO BAKER CITY

MAPS
MALHEUR NF
USGS - GREENHORN, VINEGAR HILL

Gulch. In another mile you encounter more meadows, then a long, open ridge climb with continuous views of the Elkhorns to the northeast and Dixie Butte to the west. You then enter thick forest to the townsite.

At Greenhorn there is little to see, but a primitive, unsigned road to the west leads into beautiful high-country meadows on the east slopes of Vinegar Hill, a prominent ridgetop mountain. This obscure road, not shown on maps, is also the best, least complicated route to Vinegar Hill. You find the start of it on the south side of a red house located on the west side of the central meadow opening at Greenhorn, a site identified by the only summer cabins for miles around. Ski around the south side and behind the red house, then turn north as the primitive road descends into a creekbed. Follow it as it climbs out of the creekbed and goes west 350 yards to a small meadow.

Continue along this road (Road 807) as well as possible as it follows along near the 6,400-foot contour of the south-facing hillside. The old mining road goes 4 miles from Greenhorn to Road 2010, which is a good summer access road to Vinegar Hill, but is too complicated down below to ski in winter. Vinegar Hill is an outstanding objective for Backcountry skiers on a two-day tour, but that tour is not discussed here due to the complexity of the southside access roads. The Greenhorn approach is the most direct, but there is danger of avalanches up higher on Roads 807 and 2010 as they cross steep, open, south-facing hillsides. The upper ridgecrest areas of Vinegar Hill are vast meadows in summer.

The other road to Greenhorn is Road 1042 (County Road 503), called North Fork Burnt Creek road. It is wide, monotonous, uninteresting, and used by snowmobilers. A transportation map (Long Creek Ranger District) will help on this tour, particularly if skiing to Vinegar Hill.

STRAWBERRY MOUNTAIN

(Map 86) Strawberry Mountain at 9,038 feet is the highest peak of the area and as such attracts attention in all seasons. In particular, its large basin and lake are a goal for many hikers, and for some skiers. Easily accessible in summer by a 1.3-mile trail, in winter it is a different matter, with a ski in as long as 5 miles and a climb of 1,740 feet, depending on the snowline. Most skiers go only to the near edge of the lake at 6,263 feet, take pictures, then ski back. More adventuresome skiers occasionally extend their visits to three other areas, all accessed from the same road, which is the only road that offers a practical approach in winter.

These are Slide Lake basin, the upper basin beyond Strawberry Lake, and the Onion Creek Trail. To ski to the lake or these other areas, drive south on County Road 60 from Prairie City as far as possible. The last house is 7.5 miles from town, and the National Forest boundary at 4,800 feet is 8.7 miles. From here it is 2.5 miles to the road's end and another 1.3 miles by trail to Strawberry Lake, with an elevation gain from the forest boundary of 1,500 feet. The last two miles of the road are fairly steep. The following ski

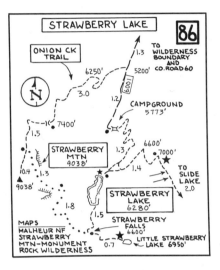

tours all use County Road 60 for access to the snowline.

Strawberry Lake. (Map 86) Drive the road as far as possible, then ski it to its end at Strawberry Campground (5,773 feet). Cross the outlet creek bridge and look for the Strawberry Lake Trail (Intermediate–Advanced rating), which makes a long zigzag northeast, then turns toward the lake. About 0.8 mile up the trail a junction to the left leads to the Slide Lake Trail, a recommended side trip. From road's end it is 1.3 miles to Strawberry Lake and a fine view of the rugged cliffs of the upper basin.

The summer trail continues along the steep east shore but is difficult to ski. The alternative follows along the surface of the lake itself, a choice to consider carefully. Inlets and outlets are always dangerous. Be very careful. The summer trail can be easily regained from the southeast corner of the lake by climbing a steep 100-yard semi-open area. From here it is 0.8 mile to the falls at 6,600 feet along the moderately climbing trail.

From the falls into the upper basin and to Little Strawberry Lake is about 0.7 mile. At the falls follow the trail southeast 200 yards then switchback to cross the stream above the falls twice to return to the stream's east side. Ski through a small meadow, climb steeply for 0.4 mile, then ski an almost level trail to the upper lake at 6,950 feet. This is a spectacular site below towering cliffs, and an area where avalanches have occurred.

Slide Lake. (Map 86) At 7,222 feet this lake sits at the head of Slide Creek in a large basin over the ridge east of Strawberry Lake. To reach it requires a 1-mile traverse of very steep slopes. Going this far is not recommended since there are great scenic rewards at a ridgecrest viewpoint only 2.5 miles from the Strawberry Campground.

Follow directions for Strawberry Lake, then take the Slide Lake Trail at the first junction, then continue southward to the next junction where the trail doubles back and goes northeast. Climb moderately to round the first ridge, then more steeply to a second ridgecrest at 7,000 feet for stunning views. You'll see Dixie Butte, Greenhorn Range, Vinegar Hill, all the Elkhorns, Prairie City, and Strawberry Mountain itself. Frankly, this viewpoint is more rewarding than going to Strawberry Lake, but requires an additional 1.2 miles of skiing and 720 feet of elevation gain.

Onion Creek Trail. (Map 86) Starting at 5,000 feet and 1.3 miles south of the forest boundary, the Onion Creek Trail is the shortest, most direct route to the summit of Strawberry Mountain at 4.5 miles and 4,038 feet above the trailhead. The trail climbs steeply out of the Strawberry Creek valley and eases off, but there are several steep sections ahead. The final distance may require climbing on foot due to windpacked snow. With care and experience it is possible to descend into the upper basin above Strawberry Lake then down to the falls for a return along the lake, trail, and road to the trailhead.

LOGAN VALLEY AND SUMMIT PRAIRIE

(Map 87) These two areas, only 7.4 miles apart, offer flat-land skiing for those seeking tranquil, scenic experiences. Although the Logan Valley is on the south side of Strawberry Mountain, it is not as scenic as Summit Prairie to the east. Roads are open almost all winter to both places. However, it is recommended that you call the Forest Service for road information.

Logan Valley. (Map 87) The extensive flats of the Logan Valley (5,200 feet) are at the south foot of Strawberry Mountain. The Lake Creek Organization Camp, a group of buildings open in winter and used as a youth camp, is the reason the road from Seneca and Highway 395 is plowed. A shelter open to the public is at the camp. Snowmobilers use the area regularly.

The Logan Valley camp is accessed from Summit Prairie via Roads 14 and 16 (check to be sure roads are open), or via Highway 395 south over Starr Summit 25 miles to Seneca, then east 17.5 miles on Road 16 to a side road that goes north 2.2 miles to the camp and the end of plowing.

This is not a particularly scenic area, but there is a lot of flat Novice terrain. Of course, roadside skiing is possible anywhere along the driving route, and there are many scenic places that will tempt you if you can park off the paved road surface. North of the camp complex a 2-mile road extends to the Clear Creek trailhead. Unfortunately, there are few if any rewards for skiing north of the camp or on this trail.

Summit Prairie. (Map 87) This wide, 2-mile-long meadow, sheltered by high, forested ridges, is the place to ski for a few relaxing hours. In summer, this is a cattle pasture so you may encounter a fence or two if the snow is shallow. North of the prairie, Road 1665 climbs a ridge to views of the prairie.

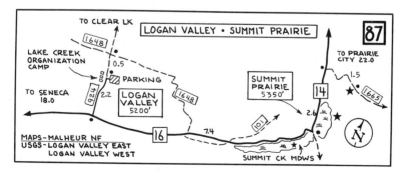

From Prairie City drive south on Road 14 following the John Day River to its headwaters, then crossing a divide at 5,920 feet and 3 miles north of the prairie for a total drive of 22 miles.

A sidetrip can be taken on Road 1665 (not shown on the Forest Service wilderness map) 2.6 miles north of Summit Prairie and 0.6 mile south of the divide, to the east of Road 14. The first views are 1.5 miles up Road 1665, and they improve if you go as far as 3.5 miles from Road 14.

Back on Road 14, continue to the junction with Road 16. A lovely ski tour from Summit Prairie parallels Road 16 as it goes southwest from the prairie uphill along Summit Creek, the driving route to Logan Valley. The narrow, continuous meadows along the creek extend almost 3 miles from Summit Prairie.

A scenic return to the town of John Day can be enjoyed by driving west 7.4 miles from the Road 14/16 junction to the Logan Valley flats, then west 18 miles to Seneca, then north on Highway 395 over Starr Summit for 25 miles to John Day.

DEARDORFF MOUNTAIN AND TABLE ROCK

(Map 88) Two Backcountry tours from the Deardorff–North Fork Malheur River divide will provide you lots of adventure and remarkable views of the John Day area, perhaps the best views of the many possible tours of the region. This is a difficult claim to support because several other area tours also provide panoramic views, such as those from easily reached Dixie Butte. County Road 62 and then Road 13 (the latter often not plowed) lead 18 miles to the 6,000-foot divide, where an obscure, primitive road leads east and north for both tours.

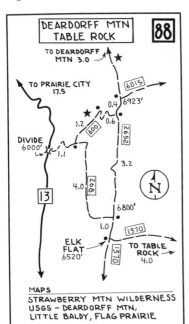

Deardorff Mountain. (Map 88) At the obvious, forested divide that is also the county line 18 miles from Prairie City, look for obscure Road 268 to the east. Ski it 0.7 mile along a winding, descending route down into a draw, then a zigzag climb 0.4 mile to Road 600. Road 600 is your route, so follow it up moderate grades through vast, open areas of the Big Cow Burn to a ridgetop route. The ridgetop is a snowmobile route, but your chance of seeing a machine here is remote. Ski the ridgetop road northward to a saddle between Baldy and Deardorff Mountains. Views from the Big Cow Burn, only 2.3 miles from the divide and your car, are of the Strawberry Range and westward along the full, spectacular length of the John Day valley.

If you are able to drive to the divide, the tour is 6 miles one-way from the divide to the 7,162-foot summit of Deardorff Mountain. The elevation gain is just under 1,200 feet. Call the Forest Service in Prairie City for road information. If the road is not plowed, ski to the divide.

Table Rock. (Map 88) The summit of a long ridge southeast of the Malheur River divide, Table Rock is an 11-mile one-way ski tour with an elevation gain of 1,800 feet. Follow directions for Deardorff Mountain, and at the junction of Road 268 with Road 600, and 1.1 miles from the divide, bear right. Go uphill on Road 268, which crosses a draw, enters forest, and heads south 5 miles to Elk Flat, a large meadow. Ski east and

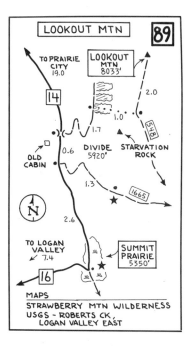

uphill 4 miles on Road 1370 to increasingly open areas and the windswept, high, ridgeside slopes below Table Rock. This route is preferred to the Road 1370 approach from Road 13, a longer route with greater elevation gain. Neither route boasts great views until quite high. However, Table Rock ridgecrest, in the Monument Rock Wilderness, is a spectacular site with views in all directions.

Note: Roads 268 and 600 appear on neither the National Forest nor the wilderness map. For Backcountry skiing, buy a transportation map of the ranger district you plan to ski in for the best road information.

LOOKOUT MOUNTAIN

(Map 89) Lookout Mountain (8,033 feet) and Sheep Mountain southeast of Prairie City form a massive, broad, gently sloping forested ridge along the top of which travels Road 548, the former lookout road. Lookout Mountain summit is open for views and entails a climb of 2,000 feet over only 4.7 miles. The ridge road route, however, is long and tedious, mostly through forest and over 9 miles long. There are two Backcountry routes: via Road 994, the shorter route, and Roads 1665 and 548, the longer.

From Prairie City drive south 19 miles on Road 14 to the 5,920-foot John Day River divide. Here at the pass, Road 994 goes east, zigzags twice, and in 1.7 miles reaches a clearcut. Ascend the rectangular clearcut and traverse through forest, at times fairly dense, to the summit ridge road about 1 mile above Road 994. Turn left (north) and ski 2 miles to the summit for extensive views.

The high ridges of the John Day are often windblown, and snow may not be perfect. The short tour to Lookout Mountain requires a good map and compass and tape to mark your route. The tape should be removed on your return, as on any ski tour or hike. Crepe paper is recommended as it is biodegradable if you miss any pieces on your return.

Interestingly, Road 994 does not show on the Strawberry Mountain Wilderness map. West of the divide 200 yards is a historic log cabin, just south of Road 101, that was used for snow surveys.

INGLE MOUNTAIN

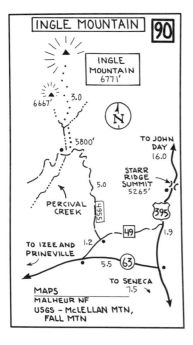

(Map 90) This 6,771-foot peak of the Aldrich Mountains southwest of John Day is reached in 8 miles of skiing with a 2,000-foot elevation gain. The road-skiing section is 5 miles, and 3 miles of off-road skiing complete the tour for Backcountry skiers to the summit, where there are sweeping views.

Although the peak is 8 miles due south of the town of Mount Vernon, it is necessary to drive Highway 395 south from John Day for 16 miles, then turn west onto County Road 63 (Izee Road). Drive 5.5 miles west to County Road 49. Turn northeast on this road (which is normally plowed) and drive 1.2 miles to Road 4955.

Drive on 4955 as far as possible. At 5 miles from Road 49 leave the road and ski into a steep-walled gully, a branch of Percival Creek. Ski up the west-curving gully, and where it forks climb the ridge between the two drainages. You'll soon have views south and west. Climb the east side of the ridge to the summit. The view down Riley Creek into the John Day valley and of the line of high peaks sweeping westward is spectacular.

A topographic map of this area will help you with route finding, although the route is quite direct.

Coyote tracks

SNOWSHOE CREEK LOOP

(Map 91) This 6-mile marked loop along winding, primitive roads will more than reward you as you ski through beautiful aspen, larch, and ponderosa forests and climb to a high ridge view of the Ochocos and Strawberry Mountains. The loop is rated Intermediate, but Novices will find the first section worthwhile, particularly if the loop is skied clockwise.

From John Day drive south on Highway 395 16 miles to the junction with the Izee Road (County Road 63). Turn west onto 63 and drive 13.3 miles to a wide spot in the road at 5,200 feet, 100 yards east of the road to Flagtail Peak, and just east of Snowshoe Summit.

The Snowshoe Creek Trail is south of the highway and starts by crossing lower Snowshoe Creek at the edge of a meadow. Ski upstream (counterclockwise on the loop) through mixed forest

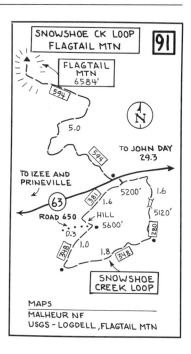

SNOWSHOE CK LOOP
FLAGTAIL MTN

91

FLAGTAIL MTN 6584'

594

5.0

594

TO JOHN DAY 29.3

TO IZEE AND PRINEVILLE

63

381

5200' 1.6

1.6

ROAD 650

HILL 5600'

5120'

280

0.3

248

1.0

1.8

348

SNOWSHOE CREEK LOOP

MAPS
MALHEUR NF
USGS - LOGDELL, FLAGTAIL MTN

and old-growth ponderosa pines. At 1.6 miles, top a ridge at 5,600 feet for a view east to the Strawberry Mountains. The climb to the ridgetop is fairly steep. The trail follows roads for its entire distance.

For the most spectacular view, however, take a side road (FS 650) 0.3 mile south along the ridgetop for a dramatic view over the south fork of the John Day River. Return to the trail, then continue on the loop south down the side of the ridge, then switchback north into a gentle valley of streamside red osier dogwood and giant larches. Along here, through a thin stand of trees, is a large meadow to explore along the creek where you'll find beaver-cut trees. At 4.4 miles you cross the Silvies River bridge, where upstream you'll see beaver-trimmed lodgepole pines.

Follow the Silvies downstream through a shallow, narrow canyon lined with lodgepole pine and ledge rock to its junction with lower Snowshoe Creek at 5 miles and the loop's low point at 5,120 feet. Turn uphill to close the loop.

FLAGTAIL MOUNTAIN

(Map 91) There are few places in the John Day area where an Intermediate skier can park conveniently at a good elevation and safely climb 1,400 feet to the top of a fine viewpoint following a 5-mile road. The summit of Flagtail at 6,584 feet is such a rewarding goal!

Follow directions for Snowshoe Creek Loop, park, then hike 100 yards west to Road 594, or park at the road itself. Ski north on 594, then west. After gaining 500 feet of elevation leave the mixed-fir forest and enter big old ponderosa pines. At 6,000 feet break into the open with great views to the south and east to Bear Valley, a vast, shallow, open basin typical of the region. The last mile requires only a short elevation gain through groves of ponderosas and firs to the summit lookout tower. The extensive views include the Three Sisters 135 miles to the west.

FIELDS PEAK

(Map 92) Site of a former fire lookout, this 7,362-foot peak is the westernmost and highest point of a rugged mountain group southwest of Mount Vernon. The peak is clearly seen from the John Day valley. The scenic lower slopes on the peak's south side are your goal, although you may want to ski higher.

Drive Highway 26 west of Mount Vernon 10 miles (18 from John Day) to Road 21, a paved forest road that you follow southward into the mountains as far as possible. The snowline is usually about 5 miles from Highway 26. At 6.8 miles from the highway turn left onto Road 2160, a primitive road, ski 3.1 miles to a saddle with a cattleguard, and turn left. Ski east 0.3 mile to where 2160 turns south. Go left here and start climbing 0.3 mile to a saddle, then onto moderately steep grades as the narrow road crosses a steep hillside eastward to the first good views. Another 0.8 mile takes you to the top of a flat-crested ridge for a breather and great views.

From here the road continues steeply upward on east-facing slopes to another ridgetop with views. The very wide, gentle saddle east of the peak is a goal for views to the north, 3.6 miles from the cattleguard and 2,000 feet higher. Views from below the upper saddle include Strawberry Mountain, Big Snow Mountain, and great expanses of the John Day.

If you ski south from the cattle-guard saddle only 0.5 mile out onto a spur ridge, you will enjoy good views of Bear Valley, a respectable goal if you are short on time or energy. The route described here is definitely the only outstanding tour from Road 21. Do not be tempted to ski west on Road 2150 from the Road 21 saddle at 5,200 feet. It is monotonous and has few views.

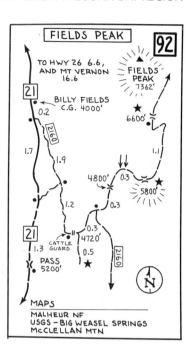

ALDRICH MOUNTAIN

(Map 93) The highest, most western point of a 10-mile, undulating, forested ridge running from Fields Peak, Aldrich Mountain (6,987 feet) is a challenging goal best approached from the north. Road 2150 going west from the Road 21 saddle along the ridgetop is not a good route unless you are doing a multi-day ski trip. The long ridge has few views, and although easy and seemingly obvious, it has little to recommend it. From the north, Aldrich Mountain is a Backcountry, 20-mile round trip with a gain of 4,500 feet from the highway, although it is usually possible to drive part of the distance.

North Route: Flat Creek and Bridge Creek. (Map 93) From Dayville, drive 5.1 miles east (1.1 miles east of an obvious relay station above Highway 26) on Highway 26 to a public access road. Drive south across the flat (2,445 feet) through a gate and climb the hillside as the gravel road turns east. In 0.8 mile reach a large field. Drive to the road at the field's east end (1.6 miles from the highway) and turn south up Flat Creek.

Reach the first shallow ford of the creek at 2.8 miles (3,200 feet) from the highway, then a second ford at 3,520 feet. Here, leave the road and hike or

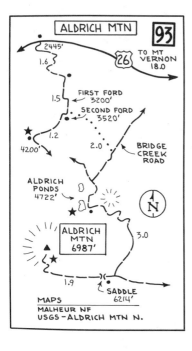

ski up a side draw east of the creek onto a wide, open ridge. Climb through scattered junipers and pines. If lucky, you might pass the aspen grove where there are trees with bear-claw scratches.

The broad ridge narrows slowly as you ascend and becomes forested. The moderately steep ridge eventually leads you to the nearby Bridge Creek primitive road, which is just over the crest of the ridge on its east side. Follow this road to the upper Aldrich pond, called Stewart Lake, at 4,873 feet. If you cross the broad ridge lower, you can avoid skiing through the forest by gaining the Bridge Creek road sooner.

From the small lake, climb a steep bank on the east and pick up an abandoned road that climbs steeply around the west side of a forested butte 3 miles through forest to Cabbage Patch Saddle (6,214 feet). From here it is an 800-foot climb and 1.4 miles on a steep road to the fire lookout on the summit of Aldrich Mountain. The view includes the Strawberry Range, Maury Mountains, Mount Bachelor, South Sister and Broken Top, Hood and Adams.

If you do not have time to go to the summit, the upper open slopes of Flat Creek at 4,200 feet, following the road, offer grand views of the John Day valley. It is a worth-the-trip goal of 10 miles round trip and a climb of only 1,800 feet from the highway, rated Advanced.

Another route to the summit climbs from the open meadows at 4,200 feet into thick forest on a complicated assortment of primitive and skid roads to Stewart Lake. You are sure to become confused if you venture this way.

Chapter 30

THE BLUE MOUNTAINS AND VICINITY

The Blue Mountains—so called by nineteenth-century immigrants due to the dark color of the range's extensive forests—cover a huge area of Northeastern Oregon. The pioneers of the Oregon Trail found the mountains to be the most difficult but beautiful section of their 2,000-mile ordeal.

Much of the area is enclosed in the Ochoco, Malheur, Wallowa-Whitman and Umatilla National Forests. Although there are high, rugged mountains in this region—such as the Strawberry, Elkhorn, and Wallowa ranges—the majority of the area is characterized by high, rolling forested ridges and plateaus, cut in many places by deep valleys. Much of the area is inaccessible in winter except by way of major snow-plowed roads, or where there is winter logging. Few suitable parking areas exist, so if you are exploring carry a shovel to improve roadside parking.

If you are a casual explorer, Umatilla and Wallowa-Whitman National Forest maps may be sufficient. If you are a serious skier, however, obtain a transportation map for the area of your interest.

This chapter explores six areas with interesting, accessible ski tours that offer a range of experiences. Four were selected for their scenic values, one for groomed tracks, and one purely for accessibility and convenience where there are no views to enjoy. There are many others to explore.

DEADMAN PASS STATE PARK

(Map 94) Located at the top of Cabbage Hill 23 miles southeast of Pendleton on Interstate 84, this state park is a popular year-round rest stop for motorists. There is parking, and in winter heated restrooms. The site is the location of a section of the Oregon Trail, still visible in several places when there is no snow. The Blue Mountains were the most difficult section of the entire Oregon Trail, and here at Deadman Pass pioneers saw for the first time the rolling prairies of the Columbia Plateau and as far as Mount Hood.

An unmarked, scenic 1-mile Novice–Intermediate ski tour goes north from the parking area north of I-84 at the state park. If you are traveling east, the parking area and restrooms are reached via an underpass. From the northside parking area walk to the entrance of the parking area then west on the plowed road (the old highway) 50 yards to a snow-covered side road. Ski this road north as it parallels the parking area and climbs gently to

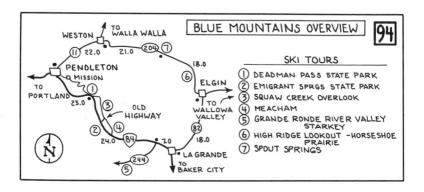

the open slopes of a wide ridge. Ski far enough to look north.

For greater views, turn westward from your northernmost point on a wide ridge and climb to the top of Emigrant Hill (radio tower 3,870 feet), a climb of 270 feet from the parking area. The Oregon Trail climbs directly to the radio tower's north side from the entrance to the parking area and proceeds along the wide ridgecrest westward, a direction you should ski for increasingly better views of Hood, Adams, and Rainier.

EMIGRANT SPRINGS STATE PARK

(Map 94) This state park is located just south of I-84 at Exit 234, 26 miles from La Grande and 29 miles from Pendleton. It has parking and heated restrooms, and at 3,800 feet there is usually skiable snow for several months. The skiing is on primitive roads and through forest with no views. Rustic overnight accommodations are available for groups, by advance reservation only.

Skiing is generally over rolling terrain on state park land and outside the park. As the roads are not marked and there are no landmarks, it is possible to become lost in the maze of forest roads outside the park. In addition, a wide swath for a pipeline runs north and south at the park's boundary 100 yards from parking. Skiing is rated Novice to Intermediate. Ski with care if you are skiing some distance.

MEACHAM AND SQUAW CREEK OVERLOOK

(Map 94) This small railroad town just 3 miles southeast of Emigrant Springs State Park and close to I-84 provides access to an open ridge to the north just off the old highway that goes through town. The old highway is plowed in winter, parallels I-84 northward to Deadman Pass, then goes down to the town of Mission near Pendleton, a scenic drive. Squaw Creek Overlook on the old highway about 5.5 miles north of Meacham has a spectacular view into a deep valley only 400 yards from the old highway across level terrain. There is only roadside parking, so have a shovel handy to clear the shoulder.

GRANDE RONDE RIVER VALLEY AND STARKEY

(Map 94) If you are staying in La Grande, or have time for a scenic side trip to an extremely beautiful area not far from I-84, consider the scenic Grande Ronde valley. The area ranges in elevation from 3,000 to 3,500 feet, and by driving only 20 miles or less from I-84 you will see magnificent natural areas, ranchlands, meadows, huge flats, creek valleys, and old barns and buildings. Much of the area is fenced, and parking is only roadside, so have a shovel handy and do not block private roads.

Take Exit 252 only 8 miles or so north of La Grande and drive Highway 244 west as it climbs gently up the Grande Ronde River valley toward Ukiah many miles to the west. The area is perfect for casual skiers and Novices who do not want to drive long distances to ski and who are looking for a unique scenic experience.

Highway 244 is paved, wide, and plowed in winter. At 4.5 miles from I-84 the Bear Creek flats appear, some 3 miles across. Another 3.4 miles bring you to a state park in a narrow valley it is possible to ski. Even if you don't find good snow or ski here, the drive is marvelous, particularly on a sunny, cold day!

HIGH RIDGE LOOKOUT AND HORSESHOE PRAIRIE

(Map 94) The open ridge where the lookout stands is 5.2 miles by road from the Highway 204 Sno-Park at 5,000 feet. Road 31, the main route to the lookout west of the highway, is 13 miles from Elgin to the south, 27 miles from Weston, and only 4.8 miles south of Spout Springs ski area. Road 31 is groomed for snowmobile use. The lookout sits at 5,303 feet, and the cumulative elevation gain for the tour is 1,300 feet.

The road to the lookout is obvious and climbs and descends for a mile or more in several places. The last 1.2 miles on the final ridge climb uphill. There are views only on the last part of the tour of deep canyons and ridges, Hood, Adams, Rainier, and Mount Emily near La Grande.

On the ski in, rated Intermediate–Advanced, the first view of the lookout is at 2.7 miles. Ski another 1.3 miles downhill to a junction with Road 270, which is followed only briefly to the first side road to the left leading the final 1.2 miles up moderate grades to the open lookout ridge. Just below the lookout to the west and south is the valley where the old La Grande-to-Mission stagecoach route lies.

Horseshoe Prairie, to the north of Road 31 and less than 2 miles from the sno-park, is visited by some skiers and snowmobilers. However, it has few attributes other than gentle, open meadows, some road skiing, and a few views west into Johnson Creek.

SPOUT SPRINGS

(Map 94) A Nordic track system is maintained at Spout Springs ski area east of Tollgate on Highway 204, 45 miles east of Pendleton. There are 12 miles of groomed tracks, and the 5,000-foot elevation usually ensures good snow. A fee is charged for skiing on the tracks.

There is a loop system north of the lodge and ski area, but the main track system is on a rolling, forested plateau at the top of the ski area at 5,500 feet. These are the most interesting tracks, and the loops range from Novice to Intermediate with only one difficult trail. They are reached by a track that climbs steeply to the plateau. There are views of the Elkhorns, Wallowas, and the Seven Devils.

Ski track through lodgepole pine forest

Chapter 31

THE ELKHORN MOUNTAINS

The Elkhorn Mountains, east of and across the Baker Valley from the Wallowa Mountains, offer a rewarding range of skiing experiences. In a magnificent setting of rugged high peaks and ridges there are groomed tracks, easy road and off-road skiing, and accessible Backcountry adventure skiing. Skiing starts at 7,100 feet, an elevation that ensures good snow. A chairlift provides easy uphill access to a fine viewpoint and a descent eastward into a safe, nearby Backcountry skiing area, and also access to the more demanding Crawfish Meadows area for serious Backcountry skiers seeking a challenge. Although the Elkhorn Range extends some 18 miles north-to-south, access to other parts of the mountains is difficult. Between 1870 and 1916 the Elkhorns were the richest gold-producing area of Oregon, and the Baker Valley saw annual drives of huge cattle herds from the surrounding region on their way to eastern markets.

Anthony Lakes is also a downhill skiing area, and the sno-park at the ski area is the starting point for most ski tours described here. The plowed access road ends at the ski area at 7,100 feet and 22 miles west of I-84, Exit 285, at North Powder. The freeway exit is approximately 20 miles south of La Grande and the same distance north of Baker City. From the freeway, follow signs to the ski area, which lead you to Elkhorn Drive and Road 73, climbing 4,000 feet from the Baker Valley to the ski area.

West of Baker City only 18 miles are three worthwhile ski tours reached by driving scenic Highway 7, which goes to the John Day area. These are good alternatives if you are staying overnight in Baker City and you do not wish to drive to Anthony Lakes in the Elkhorns or to the John Day area. At Dooley Summit there are two ski tours to extremely scenic points—Beaver Mountain, suitable for Novice skiers, and Bald Mountain, a demanding tour. There is also the low-elevation Phillips Reservoir with miles of ski trails.

From Baker City, you can drive to Greenhorn, Vinegar Hill, and Dixie Butte, just to mention three of the more accessible tours in the John Day area (see Chapter 29). Driving distance from Baker City to these tours ranges from 40 to 50 miles.

ANTHONY LAKES GROOMED TRACKS

(Map 95) The three "stacked" loops of this fee-trail system total just over 5 miles, and each of the loops, using common legs, is different and well designed for skiers ranging from Novice to Intermediate. The setting of the loops is dramatic, lying at the base of Gunsight Mountain.

The track system starts at the south end of the south sno-park, where a

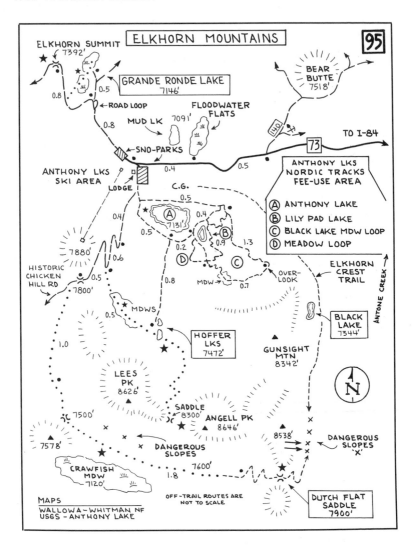

trail pass may be purchased at the lodge. Ski 150 yards to the lake and ski either clockwise or counterclockwise, using your free trail map to decide your route. The loop around Anthony Lakes is 1.2 miles and nearly level.

To the east is Lily Pad Lake with its own 1.5-mile loop, whose east leg, shared with the Black Lake Meadow Loop, will challenge Novice skiers as it is quite hilly, on a small scale. This leg climbs, twists about, and descends short, moderate grades. South of this loop is a short trail around a lovely meadow that actually forms a fourth, short loop.

Aerial view of Anthony Lake, downhill ski area, and Elkhorn Range; Gunsight Peak left of lake, Angell Basin and peak behind

The Black Lake Meadow Loop for Intermediate skiers is the longest of the three loops at 2.9 miles, and is located at the eastern end of the trail system. At the loop's farthest point there is a short side trail to an overlook of Antone Creek. This loop also includes a small meadow and several short, moderate hills, more demanding than those of the Lily Pad Lake Loop.

For Backcountry skiers headed for Angell Basin, Hoffer Lakes, or Black Lake, there is no common corridor that provides free access to areas blocked by the fee-use groomed-trail system. Local custom is for Backcountry skiers to ski through the area, staying off the groomed tracks or briefly using the tracks to get through.

GRANDE RONDE LAKE BASIN

(Map 95) Located in a small but wide shallow basin are several meadows and the lake that appears to be more meadow than lake. Although snowmobilers have their way here, it is a short 1.1 miles from the north sno-park to the basin that lies north of the ski area. The scenic area has little elevation gain or loss and is a good place for Novice skiers.

Park at the farthest sno-park and ski north on a wide road uphill 0.8 mile to a road loop turnaround (sometimes plowed to here). Here leave the main road and ski a narrow road downhill from the loop 0.5 mile through forest to the lake, taking a left branch partway down.

Ski north across the lake into open areas, then climb a clearcut for good views of the high Elkhorn peaks. On your return after crossing Grande Ronde Lake or skiing its edge if you are not sure of surface solidity, continue into meadows south of the lake and climb the hillside to the west to reach the wide road above. Ski uphill on the road to Elkhorn Summit (7,392 feet) for distant views to the west. At the summit the road crosses the ridgecrest and then drops miles to Granite, an old mining town. Elkhorn Summit is only 1.6 miles from the sno-park.

MUD LAKE AND FLOODWATER FLATS

(Map 95) These two open areas offer meadowlike skiing north of Road 73, the access road to the ski area. They are only 0.4 mile northeast of the south sno-park and are reached by skiing along the north side of Road 73.

HOFFER LAKES

(Map 95) These two small lakes 1.3 miles from the sno-park and a 350-foot climb from Anthony Lakes are a good training tour for the beginning Backcountry skier. From the south sno-park ski on the groomed tracks to the south side of Anthony Lakes to the Parker Creek sign. The summer trail here ascends 0.8 mile gently up the west side of Parker Creek to a final, moderately steep climb to the first lake. Here you'll enjoy a good view of nearby Lees Peak and a frozen waterfall.

From the lakes turn right and ski west 0.5 mile up a meadow toward the downhill ski area to a small butte and the top of the ski-area chairlift (7,880 feet) for views of the peaks. If you turn eastward at Hoffer Lakes, a draw will lead you through forest up to Angell Basin.

BLACK LAKE AND ELKHORN CREST TRAIL

(Map 95) Summer hiking trail 1611 is one access route to elusive Black Lake (7,344 feet) for Intermediate skiers, only a 350-foot climb and 1.5 miles from the sno-park. The trail starts at the snow-covered campground on the north shore of Anthony Lakes, goes southeast past Lily Pad Lake, then through forest east of Black Lake to Dutch Flat Saddle 1.5 miles beyond the lake. If you are not familiar with the trail it may be hard to locate and follow in winter.

If confused en route, look for the shallow depression of the outlet stream that flows into Lily Pad Lake and follow it to the lake, a feat not always obvious or easy. The lake lies about 200 yards west of the trail. Beyond and south of the lake, the Elkhorn Crest Trail crosses steep, dangerous slopes as it goes toward Dutch Flat Saddle. Steep slopes above the trail are deposition zones for windblown snow from the high ridges, and dangerous slab conditions are often created.

Another route to Black Lake follows the far eastern end of the groomed-track system, leaves the tracks, and curves around the shallow ridge coming off the north side of Gunsight Mountain. Look for the shallow depression of the outlet stream. Not everyone finds the lake, but it is good exercise, and an off-trail learning experience. Carry compass and map.

ANGELL BASIN AND RIDGECREST

(Map 95) This demanding tour is for Backcountry skiers only due to steepness and the need to understand snow conditions well. Splendid views of the Elkhorn Range and the Wallowa Mountains await successful skiers at the 8,300-foot pass at the head of Angell Basin, a climb of 1,200 feet from the sno-park over a one-way distance of 2.8 miles. Despite proximity to the ski area, this is a serious, steep tour.

Follow directions to Hoffer Lakes, ski to the lakes, then ski southeast up an obvious draw for 0.5 mile, then start angling up open slopes to the south. After several hundred yards of steep climbing the terrain eases off into a beautiful basin. Eat lunch here as the ridgecrest above will be cold and windy. Climb steeply along the left edge of forest to avoid avalanche danger. The saddle drops steeply off the south side, so be cautious.

For Telemark skiers, the bowl is a challenge in deep powder snow. If less experienced, do the usual traverses and kick turns on the descent. Be properly clothed and prepared for avalanche conditions. Know a lot about snow conditions and danger before you attempt this route. And be sure to take ski climbers!

ROAD 140 PAST BEAR BUTTE

(Map 95) A road system north of Road 73 permits a 7-mile descent with a prearranged car shuttle. Road 140 leaves Road 73 0.9 mile east of the ski area and goes northeast through forest, then past Bear Butte on Road 140, ultimately joining with Road 7315 and 7312 to finally arrive at Road 73 after a 2,000-foot descent. There it joins the ski-area access road at a prominent turn not far from the National Forest boundary. If you ski this, plan it with a transportation map showing all the roads for the Baker Ranger District, and be sure to verify there is sufficient snow depth at the lower end. This tour is for Backcountry skiers.

ANTONE CREEK

(Map 95) This more difficult Backcountry tour requires route finding and deep snow. It goes down Antone Creek (no trail, no road) from the east end of the Anthony Lakes Nordic Trails to the Little Alps (see Van Patten Butte) 2.6 miles below the ski area at 6,380 feet. The distance is about 5 miles with an elevation loss of over 800 feet. Depending on snow depth, brush and thick forest in places may challenge you. This tour is for Backcountry skiers only with good conditions and deep snow, and using a topographic map. From the Nordic trail system ski southeast into the Antone Creek drainage, follow it northward, then parallel Road 73 down to Little Alps.

CRAWFISH MEADOW

(Map 95) At 7,120 feet Crawfish Meadow lies in a scenic basin south of Lees and Angell Peaks. This is a Backcountry tour only for Backcountry skiers who are properly equipped and have strong knowledge of snow conditions. Several avalanche paths are crossed on the 4-mile one-way tour. Cumulative elevation gain will vary but could be up to 2,500 feet if you ski to Dutch Flat Saddle for the views.

The easiest way to start this tour is to ride the chairlift to the 7,880-foot top of the ski area, then descend southward to a saddle and continue southward through open area and scrubby forest traversing the lower west slopes of Lees Peak. The route then turns eastward, descending to Crawfish Meadow, or it can traverse above the meadow toward Dutch Flat Saddle.

Once in the meadow, or on the upper traverse, you are in the upper basin of Crawfish Creek below the rugged range of peaks and ridges forming the basin's south and east walls. Climbing 780 feet from the meadow to the 7,900-foot saddle provides stunning views. But crossing the saddle to the east is dangerous. See Black Lake and Elkhorn Crest Trail for further information on the eastside trail.

If you do not ride the chairlift up, there are two other access routes. The first goes up the Road Run ski trail, the most easterly of the downhill ski area's runs. The ski run follows a road that climbs to the saddle south of the chairlift's upper terminus. The second route to the saddle north of the chairlift butte goes to Hoffer Lakes, then turns west and climbs through open alpine areas and forest to the saddle to initiate the descending traverse to Crawfish Meadow.

To ride any chairlift, you will need runaway straps to prevent loss of skis. In fact, all Backcountry skiing requires such straps.

VAN PATTEN LAKE AND BUTTE

(Map 96) This lake and butte offer a challenge for the strong Intermediate skier who is advancing in Backcountry experience. The 4-mile one-way route itself is fairly obvious, but the terrain will be interesting and a climb of the butte will challenge anyone.

The starting point is at a turnout 2.6 miles east of Anthony Lakes on the south side of Road 73. Follow a jeep road at the turnout 1 mile south and then east past several buildings as it climbs and turns. This road went to the top of the former ski area called Little Alps, a predecessor to Anthony Lakes ski area. From the top, ski the trail to the lake at 7,396 feet. To reach the lake, slopes must be crossed that require careful thought for safety as there is some potential for avalanches.

Van Patten Butte (8,729 feet), rising about 1,300 feet above the lake, is best climbed from the south end of the lake, then northward to the summit, with some of the distance trav-

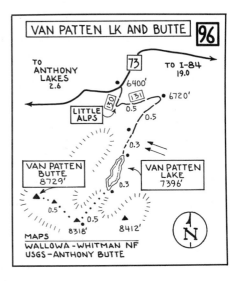

eled off your skis if necessary. The views extend to Mount Jefferson and Mount Hood. Be fully aware of snow conditions and avoid snow-deposition areas east of any crest or ridge, the result of the usual westerly storms and winds. Slab conditions are very hard to evaluate, and slab conditions can be soft snow or hardpack. The message is to stay off deposition zones below ridgetops.

Chapter 32

THE WALLOWA MOUNTAINS

Located in northeastern Oregon, the Wallowas (Wah-*lah*-wahs) lie east of the towns of La Grande and Baker City, the principal points of access for most visitors.

The Wallowa Mountains are impressive in scale, with 27 peaks exceeding 8,000 feet in elevation and several reaching nearly 10,000 feet. The range covers some 1,600 square miles, and the Eagle Cap Wilderness at its core includes 485 square miles of rugged ridges, deep valleys, many lakes, and several prominent summits, including the highest peaks. Six major valleys extend like spokes from a central hub, the Eagle Cap Peak-Lakes Basin area. These major valleys are the obvious, direct routes for penetration of the range.

With the exception of the Salt Creek Summit marked ski-trail system near the town of Joseph, there are no other developed trails on the north side of the range at this time. Occasionally a trail is broken out from Wallowa Lake, a scenic gem formed by an ancient valley glacier, and near the town of Joseph. Such trails lead out of the campground area at the lake's south end.

There is convenient lodging at the lake's south end and in the small towns of Joseph, Enterprise, and Wallowa. The Wallowa Valley, wide and fertile, lying at the north foot of the range, was the home of the Nez Perce Indians whose Chief Joseph battled valiantly against the encroaching whites. The entire valley was taken by the U.S. Army and settlers, and a poor reservation to the north was fashioned for the surviving Nez Perce tribe.

The south side of the range at the town of Halfway has a groomed-track system, but otherwise skiing on both north and south sides is on unmarked ski routes. Some of these are within the capability of Novice and Intermediate skiers, and others are strictly for Backcountry explorers. The more challenging Backcountry routes described here should be limited to skiers who have off-trail, Backcountry experience and who have a good knowledge of snow conditions and the principles of avalanche potential. Both north and south sides of the range offer a wide variety of skiing in extremely scenic areas. All skiers who ski off the marked trails of the north and south Wallowas should carry an Eagle Cap Wilderness map.

WALLOWAS—NORTH SIDE

Most of the north side of the Wallowas Range is relatively inaccessible to the average skier except for the extensive Salt Creek Summit trail system with scenic trails for all skill levels. At this time, some of the trails are groomed and no fee is charged for their use. Although the Lostine and Hurricane valleys lead for miles to the high country, they are not recommended for one-day tours. The Wallowas are mountains where a skier should maximize the scenic potential, and these two valleys are essentially in heavy timber with only occasional views of the high ridges on either side. The West Fork Wallowa River valley is the best option for a one-day tour. Following the summer hiking trail, there are views and several meadows, but there is avalanche potential, attested to by wide, treeless swaths descending from the high, steep trailside ridges.

For one-day Backcountry ski tours to high basins, the Aneroid Lake Trail and the McCully Basin are recommended, but both are long tours with lots of elevation gain on unmarked trails into the wilderness area. Both areas are superb for overnight tours that allow for further, higher exploration. See the High Wallowas section for descriptions of these and other tours on both the north and south sides of the range.

SALT CREEK SUMMIT TRAILS

(Map 97) The Salt Creek Summit marked trail system will probably satisfy most skiers as the rewards are considerable and the access road is good. Salt Creek Summit (6,150 feet) is on Road 39, the Wallowa Mountain Loop Road, which goes around the east side of the range from Joseph to Halfway, on the south side of the range. In winter the road is plowed only to Salt Creek Summit. The road is not usually open all the way until late April, depending on snow depth.

Salt Creek Summit is the only area at this time on the north side of the Wallowas with marked cross-country ski trails. There are four loops, three of which are groomed by volunteers, conditions permitting, and then there are four additional trails. One of the trails gives access to the Big Sheep Nordic Shelter, one of the two canvas-tent shelters with bunks, cooking equipment, chairs, sleeping pads, and stoves. Reservations for the shelters

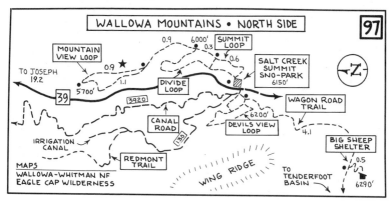

are necessary for overnight stays through Wing Ridge Ski Tours, P.O. Box 714, Joseph, Oregon 97846, 503-426-4322. If writing, include a self-addressed stamped envelope. The shelters are heavily used and reservations may be difficult to obtain for weekends.

The Canal Fire swept through this area in 1988, resulting in thousands of acres burned. The result, due to lack of normal tree cover, is better and deeper snow and the many views that were opened up. Some may find the desolation of snag forests unattractive, while others will find it a unique, open experience. The fire did not cross into the adjoining wilderness area, and all the trees were not burned in the fire area. There are many views, including the Seven Devils Range in Idaho across the Hells Canyon of the Snake River.

To ski the Salt Creek Summit trails drive east from Joseph on the Imnaha road (County Road 350) about 8.7 miles to where you turn south onto County Road 602, which becomes Forest Road 39. From the turn it is about 10.5 miles to Salt Creek Summit. To drive to the McCully Basin trailhead or to Ferguson Ridge Trail to the Ferguson Ridge Nordic Shelter, drive east from Joseph on the Imnaha road 5.2 miles then turn south onto Tucker Downs road, which becomes Forest Road 3920. This latter road is plowed and ends at the Ferguson Ski Area for downhill skiers. The McCully Basin trailhead is about 0.7 mile beyond the turnoff to the downhill ski area, and the road to the trailhead may not be plowed.

Devils View Loop. (Map 97) Excellent views of the Seven Devils are a reward for skiing this 1.9-mile loop. The trailhead is shared with the Wagon Road Trail, and there are short but steep sections at the start and end of the loop, which are difficult for Novices. Most of the loop is through burned areas, with meadows at the north end. The loop is not groomed and ranges from 6,100 to 6,300 feet.

Summit Groomed Loop. (Map 97) This excellent 1.3-mile loop for Novices on flat terrain starts at the sno-park and passes through both burned areas and forest and meadows.

Divide Groomed Loop. (Map 97) Ski either leg of the Summit Groomed Loop to reach the Divide Groomed Loop, then ski it clockwise to best manage and enjoy a short, steep descent on the west leg near the Summit Groomed Loop. Much of the loop is gentle, parts are located on a flat ridgetop, and both burned and natural forest share equally here. The loop is 1.5 miles plus the leg of the Summit Groomed Loop, and is rated Intermediate.

Mountain View Loop. (Map 97) This 2-mile Intermediate loop is reached by skiing out the east legs of the Summit and Divide Groomed Loops. There are several steep hills on the north end and west leg. The east leg is on a flat ridgetop through meadows with fine views of Wing Ridge in the Eagle Cap Wilderness. The trail passes through the burned area. Total distance out and back is 5.6 miles, with elevations ranging from 5,700 to 6,150 feet. There are also views of the Seven Devils.

Canal Road. (Map 97) This is a road tour groomed for snowmobilers (Road 3920) and is not recommended for weekend skiing. The groomed roadbed is more suitable for skating. The road goes north 3 miles, and it is possible to make a loop tour by either returning or starting out on the Upper Canal road (Road 130), a more interesting trail but out in the open and often windy. The roads are suitable for Novices as they are nearly level.

Redmont Trail. (Map 97) This 9.5-mile Intermediate trail connects Ferguson Ridge to Salt Creek Summit by using the Upper Canal Trail. The northern end is on a logging road where there are several short, steep hills and old-growth forest. Although this trail climbs to Ferguson Ridge and then descends into McCully Creek, it is not a recommended route to the McCully Basin. The route over the ridge may not be marked in the future.

Wagon Road and Tenderfoot Trails. (Map 97) This 4.7-mile trail for Advanced skiers leads to the Big Sheep Nordic Shelter at 6,290 feet at Big Sheep Creek. The trail is also the access route to one of the finest one- or two-day tours of the Wallowas, which climbs beyond the shelter up Big Sheep Creek, past Bonny Lakes, up the marvelous open valley to Dollar Lake Pass (8,400 feet) and on to Tenderfoot Pass (also at 8,400 feet), a total distance of about 12.5 miles from the sno-park, and an elevation gain of 2,400 feet.

Beyond Dollar Lake Pass (0.7 mile before Tenderfoot Pass) lies the upper Aneroid Basin, a vast area of open slopes surrounded by high ridges. The pass is easily crossed. You should have good knowledge of avalanche conditions if you venture far into the upper valley from the shelter because of the steep, south-facing slopes north of the valley.

To ski to the Big Sheep Nordic Shelter, first ski the south leg of the Devils View Loop to the Wagon Road Trail, which at first is an old road that narrows. There are several long, gentle grades up and several creek crossings. The trail follows contours southward largely through burned forest with many views of the Seven Devils. The last 0.5 mile descends steeply to the shelter on the Cutoff Trail. The shelter is available at no charge for day use, but reservations are required for overnight use and a fee is charged.

Beyond the shelter is the Tenderfoot Trail, which penetrates the Eagle Cap Wilderness, leaves the burned area behind, and puts you on your own as the route is not marked due to wilderness ethics. It is 5 miles to Bonny Lakes and another 2.5 to Dollar Lake Pass at the edge of the Aneroid Basin. (See the following description for more details.)

MIDDLE FORK BIG SHEEP CREEK AND BONNY LAKES

(Map 98) This 18-mile Backcountry round trip leads you into dramatic high country. Push yourself to reach Dollar Lake Pass to get the exceptional feeling of skiing to the top of the world. The route from the sno-park is never difficult and does not cross steep slopes or involve exceptional skiing skills. It does, however, if you are on a one-day tour, demand that you start early and that you keep pushing yourself.

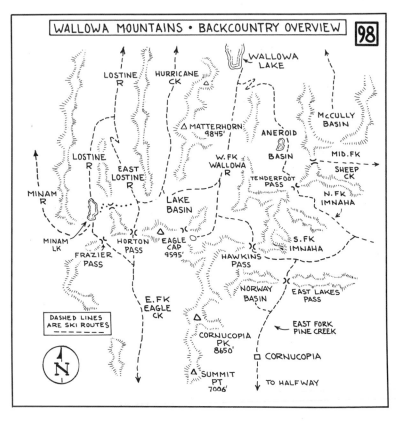

WALLOWA MOUNTAINS · BACKCOUNTRY OVERVIEW

98

WALLOWA LAKE · LOSTINE R · HURRICANE CK · MATTERHORN 9845' · ANEROID BASIN · McCULLY BASIN · MID.FK · LOSTINE R · EAST LOSTINE R · W.FK WALLOWA R · SHEEP CK · MINAM R · LAKE BASIN · TENDERFOOT PASS · N.FK IMNAHA · MINAM LK · HORTON PASS · EAGLE CAP 9595' · FRAZIER PASS · HAWKINS PASS · S.FK IMNAHA · DASHED LINES ARE SKI ROUTES · E.FK EAGLE CK · NORWAY BASIN · EAST LAKES PASS · N · CORNUCOPIA PK 8650' · EAST FORK PINE CREEK · CORNUCOPIA · SUMMIT PT 7006' · TO HALFWAY

From the Big Sheep Creek Nordic Shelter (see Wagon Road Trail) follow the trail to the wilderness boundary. In fact, do not descend the 0.5-mile trail to the shelter, but continue west. Continue on the north side of the creek all the way, often out of sight, and follow the summer trail as best you can. You will encounter thick, annoying, but skiable forest, but stay close to the creek except to negotiate steep banks. The creek becomes a minor canyon, then a waterfall where you will find a half-mile-long meadow. If you miss this you will be in timber with openings. A landmark for the meadow is a red rock ridge to the north whose foot approaches the meadow. Prior rock slides are false landmarks.

At the end of the meadow gain steeper slopes at the foot of a major rocky ridge and continue through scattered trees and openings. You will see a row of rounded forms crossing the valley—above this is a minor, sharply rounded peak. Ski above (north of) this, and in several hundred yards reach Bonny Lakes at 7,800 feet. If you feel there is low avalanche danger, continue skiing along the foot of the ridge to the north and ignore temptations to ski around low, rounded ridges to your left, a waste of time and energy.

You are now in the beautiful upper basin. Climb to Dollar Lake Pass at 8,400 feet. The wide, flat saddle gives fine views of high peaks, Tenderfoot Basin, and the Seven Devils. The scenery is awesome, and you will be thankful that you pushed on to the pass.

ANEROID LAKE BASIN

(Map 98) This basin is located southeast of Wallowa Lake on the north side of the Wallowa Mountains. The end of the road at the south end of Wallowa Lake is the trailhead for the summer trail that leads to Aneroid Lake. There are several avalanche paths along the trail, and this area should be entered only by skiers with Backcountry experience. It is 5 miles to the first meadow, your first introduction to the basin itself. Aneroid Lake at 7,520 feet is another mile, and a climb of 2,870 feet from the trailhead. The

Petes Point mountain seen to west across Tenderfoot Basin from Dollar Lake Pass (Photo: Roger Averbeck)

upper basin, called Tenderfoot Basin, reaches up to 8,400 feet to both Dollar Lake Pass and Tenderfoot Pass, 8 miles from the trailhead.

The broken ridges and peaks that surround the lake and upper basin provide a superb scene for those who persevere, and particularly for those who reach either of the passes. See the Middle Fork Big Sheep Creek description for access from the east to Dollar Lake Pass. Combining the two tours with use of a car shuttle makes for a challenging, scenic tour.

From the end of the Wallowa Lake road at 4,646 feet the trail climbs the north flank of Bonneville Mountain in long, sweeping zigzags. At first the route ascends through pines, then mixed forest, with some good views of Wallowa Lake and of the ranchlands and grassy hills to the north.

There are several narrow, obvious avalanche chutes and fans along the way. Tight zigzags lead to a small dam and pond, above which the trail crosses several "meadows," in reality avalanche fans, and reenters forest 80 yards up the far sides. The third meadow at about 6,250 feet is a dangerous avalanche area. At 6,400 feet a steep slope must be traversed directly above the stream, a tricky spot on skis.

The first large meadow in the flat valley bottom may be mistaken for Aneroid Lake, which is still a mile farther. If you have time for the upper basin, bypass the lake to the east, out of sight, to save time and to provide a direct route to Tenderfoot Basin. This basin, below the 8,400-foot pass of the same name, and Dollar Lake Pass are both worthy objectives. The scenery in the wide, open, rolling upper basin is breathtaking. This tour to the 8,400-foot level is truly a high-mountain adventure. If you do not make it to that elevation, you will be well rewarded by the parkland scenery of the lower basin.

McCULLY BASIN

(Map 98) The wide, open high-mountain basin at the head of McCully Creek southeast of Wallowa Lake lies just over the East Peak-Aneroid Mountain ridge east of Aneroid Lake. The summer trail leads about 6 miles into the upper basin, starting at 5,520 feet and climbing over 2,000 feet. The scenic basin is surrounded by rugged ridges, and is somewhat similar to the Tenderfoot Basin above Aneroid Lake. However, the access trail is safer from avalanche danger, although the upper, open basin, as are all the high-country basins, is subject to avalanche danger. When heavy snowfall, wind deposition, and temperature factors create a potential for avalanche danger, use your snow knowledge and common sense.

From Joseph drive east 5.2 miles on the Imnaha road to the Tucker Downs road. Turn south and follow this road (the downhill ski area road) 5 miles to the McCully Creek Trail parking area. The trailhead is about 0.7 mile beyond the turnoff to the downhill ski area, beyond which the road may not be plowed. This road is also used by snowmobilers who drive farther to its end for access to the Canal road snowmobile route, which goes 10 miles to

Salt Creek Summit to a system of marked ski loops. For a superb view of the Wallowa valley, drive a short distance farther east on the Imnaha road from the Tucker Downs road junction to a pulloff on a hill.

From the trailhead at the road ski upward on a primitive road that narrows to a trail at the wilderness boundary. It is about 5 miles to the lower end of the open basin. The trail climbs steadily and directly with some moderately steep sections. It is never more than 50 yards from the creek and may be hard to follow in places, particularly in the old-growth areas. There are few views until you reach the lower basin at 7,400 feet. The basin has been used by wilderness backcountry-skiing outfitters, so the trail may be broken for you. The upper basin contains beautiful parklands and open areas, hemmed in by high, rugged ridges. The basin is divided by easily crossed minor ridges. The west side of the basin offers several high benches and side basins to explore.

WALLOWAS—SOUTH SIDE

Halfway, a small town 54 miles east of Baker City, is the access point for most ski tours in the southern Wallowas. Halfway is reached by driving Highway 86 through wonderfully scenic ranch country—indeed, it is one of the most beautiful drives in Oregon. Eight miles east of Baker City on Highway 86 is the fascinating Oregon Trail Interpretive Center, a must-see for history buffs.

Halfway sits in the Pine Creek valley at 2,650 feet at the foot of the Wallowas. The valley bottom usually has skiable snow several months each winter, and has a groomed, 6-mile, no-fee track system is located north of town in rolling terrain with many views. In addition, there are several ski tours for all skill levels in the Wallowa foothills, as well as extended one-day and multi-day tours for more experienced skiers. Two of the 30-mile traverses across the range start from the mining village of Cornucopia up the valley from Halfway. The easy tour up the road to Cornucopia and beyond to forest trailheads will take you into a beautiful mountain-rimmed valley, while the Tunnel-Holbrook Creeks tour goes up a short, moderate ridge on a road closed to snowmobilers for a bird's-eye view of the Halfway valley and beyond.

The location of the snowline affects the length of all tours, both Novice and Advanced and may mean a longer tour, or perhaps even carrying skis to first snow. The 72-mile paved Wallowa Mountain Loop Road (Road 39) around the range's east side is not open in winter, and does not lead to good skiing. It is usually drivable by late April to connect Halfway with Joseph on the north.

RICHLAND, HALFWAY SUMMIT, AND ROAD 77

(No sketch map) The high ridge you drive across before entering the Pine Creek–Halfway valley provides unrestricted views in all directions, from mountains in Idaho to the south front of the Wallowas and across vast areas of lower valleys and rolling ranchlands. Road 77 (China Springs Road) at the 3,600-foot highway summit of this ridge gets you away from the highway for an easy, memorable Novice–Intermediate tour.

From Halfway, drive south to Highway 86, then drive toward Richland, which is on the way to Baker City. It is about 7 miles to the top of the Richland-Halfway Summit, where there is parking for Road 77 and a groomed snowmobile route west of the highway. Ski northwest on Road 77 for unforgettable views as the road goes from one side to the other of the ridge. The first mile climbs 400 feet on the east side, then gains the ridgecrest, then goes onto the west side to 4,400 feet at 2 miles.

BLM LANDS AND DEER CREEK

(No sketch map) In winters when there is a good layer of snow in the Pine Valley-Halfway area, rolling sagebrush lands 3 miles east of the Pine Ranger Station offer open-country Novice skiing with views in all directions. The ranger station is located beside the highway as you enter the valley from Baker City and is 1.5 miles southeast of Halfway. From the ranger station, drive east 3 miles on a country road, park, and select your direction. Most of the area is managed by the Bureau of Land Management.

PINE VALLEY GROOMED TRACKS

(Map 99) The Pine Valley Ski Club has traditionally groomed several miles of Novice tracks near Carson, a scattering of rural houses 5.3 miles north of Halfway on the road to Cornucopia. The groomed area is on private land east of the Cornucopia road on Holbrook Road, which is 0.4 mile north of Carson after crossing the Pine Creek bridge.

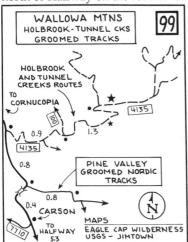

The area is not signed so you should inquire at the local bed-and-breakfast establishments or the Pine Ranger Station regarding location of the trailhead. An additional resource is Dr. Roger Sanders of Halfway (503-742-7640), who will also advise.

The groomed trails ramble across open fields, through stands of woods, and along a creek. The area is scenic and the grooming excellent. Several miles of track are usually set for skiing.

CORNUCOPIA

(Map 100) An easy yet scenic tour for Novices and anyone wanting to avoid ridge climbing is the road to the "town" of Cornucopia, really just an active mining operation and a few summer cabins. Located in a deep valley with Cornucopia Peak above to the west and the south front of the range facing down the valley, it is a dramatic site. It is worth sharing with snowmobile traffic, and is best done midweek when there are fewer machines around.

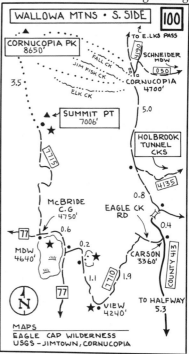

From Halfway, drive 5.7 miles up the valley on the Cornucopia road to the parking area at the end of plowing, or drive farther if plowed or if the snowline is higher. Early and late in the winter season the road to Cornucopia is often plowed to within 1.5 miles or so of the town. If it is not plowed, ski up the road 5.8 miles from the usual parking area just beyond Carson and Holbrook Road. It is a 1,300-foot climb to the mining town. At Cornucopia, a side road to the east, not shown on most maps, climbs to the ridgetop above Schneider Meadows for superb views of the range's south front and Cornucopia Peak. Ski beyond the town a half mile to the two trailheads for better views. Here, the east and west Pine Creek Trails enter forest.

Not far from your starting point is Road 4135 to the east, closed to snowmobilers and offering you a tour up moderate grades to fine views of the valley. See description for Holbrook and Tunnel Creeks Tour.

HOLBROOK AND TUNNEL CREEKS TOUR

(Map 100) This road tour has good views of the valley, is less demanding than the Summit Point tour across the valley, and is closed to snowmobilers. It is suitable for strong Novices and climbs 800 feet in 2.2 miles for the best views.

From Halfway, drive 5.7 miles north on the Cornucopia road to the Holbrook Road parking area. Ski up the Cornucopia Road 0.8 mile to Road

4135 and turn east onto this road. It is a narrow, primitive road twisting its way up moderate grades through lodgepole and ponderosa pines on steep, south-facing slopes. A pair of hairpin turns provides the first views at 2.2 miles. The second hairpin offers the best views of the Halfway valley and mountains to the south, and across the valley to Summit Point and Cornucopia Peak.

At the upper hairpin is a junction with Road 150, which can be skied northward on west-facing slopes for additional views. On Road 4135, your upward route, the only views above are another 1.8 miles as the road enters forest and a long northward draw before reaching a ridge shoulder.

SUMMIT POINT

(Map 100) This high point on the ridge leading to Cornucopia Peak and west of the town of Cornucopia is a 9-mile Advanced tour climbing 3,700 feet if you start skiing from the Halfway-Cornucopia road. However, you will probably be able to drive a distance before putting on your skis. The top of Summit Point is a noble viewpoint at 7,006 feet, but the first good view of the tour is only 1.9 miles up the road and a 880-foot climb. This open shoulder is worth the tour all by itself for views down the valley. A large meadow farther up the road is another worthy goal.

Summit Point is visible from Halfway. It is the rounded, open-topped ridge below and left of the main Wallowa peaks skyline. The highest peak in view is Cornucopia Peak.

Drive 5.3 miles north on Road 413 from Halfway to Road 7710, the Eagle Creek road, and park here at 3,360 feet or drive as far as possible. Do not block private driveways. Ski uphill through forest on a steepening road 1.9 miles to the open ridge where the road turns and goes north. There is a marvelous view here of the Halfway valley and mountains far to the south.

Unfortunately, snowmobilers use this road, and it may be hardpacked, even icy at times, but it is worth taking your chances. Conditions will improve as you gain elevation. From the shoulder meadow view at 4,240 feet turn the ridge and ski up the west side through ponderosa forest for 1.1 miles, where open hillsides beckon you to climb 300 feet to the ridgecrest for great views of Summit Point, Cornucopia Peak, the valley far below, and Fish Lake ridge to the east.

From this point, continue up the road 0.2 mile to the junction with Road 77, then circle around a large meadow with a row of tall aspens in its center. This meadow is also a worthy goal, and from its north end you will see mountains in Idaho across the Snake River.

Just west and beyond the meadow's north end turn right onto Road 7715, the road to the top of Summit Point. Just follow the obvious route upward to the top, although some maps may show a confusion of roads. In exceptional snow years, the east side of the ridge can be skied down to the Cornucopia road.

If you compare the National Forest, USGS, and Eagle Cap Wilderness maps for this route, you will see remarkable differences in roads. The answer is to not be intimidated. Just ski the obvious upward route.

EAST FORK PINE CREEK

(Map 100) This valley-bottom ski route follows a summer hiking trail 6 miles to a 7,600-foot pass overlooking the South Fork Imnaha River valley. The tour climbs over 3,000 feet to the East Lakes Pass and is for Advanced skiers. This trail is the first section of a Wallowa traverse via Tenderfoot Pass and Aneroid Lake, and also the traverse to the Lake Basin and West Fork Wallowa River.

Ski to Cornucopia, then 0.5 mile beyond the town to find summer trail 1865. On the way up, avalanche danger may exist from the steep, high ridges on either side. The upper end of the trail passes through an open basin. There is a view of the Seven Devils in Idaho from East Lakes Pass (7,600 feet), a beautiful camp spot.

An interesting one-day side trip goes up Simmons Creek on the west side of Pine Creek about 1.2 miles up the trail from Cornucopia. Climb steeply up the Simmons Creek Trail using climbers and enter the pristine, scenic Norway Basin at 7,200 feet after another 3 miles.

CORNUCOPIA PEAK

(Map 100) The ascent to the summit of this 8,650-foot peak is a serious undertaking for Backcountry skiers. It is almost 4,000 feet above the town of Cornucopia, and the views of the Wallowas are exceptional.

From Cornucopia (4,700 feet) climb the steep ridge on the north side of Fall Creek, which is immediately west of the town. Be prepared to carry your skis partway, then use ski climbers. Make the final ascent from southwest of the upper peak. The descent can be made on the ridge between Jim Fisk and Elk Creeks, which is the site of a summer trail.

An alternative descent, or ascent, is via Summit Point, but this is a longer tour, following the west side of the ridge between Summit Point and Cornucopia Peak.

FISH LAKE AND SCHNEIDER MEADOWS

(Map 100) The locals of Halfway, who are used to their backroads and driving on steep, one-lane dirt roads, may recommend that you ski to Fish Lake. It is true that there are large open slopes there and fine views, but be wary of such recommendations. Road 66 leads to both Fish Lake and Schneider Meadows, both areas north of Halfway, and as the driving distance increases so does the narrowness of the road and difficulty in turning around. This road is best driven in late spring, and don't be surprised to see snowmobilers.

If you must ski here, use a transportation map, drive as far as possible, and be prepared for a long, boring tour through forest without views until you are near Fish Lake at 6,630 feet. The same comments apply also to Schneider Meadows. Distance will vary wildly with snowline and road conditions. Be prepared to ski at least 6 miles or much more one way.

Schneider Meadows is more easily reached by skiing to the almost-abandoned town of Cornucopia 5 miles beyond the parking area at Holbrook Road (see Holbrook–Tunnel Creek Tour). East of Cornucopia ski up Road 4190 then Road 050 and climb steeply for 2 miles to the top of a ridge, then descend to the meadows. An alternative to descending is to ski north along the ridge for spectacular views of the Wallowas. This is the finest tour directly out of Cornucopia, and is for Advanced skiers who are comfortable with exploration. Surprisingly, the roads climbing east of Cornucopia to Schneider Meadows are not shown on most maps, but do appear on the transportation map.

Cornucopia has an active mine, which means the road is occasionally plowed. It is also heavily used by snowmobilers. (See description for Cornucopia for information on road plowing.)

HIGH WALLOWAS

The High Wallowas have a scenic magic and isolation unsurpassed by any other range of the Western states for tours of comparable length and elevation gain. The Wallowas are, however, a range where skiing must be taken seriously and appropriate planning done.

There are several north-to-south traverses of the range, all averaging 30 miles in length and with cumulative elevation gains of 3,500 feet to 6,000 feet. Of course, these traverses may also be done from south to north with no particular advantage in one direction or the other.

The traverses mean long car shuttles, about 175 miles each way, for a total of 350 car miles. The overall skiing distance of any traverse may vary up to 10 or more miles if the snowline is low or high. For this reason, and for the best snow and safest conditions, serious Backcountry tours are best done in late March, April, or early May after the snowpack has settled and the snowline risen, allowing deeper penetration by automobile.

These ski tours should be done with careful planning and advice on road and snowline conditions from the local ranger district offices—Pine Ranger District on the south, and Eagle Cap Ranger District on the north side of the range. The ranger stations may have suggestions concerning car-shuttle retrieval by local drivers, at least out to I-84.

Plan ahead, carry good maps, and be sure your equipment is well tested and dependable. In most cases, try to stay on trails and know where they are located. Be prepared for extremes of weather, although the inland Wallowas's snow depth and weather are not as extreme as in the Cascades.

The valleys are all deep with steep sidewalls climbing thousands of feet to high ridges and snow deposition zones. There are dozens of known avalanche paths and chutes in every valley, so be observant and cautious. Obvious signs are the absence of trees, snow debris, and damage to standing trees.

The Wallowa backcountry is unforgiving to those who are not well equipped. Carry a first-aid kit, extensive repair kit, and a shovel for emergencies and for preparing campsites and kitchen areas. Consider an extra ski pole, or a short replacement metal shaft. Tape a long cord on a wide-mouth water bottle for reaching into deep creeks using a ski pole as an extension. An avalanche cord for each person and avalanche transceivers are important safety items. Mohair or polypropylene rope climbers are necessary. Always leave a detailed itinerary with family and Forest Service. Temperatures can be very cold in January and February. Days are longer and warmer in March, April, and May.

EAGLE CREEK, HORTON PASS, AND EAST LOSTINE RIVER TRAVERSE

(Map 98) This is the most direct, "easiest" traverse of the Wallowa range. It is approximately 30 miles in length, but a low snowline could add 10 miles or more. Cumulative elevation gain is near 4,000 feet.

To ski the traverse from south to north, drive east on Highway 86 from Baker City about 22 miles, then drive north on a gravel road toward Sparta, a ghost town. About 6 miles from the highway turn onto Road 70 and continue to Forshey Meadows, about 3 miles. In times of low snowline this is the end of driving at 4,238 feet, which means skiing about 15 miles to the end of the East Fork Eagle Creek Road (Road 7740) with an extra 1,000 feet of climbing. Starting at Forshey Meadows would increase the traverse to 45 miles total. Check with the Pine Ranger District for snowline and road information. Ideally, you will be able to drive to or near to the end of the Eagle Creek road at 4,400 feet and about 23 miles from Highway 86.

From the end of Road 7740 at 4,400 feet ski the summer trail. Constantly consult your map for the trail location as it crosses the creek several times—crossings that may test your patience in finding safe passages. It is 14.3 miles to Horton Pass (8,400 feet) along the mostly forested trail. En route to the pass, you will cross many avalanche paths and will no doubt see a great deal of avalanche debris on the trail.

From the pass, on the west shoulder of Eagle Cap Mountain, it is a beautiful descent on open, moderate slopes into the Lake Basin. Ski down the East Lostine valley, a magnificent U-shaped valley of open meadows, to its north end. The trail drops through forest over a step into the Lostine River valley, where an almost level road leads miles to the snowline. In setting up a car shuttle, you will have determined where the snowline is.

An alternative route crosses Frazier Pass at 7,600 feet (before reaching Horton Pass) and then continues to Minam Lake and out of the Lostine valley. Yet another alternative crosses the trailed pass from the lake basin over the ridge (8,550 feet) to the west, then descends to Minam Lake where moderate slopes on both sides allow for easy skiing.

Yet another alternative from the lake basin goes through the basin and descends to the West Fork Wallowa River to the end of the road near Wallowa Lake. This route is the same distance as the Lostine valley route if the snowline is not below 4,400 feet.

ANEROID BASIN, TENDERFOOT PASS, IMNAHA RIVER, AND CORNUCOPIA TRAVERSE

(Map 98) All high-country skiing and traverses of the Wallowas are incredibly scenic, yet this particular traverse is probably the most varied and requires the most route finding. It will vary in length depending on snowline but will average about 30 miles (based on summer trail distances, but skiing traverses may add miles to the total). The vertical cumulative gain will also vary but will be about 7,000 feet, measuring from low to high points, which does not include the countless ups and downs of ski travel.

If it is not possible to drive to Cornucopia, add another 6 miles to the skiing total. If you are skiing this route from north to south, follow directions for Aneroid Basin and ski to Tenderfoot Pass. On this trail 200 yards above the power plant dam and pond, there is an avalanche area. If conditions here appear dangerous, reroute to the forest across the creek. If you lose the trail beyond, follow a logical route to regain it. A good camp spot is the large meadow at 5 miles.

Bypass Aneroid Lake on the east. If you camp in the Tenderfoot Basin, there is a spectacular spot below and north of the pass. Views from the pass are breathtaking. About halfway down into the Imnaha drainage you may want to go left (east) to avoid steep slopes, then cross a long, unavoidable steep slope using avalanche cords, crossing one at a time. The last person should carry the shovel.

Follow the north side of the river and stay 200 to 300 yards above it for the easiest passage. Below Mount Nebo the trees thicken, so look for the trail to get through. Cross the river on a snow bridge, then start up the north side of the South Fork Imnaha. Use Marble Mountain as a landmark for finding the obscure trail up Blue Creek on the creek's west side. East Lakes Pass at 7,600 feet is a good camp spot with views of the Seven Devils in Idaho.

From the pass, descend the upper basin going southeast to avoid dense forest. The valley narrows and the trail crisscrosses the stream. Several avalanche chutes are crossed. Stay on the trail if possible as the forest is dense. Ski past Cornucopia to the snowline to end the eventful traverse.

An alternative route from Tenderfoot Basin crosses Dollar Lake Pass and follows the north side of the ridge above Bonny Lakes then around Mount Nebo on its north side. Cross the ridge at 7,600 feet and descend directly down to the confluence of the North and South Forks of the Imnaha.

CORNUCOPIA, HAWKINS PASS, AND WEST FORK WALLOWA RIVER TRAVERSE

(Map 98) This 29-mile traverse from Cornucopia may be the most demanding as it crosses Hawkins Pass (8,400 feet), which has steep slopes on both sides. Total elevation gain is about 5,500 feet.

From Cornucopia ski up the East Fork Pine Creek trail to East Lakes Pass, then descend into the South Fork of the Imnaha, turn west, and ski up to Hawkins Pass. Both sides of the pass are very steep, so use extreme caution. Descend to Frazier Lake and follow the West Fork Wallowa River to Wallowa Lake. Below Frazier Lake there are enormous, slabby cliffs to the east, which are very dangerous and account for the absence of trees along your route. Along the West Fork are numerous avalanche paths to be crossed.

OTHER TOURS FROM BAKER CITY

The drive to several ski tours west of Baker City goes through a scenic, canyonlike valley and over a low divide. The trails offer an alternative to driving to Anthony Lakes if the weather or roads up the mountain are not appealing.

Another skiing option from Baker City is to drive Highway 7 west to the John Day area. The nearest tours range from 40 to 50 driving miles from Baker City and include Greenhorn, Vinegar Hill, Bates and Vincent Creeks, and Dixie Butte.

DOOLEY SUMMIT, BEAVER MOUNTAIN, AND BALD MOUNTAIN

(Map 101) Seventeen miles southwest of Baker City lies a long, high ridge extending many miles from east to west. High points on the ridge are Beaver Mountain and Bald Mountain. Dooley Summit at 5,456 feet is a highway pass between the two peaks and is plowed in winter. Parking is available

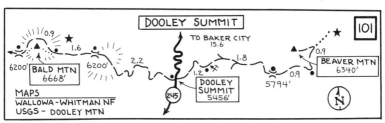

for skiers and other winter users. Roads go both east and west from the summit, both appropriately called Skyline Road.

Dooley Summit. (Map 101) From Baker City drive 8 miles southwest on Highway 7, then drive 7.6 miles south on Highway 245 to Dooley Summit. Soon out of Baker City you will see towers on a summit, your goal if you ski east of the pass. You will also see a high, bare peak to the west, Bald Mountain, the goal for experienced Backcountry skiers going west of the pass. The drive to the pass is scenic, passing through narrow gorges and steep-walled valleys.

Beaver Mountain. (Map 101) From the pass it is 4.8 miles east to the ridgecrest where the relay station towers stand, a site where a radar station was operated during World War II. The road east from the pass is wide and does not climb or descend significantly. Most of the tour is on the south side of the ridge, where there are continuous views due to forest-fire devastation. From the relay station, or better yet another 0.5 mile north, you'll see the Elkhorn and Wallowa Mountains, the Baker Valley, and distant views west and south. The entire tour is extremely scenic.

Bald Mountain. (Map 101) The road west of the pass is not wide and easy, as it is to the east. Rather, it is primitive, winding, and very steep as it clings to even steeper, south-facing slopes a mile out. Although it passes through thin forest at the beginning, the road reaches a saddle at 2.2 miles, above the steep section, switches to the north side, and passes through beautiful old growth. The final mile of the 4.7-mile tour is on a steep, open hillside facing north. Leaving the road, climb 400 feet directly to the steep summit (6,668 feet).

The road circles the north side and descends to a broad, treeless, flat saddle with marvelous views. From Dooley Summit, the total elevation gain is 1,200 feet.

Because of steepness, this tour is best suited to experienced, strong skiers who know snow conditions well and are not intimidated by steepness. The views are much the same as those from the Beaver Mountain tour. In addition, Dixie Butte and Strawberry Mountain are seen to the west.

PHILLIPS RESERVOIR

(No sketch map) Sixteen miles southwest of Baker City on Highway 7 lies the 5-mile-long reservoir with miles of Novice-Intermediate trails. The trailhead is on Black Mountain Road at the east end of the lake and across Mason Dam 0.6 mile from the highway.

The Shoreline Trail follows the south shore 4.5 miles with good views of the Elkhorn Range to the north. There are four additional trails on the south side that form four loops and total 8 miles. Two of the trails are difficult, climbing the high slopes south of the lake. Unfortunately, the low elevation of Phillips Reservoir does not always guarantee skiable snow.

Chapter 33

STEENS MOUNTAIN

The highest point in southeastern Oregon (9,733 feet), and a long way from anywhere, Steens Mountain sees a few skiers every spring. The highest road in Oregon climbs 25 miles and 5,500 feet from Frenchglen (4,230 feet) where there is a small historic hotel and a few buildings. The road climbs steadily up the rolling, tilted plateaulike western slope of Steens Mountain on a gentle to moderate grade to within 200 feet and 0.5 mile of the top of the mountain. From the summit, the east face plunges precipitously 4,000 feet to the Alvord Desert.

To reach Steens Mountain from Bend, drive 130 miles southeast to the town of Burns, then south 60 miles to Frenchglen.

Ski travel on Steens Mountain is best done in April and May, and should be done only in good weather. The endless, rolling, open terrain would be difficult to navigate in bad weather, even with a compass and map. Take your summer boots in the event you have to hike to the snowline. For information, contact BLM, Burns District, HC-74, P.O. Box 12533, Highway 20 West, Hines, Oregon 97336, 503-573-5241.

WESTSIDE STEENS MOUNTAIN

(Map 102) The ski tour up the mountain's west side follows the Steens Mountain road (the North Loop segment), and 3 miles from Frenchglen you encounter a locked gate in winter. From the gate you hike or ski upward at first through sagebrush, then grasslands, and then a 4-mile band of juniper trees that takes you to the first aspen groves just below Lily Lake, a small pond at 7,280 feet and 12 miles from the gate. Ski another 1.4 miles up to Fish Lake after passing over a hilltop viewpoint of the mountain's upper reaches. Above Fish Lake the mountain slope is all rolling grasslands to the summit.

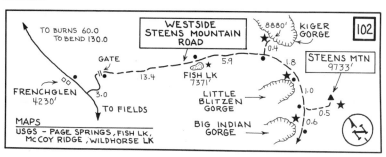

From the lake it is 5.9 miles to a side-road viewpoint of impressive Kiger Gorge, one of the three enormous glacial, U-shaped canyons. Another 1.8 miles and you reach a first view down from the head (9,360 feet) of Little Blitzen Gorge—a remarkable view. One mile farther is the road's high point. Just 0.6 mile south of the road's high point is another grand view, this time down Big Indian Gorge.

> *Something hidden. Go and find it. Go and look behind the Ranges—*
> *Something lost behind the Ranges. Lost and waiting for you. Go!*
> —Rudyard Kipling, "The Explorer"

RESOURCES

AVALANCHE INFORMATION

Forest Service Northwest Avalanche
  Forecast Center
Oregon and Southern Washington:
  503-326-2400
Washington: 206-527-6677

TOPOGRAPHICAL MAPS

U.S. Geological Survey
Denver Federal Center
Box 25286
Denver, CO 80225

CENTRAL CASCADES AND BEND

Note: Most Forest Service offices are
open 8:00 A.M. to 4:30 P.M. weekdays
and closed on weekends.

Bend and Fort Rock Ranger Districts
Newberry Volcanic National
  Monument
1230 N.E. 3rd
Bend, OR 97701
503-388-5664

Deschutes National Forest
1645 Highway 20 East
Bend, OR 97701
503-388-2715

Sisters Ranger District
P.O. Box 248
Sisters, OR 97759
503-549-2111

DIAMOND LAKE AND CRATER LAKE REGION

Crater Lake National Park
Crater Lake, OR 97604
503-594-2211 (office hours, and
24-hour road/weather report)

Diamond Lake Ranger District
HC-60, Box 101
Idleyld Park, OR 97447
503-498-2531

Umpqua National Forest
P.O. Box 1008
Roseburg, OR 97470
503-672-6601

ELKHORN AND WALLOWA MOUNTAINS

Baker Ranger District
Route 1, Box 1
Pocahontas Road
Baker City, OR 97814
503-523-4476

Eagle Cap Ranger District
612 S.W. 2nd
Enterprise, OR 97828
503-426-4978

Pine Ranger District
General Delivery
Halfway, OR 97834
503-742-7511

Wallowa-Whitman National Forest
P.O. Box 907
Baker City, OR 97814
503-523-6391

JOHN DAY REGION

Long Creek and Bear Valley Ranger
  Districts
528 E. Main
John Day, OR 97845
503-575-2110 (Long Creek)
503-575-3204 (Bear Valley)

Malheur National Forest
139 N.E. Dayton Street
John Day, OR 97845
503-575-1731

Prairie City Ranger District
327 S.W. Front
Prairie City, OR 97869
503-820-3311

Unity Ranger District (Greenhorn area)
214 Main Street
Unity, OR 97884
503-446-3351

MOUNT HOOD REGION

Barlow Ranger District
7th and Court
Dufur, OR 97021
503-467-2291

Bear Springs Ranger District
Route 1, Box 222
Maupin, OR 97037
503-328-6211

Hood River Ranger District
6780 Highway 35
Mount Hood–Parkdale, OR 97041
503-666-0701

Mount Hood Information Center
65000 E. Highway 26
Welches, OR 97067
503-622-5741 (from Portland, direct call
666-0704, ext. 684; office open seven days
per week, 8:00 A.M. to 4:00 P.M.)

Mount Hood National Forest
2955 N.W. Division
Gresham, OR 97030
503-666-0700

Ripplebrook Ranger District
61431 E. Highway 224
Estacada, OR 97023
503-630-4256

MOUNT ST. HELENS

Gifford Pinchot National Forest
6926 E. 4th Plain Blvd.
Vancouver, WA 98661–7299
206-750-5000

Mount St. Helens National Volcanic
   Monument
42218 N.E. Yale Bridge Road
Amboy, WA 98601–9715
206-247-5473, after hours 206-247-5800

Randle Ranger District
Highway 12
Randle, WA 98377–9105
206-497-7565

OCHOCOS AND MAURY MOUNTAINS

Big Summit Ranger District
348855 Ochoco Ranger Station
Prineville, OR 97754-9612
503-447-9645

Ochoco National Forest
P.O. Box 490
Prineville, OR 97754
503-447-6247

Paulina Ranger District (Buck Point
   area)
171500 Beaver Creek Road
Paulina, OR 97751–9706
503-477-3713

Prineville Ranger District
155 N. Court Street
Prineville, OR 97754–9117
503-447-9641

SANTIAM PASS REGION

Detroit Ranger District
HC-73, Box 320
Mill City, OR 97360
503-854-3366

McKenzie Ranger District
57600 McKenzie Highway
McKenzie Bridge, OR 97413
503-822-3381

Oakridge Ranger District
46375 Highway 58
Westfir, OR 97492
503-782-2291

Sisters Ranger District
P.O. Box 248
Sisters, OR 97759
503-549-2111

Sweet Home Ranger District
3225 Highway 20
Sweet Home, OR 97386
503-367-5168

STEENS MOUNTAIN

BLM—Burns District
HC-74, P.O. Box 12533
Highway 20 West
Hines, OR 97336
503-573-5241

TROUT LAKE AND MOUNT ADAMS

Mount Adams Ranger District
2455 Highway 141
Trout Lake, WA 98650–9724
509-395-2501

WILLAMETTE PASS REGION

Willamette National Forest
211 East 7th Avenue
Eugene, OR 97440
503-465-6522

Crescent Ranger District
P.O. Box 208
Crescent, OR 97733
503-433-2234

Deschutes National Forest
1645 Highway 20 East
Bend, OR 97701
503-388-2715

Oakridge Ranger District
46375 Highway 58
Westfir, OR 97492
503-782-2291

WIND RIVER, CRAZY HILLS, AND INDIAN HEAVEN

Wind River Ranger District
Hemlock Road
Carson, WA 98610–9725
509-427-5645

CLUBS

Audubon Society of Portland
515 N.W. Cornell Road
Portland, OR 97210

Chemeketans
P.O. Box 864
Salem, OR 97308

Mazamas
909 N.W. 19th Avenue
Portland, OR 97209
503-227-2345

Mount Adams Nordic Club
25 Flying L Lane
Glenwood, WA 98619

Mount Hood Nordic Ski Foundation
P.O. Box 1091
Portland, OR 97207

Mount St. Helens Club
P.O. Box 843
Longview, WA 98632

The Nature Conservancy
1234 N.W. 25th
Portland, OR 97210

Obsidians
Box 322
Eugene, OR 97440

Oregon Natural Resources Council
522 S.W. 5th Avenue, Suite 1050
Portland, OR 97204

Oregon Nordic Club/Central Oregon
2326 N.E. Ravenwood Drive
Bend, OR 97701

Oregon Nordic Club/Eugene
88313 Millican Road
Springfield, OR 97478

Oregon Nordic Club/Grants Pass
3585 Highland
Grants Pass, OR 97526

Oregon Nordic Club/John Day
Jennifer Stein Barker
Izee Route
Canyon City, OR 97820

Oregon Nordic Club/Ochoco
301145 Terrace Lane
Prineville, OR 97754

Oregon Nordic Club/Portland
P.O. Box 3906
Portland, OR 97208
Hot Line: 503-255-0823

Oregon Nordic Club/Southern Oregon
P.O. Box 9
Phoenix, OR 97535

Oregon Nordic Club/The Dalles
1801 East 16th
The Dalles, OR 97058

Oregon Nordic Club/Willamette
P.O. Box 181
Salem, OR 97308

Ptarmigans
P.O. Box 1821
Vancouver, WA 98668

Sierra Club
1413 S.E. Hawthorne Boulevard
Portland, OR 97214–3640

Trails Club of Oregon
P.O. Box 1243
Portland, OR 97207–1243

INDEX

A

Adams, Mount 94
Aiken Lava Flow 94
Aldrich Mountain 341–342
Alpine Ski Trail 126–127
Aneroid Lake Basin 360–361
Angell Basin 351
Anthony Lakes Groomed Tracks 347–349
Ape Cave 42
avalanches 33–34

B

Bailey, Mount 307
Baker City, tours from 370
Bald Peter Loops 91
Bandit Springs 314–317
Barlow Pass 111, 172–180
Barlow Ridge 180
Barlow Road 155, 172
Barlow Saddle 177–179
Barlow Trail 142
Bear Meadow 64
Beaver Ponds Loop 48
Bend 262
Bennett Pass 186–191
Bennett Ridge 186–189, 191
Big Meadow 266
Big Meadows (Mount Hood) 167
Big Obsidian Lava Flow 283–284, 284–285
Big Sheep Creek, Middle Fork 357–359
Big Springs Trails 235–236
Big Tree Loop 90
Black Butte 253–257
Black Lake and Elkhorn Crest Trail 350–351
Black Wolf Meadows and Anvil Lake 225–226
Blue Box Pass 159, 162
Blue Lake 61–62
Blue Lake Mudflow 54, 61–62, 62
Blue Mountains 343–346

Bonney Butte and Meadows 189–190
Boy Scout Ridge 179
Breitenbush Gorge, South 231
Broken Top Crater 267
Brooks Meadow 212, 215
Burnt Peak 82
Butte Camp Dome 53
Butte Camp Loop 55
Buzzard Point 155, 172

C

Cache Meadow 221–222
Cache Mountain 259
Camp Sherman 253–257
Camp Windy 190–191
Camptown-Crosstown Trail 122
Cathedral Grove 62
Cinnamon Butte and Wits End 303–305
Cinnamon Peak, North 45
Clackamas high country 219, 220
Clackamas Lake Historic Ranger Station 168–170
Clark Creek Trail 196
Clear Lake 163
Clear Lake Butte 166
Clinger Spring 212, 218
clothing 34–35
Cloud Cap Inn 210–211, 212
Coffin Mountain 233
Conboy Lake National Wildlife Refuge 100
Cooper Spur 111, 209–211
Corbett Sno-Park 250–251
Cornucopia 364
Cornucopia Peak 366–367
Corridor Tour 165
Cougar Sno-Park 52
courtesy 28–29
Crater Lake 305–306
Crater Lake National Park 308–313
Crater Lake Rim Trail 313
Crawfish Meadow 352
Crazy Hills 79–82
Crazy Hills Loop 81

Crescent Lake Trail 294–296
Crofton Ridge 98
Crystal Creek Valley and Grant
    Meadows 318–319

D

Dead Canyon 101
Deadman Pass State Park 343–344
Deardorff Mountain 336–337
Death Canyon 54
Derr Meadows 322
Devils Half Acre 175–176
Diamond Gap 102
Diamond Lake 300–307
Diamond Peak 297–299
Diamond Peak Wilderness 298
difficulty ratings 23–24
Dog River Butte 216
Dooley Summit 370
Dutchman Flat 264

E

Eagle Loop 90
East Fork Hood River Region 192–206
East Fork Trail (Pocket Creek) 205
East Leg Area 132–134
Edison Butte 276–279
Elk Lake and Gold Butte Lookout
    231–232
Elk Meadows Trail 195
Elk Mountain 197–198
Elkhorn Mountains 347–353
Emigrant Springs State Park 344
Enid Lake 119–122
Escape Ridge 62–63
ethics, wilderness 27

F

Fat Lady Trail 205
Fawn Lake 296
Fay Lake 233–235
Fields Peak 340–341
Fivemile Butte 217
Flagtail Mountain 340
Flattop Butte 52
Flattop Mountain 87–88
Frissell Point 246

Frog Lake 159–162
Frog Lake Buttes 160
frostbite 37
Fuji Creek Trail 292

G

Gates of the Mountain 198–199
Ghost Ridge 174–175
Glade Trail 127–128
Glenwood Valley 99
Goat Marsh 58
Gold Lake and Marilyn Lakes
    290
Government Camp 111, 118
Grande Ronde River Valley 345
Gravel Pit Tour 182
Green Lakes 269
Greenhorn 332–333
Grouse Saddle 93

H

Hardtime Loop 73–74
Heather Canyon 194–195
Hemlock Trail 140–142
Hidaway Lake and Shellrock Lake
    226–227
Hidden Valley 82
High Divide 147
High Ridge Lookout 345–346
High Rock 223–224
Highline Cutoff 148
Hoffer Lakes 350
Holbrook and Tunnel Creeks 364–
    365
Hood, Mount 109
Hood River, East Fork 111
Hood River Meadows 186, 192–194
Horse 'N Teal Trail 307
Horsethief Meadows 199
Howlock Mountain and Mount
    Thielsen 301–303
hypothermia 36–37

I

Ikenick Sno-Park and Fish Lake 242–
    245
Indian Heaven Trail 70

Indian Heaven Wilderness 76
Indian Ridge 227–228, 245
Ingle Mountain 338

J

Jack Pine Road 241
Jefferson Park 230–231
June Lake 46

K

Kalama River Trail 60
Kalama Springs and Overlook 59
King Mountain 88, 92–93
Kinzel Lake 152–153
Kuamaksi Butte 280

L

Lakeshore Tour 165
Lamberson Butte 197–198
Larch Mountain (Oregon) 112–113
Larch Mountain (Washington) 103–104
Lava Cast Forest 46–52
Lava Lake Trails 238–239
Lava Loop 90
Lava Plateau 53–55
Lewis River Overlook 74
Little Crater Meadows 166–167
Little Nash Trail 239
Loco Pass 80, 82
Loco Pass Loop 81–82
Logan Valley 335–336
Lone Butte Meadows 78, 80
Lone Butte Quarry 77
Lookout Mountain 213, 218, 319–321
Loowit Trail 49
Lost Canyon 55, 61–62, 62
Lost Creek 113–115
Lost Lake 115–116, 241
Lostman Trail 148
Low Rock 224

M

Maiden Peak 291
Mann Butte 84

maps 25–26
Marble Mountai 47
Marble Mountain Sno-Park 44–52
Marys Peak 246–247
Maury Mountains 322–324
Maxwell Sno-Park Trails 236–238
McBride Lake 59–60
McClellan Meadows 70
McCully Basin 361
McCumber Place Loops 100
McKenzie Pass Lava Fields 258–259
Meadows Creek 202
Medley Canyon 101–102
Meissner Trails 274–275
Mineral Jane Trail 176, 179, 184
Mirror Lake 118–119
Monitor Ridge 52–53, 54
Moraine Lake 269
Mosquito Meadows 65
Mount Adams Timberline 97–98
Mount Bachelor Nordic Sports
    Center 264
Mountain View Trail West 236
Mud Creek Ridge 146
Muddy River Canyon 51
Muddy River Lahar 50, 51
Multorpor Meadows 122–124, 124

N

Natural Bridges 84, 85
Newberry National Volcanic
    Monument 280
Newton Creek 197
No-Name Trail 74
Nordic Center
    192, 202, 248, 264, 301, 346, 347
North Shore Tours 164

O

Oak Grove Butte 222–223
Ochoco Mountains 314–324
Odell Butte and Big Marsh 296–297
Odell Lake Resort 294–296
Old Burn 216–217
Old Maid Flat 113–115
Old Man Loop 70
Old Man Pass 67
Old Santiam Wagon Road 244
Old Wagon Road 211

Outlaw Creek Clearcuts 71, 75
Outlet Falls 99–100

P

Palmateer Overlook 175
Pamelia Lake 232–233
Panorama Dome 179
Paulina Peak 283
Perry Point 217
Pete Gulch Trail 71–73
Peterson Prairie and Prairie Ridge
    86–87
Peterson Ridge and Lost Meadow 86
Pika Trail 46
Pine Creek 50
Pine Creek Connectors 50
Pine Marten Trail 44, 46
Pine Valley Groomed Tracks 363–364
Pineside Sno-Park 88
Pioneer Road Loops 156
Pioneer Woman's Grave (Beaver
    Marsh) 154–155
Pipeline Loop 90
Placid Lake 78
Plains of Abraham 51
Pocket Creek 186, 203–206, 208
Point 3670 75
Porcupine Trail 146
Powerline Tour 182

Q

Quarry Loop 146–147

R

Ramona Falls 113–115
Razorback Ridge 60
Red Top Meadow 140
Redrock Pass 53–55, 58
repair kit 35–36
Robinhood Creek 199
Rosary Lakes 290
Round Lake 251–253
Round Mountain 320, 321
Rush Creek 79
Rush Creek Clearcuts 75, 76

S

Sahalie Falls 194
Salmon Basin, Upper 157
Salmon River Basin 153–158
Salmon River Overlook 146–147
Salmon River Road 150
Salt Creek Falls Area 291–293
Salt Creek Summit 354
Salt Creek Summit Trails 355–357
Sand Mountain 239
sanitation 28
Santiam Pass Ski Trails 248–250
Santiam Pass Wilderness Areas 260
Santiam West 230–247
Sasquatch Butte 49
Sasquatch Trails 48
Sawtooth Mountain Clearcut 78
Scenic Loop: Trail 148 68–69
Sherar Burn 143, 152
Shoestring Canyon 51
Silent Creek Trail 307
Silver Star Mountain 105–107
Simcoe Mountains 107–108
Sink Holes and Cave Creek 87
Sisu Loop 150–151
Skookum Meadow 80
Skookum Peak 82
Skyliner Trails 276
Sleeping Beauty 94–96
Smith Butte 88–92
sno-park programs 26
Snow Bunny Hill 140
Snow Bunny Trail 132
Snowshoe Creek Loop 339–340
Spirit Lake Memorial Highway 64
Spout Springs 346
Squaw Creek Overlook 344–345
St. Helens, Mount 40–65
St. Helens, Mount, summit 56–58
Stagman Ridge 96–97
Starkey 345
Starr Ridge 328–330
Steens Mountain 373
Strawberry Mountain 65, 333–335
Summit Point 365
Summit Prairie 335–336
Summit Trail 122–124

Sun Notch 310
Sun Notch Trail 311
Surveyor Trail 215
Suttle Lake and Blue Lake 251–253
Swampy Lakes 267, 270–274
Swift Creek Overlook 44
Swift Creek Trail 46, 56

T

Tam McArthur Rim 256, 268
Teacup Lake 192, 202–203
Teaters Road 324
Termination Point 75
Terrible Traverse 186, 187
The John Day Region 326–342
The Right Canyon 54, 55
Three Creek Lake 256
Three Creek Loops 255
Tilly Jane Ski Trail 210
Timberline Lodge 128–130, 130
Todd Lake 264
Tombstone Pass Trails 241–242
Toutle River Overlook 60–61
Tower Point 324
trail courtesy 28
Trillium Lake 138, 142–143, 143
Trout Lake 83–93
Trout Lake Meadow 83–84
Tumalo Valley 275–276
Twin Buttes 93
Twin Lakes Trail 172–173

U

Upper Wind River 66–78

V

Valhalla Loop 149–150
Valley Ski Trail 71
Van Patten Lake and Butte 352–353
Veda Butte 151
View Point Butte 317

Vinegar Hill 332–333
Vista Trail 301

W

Wakepish Sno-Park 64
Waldo Lake 293–294
Walker Mountain 299
Wallowa Mountains 354–370
Wallowas, traverses of 367
Walton Lake and the Sheep Corrals 318
Wanoga Butte 279
Wapinitia Ridge 162
Wapiti Trails 44
Warm Springs Indian Reservation 163, 170
weather 30–32
West Leg Trail 124–126
Westview Loops 287–289
Weygandt Basin 209
White Away Trail 133
White River 111, 181–185
White River Canyon 130
White River Glacier Moraines 183
wilderness ethics 27–28
Willamette Pass 287–299
Wilson, Mount 163, 170–171
Windy Peak 190, 206
Windy Ridge 64
Wizard Island Overlook Trail 309
Worm Flows Buttress 49, 51
Wy'east Trail 131–132

Y

Yellowjacket and White River Trails Loop 183–184
Yellowjacket Trail 133, 134–137, 157, 179

Z

Zigzag Canyon 128, 129

ABOUT THE AUTHOR

As a youth Klindt Vielbig loved the outdoors but didn't start hill walking until he lived on an Oregon ranch. Serious hiking started only during a tour with the Marine Corps infantry. In 1950, the year he started climbing Northwest peaks, and before the advent of Nordic skiing, he learned to ski so he could get into the mountains in winter. He climbed actively in the Cascades for twenty-five years, including new routes on both Mounts Rainier and Baker. He has climbed Mount Hood thirty times by nine different routes, skied several times into the Wallowa Mountains to climb the higher peaks, and climbed in Canada and in the Alps. He has also served as a professional guide on several Cascade peaks and as a member of two mountain rescue groups. As a skier he was a member of both the Stevens Pass and Crystal Mountain ski patrols.

In 1965 Vielbig started cross-country skiing in Oregon and organized on Mount Hood the first Nordic ski school on the West Coast, and taught for several years. Several winter trips to Europe resulted in extensive cross-country skiing in five alpine countries.

Vielbig is a long-time member of the Mazamas, Trails Club of Oregon, Sierra Club, Audubon Society, and The Nature Conservancy, as well as a charter member of the Oregon Nordic Club. He has worked with the Forest Service on ski trail planning, and has worked extensively on volunteer maintenance and construction of cross-country ski trails. He is a native Oregonian, and is proud to note that his grandmother crossed the Plains in 1865 on the Oregon Trail to The Dalles. He is of Danish and Bavarian descent.

The publisher encourages skiers to contact the author should they have comments regarding route descriptions and route and trail changes. You can write to the author at 4214 NE Hazelfern Place, Portland, OR 97213.

THE MOUNTAINEERS, founded in 1906, is a nonprofit outdoor activity and conservation club, whose mission is "to explore, study, preserve, and enjoy the natural beauty of the outdoors...." Based in Seattle, Washington, the club is now the third-largest such organization in the United States, with 14,000 members and four branches throughout Washington State.

The Mountaineers sponsors both classes and year-round outdoor activities in the Pacific Northwest, which include hiking, mountain climbing, ski-touring, snowshoeing, bicycling, camping, kayaking and canoeing, nature study, sailing, and adventure travel. The club's conservation division supports environmental causes through educational activities, sponsoring legislation, and presenting informational programs. All club activities are led by skilled, experienced volunteers, who are dedicated to promoting safe and responsible enjoyment and preservation of the outdoors.

The Mountaineers Books, an active, nonprofit publishing program of the club, produces guidebooks, instructional texts, historical works, natural history guides, and works on environmental conservation. All books produced by The Mountaineers are aimed at fulfilling the club's mission.

If you would like to participate in these organized outdoor activities or the club's programs, consider a membership in The Mountaineers. For information and an application, write or call The Mountaineers, Club Headquarters, 300 Third Avenue West, Seattle, Washington 98119; (206) 284-6310.

Send or call for our catalog of more than 300 outdoor titles:
The Mountaineers Books
1011 SW Klickitat Way, Suite 107
Seattle, WA 98134
1-800-553-4453